THE UNITED STATES
AND WORLD WAR II

Volume I

The
New American Nation Series

EDITED BY

HENRY STEELE COMMAGER

AND

RICHARD B. MORRIS

THE UNITED STATES
AND WORLD WAR II

Volume I

By A. RUSSELL BUCHANAN

ILLUSTRATED

1817

HARPER & ROW, PUBLISHERS

NEW YORK, HAGERSTOWN, SAN FRANCISCO, LONDON

The maps in this volume are from *The War in Maps: An Atlas of the New York Times Maps, Fourth Edition*, by Francis Brown, Lucas Manditch, and others. Copyright 1946 by Oxford University Press, Inc. Reprinted by permission.

THE UNITED STATES AND WORLD WAR II, *Volume I. Copyright © 1964 by A. Russell Buchanan. Printed in the United States of America. All rights reserved. No part of this book may be used or reproduced in any manner whatsoever without written permission except in the case of brief quotations embodied in critical articles and reviews. For information address Harper & Row, Publishers, Incorporated, 10 East 53d Street, New York, N.Y. 10022.*

LIBRARY OF CONGRESS CATALOG CARD NUMBER: 63–20287

78 79 80 81 10 9 8 7 6

For Ethel, Barbara, and Joanne

Contents

VOLUME I

Illustrations

These photographs, grouped in a separate section,
will be found following page 108

1. President Franklin D. Roosevelt and Prime Minister Churchill on board the U.S.S. *Augusta* at the Atlantic Conference, August, 1941
2. Shigenori Togo, Japanese Foreign Minister
3. Premier Hideki Tojo of Japan
4. The U.S.S. *West Virginia* and the U.S.S. *Tennessee* after the Japanese attack on Pearl Harbor, December 7, 1941
5. President Roosevelt with his War Cabinet in the White House, December 19, 1941
6. Navy reconnaissance plane being catapulted from heavy cruiser
7. The infamous Death March from Bataan in 1942
8. American soldiers fording a stream in New Georgia, July, 1943
9. Infantry reinforcements landing in New Georgia
10. Wounded American and Australian soldiers in New Guinea, December, 1942
11. Admiral Raymond Ames Spruance, Commander of the Central Pacific Force
12. Admiral William F. Halsey, Commander of the South Pacific Area
13. Secretary of the Navy Frank Knox aboard the U.S.S. *Curtiss* with Lt. Col. Carlson, U.S.M.C., and Admiral Chester W. Nimitz
14. Infantrymen and tanks moving ahead on Bougainville
15. Carriers in the Pacific
16. A tank destroyer group on reconnaissance in the Kasserine Pass

Maps

Editors' Introduction

WORLD WAR II, like the Civil War, cut a gash across the surface of American history. During the decades of the twenties and the thirties the United States had reverted—or tried to revert—to isolation. President Harding had cut loose from the League, Congress had refused to adhere to the World Court, President Hoover had retreated from commitments in the Far East and thrown up tariff barriers against Europe; even Franklin Roosevelt accepted without protest the abandonment of the League and concentrated all of his energies during his first term on the domestic scene. After conceding much to the isolationists, F.D.R. in his second term found himself shackled by the Neutrality Act in his efforts on behalf of collective security.

The Nazi Blitzkrieg and Pearl Harbor together destroyed the myth that America could be insulated from European catastrophe. The course of World War II created a new climate committing the country toward intervention in world affairs. A postwar isolationist reaction never made serious headway.

President Truman, who came from what had once been the heart of isolationist country, sponsored the Truman Doctrine, the Marshall Plan and NATO. In 1952 the Republicans, long the party of isolation, picked for their standard bearer the man who had led the Allied armies in Europe. No administration could consider a retreat from existing commitments; each one—enthusiastically or reluctantly—extended those commitments. Franklin Roosevelt, like Wilson, had failed to mention foreign affairs in his First Inaugural Address; after 1945 it was difficult to imagine any major state paper that did not.

Though we were not without responsibility for the breakdown of the Western economy, and for the failure to sustain or to enlarge existing international organizations, the war itself was none of our making.

That, however, made little difference, either in our attitude toward it
or in what now appears to be our inevitable involvement, and it is
instructive to compare the initial American reaction to the First and
the Second World Wars. In 1914 President Wilson could appeal for
neutrality in spirit as well as in deed, and could—and did—manage to
preserve a very real neutrality for over two years. President Roosevelt
did not even pretend to neutrality nor, for that matter, did the great
body of the American people.

While there was a widespread suspicion of all Old World powers
and politics, and an ardent desire to keep out of the war, there was
never for a moment any question where American sympathies lay:
Hitler had taken care of that. There was, in fact, a quasi war, not
unlike that of the 1790's, before there was a real war—a quasi war by
no means all of our making. Both the moral and the practical issues
of the Second War were much clearer than those of the First, a quarter
century earlier, and—it should be added—so was American understanding. All through the thirties the totalitarian states had flagrantly
repudiated international law and torn up existing treaties and agreements; they had trampled on the rights of minorities, pursued policies
of intimidation and conquest of weaker states, erected racism into a
policy and carried it out in murderous programs; they had defiantly
announced their purpose to rule the world. In the circumstances it is
not surprising that American opinion came more and more to accept
active participation as the price of survival.

World War II differed from all previous wars in that it was truly
total. It was total in that it involved almost every great nation on the
globe, and most of the smaller ones as well: with the few notable ex-
ceptions of Sweden, Switzerland, and Spain, those nations which sought
to preserve neutrality were not permitted to do so. It was total in that
it was fought in every quarter of the globe, except South America
(and even here there were naval engagements). It was total in that it
affected every segment of society and economy: the worker and the
farmer were enlisted, the scholar and the scientist, women as well as
men. It made no distinction between combatants and civilians—indeed,
life was as safe in armies or on ships as it was in a Rotterdam, a Cov-
entry, a Warsaw, a Hamburg, or a Tokyo. And the war was almost
total in its destructive character as well; it was symbolic that it ended
with the first—and so far, happily, the only—use of the new weapon

that dramatized the fateful choice between peace and annihilation to all mankind.

Although the United States came late on the military scene, once involved she was deeply and totally involved. Her soldiers and airmen fought on or over every continent, her seamen on or in every sea. She became, almost overnight, that arsenal of democracy which President Roosevelt had invoked, her factories, her shipyards, her farms and her mines producing twice as much as anyone, friend or foe, had expected. "The Americans can't build planes, only electric ice boxes and razor blades," Hermann Göring had said. But in the end it was the sheer weight of American production that turned the tide in the war—the American ability to produce enough bombers, ships, tanks, food and oil, for her own needs, and for the needs of Britain, Russia, and even China.

All of these things impose exceptional difficulties on the historian of the war. As the war was a total war, he is called upon to be a total historian, to master and explain and synthesize the political and the diplomatic, the military, the economic, the social, the scientific conduct of the war. He is required to weave together into a coherent pattern the complex and tangled strands of war on three continents, on a dozen major fronts, in the air and on the sea. He must shuttle back and forth from the Atlantic to the Pacific, from the Mediterranean to the Caribbean and to the North Sea—and with no allowance for miscalculations. He must keep in mind, and synchronize—as the High Command never did—events in North Africa, Burma, Britain and the Pacific islands, the Russian front, the North African front, the Italian front, the Normandy front, the bombing over a hundred cities and the resistance movements of a dozen occupied countries. He must unravel domestic politics and seek to understand the politics of allies and of enemies as well. He must penetrate—something neither Churchill nor Roosevelt could ever quite do—behind the Iron Curtain to the mysteries of Russian policy and the facts of Russian warfare. He must somehow fit into all of this whatever is relevant of the conduct of the war by Germany, Italy and Japan.

It is a tribute to Professor Buchanan that he has faced these and many other problems with equanimity, approached them systematically, and somehow brought order out of what appears to be chaos. It is sobering to reflect how few historical scholars have been bold enough to undertake a historical synthesis as ambitious and as exacting as this. We have histories of battles and campaigns by the hundred; the official histories of the war, pouring relentlessly forth from the historical bureaus of a dozen governments, already constitute something of a torrent; the unofficial histories pour over us like a tidal wave. Professor Buchanan has mastered this vast mass of material, whipped it into shape with military efficiency, and given us a synthesis both original and compelling. That is a notable achievement.

This volume is one of the New American Nation series, a comprehensive co-operative survey of the history of the area now embraced in the United States from the days of discovery to the late twentieth century. Since the publication by the house of Harper of the American Nation series more than half a century ago, the scope of history has been immensely broadened, new approaches have been explored and interpretations developed. The time has come for a judicious reappraisal of the new history, a cautious application of the new techniques of investigation and presentation, and a large-scale effort to achieve a synthesis of the new findings. To this task the New American Nation series is dedicated. Each volume is part of a carefully planned whole, and fitted to the other volumes in the series; each volume, too, is designed to be complete in itself. From time to time there may be overlapping, but it has seemed to the editors that something is to be gained from looking at the same material from different points of view. Other volumes will cover the constitutional and cultural aspects of these war years.

HENRY STEELE COMMAGER
RICHARD B. MORRIS

Preface

THE purpose of this work is to present a reasonably concise account of the role of the United States in World War II. The effort to give a balanced treatment is modified by the fact that the volumes are part of a series in which appear specialized accounts of cultural and social developments. Hence, I have not included an extensive treatment of the impact of the war on these aspects of American life. Even during the war, military and other leaders were history-conscious; the result has been the accumulation of a staggering deposit of documentation and its assiduous investigation by historians either in or allied to the armed services. No one person could hope to examine all the sources available on the military phases of the war. I have, therefore, drawn heavily on the works of these trained service historians. In dealing with factors surrounding the entrance of the United States into the war, it has been feasible to work more closely with primary sources.

I should like to express my appreciation to Mr. Cass Canfield, Chairman, Harper Editorial Board, for his early and continued interest in these volumes. I wish also to thank Professor Henry Steele Commager for his careful editing and to acknowledge the suggestions made by those whom he asked to read portions of the work. Professor Richard B. Morris has been helpful in preparations of the final stages of publication, and my colleagues, Professors Robert Kelley, Charles Spaulding, and Henry Turner, made valuable suggestions about certain chapters. As always, the staff of the Library of the University of California, Santa Barbara, has been of great assistance, as has been Beulah Hagen, of Harper & Row, Publishers. Above all, I am indebted to my wife, Ethel, whose sustained help and support cannot be detailed adequately in a preface.

A. RUSSELL BUCHANAN

THE UNITED STATES
AND WORLD WAR II

Volume I

CHAPTER 1

The Coming of World War II–Europe

IN the spring and summer of 1933, while Adolf Hitler was consolidating his power in Germany, a new administration was getting under way in Washington. Concerned with the depression, President Roosevelt concentrated on domestic issues throughout his first term and much of his second. Although basically Roosevelt was an internationalist and interested in foreign affairs, need for support of his domestic program kept him from challenging isolationist sentiment, which had been strong in the United States during the 1920's and 1930's. This sentiment was varied in nature and in origin.[1] Some Americans hated war and believed that the United States, if it wished, could remain aloof from conflicts that might arise. They feared that foreign entanglements, even with the League of Nations, would lead to war rather than collective security. Anglophobia dictated an isolationist stand for some Americans, especially those of Irish or German background, since they believed the alternative would be alliance with Britain.

A significant element of isolationists, especially before the outbreak of war in Europe, consisted of liberals or progressives. Some of these had been dissatisfied with the Treaty of Versailles as a victory of power politics over the ideas which Wilson earlier had enunciated. Intellectuals were affected by the writings of the British economist,

---

[1] Discussions of isolationism include Selig Adler, *The Isolationist Impulse: Its Twentieth-Century Reaction* (London and New York, 1957); Alexander DeConde (ed.), *Isolation and Security* (Durham, N.C., 1957), pp. 3–25; 159–183.

John Maynard Keynes, who denounced the economic consequences of a harsh peace which had blocked world recovery. Revisionist writers stressed the theme that World War I had not been the diabolical product of a militaristic Germany bent on world domination, but that it had been an avoidable conflict in which economic determinism and diplomatic maneuvering figured largely and war guilt fell on not one, but every participating nation, including the United States.[2] Other Americans, including Charles A. Beard and Charles Lindbergh, Jr., believed in strength through isolation. Some extended their concept of a fortress to include the Western Hemisphere, which, insulated by broad oceans, could exist safely even in a hostile world. As involvement in the war approached, many liberals abandoned isolation and supported the Roosevelt administration. At the same time, however, some conservatives took the lead in support of isolation in the belief that Roosevelt's internationalism would lead not only to war but to the destruction of the economic institutions of the nation. This type of thinking influenced strongly the formation of the America First Committee, which, as will be noted later, came into being in the fall of 1940.[3]

Imbued with isolationist sentiment during the early thirties, many Americans came to the conclusion that if Europe went to war again, the United States should remain aloof. To this end Congress passed the Johnson Act in 1934.[4] The failure of the Allies to pay their war debts led to wishful thinking on the part of Americans that if Europe had no money it might not go to war. The Johnson Act, accordingly, prohibited the further lending of money to any nation in default on its war debts. The act proved to be an ineffective deterrent; its immediate result was the cessation of token payments on war debts.

Aroused by the Italo-Ethiopian crisis in the summer of 1935, Congress passed the first of a series of joint resolutions known as Neutrality Acts.[5] Their purpose was to prevent the United States from

[2] Helmuth C. Engelbrecht and F. C. Hannighan, *Merchants of Death: A Study of the International Armaments Industry* (New York, 1934), *passim;* Charles A. Beard, *The Devil Theory of War* (New York, 1936), *passim;* Charles C. Tansill, *America Goes to War* (Boston, 1938), *passim.*

[3] For an appraisal of the writings of this period, see Donald F. Drummond, *The Passing of American Neutrality, 1937–1941* (Ann Arbor, 1955), pp. 36–40.

[4] *U.S. Statutes at Large,* Vol. XLVIII, p. 574, reprinted in Henry Steele Commager (ed.), *Documents of American History* (New York, 1949) (5th ed.), Doc. No. 490.

[5] The neutrality legislation of 1935, 1936, 1937 is reprinted in Ruhl J. Bart-

reaching a position as a neutral that would force it into belligerency. This first resolution forbade the export of "arms, ammunition, or implements of war" to a belligerent or "to any neutral port for transshipment to, or for the use of, a belligerent country," if the President declared the existence of a state of war. The resolution also called for licensing arms manufacturers and merchants, and declared that Americans traveling on belligerent ships in wartime did so at their own risk. Amendments followed, and in 1937 Congress made a thoroughgoing revision, known as the Neutrality Act of 1937, which retained basic principles of the earlier legislation but made significant changes. It kept restrictions on munitions and loans and introduced a new principle, "cash and carry," for raw materials. Commodities listed by the President had to be paid for on delivery and carried away from American ports by the purchaser, and travel by Americans on belligerent vessels became unlawful rather than at the traveler's risk. This act, like its predecessors, met strong criticism. Some persons still argued that the President should have the power to discriminate between aggressor and attacked nations. Others asserted that it was not a neutrality law at all, since it favored belligerents who could take advantage of the cash-and-carry clause.

The neutrality laws formed but a part of the early foreign policy of the Roosevelt administration. It continued the practice of the Hoover administration of cooperation with the League of Nations in disarmament efforts, although as tension increased in Europe, such moves seemed futile. Another course of action taken by the United States reflects the influence of the Chief Executive, one of whose characteristics was a deeply ingrained belief that much could be accomplished on a personal basis at the highest governmental level. This trait helps to explain the numerous personal appeals and conferences in which the President participated during the war.

Obviously, the best way to keep the United States neutral was to prevent war from taking place. During the Sudeten crisis the President sent appeals to European leaders.[6] Historians differ on the in-

---

lett, *The Record of American Diplomacy: Documents and Readings in the History of American Foreign Relations* (New York, 1947), pp. 572–577. The Act of 1937 is in Commager (ed.), *Documents of American History,* Doc. No. 514.

[6] U.S. State Department, *Foreign Relations of the United States: Diplomatic Papers, 1938* (Washington, 1955), I, 657–658, 684–685. For Hitler's reply to the first communication, see *ibid.,* I, 669–672.

fluence these appeals may have had in producing the Munich Conference. Again, in the spring of 1939, Roosevelt unsuccessfully sought
to persuade Hitler and Mussolini to pledge not to attack other states.[7]
The dictators responded in public addresses that were critical and
even contemptuous.[8] The primary significance of the President's
overture was that it placed him on record as opposed to aggressive
action and focused attention on Mussolini and Hitler as aggressors.
Clearly the overture came from no detached observer of the world
scene.

As the war drew nearer it became apparent that the American
neutrality laws would work to the disadvantage of Great Britain and
France, for the arms embargo provisions would prevent them from
using American production to help them match the military might
which the Axis powers already had created for themselves. Roosevelt
believed that it was not a matter of indifference to Americans which
side would win. "The peace of the world," he explained two years
later, but before entry of the United States in the war, "was being
jeopardized by a handful of relentless men who sought selfish power
for themselves."[9] Consequently, in the summer of 1939 he sought
repeal of the arms embargo provisions of the Neutrality Act of 1937
as a deterrent to war, for it "would, in effect, say to the aggressor
nations that if they did declare war they would find that their enemies
would be able to obtain the needed war supplies here in America."[10]

[7] U.S. State Department, *Foreign Relations of the United States: Diplomatic
Papers, 1939* (Washington, 1956), I, 130–133.

[8] On April 17, the Secretary of State learned from the Chargé in Germany
that Hitler planned to answer Roosevelt's message in a speech before the Reichstag. The Chargé stated: "This method of replying to the President's telegram
was chosen in order to assure Hitler of a wide hearing before the world." *Ibid.,*
I, 138–139.

[9] Introduction, dated July 10, 1941, by F. D. Roosevelt to *The Public Papers
and Addresses of Franklin D. Roosevelt* (New York, 1941), VIII, xxvii.

[10] Introduction, dated July 10, 1944, in *ibid.,* VIII, xxxiv. On May 10, 1939,
Ambassador William C. Bullitt had telegraphed from Paris his conviction that
Joachim von Ribbentrop, Reich Minister of Foreign Affairs, was trying to persuade Hitler to attack France and Britain because these countries could not
secure military supplies from the United States. Bullitt asserted that Ribbentrop
was citing the debates on the Neutrality Act "as proof that the United States
in case of war would sell no military supplies or airplanes to France and England." The Ambassador continued: "The British Government therefore considered it of the highest importance that the modification of the Neutrality Act
should if possible be brought about in the near future." This modification
"would end all chance that Ribbentrop might persuade Hitler to risk immediate
war."

SEPTEMBER, 1939

The attempted revision failed in large part as a result of the opposition of Senator William E. Borah, who denied the imminence of war.[11] The issue, of course, was complicated by partisanship, by a fear of granting too much discretionary power to the President, by extreme nationalism or isolationism, and by belief on the part of some persons that the President was trying to get the nation into a war rather than out of it. Leading authorities incline to the view that revision of the law would not have dissuaded Hitler from his aggressive action, for he apparently counted heavily on the inability of the United States to mobilize in time to aid the Allies significantly.

Meanwhile, Europe moved inexorably toward war. When late in August news arrived of the Nazi-Soviet Pact, the Washington administration had been well informed of developments and apparently was less shocked than were the British or the French. Roosevelt once again tried personal appeal. Poland was the immediate danger area; there was a slim hope that the Soviet-German accord might have alienated Italy. Consequently, on August 23, 1939, the President sent messages to King Victor Emmanuel II of Italy, President Ignacy Mościcki of Poland, and Hitler.[12] Adolf A. Berle, Assistant Secretary of State, who was involved in drafting the messages, stated his opinion that the messages "would have about the same effect as a valentine sent to somebody's mother-in-law out of season; and they have all that quality of naïveté which is the prerogative alone of the United States." Even Berle felt that the messages should be sent, since no one would be "blamed for making any attempt, however desperate, for preserving peace."[13] The communication to the King of Italy antedated the others and urged him to exert his efforts to arrest war. To the others, Roosevelt offered to act as a conciliator, and he sent Hitler a second message when no reply came to the first. The only affirmative answer came from the Polish President; the Italian King declined to act, and Hitler did not bother to answer directly, but his impassioned speech to the Reichstag on August 31, 1939, giving his version of German-Polish affairs, and the subsequent invasion of

[11] Cordell Hull, *The Memoirs of Cordell Hull* (New York, 1948), I, 649–651.

[12] The communication to the King of Italy is reproduced in Commager, *Documents of American History*, No. 524. All three messages are in Roosevelt, *Public Papers*, VIII, 444–448. The date given in this source is August 24, 1939.

[13] From Berle Diaries (MS.), quoted in William L. Langer and S. Everett Gleason, *The Challenge to Isolation, 1937–1940* (New York, 1952), p. 189.

Poland constituted reply enough. Hitler had given a somewhat different reason to his Commanders in Chief on August 22, 1939, when he told them:

> I shall give a propagandist reason for starting the war, no matter whether it is plausible or not. The victor will not be asked afterwards whether he told the truth or not. When starting and waging a war it is not right that matters, but victory.
>
> Close your hearts to pity. Act brutally. Eighty million people must obtain what is their right. Their existence must be made secure. The stronger man is right. . . .[14]

The main result of Roosevelt's gestures, as the President expressed it, was to put "the bee on Germany, which no one did in 1914."[15]

Shortly before three in the morning of September 1, 1939, the United States Ambassador to France, William C. Bullitt, called Washington to tell the President that Germany had launched a war on Poland. The President's staff immediately alerted department heads and informed the press associations of developments. Later in the day Roosevelt told a press conference that he thought the nation could stay out of war and that the administration would make "every effort" in this direction.[16]

Two days later the President went on the air in a "Fireside Chat" and, making a plea for national unity, asserted, "This nation will remain a neutral nation, but I cannot ask that every American remain neutral in thought as well. Even a neutral cannot be asked to close his mind or his conscience." He reiterated his hatred of war and pledged, "As long as it remains within my power to prevent, there will be no blackout of peace in the United States."[17]

One of the first moves of the administration after the outbreak

[14] Unsigned memorandum, August 22, 1939 (Nuremberg Document 1014-PS, Exhibit USA—30). Reprinted in [Germany, *Auswärtiges Amt.*] *Documents on German Foreign Policy* (Washington, 1956), Ser. D, Vol. VII, 205.

[15] From Moffatt Diaries (MS.), quoted in Langer and Gleason, *The Challenge to Isolation*, p. 190. In his published papers, Jay Pierrepont Moffatt wrote, August 24, 1939: "I don't think that anyone felt there was more than one chance in a thousand that such messages would affect events, but it seemed that that chance should be taken and above all that the record should be abundantly clear." Jay Pierrepont Moffatt, *The Moffatt Papers: Selections from the Diplomatic Journals of Jay Pierrepont Moffatt, 1919–1943* (Cambridge, Mass., 1956), p. 253.

[16] The Five Hundred and Seventy-fifth Press Conference, September 1, 1939, Roosevelt, *Public Papers*, VIII, 457.

[17] Fireside Chat, Sept. 3, 1939, *ibid.*, VIII, 463–464.

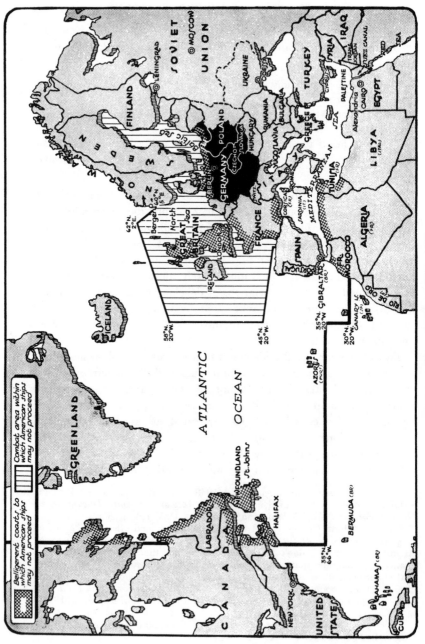

AMERICAN NEUTRALITY, 1939

of war was to bolster defenses, on the continental rather than the national level. Prompted by the United States government, a number of Latin-American states called a conference of the nations of the Western Hemisphere, opening in Panama, September 23, 1939. From the standpoint of rapport, this was one of the most successful conferences ever held by American states. The most striking resolution was Number XIV, the so-called Declaration of Panama, suggested by the United States representative, Sumner Welles, and accepted virtually unchanged by the conference. It created a zone three hundred miles in width around the Western Hemisphere, with the exception of Canada and the "colonies and undisputed possessions of European countries." This zone was to be kept free from hostile actions by any non-American belligerent. During the war, American states, either individually or collectively, as agreed upon by common consent, could patrol the waters in the area described.[18] The Declaration met fewer objections on legal grounds than had been anticipated, but practical problems of control proved complicated.

The advent of war moved the administration to attempt once again the revision of neutrality legislation. Calling a special session of Congress, Roosevelt stressed the theme that "by the repeal of the embargo the United States will more probably remain at peace than if the law remains as it stands today."[19] As the debate developed in Congress both sides agreed that they wished the United States to remain out of war; the difference of opinion was whether repeal or retention of the embargo would produce the result. The act that emerged after six weeks of debate was a compromise.[20] The arms embargo was repealed in favor of the "cash and carry" principle. American production was thus made available to the Allies, as had been the case in World War I. There was, however, a sharp difference in the type of war zone instituted. In World War I, a zone had been drawn around the British Isles by a belligerent Germany. In 1939, extensive war zones were declared to exist in waters off the coasts of belligerents, but these zones were created by the United States for the purpose of excluding its own citizens from these areas. As one expert summarized it, the act of 1939 bartered the arms embargo for

[18] The Declaration is reprinted in Commager, *Documents of American History*, No. 526.

[19] Reprinted in Roosevelt, *Public Papers*, VIII, 518.

[20] The Neutrality Act of 1939 is reprinted in Commager, *Documents of American History*, No. 527.

the danger zone and abandonment of freedom of the seas.[21]

The Neutrality Act of 1939 marked an important shift in the American relation to the war. Under the older legislation Germany stood to gain, for that country was better prepared for war; the new legislation not only gave the advantage to the Allies, but indicated where American sentiment lay. There was one possible advantage for Germany. The purpose of the war zone was to prevent loss of American life and property in incidents that might lead to war. A result of the war zone as seen by some contemporaries was to strike a blow at the American merchant marine and to increase the blockade of the British Isles.

In summarizing the struggle for revision of neutrality legislation, one is inclined to the belief that although the administration was strongly sympathetic toward the democracies and wished to aid them, it endeavored to give such assistance in the hope that by so doing the United States would stand a better chance of staying out of war.

As part of its blockade of Germany, Great Britain began to re-institute on an expanded scale practices she had employed during World War I. In an effort to avoid friction with England, Secretary Hull suggested that experts from the two countries draw up a certificate system comparable to that used in World War I.[22] Accordingly, on December 1, 1939, the British introduced the "navicert" system, under which goods would be subject to seizure if they or the materials that went into them originated in Germany, even if the goods themselves were being shipped from one neutral to another. Frictions inevitably developed, and Secretary Hull's problem was a difficult one, as he explained in his memoirs:

> While insisting on what we regarded as our rights, we still were careful not to exacerbate relations with Britain. I felt that Britain's great trial of strength lay within the coming months. I knew that Hitler, not Britain, had started the war and that a German victory would be dangerous to the best interests of the United States.[23]

Instead of making an issue of matters that might arouse public opin-

[21] Thomas A. Bailey, *A Diplomatic History of the American People* (New York, 1958) (6th ed.), p. 715; S. F. Bemis, *The United States As a World Power* (New York, 1950), pp. 367–368; Langer and Gleason, *The Challenge to Isolation*, pp. 218–235.

[22] "Memorandum of Conversation by the Secretary of State," Sept. 4, 1939, U.S. Department of State, *Foreign Relations, 1939*, I, 719.

[23] Hull, *Memoirs*, I, 734.

ion, therefore, Hull engaged with marked success in a "process of striving to work out each point amicably."[24]

The "phony" war following the conquest of Poland was accompanied in the United States by what sometimes has been called the "phony" peace. Confronted by a war that was not a war, American policy was filled with indecision. Britain's plight seemed less apparent, and irritation rose accordingly with that country's interference with neutral trade. Then when Soviet Russia turned on Finland, American sympathy with the underdog conflicted with the American desire not to become involved.[25]

The invasion of Denmark and Norway naturally aroused the interest and concern of Americans. "Force and military aggression are once more on the march against small nations," declared President Roosevelt on April 13, 1940.[26] Although highly critical of the invasion, neither the United States administration nor the people yet sensed the full power of the German *Blitzkrieg*. Thoughts did turn to Denmark's possessions, Iceland and Greenland. The United States could not with equanimity watch the Nazis move to these islands. Neither, in view of the Monroe Doctrine, could the United States welcome British seizure of these regions, for Greenland clearly lay within the Western Hemisphere as did perhaps a portion of Iceland. The administration moved cautiously at the outset. It declined the Danish suggestion of an American protectorate over Greenland, but in May, 1940, opened a consulate on the island.[27] The British did not advise

[24] *Ibid.*, I, 735. Documents relevant to the problem of neutral trade are in U.S. State Department, *Foreign Relations, 1939*, I, 717–847; *1940* (Washington, 1957), II, 2–60.

[25] At the suggestion of the Finns, the U.S. offered to negotiate a peace between Finland and Soviet Russia. When Soviet Russia dealt directly with Finland the U.S. Ambassador, Lawrence A. Steinhardt, elicited a statement from Foreign Minister V. M. Molotov that the Finns could choose their own government. Steinhardt to Secretary of State, Mar. 8, 1940, U.S. State Department, *Foreign Relations of the United States: Diplomatic Papers, 1940* (Washington, 1959), I, 305–306.

[26] Roosevelt's statement is reprinted in S. Shepard Jones and Denys P. Myers, *Documents on American Foreign Relations, July, 1939–June, 1940* (Boston, 1940), II, 410.

[27] The U.S. government secured permission to establish a consulate from the local authorities in Greenland rather than from the Danish government since the latter was unable to exercise control over its overseas possessions. See "Memorandum by Mr. Hugh S. Cummings, Jr., of the Division of European Affairs," Apr. 24, 1940. U.S. State Department, *Foreign Relations, 1940*, II, 345–346. Greenland authorities were worried over possible sabotage of the

Washington in advance of their decision to occupy Iceland. When a British landing was made in May, 1940, the American government accepted the British explanation that the occupation would be temporary.[28]

In the early evening of May 9, 1940, President Roosevelt received a telephone call from John Cudahy, American Ambassador to Belgium, reporting an anticipated German attack on Belgium before morning. Roosevelt immediately called Hull, who alerted his own staff and tried without much success to pass the alarm to embassies in Western Europe. Press flashes began to reach Washington later in the night, and other reports from Cudahy told of planes in the air and border clashes under way. Jay Pierrepont Moffatt, Chief of the Division on European Affairs, noted in his diary, "The war has now begun in earnest. . . ."[29]

While the Germans with their *Blitzkrieg* overwhelmed the Dutch, knocked out the Belgians, and pinned British and French soldiers against Dunkirk, Washington lived through what Sumner Welles called a "nightmare of frustration."[30] The ultimate promise of material support was great, but immediate returns were slow in arriving, since industrial America was just beginning to gird itself. Two major themes emerged during the "nightmare." One was the despairing hope that Mussolini might still be persuaded to remain aloof from the conflict. Through its representatives and by direct appeals the Washington administration sought to achieve this goal. A detailed examination of these efforts seems superfluous. The essential fact was that Musso-

cryolite mine at Ivigtut. The United States provided antiaircraft weapons at a fraction of their cost and assisted in procuring guards. For correspondence on this subject, see *ibid.*, 1940, II, 362–376.

[28] British Ambassador (Lothian) to the Secretary of State, May 10, 1940; Secretary of State to the British Ambassador, May 15, 1940, in *ibid.*, 1940, II, 679–680.

[29] Moffatt Diary, May 9, 1940, *Moffatt Papers,* p. 307. Cudahy on March 12, 1940, had warned Washington, "From an unimpeachable source I am advised that Germany has decided that no acceptable peace terms can be expected from France and Great Britain and is therefore determined to bring off large-scale military offensive. . . ." Cudahy to Secretary of State, Mar. 13, 1940. U.S. State Department, *Foreign Relations, 1940,* I, 184. On May 9, however, Cudahy reported that the King of the Belgians did not anticipate an attack "at the present time" and expressed his opinion that the alarm in the Netherlands was a part of the "war of nerves." Cudahy to Secretary of State, May 8, 1940, *ibid., 1940,* I, 188.

[30] Sumner Welles, *The Time for Decision* (New York and London, 1944), p. 148.

lini had made up his mind to share the rewards of victory, and these could be obtained only if Italy became an active belligerent on the victorious side. It became, as far as he was concerned, a matter of timing: to enter late enough to avoid heavy losses and the chance of defeat, but to enter before the war ended. He told his generals toward the end of May, "I need a few thousand dead so as to be able to attend the peace conference as a belligerent."[31] Neither by persuading the Allies to make modest concessions nor by appeals at the moral level could the United States turn this decision.[32]

The other theme was Washington's growing awareness not only of the serious plight of the Allies, but of the effect that their defeat might have upon America's safety. The Allies did not hesitate to tell Washington of their desperate position. Churchill asked for American nonbelligerency, the loan of forty or fifty old destroyers, and the transfer of several hundred planes being delivered to the United States Army.[33] Sympathetic though Roosevelt was, he did not comply with the request. Others, at home and abroad, advocated more direct action than was being taken. The French urged the dispatch of the American Fleet to Tangier to dissuade Mussolini from entering the war. The Australian Minister to the United States suggested that the United States declare war.[34] Alexander Kirk, United States Chargé d'Affaires in Berlin, made a similar proposal.[35]

[31] Quoted in Gaetano Salvemini, "Pietro Badoglio's Role in the Second World War," *The Journal of Modern History*, XXI (Dec., 1949), 327. See also Galeazzo Ciano, *The Ciano Diaries 1939–1943, The Complete, Unabridged Diaries of* . . . (Garden City, N.Y., 1946), May 10, 15, 29, 1940, pp. 246–247, 250–256.

[32] The principal correspondence is in U.S. State Department, *Foreign Relations, 1940*, II, 685–717. In an oral statement by direction of the President of the United States, Ambassador William Phillips advised Mussolini, through the Italian Foreign Minister, Count Galeazzo Ciano, "The further extension of the war as a result of Italian participation would at once result in an increase in the rearmament program of the United States itself and in a redoubling of the efforts of the Government of the United States to facilitate in every practical way the securing within the United States by the Allied Powers of all of the supplies and matériel which they may require." Hull to Phillips, May 30, 1940, *ibid., 1940*, II, 713–714. In reply Mussolini stated through Ciano that "the decision had already been taken to enter the war." Responding to the warning that America would increase aid to the Allies, Mussolini "says that he has no objection and that that is our decision. This proves to him, however, that America is actually giving help to the Allies and has already 'chosen the Allied side.' " Phillips to Hull, June 1, 1940, *ibid., 1940*, II, 715.

[33] Churchill, *The Second World War* (Boston, 1949), II, 24.

[34] Hull, *Memoirs,* I, 773, 775–776.

[35] Telegram from Kirk (at Rome), May 28, 1940, U.S. State Department,

The evidence shows that the President did not contemplate declaring war or intervening. A public opinion poll indicates that only 7.7 percent of the population favored immediate entrance into the war. The Allies were unhappy at the reluctance of the United States to join them, but actually it does not seem that American entrance would have aided their cause materially. Mussolini would not have been deterred from entering the struggle; Hitler would not have been checked in his war plans. In fact, an all-out submarine campaign might have been turned loose on American shipping. The United States was not psychologically or materially ready for war in the spring of 1940, and importunities of the hard-pressed Allies were not sufficient to force it into the conflict.

Although the United States at this time did not declare war, it took a step which perhaps rendered inevitable later entrance. This was what Langer and Gleason have called the "great commitment." Before May, 1940, the American government had made clear where its sympathies lay, but the material aid had come from private industry. "Almost casually," as these authors state it, toward the end of May, 1940, and on a small scale, the government made a commitment to give material support to the Allies. The President established the principle by approving the transfer of a small number of planes and equipment from the Navy and War departments to the Allies.[36]

It apparently took a further development of the war in Europe to induce the President to make a public announcement of this principle. That development was Italy's entrance into the conflict. On June 10, speaking to the graduating class of the University of Virginia at Charlottesville, Roosevelt openly made the "great commitment." First he outlined the efforts he had made to prevent Italian intervention and, against the advice of Sumner Welles, he repeated the charge current in France that "the hand that held the dagger had struck it into the back of its neighbor." Then he declared:

In our American unity, we will pursue two obvious and simultaneous courses; we will extend to the opponents of force the material resources of this nation and, at the same time, we will harness and speed up the use of

---

Foreign Relations, 1940, I, 235–236. Kirk wrote: "We are now being largely discounted as a factor in this fight because it is expected that it will be over before we are effectively a part of it and it is certain that great care will be taken by Germany to keep us out."

[36] The public was not informed of these transactions. Langer and Gleason, *The Challenge to Isolation,* pp. 503–504.

those resources in order that we ourselves in the Americas may have equipment and training equal to the task of every emergency and every defense.[37]

Insistent voices in the United States had been demanding that the government take action. William Allen White, liberal Republican editor, had become increasingly convinced that this country should aid Britain, for behind the British Fleet "we could have two years in which to prepare for the inevitable attack of the totalitarian powers upon our democracy, which must come unless Great Britain wins this war."[38] He joined others of like mind to form the Committee to Defend America by Aiding the Allies, which by July, 1940, had three hundred branches throughout the nation. A *Fortune* magazine poll of that month indicated that 67.5 percent of the people favored aid to the Allies.

As the 1940 presidential election approached, the major candidates, Roosevelt and Wendell Willkie, the Republican nominee, differed little in their views on the war. On June 8, Willkie told news correspondents that "an overwhelming number of people" in the country believed that "we should give all possible aid, short of war, of course, to the Allies."[39]

Within the Committee to Defend America by Aiding the Allies a cleavage developed as a so-called Century Group in the New York chapter wanted the United States to declare war immediately on Germany. White felt the group was moving too rapidly, and on January 1, 1941, resigned the chairmanship of the committee.[40]

In the meantime, British and French pressure on the administration continued. As France was about to fall, Churchill urged American intervention and on June 15 wrote to Roosevelt: "A declaration that the United States will if necessary enter the war might save France." He continued: "Failing that, in a few days French resistance may have crumpled and we shall be left alone."[41] The President, however, resisted this and other pressure. Full sympathy and material aid he would promise; beyond this he was not yet ready to go. Public

[37] Reprinted in Commager, *Documents of American History,* No. 530.
[38] Walter Johnson, *William Allen White's America* (New York, 1947), p. 524.
[39] Press interview, June 8, 1940, quoted in Langer and Gleason, *The Challenge to Isolation,* p. 505.
[40] Johnson, *William Allen White's America,* pp. 547–548.
[41] Reprinted in Churchill, *The Second World War,* II, 188. Reynaud sent another impassioned appeal on June 14. U.S. State Department, *Foreign Relations, 1940,* I, 252, 253.

opinion polls indicate that he was not out of tune with the majority of the people at that time.

In the United States the news of the armistice between Germany and France came as a shock. The rapid military defeat of a major power such as France threw into new perspective the matter of American security. One result was increased cooperation between the United States and Canada, which also had. been shaken by developments. In August, 1938, President Roosevelt had stated publicly that "the people of the United States will not stand idly by if domination of Canadian soil is threatened by any other Empire."[42] Prime Minister Mackenzie King had replied in kind by asserting that if the occasion ever arose, "enemy forces should not be able to pursue their way, either by land, sea, or air, to the United States across Canadian territory." With the collapse of France, the Canadian suggested staff talks to the newly appointed Minister to Canada, Jay Pierrepont Moffatt.[43] Roosevelt authorized secret staff talks, and on August 18, 1940, in a meeting the Canadian Prime Minister and the American President tightened their mutual assurances in a joint statement known as the Ogdensburg Agreement.[44] The heart of the document was an announcement that a Permanent Joint Board on Defense would be set up at once to "commence immediate studies relating to sea, land, and air problems including personnel and matériel" and to "consider in the broad sense the defense of the north half of the Western Hemisphere."

The agreement was generally praised in both countries and was quickly implemented by the appointment of members to the board. The agreement constituted a further American shift to the Allied side. Traditional concepts of neutrality could hardly encompass what was virtually a defensive alliance between a belligerent and a neutral.

After the fall of France Hitler looked to a speedy end of the war with Britain and started plans for invasion if it should become necessary. The German Foreign Office made strenuous but unsuccessful efforts to create a British Quisling out of the former King of England, Edward VII, who after abdicating his throne to marry an American

[42] Address at Queen's University, Kingston, Ontario, Aug. 18, 1938. Reprinted in Roosevelt, *Public Papers,* VII, 493.

[43] Moffatt's account of the overtures is in *Moffatt Papers,* pp. 312–318.

[44] Reprinted in Commager, *Documents of American History,* No. 535. For details of the meeting, see *Moffatt Papers,* pp. 324–330.

divorcee had been living on the Continent in self-imposed exile.[45] When they saw that the British had no intention of yielding and that invasion would be difficult and dangerous, the Germans concentrated on their air assault of the island, in what came to be called the Battle for Britain.

While the Royal Air Force fought back with all it had, and Britons bolstered their home defenses, Churchill continued his efforts to obtain destroyers from the United States as a stopgap until orders for new craft could be filled. Roosevelt was sympathetic, but legal, political, and other obstacles loomed in the way until some members of the Century Group made the proposal that with alterations was to be adopted.[46] As it ultimately worked out, Britain granted outright two bases on Newfoundland and Bermuda to the United States for ninety-nine years. In exchange for fifty overage destroyers, six other bases were leased rent-free for the same period on British possessions from Bermuda to British Guiana. Secretary Hull and Lord Lothian signed the documents on September 2, 1940, and on the following day the U.S. Chief of Naval Operations, Admiral Harold R. Stark, declared the destroyers nonessential for the national defense.[47]

The reception of the destroyers-for-bases deal on the whole was favorable. Linking the destroyers transfer with bases choked off much isolationist criticism, for leading isolationists for some time had been demanding that the United States increase its hemisphere defenses. As far as American neutrality was concerned there was no connection between this deal and neutrality, as it had been viewed by the United States before the advent of World War II. The Roosevelt administration had departed from neutrality to make two important defensive moves: to increase aid to Britain and to secure additional bases for the United States.

Isolationist sentiment was by no means dead in the United States. Two days after the signing of the destroyers-for-bases deal, the for-

[45] For numerous German documents on this subject, see analytical list of documents under Great Britain in U.S. State Department, *Documents on German Foreign Policy, 1918–1945* (Washington, 1957), X, xxiv–xxvi.

[46] Memo of Century Group meeting of July 25, 1940 (Francis P. Miller Papers MS.), quoted in Langer and Gleason, *The Challenge to Isolation,* p. 747. See also Harold L. Ickes, *The Secret Diary of Harold L. Ickes* (New York, 1954), III, 270–271, 283, 291–292, 304.

[47] The letters of Hull and Lothian are in Commager, *Documents of American History,* No. 536.

THE UNITED STATES AND BRITAIN

mation of the leading isolationist organization in this country was announced. Founded by a Yale law student, R. Douglas Stuart, Jr., son of the first vice president of the Quaker Oats Company, and influenced strongly by General Robert A. Wood, chairman of the board of Sears, Roebuck and Company, the "America First Committee" at the outset had four main objectives:

1. The United States must build an impregnable defense for America.
2. No foreign power, nor group of powers, can successfully attack a *prepared* America.
3. American democracy can be preserved only by keeping out of the European war.
4. "Aid short of war" weakens national defense at home and threatens to involve America in war abroad.[48]

Many well-known Americans lent at least their names to support the committee. Among the heaviest contributors were William H. Regnery, president of Western Shade Cloth Company, General Wood, Sterling Morton, secretary of the Morton Salt Company, and Robert Young, railway magnate. The committee from the first found itself plagued by enthusiastic fellow travelers from both the left and the right. The Communists tried to join the organization until Hitler's invasion of Russia in the summer of 1941 altered the party line toward American isolationism. More successful were representatives of the extreme right, although many leaders of the committee tried to keep it clear of any German connections. Some of the propagandist material distributed by the America First Committee came from Nazi-inspired or sponsored organizations. George Sylvester Viereck, who had performed a similar role in the neutrality period before American entry into World War I, organized several of these committees. Although the America First Committee refused to deal with the German-American Bund, it did accept the support of such extremist groups as William Dudley Pelley's Silver Shirts, the Ku Klux Klan, and Father Coughlin's Christian Front.

One of the headline speakers for America First was Colonel Charles A. Lindbergh, Jr. Son of a Swedish-born Middle Western agrarian Congressman who had opposed America's entry into World War I, young Lindbergh at twenty-five had gained world prominence by his solo flight across the Atlantic. There followed marriage, wealth, and

[48] Wayne S. Cole, *America First: The Battle Against Intervention, 1940–1941* (Madison, Wis., 1953), pp. 15–16.

the tragic kidnap-murder of the couple's infant son. Annoyed by the interest of the press in the family's personal life and by New Deal queries into his relations with commercial aviation companies, Lindbergh moved to temporary obscurity in England. In 1936 he accepted the call of the United States Embassy in Germany to assess the growing strength of the *Luftwaffe*. Feted and honored by the Nazi government, Lindbergh not only became deeply impressed by the might of the German air arm but apparently absorbed some of the Nazi ideology. In 1939 he returned to the United States as an outspoken advocate of isolationism. Instead of realizing that growing air power dwarfed the world, he stressed the view that through its own strength the United States could create an impregnable bastion of defense. Unfortunately, in an address made in Des Moines, Iowa, September 11, 1941, he made statements which brought charges of anti-Semitism against him and the America First Committee which weakened the effectiveness of the committee.[49]

The German government carefully watched American reactions to European developments. Until mid-November, 1938, its principal informant was Hans Dieckhoff, German Ambassador to the United States. Dieckhoff did not gild his reports with optimism concerning German-American relations. As early as October 9, 1937, although noting America's passive role in foreign affairs, he predicted that if Great Britain became involved in world war, "Then, of course, we will have to expect that the weight of the United States of America will soon be thrown into the scale on the side of the British."[50] He repeated this warning so often that finally he apologized for its repetition.[51]

The German Ambassador felt that American public opinion determined American foreign policy, and on December 20, 1937, he wrote that several factors recently had influenced this opinion against Germany. First was the belief that Germany was aligned with the "aggressor states," Italy and Japan. Second was a "sharper emphasis" on ideological differences between the United States and Germany, and

[49] Quoted in *ibid.*, p. 144.

[50] Dieckhoff to the German Foreign Ministry, Oct. 9, 1937 [Germany, *Auswärtiges Amt.*], *Documents on German Foreign Policy* (Washington, 1949), Ser. D, Vol. I, 635.

[51] E.g., messages Dieckhoff to German Foreign Ministry, Dec. 7, 1937, *ibid.*, Ser. D, Vol. I, 655–656; Feb. 9, 1938, *ibid.*, Ser. D, Vol. I, 690; Dieckhoff to State Secretary in the German Foreign Ministry (Baron von Weizsäcker), Mar. 22, 1938, *ibid.*, Ser. D, Vol. I, 697.

third was a growing conviction that National Socialism and Fascism threatened the United States. Dieckhoff reported that he had been making speeches expounding German policy, but he admitted, "The three above-mentioned factors form a wall against which I cannot do very much here."[52]

The German Ambassador was also pessimistic about the help his government could expect from the German-Americans in the United States. In a long message, dated January 7, 1938, he analyzed the extent of this element and noted that of a population of 130 million only four or five million "were fully cognizant of their German origin." Any attempt to organize these people was "a hopeless affair," and Dieckhoff warned vigorously against the organization of ten to twenty thousand men who "could act as a sort of assault troop and render valuable service at the crucial moment." He stated that this "conspiratorial child's play" might work in the Balkans but not in the United States. The Department of Justice would soon have the membership roll in its possession, and knowledge of such a group would inflame public opinion. The ambassador argued that his government "must abstain from seeking political contact with German-Americans."[53]

Greater hope, Dieckhoff thought, lay with the isolationists. They were not necessarily pro-German, but they sought the same goal as Germany, American isolation. On December 7, 1937, he warned his government that American isolationists opposed "foreign entanglements only through indifference or on principle," and that "if they should ever be frightened out of their lethargy, or if they should come to realize that their doctrinaire conception cannot be carried out or that it benefits the foes of liberalism and democracy, the jump from isolationism to interventionism would not be too big for them."[54]

Feeling as he did, the German Ambassador protested against the "stupid and noisy activities of a handful of German-Americans." He was referring specifically to the German-American Bund, which, under the leadership of Fritz Kuhn, was blatantly pro-Nazi and irritated many persons by its imitation of the outward forms of Nazism. The German government agreed with Dieckhoff's appraisal, ordered Ger-

---

[52] Dieckhoff to Weizsäcker, Dec. 20, 1937, *ibid.,* Ser. D, Vol. I, 658–660.

[53] Dieckhoff to the German Foreign Ministry, Jan. 7, 1938, *ibid.,* Ser. D, Vol. I, 664–677.

[54] Dieckhoff to the German Foreign Ministry, Dec. 7, 1937, *ibid.,* Ser. D, Vol. I, 655.

man nationals to resign from the Bund, and took other steps to separate itself from the organization.[55]

The assassination early in November, 1938, by a young Polish Jew of a member of the German Embassy in Paris led to vigorous reprisals against Jews throughout Germany. On November 15, Ambassador Dieckhoff reported, "The good prospects for a gradual spread of anti-Semitism have suffered a serious setback as a result of the Grünspan incidents; even the most bitter anti-Semites are anxious to dissociate themselves from methods of this kind."[56] On the same day, Roosevelt issued a statement to the press that "the news of the past few days from Germany has deeply shocked public opinion in the United States." Asserting that he "could scarcely believe that such things could occur in a twentieth century civilization," he announced that he was calling Ambassador Hugh R. Wilson from Berlin "for report and consultation."[57] Roosevelt's action ended ambassadorial representation in Berlin and Washington. Hitler at once recalled Ambassador Dieckhoff, and neither he nor Wilson returned to his post.

From Washington, Attaché Hans Thomsen carried on with reports on the American scene. Like Dieckhoff, he notified his government of adverse opinion in the United States. After the seizure of Czechoslovakia, for example, he reported stronger press support than ever of the democracies.[58] He was convinced that Roosevelt wanted war, and on May 17, 1939, asserted, "The *leitmotiv* of Roosevelt's policy is America's participation in another war of annihilation against Germany."[59] In September, 1939, when it became evident that Roosevelt would seek repeal of the arms embargo, Thomsen warned his government against using sabotage in the United States. "Alleged German acts of sabotage," he wrote, had contributed to American entry into World War I. Sabotage would "be promptly and extensively

[55] For correspondence on this subject, see *ibid.*, Ser. D, Vol. I, 635–638, 648–651, 662, 673–679, 687–688, 691. German authorities were grateful that they were separate from the Bund when its leader, Fritz Kuhn, was arrested and in October, 1939, found guilty of embezzlement. Consul General at New York to the Foreign Ministry, Dec. 8, 1939, *ibid.*, Ser. D, Vol. VIII, 504–506.

[56] Dieckhoff to Weizsäcker, Nov. 15, 1938, *ibid.*, Ser. D, Vol. IV, 640–641.

[57] The Five Hundredth Press Conference, Nov. 15, 1938, Roosevelt, *Public Papers*, VII (1938), 597. Roosevelt said, "Technically speaking, in diplomatic parlance, it is not a recall; it is a summons to come home."

[58] Thomsen to Foreign Ministry [Germany, *Auswärtiges Amt.*], *Documents on German Foreign Policy*, Mar. 18, 1938, Ser. D, Vol. VI, 36.

[59] Thomsen to Foreign Ministry, May 17, 1939, *ibid.*, Ser. D, Vol. VI, 533.

exploited by Roosevelt, interventionist circles, and enemy propaganda," and would injure the isolationists. At the same time, Thomsen wanted no tie with the isolationists for he predicted that they would lose the fight against arms repeal and he did not want this defeat to be considered one of German policy.[60]

Confronted by a hostile Roosevelt administration, the German Embassy turned to the United States General Staff. In the fall of 1939, Lieutenant General Friedrich von Bötticher, German Military Attaché, asked Nazi Army and *Luftwaffe* leaders for confidential information which would be of "considerable help in the cultivation" of friendly relations. He noted that the General Staff consulted with the President and the State Department on the war situation. While "the influence of the American General Staff, our contacts with it, or the possibility of obtaining intelligence should not be overestimated," Bötticher asserted, "the experience of the past few years has shown that it is advisable to make use of and cultivate these relations, which have proved their value."[61]

On November 21, 1939, Thomsen reported attempts to increase propagandist activity to overcome the "boycott wall of the American press," which avoided printing pro-German material emanating from the "Trans-Ocean Agency" in New York, which dispatched pro-German news to Latin America. A weekly periodical, *Facts in Review*, had been founded and reached about twenty thousand persons. Propagandist agencies included the German Information Library in New York and German Railways, which worked with travel bureaus throughout the country. According to Thomsen, "Through the press office established since the outbreak of the war, propaganda is centrally directed from the Embassy in closest collaboration with German consular officials, which is especially important in view of the size of the continent."[62] The Embassy was also interested in persuading "suitable" American journalists to visit Germany, and Thomsen also noted the use of short-wave transmitters for communications with Germany.

The German Embassy was much interested in the presidential cam-

---

[60] Thomsen to the Foreign Ministry, Sept. 18, 1939, *ibid.*, Ser. D, Vol. VIII, 89–91.

[61] Bötticher to the Foreign Ministry, Sept. 28, 1939, *ibid.*, Ser. D, Vol. VIII, 158–159.

[62] Thomsen to the Foreign Ministry, Nov. 21, 1939, *ibid.*, Ser. D, Vol. VIII, 433.

paign of 1940. Thomsen reported that Willkie was a "distinct leader-personality" who would increase Republican chances, but he added, "From the standpoint of foreign policy, Willkie's nomination is unfortunate for us." Willkie was no isolationist; rather, he belonged to "those Republicans who see America's best defense in supporting England by all means 'short of war.' "[63] Thomsen took some heart from the Republican platform, which he considered a victory for isolationism since it opposed America's involvement in a foreign war and proclaimed that the "Republican party stands for Americanism, preparedness, and peace." These statements, the attaché asserted, "were taken almost verbatim from the conspicuous full-page advertisements in the American press (e.g., the *New York Times,* June 25, p. 19), which were published upon our instigation."[64] On July 19, he notified the Foreign Ministry:

> As I have reported, isolationist Republican Congressmen at the Republican Convention succeeded in affixing firmly to the party platform the language of an isolationist foreign policy that will not let itself become entangled in a European war. Nothing has leaked out about the assistance we rendered in this.

Thomsen undertook "similar action during the Democratic Convention in Chicago." He reported:

> The special officer for press relations has seen to it that several reliable isolationist Congressmen went to Chicago in order to exert influence on the delegates with the purpose of including, at least formally, in the Democratic platform as well, a pledge of non-participation in a European war.[65]

One of the propagandist devices used was a full-page advertisement in the Chicago *Tribune,* similar to that printed in *The New York Times.*

Both Thomsen and General Bötticher looked upon Lindbergh as helpful to the German cause and as a leader in the fight against the Jews. On July 20, 1940, the two attachés reported a "circle about Lindbergh" and passed on to Germany from a member of this circle the idea that the wife of Commander P. E. Pihl, American Assistant Naval Attaché in Berlin, who was Wendell Willkie's sister, had "pro-

---

[63] Thomsen to the Foreign Ministry, June 28, 1940, *ibid.,* Ser. D, Vol. X, 49.
[64] Thomsen to the Foreign Ministry, July 3, 1940, *ibid.,* Ser. D, Vol. X, 102.
[65] Thomsen to the Foreign Ministry, July 19, 1940, *ibid.,* Ser. D, Vol. X, 250.

nounced sympathies for Germany and might greatly influence her brother."[66]

Despite Thomsen's optimistic reports on German propaganda, the Roosevelt administration's foreign policy was not at stake in the presidential campaign. Aside from the last-minute flailing of issues, which later he passed off as "campaign oratory," Willkie's ideas on America's relation to the conflict were basically those of the President. After his re-election, Roosevelt began to speak more plainly concerning the Germans. On December 20, 1940, he addressed the nation in a Fireside Chat, in an effort to arouse the American people to a realization of the Nazi menace. This danger was justification for his ringing assertion that the United States would become "the great arsenal of democracy."[67]

The implementation of this phrase led to the passage of novel legislation for a nation ostensibly at peace. Once before, the United States had been an "arsenal of democracy," and one result had been the war-debts muddle. Early in 1941 the administration concluded that different financial arrangements should be made than those of World War I. Roosevelt had indicated the way in a story to press correspondents, December 7, 1940. Suppose a neighbor's house is on fire, said the President in effect, and I have a hose to help put out the blaze. I don't sell the hose to him. I want my garden hose back after the fire is over. Roosevelt explained, "What I am trying to do is to eliminate the dollar sign."[68]

From this simple analogy came a far-reaching piece of legislation. In the struggle for Selective Service, Roosevelt had hesitated and permitted others to direct; in the struggle for Lend-Lease the President definitely assumed the leadership. Unlike the destroyers-for-bases deal, Lend-Lease was an act of Congress. Its passage was bitterly contested both in Congress and in the country. Pressure groups lined up on each side; the Committee to Defend America by Aiding the Allies, of course, supported the bill, and the America First Committee fought it as a device to push the nation into war.

The Lend-Lease Act, which became law March 11, 1941, was

[66] Bötticher, Thomsen to the Foreign Ministry, July 20, 1940, *ibid.*, Ser. D, Vol. X, 255.

[67] Reprinted in Roosevelt, *Public Papers*, IX, 633–644.

[68] The Seven Hundred and Second Press Conference, Dec. 17, 1940, *ibid.*, IX, 607.

one of the most significant acts of the war period.[69] It gave the President broad powers to procure defense articles and "to sell, transfer title to, exchange, lease, lend, or otherwise dispose" of them to "the government of any country whose defense the President deems vital to the defense of the United States." Virtually the only limitation placed upon the President was the amount of money to be made available to him, and the act indicated that further sums were to be allocated. The sum of $1.3 billion was appropriated in the act. By November there were Lend-Lease commitments of more than $13 billion; by June, 1942, the figure had skyrocketed to $30 billion.

The Lend-Lease Act cleared the way for fulfillment of the pledge that America would become the "arsenal of democracy." According to Secretary Stimson it broke two bottlenecks; it provided for the financing of the British supply program, and it gave the American government "badly needed authority over the whole field of military supplies."[70]

As for American policy, if the destroyers-for-bases deal had taken the United States into "limited war," Lend-Lease most certainly constituted, as Stimson declared, "a declaration of economic war."[71] A formal declaration of war merely awaited the convenience of one side or the other. The die had already been cast, and the ensuing months saw the United States gradually draw into a shooting war with Germany. The next step was inevitable and will be discussed later in connection with military operations, for once the United States had committed itself to become an "arsenal," it almost automatically became concerned with the transportation of war materials to Britain. The Lend-Lease Act had stated that America was not authorized by the act to convoy vessels or take American ships into the war zones, but such developments came within a few months.

The course of American history in the early years of World War II stands in sharp contrast to American actions before our entry into World War I. As long as we were at peace Wilson had sought to maintain neutrality. Neutrality, as we have seen, had long since vanished when the United States and Germany in December, 1941, went formally to war against each other. The United States had seen one small nation after the other that had sought security through ad-

---

[69] Reprinted in Commager, *Documents of American History,* No. 538.

[70] Henry L. Stimson and McGeorge Bundy, *On Active Service in Peace and War* (New York, 1947, 1948), p. 360.

[71] *Ibid.*

herence to law go down under the heel of the aggressor. The American people had seen France collapse and Britain fighting for its life. The administration and, it would appear, the American people reached the conviction that the United States was marked for attack and determined to aid the nations already fighting as a means of defending themselves.[72] There was also, of course, the Far East to be considered.

[72] For a few of the many appraisals of America's departure from neutrality, see Bemis, *The United States as a World Power,* pp. 390–391; Bailey, *Diplomatic History of the American People* (6th ed.), p. 725; Drummond, *The Passing of American Neutrality,* pp. 376–381. For accounts sharply critical of the Roosevelt administration, see Charles C. Tansill, *Back Door to War: The Roosevelt Foreign Policy, 1933–1941* (Chicago, 1952), *passim;* Charles A. Beard, *President Roosevelt and the Coming of the War, 1941: A Study in Appearances and Reality* (New Haven, 1948), pp. 3–117.

CHAPTER 2

The Coming of World War II–The Far East

ALTHOUGH the United States was in effect an economic belligerent against Germany by the summer of 1941, it was action in the Pacific that thrust this country openly into World War II. The path to Pearl Harbor was as tortuous as that leading to Lend-Lease.

During the latter half of the nineteenth century, an oligarchy had modernized the Japanese Empire.[1] Its leaders accepted the ideas of Western imperialism and saw opportunities for expansion on the nearby mainland of Asia. In some instances using techniques which Western powers had employed against them, the Japanese launched and enlarged their colonial expansion. In 1894–95, Japan engaged in war with China to advance her own interests, in 1904–05 she fought Russia, in 1910 she annexed Korea, and as a result of World War I she extended her empire by taking over as mandates islands in the Pacific seized from Germany.

Then in the 1920's Japan for a time appeared to be reversing herself. As a result of the great economic growth of the nation, businessmen seemed to be more important than Army officers or politicians. During the decade they tended to oppose the high taxes needed to support a large Army and Navy and to believe it better to build foreign trade and gain concessions through diplomacy than to expand

[1] For accounts of the modernization of Japan, see Edwin O. Reischauer, *Japan Past and Present* (New York, 1958), pp. 108–195; Hugh Borton, *Japan's Modern Century* (New York, 1955), pp. 69–372. For the period since 1932, see Joseph C. Grew, *Turbulent Era: A Diplomatic Record of Forty Years* (Boston, 1952), II, 921–1243.

by military conquest, particularly against an aroused Chinese nationalism. Therefore the government withdrew Japanese troops from Siberia in 1922, participated in the Washington Conference on the Limitation of Naval Armament, pulled troops from certain Chinese mainland areas taken from the Germans, and in 1925 reduced the standing Army by four divisions out of twenty-one. During this period Japan went through its version of the "jazz age," in which many young men and women threw off former customs along with their inhibitions. The electorate grew and in 1925 was increased to full manhood suffrage. Numerous new parties came into being, although despite suffrage the masses of the people remained uninterested in politics.

Ultranationalism rose as a reaction to some of these developments. The peasantry objected to the liberalism and new ways of city life, and Army officers and men, having stemmed from the country, shared in the dissatisfaction. Some Japanese, particularly from rural and military groups, began to feel that military expansion was the only answer to Japan's problems. Within the Army there were two main schools of thought. One known as the Kodoha, or Imperial Way Group, appealed especially to young field officers, mainly with a rural background. It sought the overthrow of the capitalistic system and advocated the use of violence. This group was not well organized, and some of its adherents were closely associated with civilian terrorist groups. It had some support among senior staff officers. The other school of thought, the Toseiha, or Control Group, consisted of more senior officers, especially members of the General Staff, who saw the futility of trying to return to a primitive, decentralized society. They worked to preserve the existing bureaucratic administration and to control it by merging all political parties into a single system which they would dominate while making industrialists and court officials subordinate to them. They believed in evolutionary means but did not mind if terrorists killed some of the moderate opposition.

And there was terrorism. In 1932, assassins killed a former finance minister and a few months later the premier. In February, 1936, some fourteen hundred soldiers, attempting a *coup d'état,* seized a portion of Tokyo and killed three high officials. Suppressing the uprising, the government executed thirteen Army officers and four civilians. The incident ended the Kodoha as a strong group and gave Toseiha firm control over the policy of the Army. It also resulted in *rapprochement* between Toseiha and large business interests, or *zaibatsu*.[2] In time Army leaders realized that they needed the cooperation of politicians as well as businesmen and in May, 1937, they found the man who seemed to fit their purpose; Prince Fumimaro Konoye, scion of one of the oldest noble families and a distant relative of the Emperor, was acceptable to court and business circles as well as to the military.

In the early thirties, Manchuria became the objective of resurgent Japanese extremists, who wished to develop it as a source of food and other raw materials and as a possible outlet for the surplus Japanese population. Further, it would be a buffer against Russian Communism to the north, and its control would be an important step toward an economic bloc with China and toward Japanese leadership on the mainland. How much of this concept was national policy and how much the ideas of extremists is difficult to determine. It is also hard to be sure whether Japanese military action in Manchuria in 1931 was a move by Japanese military leaders in the area to force the home government to act or whether it was the result of the home government's decision. Whatever the cause, the Japanese Army continued operations and by January, 1932, had virtual control of Manchuria.

The American government at first moved slowly in its reaction to the Manchurian affair in the hope that moderates in Japan could regain control from the military. After the bombing of Chinchow, however, Secretary of State Henry L. Stimson gave moral support to the League of Nation's inquiry into the matter. When the League accomplished nothing, Stimson resorted to a statement made to both China and Japan announcing a policy of nonrecognition of forcible changes of government.[3] Stimson also stated that the United States would continue to support the Open Door and China's territorial and administrative integrity.

Stimson would have liked to have gone farther, but President Hoover declined to go beyond moral sanctions, stating, "First, this is primarily a controversy between China and Japan. The United States has never set out to preserve peace among other nations by force, and so far as this part is concerned we shall confine ourselves to friendly

[2] Chitoshi Yanaga, *Japan Since Perry* (New York, Toronto, London, 1949), pp. 508–518; Reischauer, *Japan Past and Present*, pp. 179–180.
[3] Henry L. Stimson and McGeorge Bundy, *On Active Service in Peace and War* (New York, 1947, 1948), pp. 225–239.

counsel."[4] Stimson had made it clear that American policy ran counter to Japanese military expansion. On the other hand, as long as the United States sought to impose only moral sanctions, war was not likely to occur between the two countries. There was little change during the early years of the Roosevelt administration, although there were periods of friction.

Matters became infinitely worse when in the so-called China affair in July, 1937, Japanese armed forces moved ahead to carve out the new autonomous states, Inner Mongolia and North China. Focusing attention on Russian Communism, the Japanese felt that the Chinese should cooperate economically and politically against this menace. Virtually all factions in China, however, united against pressure, and undeclared war broke out in 1937.[5] During 1937 and 1938 Japanese forces seized much of northern and central China and key ports and other areas on the southern coast. They did not conquer either the Chinese Communists in the north or the Chinese Nationalist forces which had retired to Chungking. In November, 1938, Prince Konoye announced that Japan intended to create a Greater East Asia Co-Prosperity Sphere, which would involve the cooperation of China, Japan, and the puppet state, Manchukuo, against Communism. Chiang Kai-shek, hoping for aid from the West, rejected the proposals.[6]

Help from the United States did not appear imminent. The outbreak of hostilities in China raised the question of American neutrality. If the President declared the existence of war, the restrictions on trade provided by the act would go into effect and give the advantage to Japan. The sympathy of the American people and government was with the Chinese; consequently President Roosevelt chose not to see that there was a war in progress, and the neutrality law did not go into effect for the Far Eastern struggle.

In October, 1937, Roosevelt sent up a trial balloon known as his quarantine speech, in which he condemned war as a disease and sug-

[4] Herbert Hoover, *The Memoirs of Herbert Hoover: The Cabinet and the Presidency, 1920–1933* (New York, 1952), [II], 368.

[5] For diplomatic correspondence, see U.S. State Department, *Papers Relating to the Foreign Relations of the United States, Japan* (Washington, 1943), I, II, *passim;* U.S. State Department, *Foreign Relations of the United States: Diplomatic Papers, 1937,* Vol. III, *The Far East* (Washington, 1954), 1–848.

[6] For example, see message Generalissimo Chiang Kai-shek to President Roosevelt, dated October 15, 1938, U.S. State Department, *Foreign Relations, 1938,* III, 321–322.

gested "a quarantine of the patients in order to protect the health of the community against the spread of the disease."[7] Widespread criticism of the speech led the President to drop the idea. Secretary Stimson, who expressed similar views at the same time, later commented that "in the months that followed Mr. Roosevelt seemed to conclude that the country was not ready for strong medicine, and the speech remained an isolated episode in a continuing pattern of inaction."[8]

More serious in their possible immediate effect on Japanese-American relations than Japanese aggression in China were incidents involving American property and lives in the area. Outstanding among hundreds protested by the United States was the sinking of the American gunboat *Panay* in the Yangtze River by Japanese planes on December 12, 1937. The Japanese government promptly acknowledged responsibility and closed the incident by paying indemnities. Despite the conviction of Secretary of State Hull and other American diplomats that Japan was trying to drive all other foreigners from China and dominate the Far East, it does not appear that the United States contemplated using force. The medium of protest continued to be diplomatic.[9] In the summer of 1938, the United States attempted a variant on the theme of moral pressure to check aggression when it instituted a so-called "moral embargo" on the shipment of airplanes and parts to Japan and urged American manufacturers to refrain from making such exports.[10]

Japan was not pleased by the moral embargo, but she was not especially hurt by it. The crucial materials needed were not planes

[7] Franklin D. Roosevelt, *The Public Papers and Addresses of Franklin D. Roosevelt* (New York, 1941), VI, 410.

[8] Stimson and Bundy, *On Active Service*, p. 312.

[9] On November 14, 1938, Stanley K. Hornbeck, Adviser on Political Relations to the State Department, wrote a memorandum stating that in recent years the United States had been "opposing Japan by use of words." Victories in this field would "not halt the forward march of Japan's military machine." Continuance along this line, predicted Mr. Hornbeck, would be "almost certain to lead to the development of a situation in which this country will have either to accept a diplomatic defeat or find itself forced to resort to arms." Hornbeck recommended that the United States take steps which would "include a combination of diplomatic, economic and potential military pressures." *Foreign Relations, 1938,* III, 573.

[10] American action resulted from objections to Japanese bombing of the civilian population in China. For some of the diplomatic correspondence, see *ibid.,* III, 613–626.

but oil and scrap iron. The United States made no attempt to embargo these commodities, "morally" or otherwise. Such an embargo would have been in violation of the existing trade treaty with Japan. More fundamentally, the United States feared that such a move might lead Japanese militarists to seize control of their own country and then attempt to secure oil elsewhere, probably in the Dutch East Indies. Realizing, however, that the threat of imposing an embargo might constitute a good diplomatic weapon, in the summer of 1939, the United States government gave the prescribed six months' notice that the trade agreement would be terminated.[11] When the period ended, the United States decided not to use the weapon, but at the same time it declined to negotiate for the extension of the treaty or the formulation of a new one.

Beginning in 1940, the United States and Japan began to view their relations with each other in a new light, shed by the conflagration in Europe. To the Japanese, the phenomenal Nazi successes in Western Europe made what might earlier have seemed only visionary ideas become attainable goals. Viewing the scene in the same light, the United States began to think less of separate incidents occurring in China and more of the broad implications of Japanese expansion in terms of the European conflict.

During the summer of 1940, tension in the Far East increased as Japan exerted pressure on Britain and France while they were fighting for their existence against Germany. China had been equipping herself through Hong Kong, French Indo-China, the Burma Road, and Soviet Russia. Taking advantage of the Munich crisis, Japanese forces launched an offensive against South China and by capturing the mainland behind the island of Hong Kong and the Kowloon leasehold had reduced the effectiveness of this avenue of supply. While Hitler was preparing to take Czechoslovakia in 1939, Japan occupied the Chinese island of Hainan, controlling the Gulf of Tonkin.[12] Then during the summer and fall of 1940, the Japanese moved

---

[11] Cordell Hull to Japanese Ambassador (Kensuke Horinouchi), July 26, 1939, *ibid., 1939* (Washington, 1955), III, 558–559.

[12] In a message to the Secretary of State, Ambassador Grew stressed the importance of Hainan and stated, "If converted into a well equipped naval and air base, this Island will dominate the whole coast of the mainland between Hong Kong and the southern tip of the Indo-China peninsula." Grew to Hull, February 10, 1939, *ibid., 1939,* III, 103.

against both Indo-China[13] and the Burma Road. A treaty of mutual guarantees was signed with Thailand, and after the fall of France the Japanese government brought pressure for concessions in Indo-China. A distraught Vichy government could secure no help from Britain and the United States and, although there was some local French opposition, acquiesced in the advance of Japanese troops into northern Indo-China. The Japanese did not move directly against the Burma Road, but pressed the British to stop sending war materials to China by this route. Unable to get American support, the British told the Chinese that they had no other choice but to close the road.[14]

While this crisis continued, there was a strong difference of opinion within the American government. Such Cabinet members as Henry L. Stimson and Henry Morgenthau, Jr. felt that there should be no yielding to Japan and that in the last analysis Japan would shrink from provoking war with the United States. Some members of the State Department, especially Sumner Welles, Under Secretary of State, counseled caution and emphasized the possibility that a strong stand by the United States would force Japan into an attack on the Dutch East Indies.[15] Persuaded by advocates of a stiff policy and spurred on by reports that Japanese agents were cornering the aviation gasoline supply on the West Coast, President Roosevelt on July 25 signed an order placing under the licensing system "petroleum products, tetraethyl lead, and iron and steel scrap." State Department pressure and a Cabinet discussion prompted the administration to publish a note on the following day that "petroleum products" meant

[13] The Japanese first induced Indo-China to stop trade with China. Grew to Hull, June 20, 1940, *ibid., 1940,* IV, 30–31.

[14] Grew to Hull, June 19, 1940, June 24, 1940, *ibid.,* IV, 26–27, 36–37. When informed of Japanese interest in Indo-China, General Eugen Ott, German Ambassador in Japan, reported a conversation with the Japanese Colonial Secretary: "I called attention to the well-known statement of the Reich Government according to which Germany was not interested in the Netherlands Indies question and added that we would probably also have nothing against Japanese action in Indochina, provided Japan pledged herself to keep America occupied in the Pacific area, possibly by promising to attack the Philippines and Hawaii in case America should enter the war against Germany." The Ambassador in Japan to the Foreign Ministry, June 24, 1940, U.S. State Department, *Documents on German Foreign Policy, 1918–1945* (Washington, 1957), Ser. D, Vol. X, 5.

[15] Sumner Welles, "Roosevelt and the Far East," *Harper's Magazine,* Vol. 202 (Feb., 1951), 33.

only aviation gasoline and "iron and steel scrap" meant only a certain type of scrap.[16] The actual check on the flow of goods to Japan was slight, but the move indicated some resistance to the Japanese and showed that the United States was assuming the dominant role in dealing with Japan.

In addition to the threat of an embargo, the United States had another weapon that it attempted to use in the diplomatic struggle with Japan. This was the United States Fleet, which found itself shuttled about as a diplomatic pawn. In April, 1940, the fleet was ordered to Hawaii ostensibly for maneuvers; actually it was sent to the islands as a deterrent to Japanese aggression in the Far East, and, despite strong Japanese criticism, the fleet remained in Hawaii after the maneuvers were over. Primarily for the purpose of restraining Japan, Roosevelt came to the conclusion that the fleet should be permanently based in Hawaii instead of on the West Coast. Admiral J. O. Richardson, Commander in Chief of the fleet, interested in operations rather than diplomacy, felt that a move to Pearl Harbor was logistically inadvisable; the fleet could be supplied better at San Diego, and the morale of the personnel would be higher when they could be permanently based nearer their families. Richardson went to Washington to protest, but the administration refused to change its plans, and in February, 1941, Admiral Richardson was relieved of his command. The United States Fleet was renamed the Pacific Fleet and stayed in Pearl Harbor.[17]

One of Japan's principal aims, as we have seen, was to prevent the flow of war materials into China. Another diplomatic goal was to maintain satisfactory relations with Germany. At first this aim was dictated by fear of Soviet Russia, whose strategic position in the Far East menaced Japanese designs on the Asiatic Continent. To this end Japan joined Germany and Italy in signing the so-called Anti-Comintern Pact in 1936, directed ostensibly against Communism and

[16] Herbert Feis, *The Road to Pearl Harbor: The Coming of the War Between the United States and Japan* (Princeton, 1950), pp. 91–93; W. L. Langer and S. E. Gleason, *The Challenge to Isolation, 1937–1940* (New York, 1952), pp. 719–723.

[17] S. E. Morison, *History of United States Naval Operations in World War II* (Boston, 1948), III, 42–43, 46–47. For Admiral Richardson's objections to Pearl Harbor, see his Memorandum for the Secretary, September 12, 1940, in U.S. Congress, Joint Committee on the Investigation of the Pearl Harbor Attack, *Hearings . . .* (Washington, 1946), Part 14, pp. 955–956.

especially against Soviet Russia. Although there were overtures, numerous factors prevented the pact from expanding into a military alliance.[18]

Then in 1940 the situation changed as the startling successes of Germany in the spring and the collapse of the French and Dutch made vividly possible a realignment of colonial power in the Far East. The nation immediately to be watched was Germany, not Soviet Russia. Because of its preoccupation with Europe, Germany was willing to come to an understanding. The result was the Tripartite Pact of September 27, 1940, signed by Germany, Italy, and Japan. The agreement parceled the world into spheres of influence and potential control, Europe for Germany and "the leadership of Japan in the establishment of a New Order in Greater East Asia." From the standpoint of the United States another phase of the treaty was of marked significance. In contrast to the Anti-Comintern Pact, which was aimed at Soviet Russia, the new treaty was pointed at the United States, for it stated that each ally would aid the other "if attacked by a power at present not involved in the European war or in the Sino-Japanese conflict."[19]

A shift in the Japanese government had paved the way for the Tripartite Agreement when in July, 1940, Prince Konoye, who had been the "front" for the militarists in 1931, returned to power.[20] By the beginning of 1941, the Japanese government embarked upon two programs, one diplomatic and the other military. Japanese diplomats endeavored to avoid war with the United States and at the same time to secure fundamental objectives from this country. They continued their efforts to persuade the United States to give Japan a free hand in China and also to gain assurances that America would remain aloof in case of Japanese expansion southward in Asia. At the same time that Japanese emissaries were seeking these goals diplo-

[18] Localized fighting between Soviet and Japanese troops on the Mongolian border came to an end in September, apparently with the consent of both parties. The Ambassador in the Soviet Union (Laurence Steinhardt) to the Secretary of State, Sept. 8, 1939, and the Chargé in Japan (Eugene H. Dooman) to the Secretary of State, Sept. 8, 1939, U.S. Department of State, *Foreign Relations, 1939*, III, 62–63. The German-Soviet nonaggression pact complicated the problem. For correspondence on this subject see *ibid.*, 34–102. See also Feis, *The Road to Pearl Harbor*, pp. 25–37.

[19] U.S. State Department, *Foreign Relations, Japan*, II, 165.

[20] For a study of the Tripartite Pact and Japanese-American relations, see Paul W. Schroeder, *The Axis Alliance and Japanese-American Relations* (Ithaca, N.Y., 1958), *passim*.

matically, Japanese militarists were preparing for offensive war against the United States in case the diplomats failed. There were leaks of information even in Japan. On January 27, 1941, Ambassador Joseph C. Grew sent the following message to Washington:

> My Peruvian colleague told a member of my staff that he had heard from many sources including a Japanese source that the Japanese military forces planned, in the event of trouble with the United States, to attempt a surprise mass attack on Pearl Harbor using all their military facilities. He added that although the project seemed fantastic the fact that he had heard it from many sources prompted him to pass on the information.[21]

The plan evidently "seemed fantastic" also to American officials as the message was routed through appropriate channels in Washington. The Chief of Naval Operations noted that the Division of Naval Intelligence placed "no credence in these rumors" and further stated that "based on known data regarding the present disposition and employment of Japanese naval and army forces, no move against Pearl Harbor appears imminent or planned for in the forseeable future."[22] In that same month of January, 1941, or not later than February 1, Admiral I. Yamamoto launched a serious study of the Pearl Harbor operation and stated that if Japan were to have war with the United States "we will have no hope of winning unless the U.S. Fleet in Hawaiian waters can be destroyed."[23] Although the warnings of Am-

---

[21] Grew to Hull, Jan. 27, 1941, *Pearl Harbor Attack,* Part 14, p. 1042.

[22] Chief of Naval Operations to Commander-in-Chief, Pacific Fleet, Feb. 1, 1941, *ibid.,* Part 14, 1044.

[23] The majority report of the Joint Congressional Committee on the Investigation of the Pearl Harbor Attack asserts that the planning was "originally conceived and proposed early in January of 1941 by Admiral Isoroku Yamamoto." *Ibid., Report,* p. 53. The quotation attributed to Admiral Yamamoto is from an interrogation, dated November 28, 1945, of Captain Minoru Genda, Air Operations officer on the staff of Admiral Nagumo during the attack on Pearl Harbor. Genda stated that Admiral Yamamoto made the remark in a conversation "about February 1, 1941." *Ibid.,* Part 13, p. 426. In a telegram dated January 31, 1941, Eugen Ott, German Ambassador to Japan, informed his Foreign Minister, "The [Japanese] Government is trying to scare America from entering the war by a threatening attitude, armament measures, and sharp speeches in the Parliament and press.

"In contrast to this, activist circles demand a preventive attack on Singapore as the key position in the Western Pacific. They expect by a surprise action to deprive America of the possibility of military warfare in the Pacific or to render it difficult. This minority group is under the leadership of Admiral Suetsugu and Ambassador Shiratori, and has the support of the young officers corps and

bassador Grew and others were to be forgotten or ignored, the Tri-partite Agreement made it clear that expansion southward was a distinct possibility and that war between the United States and Japan might result.

Early in 1941, a move came from private individuals to improve relations between the United States and Japan. A so-called "John Doe" group, spearheaded by two Catholic clergymen, Father James M. Drought and Bishop James E. Walsh, leaders of the Catholic Mission Society of America, known as "Maryknoll Fathers,"[24] worked with Japanese diplomats in Washington and the State Department in an effort to draft a satisfactory agreement between Japan and the United States.[25] Father Drought enlisted the support of Postmaster General Frank C. Walker and also sought to interest President Roosevelt and Secretary Hull. The latter was cautious, but he and the President felt that "we could not afford to neglect any chance to avoid a war in the Pacific."[26] Discussions continued at various levels into July, as participants considered interminably particulars and generalities. Half a dozen draft proposals appeared, but the conversations never passed the preliminary stage. The Japanese wanted to separate the China problem from relations with the United States and to retain troops in northern China. Hull agreed that the main purpose was peace in the Pacific between the United States and Japan and insisted, "But a peaceful settlement between Japan and China is an essential element in the situation."[27]

From Tokyo, Ambassador Grew strongly urged a continuation of negotiations and he warned, "The alternative might well be progressive deterioration of Japanese-American relations leading eventually to war."[28] Of a different opinion was one of Hull's principal counselors, Stanley K. Hornbeck, Adviser on Political Relations to the Secretary of State. A long-time State Department official, Hornbeck was strongly pro-Chinese and looked upon Japan as an overrated

---

some high leaders of the Army and Navy." Ott to the Foreign Minister, Jan. 31, 1941, U.S. State Department, *Documents on German Foreign Policy*, Ser. D, Vol. XI (1960), p. 1232.

[24] "Memorandum of Conversations, by Mr. Joseph W. Ballantine," Mar. 28, 1941. *Foreign Relations of the United States, 1941*, IV, 113.

[25] *Ibid.*, IV, 117.

[26] Cordell Hull, *The Memoirs of Cordell Hull* (New York, 1948), II, 985.

[27] *Ibid.*, II, 1004; "Memorandum of a Conversation," *Foreign Relations of the United States, Japan: 1931–1941*, II, 435.

[28] Grew to Hull, May 27, 1941, *ibid.*, *1941*, IV, 232.

power which "had achieved one diplomatic victory after another by processes of diplomacy backed by threats, implied threats, or inferred threats of force." He firmly believed that the United States should "cultivate rather than destroy an impression" on the part of the Japanese "that adventure southward by them would meet with armed resistance on our part."[29] He was continually suspicious of the Japanese and viewed critically such moves as those of the John Doe group toward a draft agreement.

Within the Japanese government there was increasing friction between Prince Konoye, who wished to reach some sort of an agreement with the United States, and the strongly pro-German Foreign Minister Yosuke Matsuoka.[30] After Germany invaded Soviet Russia, despite the fact that he had just negotiated a nonaggression pact with that country, Matsuoka eagerly advocated attacking the Soviet Union. After deliberation, the Japanese government rejected the idea as being too costly and a weakening of preparations for advance southward. Furthermore, the Japanese thought Germany would win without help and would remove the Soviet Union as a menace to Japanese expansion. The government's decision was clearly outlined in a resolution adopted by the leading civilian and military figures of Japan meeting before the Emperor, July 2, 1941.[31]

This resolution stated that the Imperial government was determined to follow a policy that would "result in the establishment of the Greater East Asia Co-Prosperity Sphere and world peace, no matter what international developments take place." Further, the Imperial government planned to continue its effort "to effect a settlement of the China Incident," and would carry out its program "no matter what obstacles may be encountered." That the United States and Great Britain were considered to be "obstacles" was indicated later in the resolution: "In carrying out the plans outlined in the foregoing article, we will not be deterred by the possibility of being involved in a war with England and America." The resolution stated that Japan's relations to the German-Soviet war would be "based on the spirit of the Tri-Partite Pact" but that it would not enter the

[29] Memorandum by Hornbeck, Apr. 11, 1941, *ibid.,* IV, 147–148.
[30] "Memoirs of Prince Konoye," *Pearl Harbor Attack,* Part 20, pp. 3995–3997; Grew to Hull, May 14, 1941, *Foreign Relations of the United States, 1941,* IV, 188.
[31] "An Outline of the Policy of the Imperial Government in View of Present Developments," *Pearl Harbor Attack,* Part 20, pp. 4018–4019.

conflict "for some time." Any such military plans against the Soviets would be carried out in such a way as "to place no serious obstacles in the path of our basic military preparations for a war with England and America."

During July Matsuoka went too far with his extreme pro-Germanism and obstructionist tactics toward Japanese-American relations and on the sixteenth of the month was eased out of office. Ambassador Grew's cautious optimism over this development[32] proved unconfirmed, for Washington was already receiving reports of planned Japanese moves into Indo-China. On hearing these reports, Roosevelt and his Cabinet began to consider a significant change in policy from mere protest to the addition of economic sanctions. Through carefully guarded discussions with the British, the State Department learned that the British and the Dutch would probably go along with an oil embargo.[33] On the other hand, the Chief of Naval Operations recommended against an embargo "at this time." Admiral R. K. Turner, Director of the Navy's War Plans Division, warned that an embargo would be "almost certain to intensify the determination of those now in power [in Japan] to continue their present course." He further predicted that if Japan should move against the British and the Dutch, "She would also include military action against the Philippines, which would immediately involve us in a Pacific war."[34]

Despite these predictions, the President decided to impose sanctions if Japan moved into Indo-China. He made a last attempt to dissuade the Japanese from taking this step, when in a meeting with Ambassador Nomura on July 24 he proposed the neutralization of Indo-China, comparable to that of Switzerland.[35] For reasons that are not clear, Nomura did not forward a complete report of the President's suggestion for three days.[36] Whether the recommendation would have altered developments is impossible to determine. It merited serious

[32] Grew to Hull, July 23, 1941, *Foreign Relations of the United States, 1941,* IV, 337.
[33] E.g., "Memorandum of Conversation, by the Assistant Secretary of State [Acheson]," July 23, 1941, *ibid.,* IV, 841.
[34] Turner to Stark, July 19, 1941, *ibid.,* IV, 836–840.
[35] "Memorandum by the Acting Secretary of State [Welles]," July 24, 1941, *ibid., Japan: 1931–1941,* II, 529.
[36] Grew to Hull, July 27, 1941, *ibid.,* 1941, IV, 345; Roosevelt to Hopkins, July 26, 1941, *Pearl Harbor Attack,* Part 20, p. 4373; Hopkins to Roosevelt, July 25, 1941, *ibid.,* Part 20, p. 4384.

consideration by the Japanese government, however, and it was unfortunate that it was delayed in reaching Tokyo.

By July 24 it was known to the Washington government that Japan had started its move on Indo-China. The new Japanese Foreign Minister, Admiral Teijiro Toyoda, explained to Nomura that occupation would be carried out "peacefully, for the purpose of jointly defending French Indo-China."[37] In the evening of July 26, a President's office press release announced the issuance of an Executive Order freezing Japanese assets in the United States.[38] There was sharp reaction in Japan; Ambassador Grew reported the "astonishment and profound concern of the Japanese" and "the bitter resentment engendered by the action of the United States."[39] In return, the Japanese placed heavy restrictions on foreign business transactions in Japan.

In Washington, Ambassador Nomura was deeply perturbed and in a message to Tokyo dated July 30 reported that Washington officials "meant business" and he urged his government "to take without one moment's hesitation some appeasement measures."[40] In his reply, the Foreign Minister explained that commercial and economic relations between Japan and England and the United States were becoming "so horribly strained that we cannot endure it much longer." Consequently, Japan was moving into Indo-China after raw materials to break the "ever-strengthening chain of encirclement" being woven under the guidance of Britain and the United States.[41]

By the summer of 1941, top officials in Washington were being aided greatly by intercepted and decoded Japanese messages, called "Magic," for, unknown to the Japanese, the United States War and Navy departments had been able to crack the principal Japanese diplomatic codes. Stations in the United States and the Pacific in-

[37] Teijiro Toyoda to Nomura, July 23, 1941, *ibid.*, Part 12, p. 4.

[38] "Press Release Issued at Poughkeepsie, New York, by the White House on July 25, 1941," *Foreign Relations of the United States, Japan: 1931–1941*, II, 266–267.

[39] Grew to Hull, July 26, 1941, *Foreign Relations of the United States, 1941*, IV, 344.

[40] Nomura to Toyoda, July 30, 1941, *Pearl Harbor Attack*, Part 12, p. 8. On July 30 Japanese planes bombed the U.S. gunboat, *Tutuila*, during an air attack on Chungking. The Japanese quickly apologized to the United States. *Foreign Relations of the United States, Japan: 1931–1941*, I, 719–726.

[41] Toyoda to Nomura, July 31, 1941, *Pearl Harbor Attack*, Part 12, p. 9.

tercepted and forwarded messages to Washington for decoding and translating. The station at Corregidor in the Philippines, because of its location, received facilities which enabled it to decode messages.[42] The Japanese had been attempting to break American codes and apparently had been successful with all but the top diplomatic code.[43]

Roosevelt and Hull had learned of the plan to occupy Indo-China through Magic and through the same source they learned that Thailand might be next. Hull, recuperating at White Sulphur Springs, West Virginia, from an illness, expressed the belief that the Japanese had reached a point from which they must either go forward to Thailand and the Burma Road area or "turn around and come back toward the road of friendship and peace." The United States, said Hull, must watch lest it be surprised. "Nothing will stop them except force. Unless we figure that they are going to turn back we should not figure that they are going to be satisfied where they are. The point," he continued, "is how we can maneuver the situation until the military matter in Europe is brought to a conclusion."[44]

In August, Prime Minister Churchill and President Roosevelt in a bay off Argentia, Newfoundland, held a meeting which produced the Atlantic Charter. They and their advisers also considered the Far East and agreed that they did not want war in the Pacific but that Japan should be checked. Roosevelt and Churchill decided to deal with the Japanese individually on the basis of a statement jointly agreed upon. State Department officials who saw this statement after Roosevelt returned to Washington thought it too strong and were able to secure its modification.[45]

The occupation of Indo-China and the retaliatory action of the United States had halted Japanese-American informal discussions. Prince Konoye, concerned over the dangerous trend of relations with the United States, told his Ministers of War and the Navy that he planned to propose a meeting with President Roosevelt. The Navy Minister assented; the War Minister predicted failure but said the Army would not oppose the venture if it was the Prime Minister's

[42] There is much about "Magic" in *ibid*. E.g., *Report*, pp. 179–181. There were also so-called "Purple" special decoding machines in London and Singapore.

[43] Feis, *The Road to Pearl Harbor*, p. 173 *n*.

[44] "Memorandum by Mr. Cecil W. Gray, Assistant to the Secretary of State," Aug. 2, 1941, *Foreign Relations of the United States, 1941*, IV, 358–359.

[45] "Draft of Proposed Communication to the Japanese Ambassador [Nomura]," *ibid.*, IV, 372. "Oral Statement Handed by President Roosevelt to the Japanese Ambassador [Nomura] on August 17, 1941," *ibid., Japan: 1931–1941*, II, 557.

determination "to carry out a war against America if the President of the United States still fails to comprehend the true intentions of the Empire after this final effort is made."[46] The Japanese Emperor, concerned for the effect an oil embargo would have on the Japanese Navy, urged a meeting with the President as soon as possible.

On his return from the Atlantic Conference, President Roosevelt met Ambassador Nomura and delivered his statement. It was hardly an ultimatum and was certainly milder than a public statement soon to come from Churchill. In this same conference, Nomura broached the subject of a meeting with Prince Konoye. In his initial reaction the President seemed interested, and he expressed optimism over the proposal in a subsequent meeting. Roosevelt and Hull found their advisers differing sharply on the matter. From Tokyo, feeling that the Prime Minister's startling break with tradition in making such an offer attested to his sincerity, Ambassador Grew in a series of dispatches strongly urged the President to meet Konoye. On September 29, Grew sent a long message summarizing his views and contending that failure to meet Konoye would result in the downfall of his Cabinet and "its replacement by a military dictatorship with neither the temperament nor the disposition to avoid a head-on collision with the United States." He also asserted that the Japanese government, while refusing to renounce the Tripartite Pact openly, had "in actual fact shown itself ready to reduce to a dead letter Japan's adherence to the alliance by indicating readiness to enter into formal negotiations with the United States." Grew's conclusion was that the only alternative to war was "to endeavor to bring about a regeneration of thought and outlook in Japan, along the lines of our present efforts through constructive conciliation."[47]

Within the State Department there was quite a different reaction to the Konoye proposal. Hornbeck expressed the view most sharply, but others shared it and voiced it. Hornbeck wrote that Japan was "already more than half beaten" and that "worse things could happen in Japan and between Japan and the United States" than the fall of the Japanese government.[48] In Hornbeck's opinion the Japanese suggestion of a conference was "a confession of internal weakness

[46] "Memoirs of Prince Konoye," *Pearl Harbor Attack*, Part 20, pp. 3999–4000.

[47] Grew to Roosevelt, September 29, 1941, *Foreign Relations of the United States, 1941*, IV, 483–489.

[48] "Memorandum by the Adviser on Political Relations [Hornbeck]," Aug. 30, 1941, *ibid.*, IV, 412–416.

and external weakness."[49] A few days later he wrote that there was a "low minimum of likelihood that Japan will make war on us," and his assertion that Japan was "half-whipped" seemed to be borne out by messages from China.[50] On September 23, Joseph W. Ballantine of the State Department reviewed the progress of negotiations and stressed the point that the Japanese had narrowed the matters to be discussed to such an extent that a conference would be disadvantageous to the United States. President Roosevelt concurred and on September 28, wrote:

> I wholly agree with your penciled note—to recite the more liberal original attitude of the Japanese when they first sought the meeting, point out their much narrowed position now, earnestly ask if they cannot go back to their original attitude, start discussions again on agreement in principle, and re-emphasize my hope for a meeting.[51]

On October 2, Hull relayed these views to Nomura and reiterated the general principles with which Konoye earlier had concurred. Hull suggested that the Japanese give clear manifestation of this agreement by a statement of intentions about withdrawal of troops from China and French Indo-China.

As the negotiations continued, Konoye encountered pressure from Army and Navy leaders who were becoming increasingly impatient with diplomacy. The issue came to a head in a meeting before the Emperor on September 6 and resulted in the following statement of policy for "carrying out its plans for the southern territories." Blame for the critical situation was laid to "especially the aggressive plans being carried out by America, England, Holland and other countries, the situation in Soviet Russia and the Empire's latent potentialities."

> 1. Determined not to be deterred by the possibility of being involved in a war with America (and England and Holland) in order to secure our national existence, we will proceed with war preparations so that they be completed approximately toward the end of October.

[49] Memorandum, Hornbeck to Hull, Sept. 2, 1941, *ibid.*, IV, 419.

[50] "Memorandum by the Adviser on Political Relations [Hornbeck]," Sept. 5, 1941, *ibid.*, IV, 428.

[51] Roosevelt to Hull, Sept. 28, 1941, *ibid.*, IV, 483. During the fall of 1941 a prominent Methodist clergyman, Dr. E. Stanley Jones, tried unsuccessfully to persuade the Roosevelt administration to help Japan acquire New Guinea as a solution of its expansionist desires. See numerous memoranda and letters in *ibid.*, IV, 455–457, 501–502, 555–558, 561–562, 641, 702–703. He made his last attempt on December 1, 1941.

2. At the same time, we will endeavor by every possible diplomatic means to have our demands agreed to by America and England. Japan's minimum demands in these negotiations with America (and England), together with the Empire's maximum concessions are embodied in the attached document.

3. If by the early part of October there is no reasonable hope of having our demands agreed to in the diplomatic negotiations mentioned above, we will immediately make up our minds to get ready for war against America (and England and Holland).

This policy of dual initiative, as Herbert Feis calls it, set the machinery of war into motion, to be stopped only by successful diplomacy. Japan's minimum demands fell into three categories. First, the United States and Britain should not interfere in the settlement of the China "Incident." They should close the Burma Road and cease aiding Chiang Kai-shek. Second, Britain and the United States would take no action in the Far East which offered a "threat to the defense of the Empire." They would not establish military bases in Thailand, the Netherlands East Indies, China, or Far Eastern Soviet Russia, nor would they increase their Far Eastern military forces over their present strength. Third, the United States and Britain would cooperate with Japan's attempt to secure raw materials. They would restore trade relations with Japan, provide her with needed raw materials from their possessions and help her to establish close economic relations with Thailand and the Netherlands East Indies. Then, after these demands were agreed to, Japan would make the following maximum "concessions": Japan would not use Indo-China as a base for operations against any neighboring country except China, and she would be prepared to withdraw her troops from French Indo-China "as soon as a just peace is established in the Far East." Japan also, after securing her minimum demands, would be "prepared to guarantee the neutrality of the Philippine Islands."[52]

Caught between this policy and the conflicting demands for concessions by the United States, the Konoye government moved toward collapse. On September 18, Prince Konoye escaped without injury from an assassination attempt made on him. On September 27, the Japanese Foreign Minister met with Ambassador Grew and urged American agreement to a meeting between Konoye and Roosevelt to be held as early as possible. From Tokyo on October 13 came a

[52] "Plans for the Prosecution of the Policy of the Imperial Government," *Pearl Harbor Attack,* Part 20, pp. 4022–4023.

warning to Nomura (intercepted by Magic) that the situation was "fast approaching a crisis" and that it was "becoming absolutely essential that the two leaders meet if any adjustment of Japanese-U.S. relations is to be accomplished."[53] The American comment of October 2, noted above, not only had doomed the conference but also the Konoye Cabinet, which on October 16 submitted its resignation.

General Hideki Tojo, Konoye's War Minister, headed the new Cabinet, which was loaded with military personnel. A State Department official reported, "In Manchuria General Tojo had a reputation of being a taciturn, clear-thinking, quick-deciding executive, with ideas leaning toward the conservative, sound side." The report predicted that Tojo would continue Konoye's policies, "including continuation of conversations with the United States."[54] A military intelligence appraisal of the General marked him as anti-Russian and pro-German and reported him as saying that Japan's road was "definitely decided" when Japan signed the Tripartite Pact, and there was no turning back. His associates, the report continued, termed him a man of "unshakable" determination. "He cites reverence and filial piety as the two most important attributes of a Japanese soldier. He has little patience for arguments or other people's views."[55] After the selection of Tojo's Cabinet, the State Department said that it appeared to be "a strong cabinet, predominantly military in character and with a large representation from among military leaders who have been directly involved in Japan's program of aggression on the continent." The report made the following prediction:

It is not believed that the new cabinet will reject a negotiated solution of Japan's international relations, but at the same time will take every measure possible to insure that, if such negotiated solutions are not forthcoming or are not successful, the opportunity for a solution by force will not be lost through lack of preparation or deployment of forces.

The new Foreign Minister, Shigenori Togo, was described as a career diplomat with a reputation as an "experienced, patient and capable negotiator."[56]

---

[53] Toyoda to Nomura, Oct. 13, 1941, *ibid.*, Part 12, p. 64.

[54] "Memorandum by Mr. William R. Langdon, of the Division of Far Eastern Affairs," Oct. 17, 1941, *Foreign Relations of the United States, 1941,* IV, 519.

[55] Acting Assistant Chief of Staff, Military Intelligence Division (Brigadier General Sherman Miles to General George C. Marshall), Oct. 17, 1941, *ibid.,* IV, 520.

[56] Maxwell M. Hamilton, Chief of the Division of Far Eastern Affairs, to Hull, Oct. 18, 1941, *ibid.,* IV, 522–523.

A United States Navy Department memorandum presented a somewhat different appraisal and asserted, "With the advent of the Tojo Cabinet Japan swings back to closer Axis ties under the aegis of the jingoistic military clique." According to the memorandum, "The maximum of Japanese manpower is being placed on a war footing," and "The naval forces of Japan may now be considered to be fully mobilized for imminent action."[57]

In Washington, feeling out of touch with the Tojo Cabinet and that he had lost his influence with the Washington administration, Admiral Nomura pleaded for permission to return to Japan, but he was told to remain at his post. Soon, however, the Japanese government decided to send a special emissary, Ambassador Saburo Kurusu, to assist Nomura. Kurusu, former Ambassador to Belguim and later to Germany, had an American wife and much greater fluency in English than did Nomura.[58] Aided by the American State Department in working out a plane schedule, Kurusu flew to Washington by way of the Philippines, Hawaii, and the West Coast. Tokyo informed Nomura in a message decoded by Magic that Kurusu would be his "right-hand man in these parleys." The message continued: "He is carrying with him no additional instructions, so in order to prepare him for the talks, will you please tell him all, and I hope that you can, by all means, arrange for an interview between him and PRESIDENT ROOSEVELT."[59]

On November 5, an Imperial conference reaffirmed the doctrine of dual initiative by directing that a last diplomatic effort be made and that if the diplomats were unsuccessful by November 25 the issue of war would go to the Emperor. The diplomats had two proposals; proposal A was a restatement of the Japanese position, and proposal B was a somewhat more moderate temporary solution or *modus vivendi*.[60] Confronted with the deadline of November 25, Japanese diplomats felt a great sense of urgency and tried to instill American leaders with the same feeling.[61] Grew became convinced of the danger

[57] "Memorandum for the Chief of Naval Operations, October 21, 1941," *Pearl Harbor Attack*, Part 15, pp. 1845–1847.

[58] For Grew's analysis of Kurusu's appointment, see *Pearl Harbor Attack*, Part 2, pp. 600–601.

[59] Togo to Nomura, Nov. 4, 1941, *ibid.*, Part 12, p. 97.

[60] Proposal A, as presented to the United States, is in *Foreign Relations of the United States, Japan: 1931–1941*, II, 709–710, 715–717. Proposal B is on pp. 755–756.

[61] "Memorandum by the Ambassador in Japan [Grew]," Oct. 30, 1941, *ibid.*, II, 699.

and on November 3 sent a sharp warning to Washington that if conciliation efforts failed the pendulum might swing to an "all-out, do-
or-die attempt, actually risking national hara-kiri, to make Japan
impervious to economic embargoes abroad rather than yield to foreign
pressure." Such action might come "with dangerous and dramatic
suddenness."[62]

Word went from Tokyo to Nomura on November 5 to present
proposal A to the United States government, and at this time
Nomura, and Magic, learned of the deadline of November 25.[63] When
the ambassador presented the proposal to Roosevelt on November
10, he said it contained Japan's "utmost efforts" for the maintenance
of peace, and he asked for the views of the United States government
at "the earliest possible opportunity." Roosevelt in reply gave no
evidence that he sensed any emergency; it took time, he said, to
dispose of diplomatic problems, and patience was necessary.[64] Concerned by the slowness of the Washington discussions, Togo wired
Nomura (in a message decoded by Magic) that the United States
was "still not fully aware of the extreme criticalness of the situation
here," and he stated that the deadline was still the twenty-fifth.[65] In
Tokyo Japanese officials tried to impress both the British Ambassador
and Ambassador Grew with the urgency for a quick agreement, and
on the thirteenth the Tokyo government again advised Nomura to
try to convince Washington of the seriousness of the situation.[66] Two
days later Togo once more told Nomura that the deadline of November 25 was immovable.[67] On the same day, November 15, orders went
out from Tokyo to Washington giving detailed instructions for the
"order and method of destroying the code machines in the event of
an emergency."[68] On the next day, Tokyo repeated the warning of
the deadline date and, importuning the ambassador to try harder

[62] Grew to Hull, Nov. 3, 1941, *ibid.*, II, 701–704.

[63] Togo to Nomura, Nov. 5, 1941, *Pearl Harbor Attack*, Part 12, p. 100.

[64] "Memorandum by the Secretary of State," *Foreign Relations of the United
States, Japan: 1931–1941*, II, 717–718.

[65] Togo to Nomura, Nov. 11, 1941, *Pearl Harbor Attack*, Part 12, p. 116.

[66] The British Embassy to the Department of State, Nov. 11, 1941, *Foreign
Relations of the United States*, 1941, IV, 585–586; Grew to Hull, Nov. 13,
1941, *ibid.*, IV, pp. 587–588; Togo to Nomura, Nov. 13, 1941, *Pearl Harbor
Attack*, Part 12, p. 123 (intercepted by Magic).

[67] Togo to Nomura, Nov. 15, 1941, *ibid.*, Part 12, p. 130 (intercepted by
Magic).

[68] Togo to Nomura, Nov. 15, 1941, *ibid.*, Part 12, p. 137 (intercepted by
Magic).

than ever for an agreement, stated, "The fate of our Empire hangs by the slender thread of a few days."[69] On November 17, Grew sent another warning, emphasizing "the need to guard against sudden Japanese naval and military action in such areas as are not now involved in the Chinese theater of operations."[70]

Meanwhile, Kurusu had arrived in Washington, and he and Nomura began to meet almost daily with Hull. The Japanese diplomats reported little headway on proposal A to the Japanese government and they stated that the principal stumbling blocks were the China question and Japan's relations to the Tripartite Pact. They felt that the United States leaders were "of a mind to bring about a compromise after making sure of our peaceful intentions." Consequently, they urged that instead of presenting proposal B immediately it would be better to reach a "practical settlement" first on the matter of American freezing legislation. The United States, they reported, was not interested in "mere promises" as much as she was in "putting said promises into effect."[71] On the eighteenth, the Japanese diplomats in Washington suggested the possibility of a temporary agreement to revert to the status quo before the occupation of French Indo-China and the American freezing order.[72] Tokyo replied that "the internal situation in our country is such that it would be difficult for us to handle it if we withdraw from Southern French Indo-China, merely on assurances that conditions prior to this freezing act will be restored." Togo, therefore, instructed Nomura and Kurusu to present the B proposal, "and no further concessions can be made." He further stated that if American consent could not be secured, "the negotiations will have to be broken off."[73] These instructions crossed a request from Kurusu and Nomura for permission to seek a temporary truce, which Tokyo promptly rejected.

Accordingly, on November 20, the Japanese diplomats in Washington presented the following proposal (B) to Secretary Hull:

1. Both the Governments of Japan and the United States undertake not to make any armed advancement into any of the regions in the South-eastern

[69] Togo to Nomura, Nov. 16, 1941, *ibid.*, Part 12, pp. 137–138.

[70] Grew to Hull, Nov. 17, 1941, *Foreign Relations of the United States, Japan: 1931–1941*, II, 743.

[71] Nomura to Togo, Nov. 18, 1941, *Pearl Harbor Attack*, Part 12, pp. 152–153.

[72] Nomura to Togo, Nov. 18, 1941, *ibid.*, Part 12, p. 149.

[73] Togo to Nomura, Nov. 19, 1941, *ibid.*, Part 12, p. 155.

Asia and the Southern Pacific area excepting the part of French Indo-China where the Japanese troops are stationed at present.

2. The Japanese Government undertakes to withdraw its troops now stationed in French Indo-China upon either the restoration of peace between Japan and China or the establishment of an equitable peace in the Pacific area.

In the meantime the Government of Japan declares that it is prepared to remove its troops now stationed in the southern part of French Indo-China to the northern part of the said territory upon the conclusion of the present arrangement which shall later be embodied in the final agreement.

3. The Governments of Japan and the United States shall cooperate with a view to securing the acquisition of those goods and commodities which the two countries need in Netherlands East Indies.

4. The Governments of Japan and the United States mutually undertake to restore their commercial relations to those prevailing prior to the freezing of the assets.

The Government of the United States shall supply Japan a required quantity of oil.

5. The Government of the United States undertakes to refrain from such measures and actions as will be prejudicial to the endeavors for the restoration of general peace between Japan and China.[74]

Hull had already received this document through Magic, and he later wrote: "The intercepted message had apprised us of the fact that this was Japan's final proposition. It was an ultimatum."[75]

The Secretary's problem was a serious one. To accept the Japanese suggestions would have meant a complete reversal of American policy. However, the American military authorities were asking for more time. A rejection of the Japanese proposal or even a failure to reply might be used as the occasion for hostilities. Roosevelt and Hull, therefore, considered a counterproposal, or *modus vivendi,* primarily as a time-consuming device. This was a plan for a three months' truce, during which a certain amount of trade would be permitted. Before deciding to present this proposal to the Japanese, the Washington administration sought the opinion of representatives of the British, Dutch, Australian, and Chinese governments. The Chinese reacted violently, and Chiang Kai-shek sent importunate cablegrams to Cabinet members and other Washington officials. The British Ambassador

[74] "A Proposal Handed by the Japanese Ambassador [Nomura] to the Secretary of State on November 20, 1941," *Foreign Relations of the United States, Japan: 1931–1941,* II, 755–756.

[75] Hull, *Memoirs,* II, 1068.

in general favored the *modus vivendi*, although he questioned portions of it.[76] The turning point seems to have been a cabled comment from Churchill. The Prime Minister said the matter was for the United States to decide and "we certainly do not want an additional war." However, asked Churchill, "What about Chiang Kai-shek? Is he not having a very thin diet? Our anxiety is about China."[77]

An intercepted message from Togo to Nomura should have had a sobering effect on those who read it. Togo said that he would extend the deadline from November 25 to the twenty-ninth (Tokyo time). "This time," he warned, "we mean it, that the deadline cannot be changed. After that, things are automatically going to happen."[78]

On November 25, the President conferred with a group of his top political advisers, sometimes called the War Cabinet. Present were General Marshall, Admiral Stark, and Secretaries Hull, Knox, and Stimson. Much has been made of that part of Stimson's diary dealing with the meeting in which he wrote that the President

brought up the event that we were likely to be attacked perhaps (as soon as) next Monday, for the Japanese are notorious for making an attack without warning, and the question was what we should do. The question was how we should maneuver them into the position of firing the first shot without too much danger to ourselves.[79]

This last sentence has been used by some postwar writers as evidence that Roosevelt deliberately plotted to force Japan into war against the United States and used Pearl Harbor as the bait. Others insist, more reasonably, that the War Cabinet did not anticipate that the Japanese would actually attack American soil at the outset and thought of maneuvering them into a position of appearing to be firing the first shot even though the shot might be fired at Thailand or Singapore.[80]

In the same meeting Secretary Hull pointed out the critical nature of Japanese-American relations, and he predicted, "The Japanese are likely to break out at any time with new acts of conquest by force." Warning against possible surprise, he stated, "The question of safe-

[76] For correspondence and other materials on the proposed *modus vivendi*, see *Foreign Relations of the United States, 1941*, IV, 635–665.
[77] Churchill to Roosevelt, Nov. 26, 1941, *ibid.*, IV, 665.
[78] Togo to Nomura, Nov. 22, 1941, *Pearl Harbor Attack*, Part 12, p. 165.
[79] Henry L. Stimson Diary, Nov. 25, 1941, *ibid.*, Part II, p. 5433.
[80] For a discussion of this matter, see Richard N. Current, "How Stimson Meant to 'Maneuver' the Japanese," *The Mississippi Valley Historical Review*, XL (June, 1953), 67–74.

guarding our national security lies in the hands of the Army and the Navy."[81]

When Stimson returned to the War Department in the afternoon he received word from Army Intelligence that a Japanese expeditionary force of from thirty to fifty ships was leaving Shanghai and heading down the China Coast south of Formosa.[82] This news, when relayed to them, disturbed both Hull and Roosevelt and may have reinforced their feeling that Japan would reject even the *modus vivendi*.

Tension was also mounting among the Japanese officials. Tokyo urged Kurusu and Nomura to do their utmost to persuade the United States authorities to accept the Japanese proposal. Togo also wrote: "I need not suggest the following, for you, no doubt, have already thought of it. I would like to have you make full use of influential Americans about whom you have wired me in the past and put pressure on the United States authorities indirectly as well."[83] Reporting by telephone code on November 26, Kurusu said, "I have made all my efforts, but *they will not yield*." The response from Tokyo was: "The situation in Tokyo is extremely critical also."[84]

On the same day, convinced that there was little chance that the Americans would accept the B proposal and believing that Britain and the United States might be conspiring to gain control of the Netherlands East Indies, Kurusu and Nomura suggested that Japan propose the "establishment of neutral nations, including French Indo-China, Netherlands, India and Thai."[85] They reminded Togo that Roosevelt had made such a proposal for French Indo-China and Thai in the preceding September. Unconvinced, the Tokyo government rejected the suggestion.

By the twenty-sixth, impressed by unfavorable Chinese and British reactions and possibly sure that it would not be accepted anyway, Hull, with Roosevelt's approval, dropped the *modus vivendi* and in its place offered the Japanese a statement of views which the United States had been presenting during the preceding months of discussion.[86] The first section of the document consisted of a draft Mutual Dec-

[81] Hull, *Memoirs*, II, 1080.

[82] Stimson Diary, Nov. 25, 1941, *Pearl Harbor Attack*, Part 11, p. 5433.

[83] Togo to Nomura, Nov. 26, 1941, *ibid.*, Part 12, p. 176.

[84] Telephone code, Transpacific Telephone, Kumaicho Yamamoto, Head of American Division of Japanese Foreign Office, and Kurusu, Nov. 26, 1941, *ibid.*, Part 12, p. 179.

[85] Nomura and Kurusu to Togo, Nov. 26, 1941, *ibid.*, Part 12, p. 180.

[86] Hull to Roosevelt, Nov. 26, 1941, *Foreign Relations of the United States, 1941*, IV, 665–666.

laration of Policy and included general principles earlier enunciated by the United States officials. The second part listed ten steps to be taken by the United States and Japan. Briefly, they were:

1. The two governments would attempt to conclude a multilateral non-aggression pact among the British Empire, China, Japan, the Netherlands, the Soviet Union, Thailand, and the United States.

2. Both governments would attempt to conclude an agreement among the American, British, Chinese, Japanese, the Netherlands, and Thai governments to pledge respect for the territorial integrity of French Indo-China and for equality of treatment in trade and commerce with that country.

3. Japan would withdraw all military, naval, air, and police forces from China and Indo-China.

4. Both governments would not support—militarily, politically, economically—any government or regime in China except the National Government of China with capital temporarily at Chungking.

5. Both governments would give up all extraterritorial rights in China, including rights and interests in international settlements and concessions, and rights under the Boxer Protocol of 1901.

6. Both governments would enter negotiations for the conclusion between the United States and Japan of a most-favored-nation treatment and reduction of trade barriers by both countries, including an undertaking by the United States to bind raw silk on the free list.

7. Both governments would, respectively, remove freezing restrictions on Japanese funds in the United States and on American funds in Japan.

8. Both governments would agree on a plan for the stabilization of the dollar-yen rate, with equal allocation of funds for the purpose.

9. "Both Governments will agree that no agreement which either has concluded with any third power or powers shall be interpreted by it in such a way as to conflict with the fundamental purpose of this agreement, the establishment and preservation of peace throughout the Pacific area."

10. Both governments would use their influence to cause other governments to adhere to and give practical application to the basic political and economic principles set forth in this agreement.[87]

The reaction of the Japanese diplomats is reflected in their report to Tokyo: "In view of our negotiations all along, we were both dumbfounded and said we could not even cooperate to the extent of reporting this to Tokyo. We argued back furiously, but HULL remained solid as a rock."[88] On the twenty-eighth came a message from Tokyo which was decoded by Magic. The United States had pre-

[87] "Document Handed by the Secretary of State to the Japanese Ambassador [Nomura] on November 26, 1941," *ibid., Japan: 1931–1941*, II, 768–770.

[88] Nomura to Togo, Nov. 26, 1941, *Pearl Harbor Attack*, Part 12, p. 182.

sented a "humiliating proposal," which the Japanese government could "by no means use" as a basis for negotiations. The message continued:

Therefore, with a report of the views of the Imperial Government on this American proposal which I will send you in two or three days, the negotiations will be *de facto* ruptured. This is inevitable. However, I do not wish you to give the impression that the negotiations are broken off. Merely say to them that you are awaiting instructions. . . .[89]

After the war, Japanese leaders claimed that the American note forced war on Japan, and Foreign Minister Togo, for example, pleaded, "Japan was now asked not only to abandon all the gains of her years of sacrifice, but to surrender her international position as a power in the Far East."[90] This explanation is based on the premise that Japan was entitled to hold what she had seized on the mainland. The American note threatened Japanese expansion, but not Japan, nor the Japanese people, nor even Japanese right to trade in the Far East. It was not an ultimatum in the sense that if Japan rejected the proposals the United States would sever diplomatic relations, declare war, or launch an attack. On the other hand, Hull realized that since Japan almost certainly would not accept the American reply to the Japanese "last word," diplomacy had failed to solve Japanese-American relations. Early in the morning of the twenty-seventh, Hull phoned Secretary of War Stimson, "I have washed my hands of it and it is now in the hands of you and Knox—the Army and the Navy."[91] Hull also told General Marshall, "Those fellows mean to fight and you will have to watch out."[92]

Military leaders in Washington decided to send a warning to the West Coast, Panama, Hawaii, and the Philippines. This was by no means the first warning to the outlying areas. On April 1, 1941, the Chief of Naval Operations sent the following notice to commandants of all naval districts:

[89] Togo to Nomura, Nov. 28, 1941, *ibid.*, Part 12, p. 195.

[90] Quoted in Feis, *The Road to War*, p. 327. For an elaboration of Togo's views, see Shigenori Togo, *The Cause of Japan* (New York, 1956), pp. 170–192. Togo insists that the note gave Japan only the alternatives of war or surrender.

[91] Stimson Diary, Nov. 27, 1941, *Pearl Harbor Attack*, Part 11, pp. 5434–5435.

[92] Statement by Marshall to Pearl Harbor Congressional Investigation Committee, *ibid.*, Part 3, p. 1148.

Personnel of your Naval Intelligence Service should be advised that because of the fact that from [sic] past experience shows that Axis powers often begin activities in a particular field on Saturdays and Sundays or on national holidays of the country concerned, they should take steps on such days to see that proper watches and precautions are in effect.[93]

Admiral Stark in a series of letters kept both Admiral Thomas C. Hart in Manila and Admiral Husband E. Kimmel in Hawaii informed of diplomatic developments. On September 22, he told Hart that although Hull was working hard the chances for settlement were slight, and on the following day he wrote Kimmel that conversations with the Japanese had "practically reached an impasse."[94] When the Konoye Cabinet fell in October, the Chief of Naval Operations notified the commanders in the Pacific of the "grave situation" and further stated, "Since the U.S. and Britain are held responsible by Japan for her present desperate situation there is also a posibility [sic] that Japan may attack these two powers." He ordered the commanders, consequently, to "take due precautions, including such preparatory deployments as will not disclose strategic intention nor constitute provocative action against Japan."[95] Other action indicating the approach of crisis included orders to reroute United States transpacific flag shipping to keep clear of the Japanese mandated islands and of Japan itself. Orders went out to take "all practical precautions for the safety of the airfields at Wake and Midway," because of their usefulness in flying bombers to the Philippines.[96] Early in November came word that Japanese merchant vessels were disappearing from the western Pacific. On November 25, Stark wrote Kimmel that he had been talking with Roosevelt and Hull and that neither "would be surprised over a Japanese surprise attack."[97]

Then on November 27 came the decision to send out a more direct warning. The message to Admiral Kimmel was more direct than that to General Short. It started with the words, "Consider this dispatch a war warning," and stated that attempts to negotiate with Japan had

---

[93] "From OPNAV Action: Com al Nav Districts N.Y. Wash Governors of Guam and Samoa," Apr. 1, 1941, *ibid.,* Part 14, pp. 1395–1396.

[94] H. R. Stark to H. E. Kimmel, Sept. 23, 1941, *ibid.,* Part 16, p. 2213.

[95] CNO to CINCLANT, CINCPAC, CINCAF, Oct. 16, 1941, *ibid.,* Part 14, p. 1402.

[96] CNO to CINCPAC, Oct. 17, 1941, *ibid.,* Part 14, p. 1403.

[97] Stark to Kimmel, Nov. 25, 1941, *ibid.,* Part 16, p. 2224. Stark gave no indication that he thought Pearl Harbor would be attacked and mentioned such places as Thailand, Indo-China, the Burma Road, and the Philippines.

ended. Japan was expected to make an aggressive move "within the next few days." The number and nature of the Japanese task force indicated an amphibious attack on the Philippines, the Kra Peninsula, or possibly Borneo. Kimmel was to execute a defensive deployment. The notification to General Short was not quite so definite about the ending of diplomatic conversations but predicted that the chances of further discussions were slight. If hostilities could not be avoided, "the U.S. desires that Japan commit the first overt act." Short should prepare his defenses, but not in such a way as to "alarm the civil population or disclose intent."[98] On the same day the following message also went to General Short:

> Japanese negotiations have come to practical stalemate stop Hostilities may ensue stop Subversive activities may be expected Inform commanding general and Chief of Staff only.[99]

After receiving the warning message, General Short unwittingly took steps which were to have tragic consequences. Military authorities were disturbed by the thought that some of the 160,000 persons of Japanese ancestry on the islands might engage in subversive activity. Short replied to the warning with the message, "Report Department alerted to prevent sabotage. Liaison with the Navy." He then decided to institute the first of three alerts which were to be put into operation. The first was against sabotage, and included bunching planes so that they could be protected more easily from sabotage. The second alert was against both sabotage and air attack and involved the posting of antiaircraft batteries and dispersal of planes. The third was preparation for sea-borne invasion as well as air attack, and put everyone in the field.[100]

At the same time the Navy seemed more preoccupied with submarine attack than air assault. Fortunately, Admiral Kimmel decided to send Marine fighter plane replacements to Wake and Midway islands, and this move resulted in the absence of the aircraft carriers, *Lexington* and *Enterprise,* from Pearl Harbor on December 7, 1941.

---

[98] The messages to General Short and Admiral Kimmel may be examined in parallel columns in *ibid., Report,* p. 535.

[99] Miles [General Sherman] to Hawaiian Department, Nov. 27, 1941, *ibid.,* Part 14, p. 1329.

[100] This message appears in many places in *ibid.,* e.g., *Report,* p. 120. The failure of the War Department to see the danger implicit in the reply is one of the most serious charges against the War Department.

Not all the Washington officials felt that the United States was headed toward war. Over in the State Department Stanley K. Hornbeck drew up an estimate of the situation, dated November 27. In his opinion Japan did "not desire or intend or expect to have forthwith armed conflict with the United States." While Japan would launch new military operations in the Far East, it would "endeavor to avoid attacking or being attacked by the United States." In fact, continued the expert, "Were it a matter of placing bets, the undersigned would give odds of five to one" that the United States would not be at war on or before the fifteenth of January, 1942, and he would give even money that war would not come by March, 1942.[101]

After receiving the American note, Japan advised the German government of the possibility of war in the Pacific and drew attention to the Tripartite Pact. The German Foreign Minister, Joachim von Ribbentrop, promised orally that if Japan and the United States went to war Germany would join the war immediately.[102]

On December 1, Togo sent a message to Kurusu and Nomura; the deadline date of November 29 had "come and gone," and the situation was becoming increasingly critical. He continued:

However, to prevent the United States from becoming unduly suspicious we have been advising the press and others that though there are some wide differences between Japan and the United States, the negotiations are continuing. (The above is for only your information).[103]

Kurusu and Nomura made one final effort to win the diplomatic battle and avert war. They reported that the indications were that the United States wished to continue negotiations. If a conference of leaders was impossible for political reasons, could not there be a meeting of persons in whom the leaders had confidence, say Vice President Henry A. Wallace or Harry Hopkins from the United States and Prince Konoye or Adviser to the Imperial Privy Council Ishii from Japan? The diplomats urged, "Have them make one final effort to reach some agreement, using as the basis of their discussions the latest

101 "Memorandum by the Adviser on Political Relations [Hornbeck]," Nov. 27, 1941, *Foreign Relations of the United States, 1941,* IV, 672–675.

102 Berlin to Tokyo, Nov. 29, 1941 (Magic interception), *Pearl Harbor Attack,* Part 12, p. 202. Benito Mussolini made a similar pledge for Italy on December 3, 1941. Rome to Tokyo, Dec. 3, 1941 (Magic interception), *ibid.,* Part 12, p. 229.

103 Togo to Nomura, Dec. 1, 1941 (Magic interception), *ibid.,* Part 12, p. 208.

proposals submitted by each."[104] Togo replied on December 3; an earlier Japanese Cabinet had suggested a meeting of leaders but it had not materialized. "It is felt that it would be inappropriate for us to propose such a meeting at this time."[105]

Since October, President Roosevelt had considered writing a letter to Emperor Hirohito. His advisers had talked him out of the idea until early in December, when he reconsidered and on the sixth sent a message to Grew with instructions to deliver it to the Emperor.[106] Pointing out that a continuation of the current situation was "unthinkable," Roosevelt called on the Emperor to give thought, as he, himself, was doing, "in this definite emergency to ways of dispelling the dark clouds."[107] The President's action came too late, and offered too little. Tojo and Togo felt the proposal could accomplish nothing, and they sent a reply after the bombing of Pearl Harbor.[108]

As the crisis deepened, Kurusu and Nomura received orders for the destruction of codes and for members of the Embassy to prepare to leave Washington. Then, on the sixth, Toyko informed Kurusu and Nomura that a fourteen-part response would shortly be on its way. "The situation is extremely delicate," advised Togo, "and when you receive it I want you to keep it secret for the time being." The Foreign Minister further said that he would send a separate message telling the diplomats when to present the memorandum to the United States government.[109]

The first thirteen parts of the fourteen-point memorandum were intercepted and arrived in the Navy Department between 11:49 A.M. and 2:51 P.M. on December 6. They were decoded, typed, and ready for distribution by about 9 P.M. Captain A. D. Kramer arrived at the White House between 9:30 and 10:00 and delivered the first thirteen parts to Commander L. R. Schultz, who in turn took the materials to the President. Roosevelt was with Harry Hopkins, and the two men

---

[104] Nomura to Togo, Dec. 1, 1941 (Magic interception), *ibid.*, Part 12, p. 213.

[105] Togo to Nomura, Dec. 3, 1941 (Magic interception), *ibid.*, Part 12, p. 224.

[106] See early drafts and State Department objections to sending the note in *Foreign Relations of the United States, 1941*, IV, 513–515.

[107] President Roosevelt to Emperor Hirohito, Dec. 6, 1941, *ibid.*, *Japan: 1931–1941*, II, 784–786.

[108] Togo, *The Cause of Japan*, pp. 219–221.

[109] Togo to Nomura, Dec. 6, 1941, *Pearl Harbor Attack*, Part 12, pp. 238–239.

read the intercepted document. The only record of the President's re-action comes from Commander Schultz' statement that he heard Roo-sevelt comment in essence, "This means war." Hopkins and Roosevelt discussed the matter for about five minutes. Hopkins apparently ex-pressed the view that since war was going to come it was too bad the United States could not strike the first blow and avoid being sur-prised. The President, however, said, "No, we can't do that. We are a democracy and a peaceful people." Schultz left with the impression that the United States would have to wait for the Japanese to make the first move. He later recalled no mention of Pearl Harbor and stated that Indo-China was the only area mentioned by Roosevelt and Hopkins.[110]

Kramer next took the dispatches to Secretary Knox and then to several high-ranking officers, who were attending a dinner party. None felt that the message had military significance. Kramer returned to the Navy Department and, finding that the fourteenth part of the message was not yet in, retired for the night. Although the evidence is conflicting, it does not appear that similar distribution was made that night to Secretary Hull, Secretary Stimson, General Marshall, Admiral Stark, or General L. T. Gerow, of the War Plans Division.

The fourteenth part of the Japanese message was intercepted, de-coded, and made available between 7:30 and 8:00 in the morning of the seventh. Roosevelt received it at about 10 A.M. Rear Admiral John R. Beardall, who delivered the message, recalled that the Presi-dent remarked that it looked as if the Japanese were going to sever negotiations.[111] The first thirteen parts of the memorandum had con-sisted of a recital of recent Japanese-American relations from the Japanese point of view. Criticizing American support of China and charging that the United States and Britain were attempting to en-circle Japan, the note asserted that the Japanese had always been fair and moderate and tried to reach a settlement for which "it made all possible concessions in spite of great difficulties." The note tore the American ten-point memorandum apart and rejected it as a basis for negotiations. In the fourteenth part, the Japanese charged that the United States and Britain were attempting through aid to China to "obstruct Japan's efforts toward the establishment of peace through the creation of a New Order in East Asia." The note concluded:

110 Testimony of Commander L. R. Schultz in *ibid.*, Part 10, pp. 4662–4663.
111 Testimony of Rear Admiral John R. Beardall, *ibid.*, Part 11, p. 5274.

The Japanese Government regrets to have to notify hereby the American Government that in view of the attitude of the American Government it cannot but consider that it is impossible to reach an agreement through further negotiations.[112]

During the night another message from Tokyo addressed to the Japanese Embassy in Washington was intercepted and decrypted. Ready for distribution about 9 A.M., this note referred to the fourteen-point memorandum and stated:

Will the Ambassador please submit to the United States Government (if possible to the Secretary of State) our reply to the United States at 1:00 P.M. on the 7th, your time.[113]

Arriving at the Navy Department at about 10:20, Captain Kramer discovered the message ten or fifteen minutes later and sensed its significance. He got the message to a presidential aide in another twenty minutes. That morning General Marshall had gone for his customary horseback ride across the river in Virginia. On his return he received word of an important message and reached his office between 11:15 and 11:30 A.M. Reading first through the fourteen-point memorandum, he finally reached the shorter message and felt that it was very significant, "relating to a specific hour for some specific act somewhere."[114] He called Admiral Stark and suggested sending a warning to all theaters concerned. Stark at first demurred on the ground that a warning had already been issued, and another one might cause confusion. Marshall insisted that he was going to send a message and wrote it out in longhand. Stark, meanwhile, reconsidered and called back to ask that the note include a request to inform naval authorities. Marshall's message was addressed to the Western Defense Command, the Panama Command, the Philippine Command, and the Hawaiian Command. Marshall sent officers back twice to the message center to find out how long it would take to transmit the message until he was reassured that all to whom it was addressed would receive the message before 1 P.M. His message read:

The Japanese are presenting at 1 P.M. Eastern Standard Time, today, what amounts to an ultimatum. Also they are under orders to destroy their code

[112] The note as intercepted by Magic is in *ibid.*, Part 12, pp. 239–245.
[113] Togo to Nomura, Dec. 7, 1941 (intercepted by Magic), *ibid.*, Part 12, p. 248.
[114] Testimony of General George C. Marshall, *ibid.*, Part 3, p. 1513.

machine immediately. Just what significance the hour set may have we do not know, but be on the alert accordingly.[115]

Colonel Edward F. French, in charge of the message center, took personal charge of the communication for Hawaii.[116] Finding that the War Department radio was out of contact with Hawaii, a customary condition at that time of day and year, French felt that he could send the message through faster by commercial facilities than by using Navy services. The message went by Western Union to San Francisco and by RCA radio to Honolulu and arrived in the RCA office at 12:33 Washington time or 7:33 A.M. Hawaii time. Apparently the teletype arrangement between the Honolulu office and Fort Shafter was not operating at the time, and a messenger started out on his bicycle with the message. He was on his way when the attack started and he was understandably delayed. When the message finally arrived at 11:45 A.M. Hawaii time, it was only an historical curiosity.

General Marshall could have called Hawaii by telephone. He did not know what was going to happen at one o'clock, nor did he think that Hawaii would be attacked. He said later that if he had called anyone it would have been MacArthur, and a second phone call could not have been put through in time to reach Hawaii before the deadline. Security reasons also dictated against using the telephone, for the United States authorities did not want the Japanese to find that they had broken the Japanese code.[117]

There remained the final scene in the diplomatic play in Washington. Ironically, the Japanese were slower in decoding the fourteen-part message than were the Americans and they missed the careful timing required of them. Kurusu and Nomura made an appointment with Hull for 1 P.M., and later called to postpone the meeting until 1:45. It was actually a little after two when they appeared. As they moved to the diplomatic waiting room, Hull received a call from the President, "There's a report that the Japanese have attacked Pearl Harbor."

Hull asked, "Has the report been confirmed?"

Roosevelt replied, "No."

[115] This message appears in many places in *ibid.*, e.g., *Report*, p. 224.

[116] Testimony of Colonel Edward F. French before Army Pearl Harbor Board, *ibid.*, Part 27, pp. 105–115.

[117] For differing views on the sending of this message, see majority and minority reports of the Joint Committee on the Investigation of the Pearl Harbor Attack, *ibid.*, *Report*, pp. 225–226, 540.

Coldly, the Secretary met the Japanese diplomats, read rapidly through the document, which, thanks to Magic, he had already seen, and with the President's message ringing in his mind told the delegates that in his fifty years of public service he had never seen a document that was "more crowded with infamous falsehoods and distortions—infamous falsehoods and distortions on a scale so huge that I never imagined until today that any Government on this planet was capable of uttering them."[118]

Hull was not starting a debate; he was pronouncing his judgment. He waved the ambassadors from the room without further word. A few minutes later he received verification of the news that Pearl Harbor had been attacked.

[118] Hull, *Memoirs*, II, 1095–1096.

CHAPTER 3

War Plans and the Start of the War in the Pacific

E ARLY in the 1920's, American military planners began to consider the possibility of war with Japan and in July, 1924, they
prepared a so-called "Orange" plan for such a contingency.[1] They
continued to study this and other "color" plans for possible war with
other nations, mainly as exercises and as bases for budgetary presenta-
tions to Congress, while the peacetime Army dwindled in size.[2] In
the 1930's, planners replaced Orange with "Rainbow 5," which envisaged war not with one state but with the Axis, either with or without Japan, and which sought to prevent violation of the Monroe
Doctrine, to protect the United States, its possessions, and its sea
trade, and to defend the Western Hemisphere.[3]

[1] For extracts from the Orange plan (1938), see U.S. Congress, Joint Committee on the Investigation of the Pearl Harbor Attack, *Pearl Harbor Attack,
Hearings* . . . (Washington, 1946), Part 15, pp. 1423–1425. For studies of
prewar planning, see Mark S. Watson, *Chief of Staff: Prewar Plans and Preparations (United States Army in World War II: The War Department)* (Washington, 1950), *passim;* Maurice Matloff and Edwin M. Snell, *Strategic Planning
for Coalition Warfare, 1941–1942 (United States Army in World War II: The
War Department)* (Washington, 1953), pp. 32–96; Louis Morton, *The Fall of
the Philippines (United States Army in World War II: The War in the Pacific)*
(Washington, 1953), pp. 61–73.

[2] See letter, Admiral J. O. Richardson to Admiral H. R. Stark, Jan. 26,
1940. *Pearl Harbor Attack,* Part 14, pp. 924–925. As far as the Philippines
were concerned, the plan was tactically good. Morton, *The Fall of the Philippines,* p. 61.

[3] "Navy Basic War Plan—Rainbow No. 5 (WPL-46)" and appendices are
printed in *Pearl Harbor Attack,* Part 33, pp. 926–985.

Meanwhile, the British had been thinking of possible war in the Pacific, and held discussions which led to an Anglo-Dutch-Australian (ADA) plan for the defense of common interests in the Far East.[4] Not satisfied, the Australians sought another meeting with American participation. In November, 1940, Admiral H. R. Stark, Chief of Naval Operations, wrote Admiral T. C. Hart, Commander in Chief, U.S. Asiatic Fleet, that the Navy could make no political commitments or "specific military plans for an allied war." Hart could, however, "perform a useful service by laying, with the British and possibly the Dutch, a framework for a future plan of cooperation, should we be forced into the war."[5] At about the same time, the United States government gave Chiang Kai-shek $100 million and a promise of a supply of fighter aircraft.

In January, 1941, British and American staff conversations in Washington resulted in the production two months later of a joint basic war plan, known as ABC-1.[6] According to this plan, the United States would increase its forces considerably in the Atlantic and somewhat in the Mediterranean to enable Britain to release vessels for the Far East, where forces of both powers would guard against Japanese aggression. In case of war, the strategy of both powers would be defensive, although the U.S. Pacific Fleet would be used offensively to weaken Japanese economic power and to divert Japanese strength away from the Southwest Pacific. There was no obligation on the part of the United States to enter the war. The military of both governments accepted the plan in principle although the political leaders did not give it formal approval, and the United States began its neutrality patrol in the Atlantic. This action reduced American naval strength in the Pacific.

When Japan signed a neutrality pact with Soviet Russia on April 13, 1941, the British suggested a statement by the British, Americans, and Dutch that they had a joint strategic plan to check any open act of Japanese aggression.[7] The United States government was starting discussions in Washington in an effort to reach a solution of the Far Eastern problem and preferred this course of action. The Americans

[4] British planning is described in S. Woodburn Kirby, *The War Against Japan* (*History of the Second World War: United Kingdom Military Series*) (London, 1957), I, 1–88.

[5] Stark to Hart, Nov. 12, 1940, *Pearl Harbor Attack,* Part 14, p. 972.

[6] ABC-1 is in *Pearl Harbor Attack,* Part 15, pp. 1485–1541.

[7] Kirby, *The War Against Japan,* I, 61.

did agree to discuss strategic plans with the British and the Dutch, and military leaders met in Singapore from April 22 to 26, 1941. Australia, New Zealand, and India also were represented, and in the resultant ADB Agreement the military leaders recommended long-range economic pressure on Japan until offensive action could be taken.[8] They based their recommendations primarily on the employment of naval forces, mainly American, until a British battle fleet arrived in the area. American military leaders in Washington refused to accept the plan.[9] They felt that it covered too wide an area, all the way from Africa to Australia, and that the Commander in Chief, U.S. Asiatic Fleet, might lose his identity and be ordered to operate in waters of no strategic significance to the United States. No joint plan resulted at this time. In August, while Churchill and Roosevelt met in the Atlantic Conference, military leaders with them drew up a revised draft agreement, ABD-2, which they hoped would meet most of the American objections, particularly on limitation of area and command of naval forces.

Meanwhile, the U.S. Army and Navy, profiting by the discussions with the British early in 1941, as well as by conversations with the Canadians,[10] had proceeded with the refinement of Rainbow 5. The task of the Army and the Navy in the Far East, as visualized in the Navy's version of Rainbow 5 was to destroy Axis sea communications in the Pacific area east of 180° (the International Date Line), to raid Axis forces in the Pacific and Far Eastern areas, to protect sea communications in the Far East and to the east of Australia.[11] The plan also included preparations to seize the Marshall and Caroline Islands in order to establish an advanced fleet base at Truk in the Carolines.

In October, United States naval leaders indicated that they would not accept ABD-2. Their main criticism was that British naval weakness in the Far East made an effective combined plan seem impossible. On November 3, Rear Admiral R. E. Ingersoll, Assistant Chief of Naval Operations, told the Joint Board that the policy already set

---

[8] The report of the American-Dutch-British conversations is in *Pearl Harbor Attack*, Part 15, pp. 1551–1584.

[9] Letter, Chief of Naval Operations and Chief of Staff to Special Naval Observer, London, and Special Army Observer, London, July 3, 1941, *ibid.*, Part 15, pp. 1677–1679.

[10] "Joint Canadian–United States Basic Defense Plan No. 2 (Short Title—ABC-22)," *ibid.*, Part 15, pp. 1585–1593.

[11] U.S. Pacific Fleet Operating Plan Rainbow Five (Navy Plan O-1, Rainbow Five (WPPac-46), *ibid.*, Part 33, pp. 995–996.

in U.S. British Conversations Report ABC-1 was that the major effort should be in the Atlantic and that if forced to fight in the Pacific the British and Americans should "engage in a limited offensive effort." A major Pacific war would reduce the effort in the Atlantic, Singapore was inadequately protected, and there were no repair facilities at either Singapore or Manila. General Marshall expressed the opinion that when the United States had a powerful air and submarine force in the Philippines, Japan could hardly risk a flank attack on their supply lines in a southern move. He also commented that "until powerful United States forces have been built up in the Far East, it would take some very clever diplomacy to save the situation." After the discussions, the Joint Board proposed that the War Plans Division of the War and Navy departments prepare a memorandum for the President opposing the issuance of an ultimatum to the Japanese and suggesting that the State Department postpone hostilities with Japan as long as possible and make "agreements with Japan to tide the situation over for the next several months."[12]

Two days later, on November 5, General Marshall and Admiral Stark presented a memorandum to the President which expressed similar ideas. They wrote:

> At the present time the United States Fleet in the Pacific is inferior to the Japanese Fleet and cannot undertake an unlimited strategic offensive in the Western Pacific. In order to be able to do so, it would have to be strengthened by withdrawing practically all naval vessels from the Atlantic except those assigned to local defense forces. An unlimited offensive by the Pacific Fleet would require tremendous merchant tonnage, which could only be withdrawn from services now considered essential. The result of withdrawals from the Atlantic of naval and merchant strength might well cause the United Kingdom to lose the battle of the Atlantic in the near future.[13]

The two military leaders informed the President that the only current plans for war against Japan were "to conduct defensive war, in cooperation with the British and the Dutch, for the defense of the Philippines and the British and Dutch East Indies." They predicted that by the middle of December, the U.S. air and submarine strength

[12] The Joint Board, "Minutes of Meeting, November 3, 1941," *ibid.*, Part 14, pp. 1062–1065.
[13] "Memorandum for the President, November 5, 1941," *ibid.*, Part 14, pp. 1061–1063.

would be "a positive threat to any Japanese operations south of Formosa" and that U.S. Army air forces would reach their projected strength in the Philippines by February, 1942. By that time, "The potency of this threat will have then increased to a point where it might well be a deciding factor in deterring operations in the areas south and west of the Philippines." Increase in British defenses at Singapore would furnish a similar deterrent in that area.

Toward the end of the month, Marshall and Stark, in another memorandum to the President, wrote: "The most essential thing now, from the United States viewpoint, is to gain time. Considerable Navy and Army reinforcements have been rushed to the Philippines but the desirable strength has not been reached."[14] They recommended that the United States government seek an agreement with the British and the Dutch to warn the Japanese that an advance west of 100° East or south of 10° North into Thailand might "lead to war." It was on this same day that war warnings were sent to the outlying possessions of the United States.

On December 5, Admiral Sir Tom Phillips, commander of the British Far Eastern Fleet, arrived in Manila to discuss joint plans for defense with Admiral Hart and General MacArthur. Hearing on the next day that a Japanese force had been sighted in the Gulf of Siam, Phillips left immediately by plane for Singapore and his flagship, *Prince of Wales*. On December 7 (Manila date), Hart sent a report of his meeting with the British Admiral to Naval Operations in Washington.[15] He included a joint statement with Phillips which outlined defensive naval action on a cooperative basis rather than through the institution of joint headquarters. In his own message Hart urged immediate strengthening of Manila for use by the British Fleet by April, 1942. Very favorably impressed by the British Admiral, Hart sent a second message reporting that he had sent Admiral William A. Glassford to command Task Force 5 and recommended "you empower me put all or part his command under British strategic direction or even direct command and to withdraw same at discretion anytime."[16] Admiral Hart's report of his meeting with Phillips reached Washington about 11 P.M. on December 6. A dispatch of

[14] "Memorandum for the President, November 27, 1941," *ibid.*, Part 14, p. 1083.

[15] CINCAF to OPNAV, Dec. 7, 1941, *ibid.*, Part 19, pp. 3547–3553.

[16] CINCAF to CNO, Dec. 7, 1941, *ibid.*, Part 19, p. 3555.

approval went to him after receipt of news about the attack on Pearl Harbor.[17]

Thus, in the prewar months there had been discussions with the British and the Dutch, there had been proposed plans of operation if war should come, but none had received final authorization. Consequently, when the war started, the United States placed in operation its own war plan, as did the British. The Japanese evidently expected joint action against them, and British-American military discussions apparently had little to do with Japan's decision to make war.[18]

Japanese military planning for a southward move, which had begun early in 1941, developed in earnest after Japanese assets had been frozen in July in response to the Japanese occupation of southern Indo-China. The planning, which was based on the assumption that war would come before the end of the year, centered about the accomplishment of the national objective—the Greater East Asia Co-Prosperity Sphere.[19] The planners found their problem complicated by the fact that they had to plan a short war in view of the nation's resources and industrial potential. Japan, an insular power, depended on a merchant marine which was barely adequate in peacetime. Its industries needed foreign markets for strategic materials, most of which were closed by embargoes; by fall Japan would be drawing on reserves, of which oil reserves were the most critical. War plans, therefore, included early seizure of oil-producing regions in the East Indies, capture of Singapore and the Philippines to protect lines of

[17] *Ibid., Report,* p. 170.

[18] The majority report of the Joint Committee on the Investigation of the Pearl Harbor Attack states: "There is no evidence to indicate that Japanese knowledge of the 'ABC' and 'ADB' conversations was an inducing factor to Japan's decision to attack the United States coincident with her thrust to the south. Indeed, the idea of attacking us at Pearl Harbor was conceived before these conversations were initiated." *Ibid., Report,* p. 171.

[19] After the war a Liaison Committee (Tokyo) for the Imperial Japanese Army and Navy provided information on Japanese war plans, which General MacArthur's headquarters forwarded to the War Department. The material included captured documents and answers by Japanese military and naval leaders to questions presented to them. They form part of the documentation of the Joint Congressional Committee on the Investigation of the Pearl Harbor Attack. E.g., "Japanese Combined Fleet Top Secret Operation Order #1," *ibid.,* Part 13, pp. 431–484. For analyses of Japanese military planning, see Morton, *The Fall of the Philippines,* pp. 51–61; Kirby, *The War Against Japan,* pp. 89–96.

communication, and a blow at the U.S. Pacific Fleet to prevent its interference. Weather and the Russians entered the planning; war should start in December before the northeast monsoon in the South China Sea and the winter storms in the North Pacific could reach their full force, and a winter offensive would be less likely to tempt the Russians into a flank attack in the north.

There was no over-all command; but both the Japanese Army and Navy agreed to essentially a final plan on October 20. There would be three periods in its development: the first, an attack on Pearl Harbor, seizure of the southern regions, and capture of a defensive perimeter, extending from Wake through the Gilberts, Bismarck Archipelago, New Guinea, Timor, Java, Sumatra, Malaya, and Burma to the Indian border; the second, consolidation and strengthening of the perimeter; the third, repulse of attempts to break the ring until the enemy tired of fighting. From one standpoint, the plan was aggressive and expansionist, for by it the Japanese sought to extend their domination over vast expanses of land and sea. From another point of view, the plan was defensive. The Japanese intended to strike quickly and *hold* what they had won. There is no evidence that they planned to defeat or destroy the United States or Britain.

The first period in the Japanese planning fell into three phases. The first of these centered about initial attacks, counting on surprise to throw the opposition off guard and prevent the sending of replacements. Occurring closely together, therefore, would be the air attack on Pearl Harbor, occupation of Thailand (Siam) as necessary for operations against Malaya and Burma, seizure of Hong Kong, air attacks on Luzon, occupation of Guam, Wake, and the Gilbert Islands. Then the Japanese would follow up the air attacks on the Philippines with invasion of Luzon and Mindanao to get the ports of Manila and Davao. They would take Jolo in the Sulu Sea and North Borneo as part of the preparations for the move on Sumatra and Java.

The second phase envisaged operations to seize the southeastern part of the perimeter, including the Bismarck Archipelago. At this time, also, the Japanese would complete their conquest of Malaya, culminating in the seizure of Singapore. To the north, there would be air attacks on Burma, which the Japanese had decided to take partly to protect their flank and partly for its oil and rice. In the East

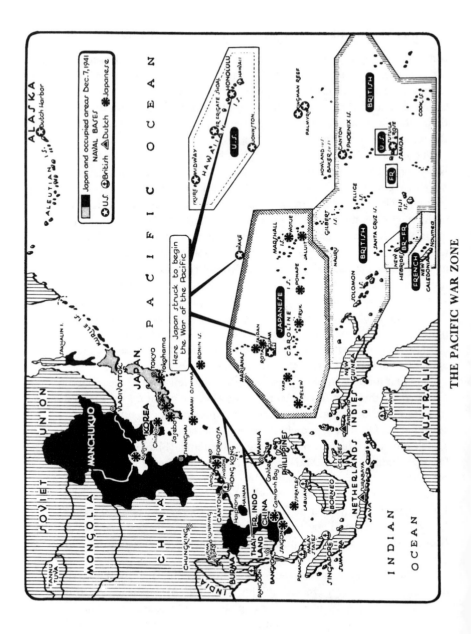

THE PACIFIC WAR ZONE

Indies, the Japanese planned to occupy strategic parts of southern Sumatra, Dutch Borneo, Celebes, Amboina, and Timor preparatory to conquest of Java.

In the third phase the Japanese forces would capture Java, extend their hold on Sumatra to the entire island, and conquer Burma. The timetable estimated for the major moves included 50 days for the Philippines, 100 days for Malaya, and 150 days for the Netherlands East Indies.

Anticipating that certain developments might necessitate a change of plans, Japanese military planners drew up alternatives. If the Japanese diplomats should be successful in their negotiations with the United States, there would be no need of war, and it would be called off even if the final order for the attack had been given. If the United States should send part of its Pacific Fleet to the Far East, the Japanese Navy should deploy forces to meet it and go on with the invasions. If the British or the United States should start operations, the Japanese forces should wait for orders from the Imperial General Headquarters.

The Japanese attack on Pearl Harbor was carefully planned and carried into execution. In January, 1941, Admiral I. Yamamoto, Commander in Chief of the Japanese Combined Fleet, ordered a staff study of a carrier strike against Hawaii. By August the plans were sufficiently advanced to warrant a start of actual preparations.[20] The air striking force that was organized consisted of six carriers, screened by a squadron of nine destroyers. It was supported by a force that included two battleships, two cruisers, three submarines, and a train of eight tankers and supply ships. In addition, there was an advance expeditionary force of about twenty submarines. Eleven bore small planes, and five were equipped with midget submarines. The latter were operated by two men and powered by storage batteries. They carried two small torpedoes and were designated as the Special Naval Attack Unit.

The Air Attack Force left the Kure naval base in echelons between November 10 and 18. Keeping strict radio silence, the force headed for the Kurile Islands to the north of Japan. Although the Kure base increased the flow of other radio messages to cover the silence of the attack force, the Pacific Fleet Intelligence Officer at Pearl Harbor

[20] *Pearl Harbor Attack*, Part 13, pp. 329–426. Information gained from interrogation of Japanese officers.

noted that the call signs of two Japanese carrier divisions were not on the air. Unfortunately, his superiors saw no significance in his report.[21]

In its move toward the target, the Japanese force had the choice of three routes. One, leading east from Japan, and a second approaching Hawaii from the Marshalls offered the advantage of good weather and greater ease of refueling, but the danger of discovery. The third was the approach to Hawaii from the north.[22] The customary bad winter weather might make refueling difficult, but the chance of carrying through a surprise attack was much greater. The Japanese had selected the latter route, and for this reason the force headed for Tankan Bay in the Kuriles for its last rendezvous. It was at this spot that the men of the attack force were told what their mission would be. There seems to have been nothing but elation at the thought of thus launching two great nations into war. One of the Japanese seamen wrote: "An air attack on HAWAII! A dream come true. What will the people at home think when they hear the news? Won't they be excited! I can see them clapping their hands and shouting with joy! These were our feelings. We would teach the arrogant Anglo-Saxon scoundrels a lesson!"[23]

On the twenty-sixth of November, the force left Tankan Bay. As anticipated, it encountered adverse weather conditions, fog, gales, and heavy seas, but it avoided detection. The attacking force actually started toward Hawaii before the final order to attack was given, and Admiral Yamamoto had ordered the striking force to turn back if detected prior to December 6. If the force was detected December 7 (east longitude date), the Admiral in command would decide whether or not to attack. On December 2, the code signal to commence hostilities was sent, and the date of the attack was set at December 8 (December 7, Hawaii time).

On the morning of December 7, the striking fleet reached its pre-

[21] S. E. Morison, *History of United States Naval Operations in World War II* (Boston, 1948), III, 88–89. Communication Intelligence Summaries Concerning Locations of Japanese Fleet Units (14th Naval District) from Nov. 1 to Dec. 6, 1941, are in *Pearl Harbor Attack*, Part 17, pp. 2601–2642.

[22] From interrogation of Japanese officers, *ibid.*, Part 13, pp. 401–402.

[23] Iki Kuramoti, "The Southern Cross," an account by presumably an enlisted man in the attack force. *Ibid.*, Part 13, p. 516. See also Andrieu d'Albas, *Death of a Navy: Japanese Naval Action in World War II* (New York, 1957), p. 17.

determined launching position, about 275 miles north of Oahu.[24] From carrier decks pitching somewhat from a moderate sea, the planes began their flight. There were forty "Kate" torpedo bombers, armed with torpedoes especially fitted for dropping in shallow water, and fifty more "Kates," prepared for high-level bombing. In addition, there were fifty dive bombers and an equal number of fighter planes.[25] A second wave consisted of fifty Kates, eighty Vals, and forty Zekes.

Weather conditions were ideal for a surprise attack, and, as we have seen, Pearl Harbor was unprepared for the blow. The American tradition of weekends in port, on which the Japanese were counting so heavily, was being upheld. The vessels were lined up in a row, and officers and men in general were relaxed. There was no advance warning that counted. The destroyer *Ward* discovered one of the Japanese midget submarines near the harbor entrance and sank it with depth charges at 6:45 A.M., with a Navy patrol bomber assisting in the attack. The matter was reported to Pearl Harbor, but the only response was to order another destroyer to the area.[26] Another direct warning was unheeded. Permanent radar stations had not yet been installed on the island. Of the six temporary stations only one was in operation after 7 A.M. Private George Elliott wanted some practice, and the operator in charge, T/3 Joe Lockard, had consented to keep the set operating for a time. At 7:02 Lockard detected signals of approaching aircraft. Unfortunately, the watch officer, to whom the information was reported, was inexperienced in the use of radar and confused the aircraft with some B-17's expected from the mainland or planes due in from the carrier *Enterprise* on its way back from Wake Island. Consequently, he did not forward the information.[27]

[24] For charts showing route of the attack force, see *Pearl Harbor Attack*, Part 21, Item No. 15; Morison, *History*, III, 91. A Japanese naval officer who was with the attack force stated in an interview after the war that on the night before the attack he heard that there were no carriers at Pearl Harbor. *Pearl Harbor Attack*, Part 13, p. 645.

[25] The Congressional Joint Committee on the Investigation of the Pearl Harbor Attack stated in its report that the Japanese aircraft taking part in the operation included 81 fighters, 135 dive bombers, 104 horizontal bombers, and 40 torpedo bombers. *Ibid., Report*, p. 58.

[26] A small converted mine sweeper, U.S.S. *Condor*, made the first sighting and notified the *Ward*. *Ibid.*, Part 13, p. 494; Morison, *History*, III, 96–97.

[27] For statements by the persons involved, see *Pearl Harbor Attack*, Part 18, pp. 2966–2968. See also G. R. Thompson, D. R. Harris, P. M. Oakes, and D. Terrett, *The Signal Corps: The Test (December 1941 to July 1943)*

Without initial opposition, therefore, the Japanese swept down over Pearl Harbor and its surrounding military installations. The first phase of the attack started at 7:55 and lasted a half-hour. During this time torpedo and dive bombers attacked the battleships and made strafing runs on the Naval Air Station on Ford Island and adjoining Marine and Army airfields. Then there was a lull for about fifteen minutes. Next came a series of high-level bombing attacks on Pearl Harbor, from 8:40 to 9:15. Then the dive bombers came in once again to attack the harbor with devastating blows for about thirty minutes. At 9:45 the planes withdrew, and the attack was over.

Although it is clear that the American forces in Hawaii were caught off guard, they recovered quickly and fought courageously. The official accounts are filled with acts of heroism, pilots taking to the air in obsolete planes to attack the enemy, men with no thought of personal safety firing antiaircraft weapons from exposed positions, others performing acts of valor on or near the ships under attack.

The odds, however, were hopeless, and the punishment inflicted by the Japanese was heavy. The death total was 2,403 of whom 2,008 were Navy personnel, and there were 1,178 wounded, of whom the heavy percentage (710) came from Navy ranks. The Battle Force of the Pacific Fleet took a terrific beating, and Battleship Row along the southeast shore of Ford Island was a shambles. *West Virginia* took six or seven torpedoes and two bombs and sank. Fortunately for later salvage operations, prompt counterflooding prevented the vessel from capsizing. *Tennessee,* moored inboard of *West Virginia,* was thus protected from aerial torpedoes, and most of its damage came from flaming debris and burning oil from adjacent vessels. *Arizona,* moored astern of *Tennessee,* was the hardest hit of all the battleships. An explosion of the forward magazines wrecked the forward part of the vessel. Then a series of bombs struck, one actually going down the stack, and the *Arizona* sank, taking to their death over a thousand men. *Nevada* suffered heavy damage to its superstructure by at least five bombs, and a torpedo ripped a hole thirty feet high and forty-five feet long. *Oklahoma* was struck by three torpedoes and capsized. In the next berth *Maryland,* like *Tennessee,* was screened from aerial torpedoes, receiving but two bombs and suffering the least damage of all the battleships. *California,* the flagship of Vice Admiral W. S.

(*United States Army in World War II: The Technical Services*) (Washington, 1957), pp. 3–5.

Pye, was poorly prepared for attack. Hit by two torpedoes and a couple of bombs, the vessel attempted to get under way. The damage was too great, and the vessel sank in shallow water and mud until only the superstructure remained above the surface. *Pennsylvania,* in dry dock, although taking a bomb hit that exploded below with considerable loss of life, was not seriously damaged. Smaller naval craft in the harbor also received heavy punishment during the attack. The alert against sabotage resulted in severe damage to aircraft. Two-thirds of the naval aircraft had been destroyed, and there were only sixteen serviceable Army Air Force bombers left in the area. The Japanese, in contrast, had lost twenty-nine planes and three midget submarines.[28]

A few bombs fell on nearby Honolulu, and there were occasional machine-gun bursts at nonmilitary targets, but these were incidental to the main purpose of the attack, which was to strike at the U.S. Pacific Fleet and its supporting military establishments. In Honolulu people hearing the bombs exploding received through their radios the warning: "Oahu has been subjected to a sporadic air raid. Do not drive in the streets or highways. Keep off the streets." At about 8:30 military officials told the press that the planes were definitely Japanese, at 10:00 the Governor declared the territory to be in a state of emergency, and at 3:45 General Short proclaimed martial law and instituted a black-out. Throughout the day rumors, soon to be discounted, poured into the Army Intelligence Office: parachute troops were landing near Barbers Point, parachute troops wearing blue coveralls with a red shield on the shoulder had landed on the North Shore, a landing party between Barbers Point and Nawakuli was being fired on by P-40's, a sampan was about to land in front of Lualualei, parachutists were landing in Pauva Valley, others were dropping on St. Louis Heights.[29]

Successful and destructive though the Pearl Harbor attack was,

[28] For a factual account of the attack, see *Pearl Harbor Attack, Report,* pp. 57–62. For damage done to vessels, see *ibid.,* Part 33, pp. 1341–1343. For other descriptions of the attack, see Morison, *History,* III, 98–125; W. F. Craven and J. L. Cate, *The Army Air Forces in World War II* (Chicago, 1948), I, 194–201; A. R. Buchanan (ed.), *The Navy's Air War: A Mission Completed* (New York [1946]), pp. 4–14. For Japanese versions, see d'Albas, *Death of a Navy,* pp. 16–37; Masatake Okumiya and Jiro Horikoshi, *Zero* (New York, 1956), pp. 44–52.

[29] Work sheet of Journal in Combat Intelligence Section, 7 December 1941, *Pearl Harbor Attack,* Part 19, pp. 3628–3629.

it will probably be ranked in history as one of the worst blunders ever committed by a major power. No other act could have pulled the American people more quickly together behind a declaration of war. To the American who heard of the attack there was no longer any question of peace or war. The unprovoked character of the assault strengthened still more the American will to win the struggle.

The Japanese no doubt anticipated the nature, if not the extent, of the American reaction, and reckoned it as a calculated risk, to be more than counterbalanced by the military gains. Sober judgment, however, inclines to the view that the Pearl Harbor attack was a military as well as a psychological error. The main purpose of the blow was to knock the Pacific Fleet out of interference with Japanese expansion southward. Such a move was unnecessary, Morison insists, since the Pacific Fleet was too weak to have ventured into waters within reach of land-based aircraft. Prewar American plans called for a slow movement into the Pacific,[30] and had there been no Pearl Harbor attack, the Japanese could have seized their objectives in the Pacific before the United States could have brought its forces to bear in the area. Morison even suggests that one of the reasons for the surprise at Pearl Harbor was that American military leaders thought the Japanese would realize that an attack was unnecessary.

The attack was not only a strategic blunder; it was even an error on the tactical level. Rather than centering the blows on the vessels in the harbor, it would have been more effective in the long run to blast the permanent installations and the oil tanks. The bulk of the vessels left helpless on Battleship Row gradually were restored to

---

[30] American-Dutch-British conversations, Singapore, April, 1941, rejected by the Americans, stated that the U.S. Fleet should operate offensively against the Japanese mandated islands. *Ibid.*, Part 15, p. 1568. On November 3, 1941, the Joint Board advocated State Department efforts to avoid war as long as possible with Japan, noted the effect a war with Japan would have on aid to Britain and other nations in the European war, and pointed out the existing limitations on shipping and the inability of the United States to wage offensive war in the Pacific without transferring "the major portion of shipping facilities from the Atlantic to the Pacific." The discussion also brought out the fact that if the fleet should move to the Far East "no repair facilities are available at either Manila or Singapore; while there are docks, nevertheless the necessary machinery and facilities for making repairs are not present." Rear Admiral R. E. Ingersoll, Assistant Chief of Naval Operations, also told the Board, "Manila is not as yet a secure base for the Fleet due to the lack of adequate antiaircraft protection for the anchorage." "Minutes of Meeting, November 3, 1941," Joint Board, *ibid.*, Part 14, 1062–1065. See also Part 14, p. 1083.

fighting trim and participated in the later strikes that were to bring Japan to defeat.[31] Fortunately for the United States, there were no carriers in Pearl Harbor; the *Lexington* and *Enterprise* were at sea, and the *Saratoga* was on the West Coast.

These were interpretations to be expressed at a later date.[32] On December 7, 1941, a stunned America merely knew that a savage blow had been dealt our armed forces in Hawaii. In Washington, the President conferred with administration leaders about the message to be delivered. There was no debate over the main theme. Roosevelt

[31] Morison, *History*, III, 125–132; Kirby, *The War Against Japan*, I, 99–100. This British military historian notes the failure of the Japanese to seek out and destroy the United States carriers in the area.

[32] There have been eight investigations of the Pearl Harbor Attack, as follows:

The Roberts Commission, organized under Executive Order dated December 18, 1941. The inquiry lasted from December 18, 1941, to January 23, 1942, and was headed by Justice Owen J. Roberts.

The Hart Inquiry, initiated by Secretary of the Navy Frank Knox, lasted from February 12 to June 15, 1944.

The Army Pearl Harbor Board, appointed pursuant to provisions of Public Law 339, approved June 13, 1944, was initiated by an order of the Adjutant General, War Department, dated July 8, 1944. Its investigation lasted from July 20 to October 20, 1944.

The Navy Court of Inquiry also originated from Public Law 339 and came into being as a result of an order by Secretary of the Navy James Forrestal dated July 13, 1944. It held sessions from July 24 to October 19, 1944.

The Clarke Inquiry, conducted by Colonel Carter W. Clarke, "regarding the manner in which certain Top Secret communications were handled," resulted from oral instructions from General George C. Marshall. This inquiry was held from September 14 to 16, 1944, and July 13 to August 4, 1945.

The Clausen Investigation came from an order by Secretary of War Henry L. Stimson and extended from November 23, 1944, to September 12, 1945. It was conducted by Major Henry C. Clausen, JAGD.

The Hewitt Inquiry, conducted by Admiral H. Kent Hewitt, came from an order of Secretary of the Navy James Forrestal and lasted from May 14 to July 11, 1945.

The Joint Congressional Committee on the Investigation of the Pearl Harbor Attack came into being as a result of Senate Resolution No. 27 (as extended). It held its first hearings November 15, 1945, and submitted its report July 20, 1946. This committee published not only its own hearings and supporting exhibits but also the records of the other investigating agencies in 39 volumes.

No clear-cut findings have emerged. The Congressional Committee, for example, published a majority and a minority report. While critical of many persons and actions, the majority report tended to absolve the Washington administration of responsibility and to place the blame on those in command in Hawaii. The minority report put the blame on officials in both Washington and Hawaii. See *Pearl Harbor Attack, Report, passim.*

pushed aside the suggestion of Hull that a detailed review of Japanese-American relations be given, and determined upon a brief call to arms.

Accordingly, on December 8, referring to the previous day as a "date which will live in infamy," President Roosevelt asked Congress to declare the existence of a state of war with Japan.[33] Congress hastened to comply. In the Senate the vote was unanimous, and in the House of Representatives there was but one dissenting vote. Jeannette Rankin, who had opposed the entrance of the United States into World War I, repeated her protest vote in December, 1941.

The United States was in World War II, but there remained an important question. What of Germany and Italy? Nazi Germany was viewed as the principal enemy and we were actually in a state of undeclared war with her on the Atlantic, but how and when should the shift be made from undeclared to open war? There was some pressure on Roosevelt to declare war on Germany and Italy, but he preferred to wait for them to act. "Magic" intercepts of Berlin-Tokyo correspondence helped him decide to wait. Fortunately for the Roosevelt administration, the German government solved the problem.[34]

Japan had made its fateful move without consultation with Germany, and in fact was prepared to carry on the war alone if her European allies remained aloof.[35] However, drawing on the Tripartite Alliance of 1940, Japan officially requested Germany to declare war on the United States. Hitler, pleased that Japan was in the conflict, promptly agreed. On December 11, 1941, charging the United States with "open acts of war," Germany declared war on this country.[36]

[33] Franklin D. Roosevelt, *The Public Papers and Addresses of Franklin D. Roosevelt* (New York, 1950), X, 514–516. See also "Memorandum. Remarks of the President on the occasion of the meeting of his Cabinet at 8:30 and continuing at 9:00 with legislative leaders, on December 7, 1941," *Pearl Harbor Attack,* Part 19, 3503–3507.

[34] Roosevelt knew through "Magic" interceptions of the probability that Germany and Italy would declare war on the United States, and he decided to await their move. Robert E. Sherwood, *Roosevelt and Hopkins: An Intimate History* (New York, 1948), pp. 441–442. An intercepted message from Berlin to Tokyo, dated November 29, 1941, quoted Foreign Minister Joachim von Ribbentrop as telling the Japanese emissary, "Should Japan become engaged in a war against the United States Germany, of course, would join the war immediately. There is absolutely no possibility of Germany's entering into a separate peace with the United States under such circumstances. The Fuehrer is determined on that point." *Pearl Harbor Attack,* Part 12, p. 202.

[35] Togo Shigenori, *The Cause of Japan* (New York, 1956), pp. 212–213.

[36] Message, Foreign Minister, Tokyo, to Japanese Ambassador, Berlin, De-

Italy, using the same arguments, followed her major ally's example. There was no question of the response in Congress. The Senate, unanimously, and the House, without record vote, passed a joint resolution that a state of war "which has been thrust upon the United States is hereby formally declared."

The United States entered a war which at the time looked promising for her enemies. Continental Europe, with the exception of Sweden, Switzerland, and Portugal, was under the direct or indirect influence of Germany. The Franco regime in Spain was pro-Axis, Italian Fascism had been subordinated to Nazism, the Vichy government was collaborating both in France and in North Africa, and Sweden, though neutral, was bound closely by economic ties to Germany. Soviet Russia had been pushed deep into her own territory, and although her counteroffensive began on December 6, 1941, its prospects for success certainly could not be seen at the time.[37] In North Africa, the outlook was equally dim for the Allies. The gains made earlier in the year by General Sir Archibald P. Wavell had been wiped out when General Erwin Rommel led the Germans to the aid of the hard-pressed Italians. Between November, 1941, and January, 1942, Axis forces thrust the Allies to within fifty or seventy-five miles of Alexandria.

Having immobilized the Pacific Fleet at Pearl Harbor, the Japanese moved rapidly in the Far East. One of their immediate objectives was Singapore, regarded as the outstanding Far Eastern bastion of the British Empire. As war approached, the British sought to bolster Singapore's defenses; looking upon it as a great naval base, they relied on sea power for protection and planned enough ground and air units to withstand siege until the Navy could go to the rescue.[38] Ground forces were dispersed to protect an inadequate air force in Malaya and were in a position to meet defeat piecemeal at the hands of an aggressive, well-trained invader.[39]

---

cember 12, 1941, *Pearl Harbor Attack*, Part 35, pp. 691–692. See also F. C. Jones, *Japan's New Order in East Asia: Its Rise and Fall, 1937–1945* (London, 1954), pp. 328–329.

[37] Wladyslaw Anders, *Hitler's Defeat in Russia* (Chicago, 1953), p. 66.

[38] Winston Churchill, *The Second World War* (Boston, 1949), II, 668. Churchill in a letter to General Ismay, September 10, 1940, asserted: "The defence of Singapore must, therefore, be based upon a strong *local* garrison and the general potentialities of sea-power." Malaya was too large, he wrote, and the idea of trying to defend it "cannot be entertained."

[39] S. Woodburn Kirby, *The War Against Japan*, I, 456–457; Lionel Wigmore,

On December 8, Japanese forces landed on the east coast of Malaya, farther south than had been anticipated, hampered but not repelled by fire from ground troops and Australian air attacks.[40] Thailand was also attacked and fell into Japanese hands after little more than token resistance. The Japanese then began to develop their plan of campaign in Malaya, which was to push across to the west coast and advance down through Johore at the end of the peninsula for an attack on Singapore on the island across the narrow strait of Johore.

The Japanese quickly punctured the myth of sea power as Singapore's greatest defense when a Japanese air force tracked down and sank the battleship *Prince of Wales* and the battle cruiser *Repulse*.[41] On land British Lieutenant General Sir Archibald Wavell, arriving as the newly appointed head of a united Australian, British, Dutch, American (ABDA) command, was shocked to find that "no defences had been made or even planned" on the northern part of Singapore Island.[42] He ordered a start of such defenses, while the Japanese were relentlessly battling their way down the Malay Peninsula. Johore was lost on January 27; on the thirty-first the last of the retreating forces marched onto the island, and demolition squads blasted a seventy-foot gap in the huge causeway which had linked the island with Johore.

From England Churchill sent word that this would be the last retreat. "I want to make it absolutely clear that I expect every inch of ground to be defended, every scrap of material or defences to be blown to pieces to prevent capture by the enemy, and no question of surrender until after protracted fighting among the ruins of Singapore."[43] Regrettably, on this island where these things were to take place were hundreds of thousands of civilians, men, women, and children, with no place to go and no place to hide.

Enemy bombers made two or three raids daily, virtually unhindered

---

The Japanese Thrust (*Australia in the War of 1939–1945*, Series 1, *Army*, Volume IV) (Canberra, 1957), pp. 90, 114–117.

[40] For descriptions of the Malayan campaign, see *ibid.*, pp. 121–283; Kirby, *The War Against Japan*, I, 177–199, 229–249, 301–346; Churchill, *The Second World War*, IV (1950), 36–59.

[41] For accounts of the sinking, see S. W. Roskill, *The War at Sea, 1939–1945* (*History of the Second World War: United Kingdom Military Series*) (London, 1954), 564–569; Kirby, *The War Against Japan*, pp. 193–199.

[42] Wigmore, *The Japanese Thrust*, pp. 202–203.

[43] Churchill, *The Second World War*, IV, 53.

after the middle of January.[44] The Allied air defenses were practically and finally completely nonexistent. The bulk of the seventy thousand combatant forces were raw recruits. The heavy guns which had contributed to the myth of Singapore's impregnability were pointed out to sea; some could not be turned around against the enemy approaching by land, and those that could had mostly armor-piercing ammunition instead of the high-explosive ammunition needed for land warfare.

After preliminary bombardment, the Japanese began the assault of the island, and although Australians fought desperately in hand-to-hand encounter, wave after wave of the invaders extended the beachhead. By the thirteenth, the enemy was within five thousand yards of the main sea front and was bringing the entire city into artillery range. Seagoing craft evacuated, but the land forces were told to keep fighting. On the fourteenth, the Governor of the Straits Settlement reported to the Colonial Office:

There are now one million people within radius of three miles. Water supplies very badly damaged and unlikely to last more than twenty-four hours. Many dead lying in the streets and burial impossible. We are faced with total deprivation of water, which must result in pestilence. I have felt that it is my duty to bring this to notice of General Officer Commanding.[45]

When a similar report reached Wavell, he said fighting should continue as long as there was water for the troops. He sent a somewhat different message to Churchill and, asking for discretionary power, stated, "There must come a stage when in the interests of the troops and civil population further bloodshed will serve no useful purpose."[46] Churchill agreed, and the worn and depleted forces surrendered the city on February 15. A seventy-day campaign by the Japanese, thirty days shorter than they had anticipated, had resulted in the conquest of Malaya and the "Gibraltar of the East."

While the campaigns in Malaya and the Philippines continued, the Japanese made other conquests in their southward sweep. Hong Kong's cause was hopeless from the start. For reasons of prestige, the British could not abandon it before war began, and its vulnerable

---

[44] For accounts of the attack on Singapore Island, see Kirby, *The War Against Japan*, pp. 375–415; Wigmore, *The Japanese Thrust*, pp. 284–389; Churchill, *The Second World War*, IV, 92–107.

[45] Quoted in Churchill, *The Second World War*, IV, 103.

[46] Quoted in *ibid.*, IV, 104.

location just off the coast of China, with the hinterland in Japanese hands, made it certain of capture in case of war. British leaders hoped, however, to pin down numbers of the enemy in an extended siege and deprive them of the use of an excellent harbor. A few hours after the attack was launched on Malaya on December 8, Japanese forces began the attack on Hong Kong. Seizing first the leasehold of Kowloon on the mainland, the Japanese forced their way on the island. Hong Kong fell on December 25, after only eighteen days of fighting. Like Singapore it had proved to be no significant block to Japanese advance.[47]

About a week after the first invasion, a Japanese force struck at British Borneo and with little difficulty conquered this rich oil-producing area.[48] Also, as soon as the war started, the Japanese moved quickly to seize Guam, the only island in the Marianas group which they did not control already, and which had been a possession of the United States since the Spanish-American War. Congress had failed to authorize funds for an expansion of fortifications on Guam, which at the outbreak of the war provided a fueling station for naval vessels, a naval radio station, a relay for the transpacific cable, and a stop for Pan American clippers. After a series of air attacks from December 8 to 10, the Japanese landed with a force of about six thousand. Not wishing to endanger the lives of the twenty thousand Guamanians on the island and realizing that the chance of survival was slight, the senior officer of the defenders quickly surrendered, and the Japanese had another important American possession.[49]

As another part of the effort to break American communications across the Pacific, the Japanese advanced toward Wake, Midway, and other islands in the Pacific. In order both to guard communications and to protect the flank of Pearl Harbor, the United States had started the military strengthening especially of Midway and Wake. Work on the naval air base at Wake was well advanced by the summer of 1941; by late October there were about four hundred

[47] For a description of the fall of Hong Kong, see Kirby, *The War Against Japan*, I, 107–151. The only naval vessels to escape destruction were two destroyers which left Hong Kong on the day of the attack.

[48] *Ibid.*, I, 221–227.

[49] For a description of the capture of Guam, see O. R. Lodge, *The Recapture of Guam* (Marine Corps Monographs [12]) ([Washington] 1954), pp. 6–8; Frank O. Hough, Verle E. Ludwig, Henry I. Shaw, *Pearl Harbor to Guadalcanal: History of U.S. Marine Corps Operations in World War II* (Washington, 1958), I, pp. 75–78; S. E. Morison, *History*, III, 184–186.

Marines in the advanced defense detachment, and about twelve hundred civilians working on military construction.[50] On December 4, twelve Grumman Wildcats of a Marine Fighter Squadron arrived from the carrier *Enterprise* and began regular flights. The planes were not armored, lacked self-sealing fuel tanks, and had bomb racks which did not fit the bombs in supply on the island. The Marines, a fifth of whom had no arms nor equipment, had three months' food supply; the construction workers had half a year's provisions. All had to rely on evaporators for there was no natural water supply. The island, like many others in the Pacific, consisted of a lagoon surrounded by a coral group, somewhat higher and more wooded than many. The Marines had partly completed placement of guns, but there had been no time to test-fire them. Warning devices were practically nonexistent; there was no radar, the fighters could provide only limited coverage, and from an observation post atop a steel water tower one could see twelve miles out to sea.

Like those on Guam, the people on Wake had a few hours' warning of war. It did not help much; shortly after nine in the morning of December 8, thirty-six twin-engine Japanese bombers from the Marshalls, taking advantage of a rain squall and profiting from the noise of the heavy surf, dropped suddenly over the island in an attack that killed or wounded more than half of the naval air personnel. Hastily the men dug in, mined the air strip, and placed a barge loaded with dynamite surrounded by concrete blocks near the dredged channel. When the second attack came, Marine fighters were able to isolate and down one bomber, yet the effect of the raid was devastating; direct hits destroyed the hospital, barracks buildings, garage, the partly completed naval air station, and the radio station with most of its gear. The defenders, however, were learning, and as long as their forces held out gave a good account of themselves. The Japanese air raids came almost on schedule, and for a time their bombing tactics remained the same.

On December 9 (west longitude time), Admiral Kimmel at Pearl Harbor decided to send a relief force to Wake. This Task Force 14 centered about the carrier *Saratoga* and included six cruisers, nine destroyers, and a seaplane tender carrying relief troops and equipment.

<hr/>

50 Accounts of Wake, its preparations and its seizure, include Robert D. Heinl, *The Defense of Wake* (Marine Corps Monographs [1]) ([Washington] 1947), *passim;* Hough, Ludwig, Shaw, *Pearl Harbor to Guadalcanal,* pp. 95–149.

Two other task forces, including the carriers *Lexington* and *Enterprise,* were to give general support by diversionary strikes. While Task Force 14, after numerous delays, was getting under way, Vice Admiral N. Inouye, at headquarters of the Japanese Fourth Fleet at Truk, in the Carolines, turned his attention to Wake after the successful invasion of Guam. Bombers from the Marshalls continued to "soften up" the island, and on December 11 a surface force, which under cover of bad weather had reached the island undetected, began bombardment preparatory to landing. Determined Marines manned their guns and using their meager stock of planes fought off the enemy, which instead of landing sailed away, having lost two destroyers and suffered damage to other vessels. The Marines were jubilant at their stand. As the siege continued, however, the war of attrition went heavily against the defenders, although they performed herculean tasks of remaking flyable aircraft from shattered wrecks. Japanese carrier aircraft arrived to add to the softening-up process. Marine fighters fought the unequal battle for fifteen days; at the end of that time there were no planes left.

On December 21, a second and much stronger assault force left Roi in the Marshalls for Wake; in the meantime the relief force from Pearl Harbor headed toward the same objective. On December 22, Rear Admiral F. J. Fletcher's Task Force 14, about 550 miles from Wake, paused a day to refuel. The delay was fatal to the relief venture, for by the time Fletcher got under way again, the Japanese were within fifty miles of Wake and at about two-thirty the following morning began landings. The dark and the intermittent rainfall made things difficult for both invader and invaded, but although the Marines fought desperately and sank a destroyer transport and damaged another, the enemy gradually placed a thousand men ashore against the five hundred defenders. Communications were severed, and isolated Marine groups fought their separate battles. In the meantime, authorities at Pearl Harbor considered the risk of losing a task force as well as an island and called off the relief expedition.[51] Once hope of reinforcement was gone, the military leaders on Wake decided to surrender. It took time to inform all the Marines. In their own battle on another island in the group, Captain W. M. C. Platt and his men had wiped out twice their number of Japanese and were looking for more when they encountered Major J. P. S. Devereux and his captors,

[51] *Ibid.,* p. 143; Morison, *History,* III, 235–254.

who told them of the decision to surrender. In the defense of Wake, the Marines demonstrated great courage, and they learned the need of an adequate mobile infantry reserve, underground communications, and radar. They had suffered about 20 per cent casualties and had killed about seven hundred Japanese.

With little effort the Japanese took over the British-controlled Gilbert Islands. From bases in the Marshalls a small force occupied Makin without encountering resistance. A token force which landed at Tarawa proved unnecessary, for airplanes from Makin were soon patrolling the area.

Midway, outlying island of the Hawaiian chain some 1,137 miles northwest of Oahu, was early seen to be of strategic importance. In 1938, the Hepburn Board reiterated: "From the strategic point of view an airbase at Midway Island is second in importance only to Pearl Harbor," and it recommended military development of the small circular atoll which surrounded two low, sandy islands.[52] Like Wake, Midway was a stopover for Pan American clippers and a relay station for the transpacific cable. The Marine detachment at the outbreak of the war included 33 officers and 810 men. Midway had the same number of five-inch guns (6), three-inch guns (12) and .30-caliber machine guns (30) as Wake and almost twice as many .50-caliber machine guns. There were actually more guns than the number of men could handle satisfactorily, and as on Wake there was lack of a mobile infantry reserve. Fortunately, at first the Japanese planned only a hit-and-run attack.[53] A task unit of two destroyers and a tanker proceeded directly from Tokyo Bay to shell the air base at Midway while the main Japanese striking force retired from its attack on Pearl Harbor. Arriving at their destination, the destroyers began firing on Midway on the night of December 7. The raid killed four persons and wounded about two score. Property damage was not irreparable, and the attack underlined the need for greater defenses. The Marine reinforcements called back from the expedition to Wake went instead to Midway, and by the end of the year Midway had a garrison of a heavily reinforced defense battalion, a Marine scout bomber and a fighter squadron, and some patrol bombers. The

[52] Robert D. Heinl, *Marines at Midway* (Marine Corps Monographs [3]) ([Washington] 1948), p. 1.
[53] The Midway attack is described in *ibid.*, pp. 11–22; Hough, Ludwig, Shaw, *Pearl Harbor to Guadalcanal*, pp. 78–81.

next year saw steady increases in the island's defenses, which went largely underground.

Johnston Island, to the south and somewhat nearer Oahu than was Midway, was too small and too near Pearl Harbor for the Japanese to risk a surface attack. During December, however, Japanese submarines fired on the island, causing little damage. Although return fire from the shore was equally ineffective, the island was not subjected again to surface shelling. Palmyra Island also received minor shelling from a Japanese submarine.[54]

The conquest of Guam paved the way for the seizure of Rabaul, at the northern tip of New Britain, which the Japanese early in their planning visualized as an important bastion in their perimeter of empire. In December, aircraft from Truk began a series of raids which at first did little damage but which increased in intensity in January. A small force of Australians guarded the city, which boasted the finest natural harbor in the Southwest Pacific. After the outbreak of war most of the European women and children had been evacuated from the island. On January 20 approximately 120 Japanese planes struck Rabaul a devastating blow; they quickly put out of action the half-dozen obsolete Australian aircraft, whose pilots valorously but hopelessly engaged in unequal combat. High-level bombers picked targets on the docks and airfields while fighters strafed vessels in the harbor. Two days later, when another raid destroyed the coastal guns, the way was clear for the entrance of a convoy that had left Guam on January 14. The invasion force, about 5,300 in number, had little difficulty defeating a disorganized enemy of some fourteen hundred. Of these approximately four hundred escaped to Australia; the rest were either killed or imprisoned.[55]

While these invasion forces were taking over Rabaul, others were engaged in making other conquests in the Southwest Pacific; one took Balikpapan in Dutch Borneo, another Kendari in the Celebes, and still another Kavieng on New Ireland. In no case was resistance sufficient to forestall the Japanese advance.

---

[54] *Ibid.*, pp. 81–83.

[55] Accounts of the capture of Rabaul include Wigmore, *The Japanese Thrust,* pp. 392–417; G. H. Gill, *Royal Australian Navy* (*Australia in the War of 1939–1945,* Series 2, *Navy,* Volume IV) (Canberra, 1957), pp. 542–544.

CHAPTER 4

Japanese Conquest of the Philippines

ONCE Pearl Harbor was attacked, Americans realized that the Philippines might be the object not only of attack but of conquest. Japanese interest in the Philippines was linked to a more vital objective, the Netherlands East Indies, with their all-important oil supply. Aside from copper, the Philippines had little to offer the Japanese, but they felt it essential to seize the islands to keep the United States from using them as bases of operations, especially with the new long-range bombers.[1]

The Tydings-McDuffie Act of 1934 had provided for the recognition of Philippine independence after ten years. During the transitional period the United States retained the right to maintain military establishments and call out military forces of the Philippine government. Anticipating independence, the Philippine government began development of a Philippine Army under the guidance of General Douglas MacArthur and his two main assistants, Majors Dwight D. Eisenhower and James B. Ord.

By the summer of 1941, the Philippine Army was still far from being an adequate fighting force, and with a coastline longer than that of the United States to guard, torpedo boats obviously could not stand off attacks from the sea. As international tensions mounted, the United States government moved to increase defenses in the Philippines. On July 26, the same day that he ordered the freezing of

---

[1] S. E. Morison, *History of United States Naval Operations* (Boston, 1948), III, 165; Louis Morton, *The Fall of the Philippines* (*United States Army in World War II: The War in the Pacific*) (Washington, 1953), p. 52.

Japanese assets, President Roosevelt established a new Army command known as U.S. Army Forces in the Far East and he recalled General MacArthur to active duty to become its head. Implementing the decision to strengthen American holdings in the Far East was a slow process that was not completed when war came.[2] One factor behind the decision to protect the Philippines was General MacArthur's reputation, for it was felt that a man of his ability, experience, and leadership increased greatly the chances of the Philippines for survival. More important was growing confidence in air power. The success of the Flying Fortress, B-17, in the European Theater made Army officers believe that it could be used to advantage in defending the Philippines. In fact, as a potential striking force against Japanese territory, the bomber might even be a deterrent to war. A successful flight of a squadron of B-17's from the West Coast to the Philippines in September increased this confidence. More B-17's went to the Philippines, and on December 1, General H. H. Arnold wrote: "We must get every B-17 available to the Philippines as soon as possible."[3] Meanwhile, work proceeded on the construction and expansion of airfields, particularly on Luzon. The bottleneck in supplies and men was in transportation from the United States. Attempting to break the block, the government established a shipping schedule about the middle of November which gave the Philippines a priority over the Hawaiian Islands. Nine vessels with vital war materials and men were assigned to sail to the Philippines during November and December. War prevented their arrival.

In the islands, strengthening of the defenses continued. By December, 1941, the Air Force had been reorganized, and there were about 250 aircraft, mainly on Luzon, although only about half were suitable

[2] *Ibid.*, pp. 8–31.

[3] H. H. Arnold to F. L. Martin, Dec. 1, 1941, quoted in W. F. Craven and J. L. Cate, *The Army Air Forces in World War II* (Chicago, 1948), I, 193. On July 31, 1941, Admiral Stark had written: "Regarding the Philippines, as you know, ever since I came here I have urged increasing their defenses. The Navy's contribution has not been great, but it has been about all Hart can handle with the facilities he has or which we have been able to make available. Still, the increase is a factor, namely 28 PBYs and 11 modern submarines.

"We are delighted with the Army move putting the Filipinos in harness; we recommended this. Also it is being supplemented by a considerable number of planes, fighters and bombers." H. R. Stark to Charles M. Cooke, Jr., July 31, 1941, U.S. Congress, Joint Committee on the Investigation of the Pearl Harbor Attack, Hearings . . . (Washington, 1946), Part 16, p. 2176.

for fighting.[4] An aircraft warning system of sorts was in operation at Clark Field, outside Manila, which was also protected by an anti-aircraft artillery regiment. Inadequate though American air power in the Philippines appears in retrospect, it was a stronger complement than that of either the Hawaiian Islands or the Panama Canal Zone. The ground forces also had shipping difficulties; General MacArthur evidently felt that U.S. Army forces would be prepared by April, 1942, and the Philippine Army by the following July. Admiral Thomas C. Hart's United States Asiatic Fleet included the heavy cruiser *Houston,* two light cruisers, four old destroyers, twenty-nine submarines, thirty-two PBY's (Catalina torpedo bombers), and numerous torpedo boats and other craft. There were supplementary forces in Borneo, including a light cruiser and nine destroyers.[5]

Japanese military leaders completed their plans for the conquest of the Philippines in mid-November. Briefly, they contemplated striking first at the most important island, Luzon, on which combined land and naval air units would knock out American aircraft and installations, aided by seizure and use of outlying airfields. Meanwhile, major landings would be made on Lingayen Gulf and a smaller landing at Lamon Bay, southeast of Manila. The forces would converge on Manila and defeat the enemy; afterward they could easily conquer the rest of the islands. General Masaharu Homma, in command of the Fourteenth Army, which was to land on Luzon, was expected to conquer the island in fifty days. The Japanese had prepared carefully and had a good knowledge of the terrain and the nature of American and Philippine defenses. Their only miscalculation was to anticipate that their enemy would make a last stand in Manila instead of withdrawing, as they did, to Bataan, the peninsula west of the capital.[6]

Because of the variations in time zones, the news of the attack on Pearl Harbor reached Manila at about 3:30 A.M., December 8. The notification was unofficial but authentic. A naval radio operator intercepted a message from Pearl Harbor announcing: "Air Raid on Pearl Harbor. This is no drill." Recognizing the sending technique as being that of a friend of his based in Hawaii, the naval operator knew

[4] Walter D. Edmonds, *They Fought With What They Had* (Boston, 1951), p. 33.
[5] Morison, *History,* III, 158–160.
[6] For a discussion of the Japanese plan, see Morton, *The Fall of the Philippines,* pp. 56–59.

the message was genuine and passed it on to the duty officer. Shortly thereafter, Admiral Hart was advised, and he promptly sent the following message to the Asiatic Fleet: "Japan started hostilities. Govern yourselves accordingly."[7] The Admiral apparently was not so zealous in having the word passed to the Army in Manila. General Richard K. Sutherland received information of the Pearl Harbor attack through commercial broadcasts and notified General MacArthur and other top Army officers.[8]

By dawn the news of the Pearl Harbor attack had spread throughout the ranks. By morning, also, hostilities had commenced. The seaplane tender, *William B. Preston,* lying at anchor at Malalag Gulf far to the south on Mindanao, was suddenly attacked by thirteen Japanese dive bombers and nine fighters from the carrier *Ryujo.* One of the *Preston's* three planes was on patrol, but the other two were destroyed at their moorings and Ensign R. G. Tills was killed. After the raid, the *Preston* cautiously moved to other waters.[9]

At 8 A.M. the heavy bombers at Clark Field were ordered to go on patrol without bombs to avoid being caught on the ground. There was some talk of a raid on Formosa, five hundred miles away, and orders were signed for the B-17's to make ready; just why the attack was not made has provided fuel for a bitter postwar dispute among the principals. In any case, the bombers were back on the field by 11:30. Some were being loaded with bombs, some were being fueled, and others waited for photographic equipment. Only two bombers were in the air.[10]

One of these B-17's returned to base shortly after noon. As the pilot came down through the overcast and lowered the wheels for landing, he and his crew saw bombs exploding in some of the quarters and on the landing field. The Japanese attack had just begun. Hastily, the bomber left the area and after a struggle with Japanese fighters ultimately reached an adjoining airfield.

The Japanese attack on Clark was heavy and devastating. At midmorning 108 twin-engine bombers and an escort of 84 Zeros had left Formosa. Their approach was not unnoticed. Radar picked them up,

[7] Morison, *History,* III, 168–169.
[8] Morton, *The Fall of the Philippines,* p. 79.
[9] A. R. Buchanan (ed.), *The Navy's Air War: A Mission Completed* (New York [1946]), pp. 113–114.
[10] Morton, *The Fall of the Philippines,* pp. 80–82; Craven and Cate, *The AAF in World War II,* I, 207–209.

and as they crossed the coastline numerous civilians spotted them and reported their arrival. This information began to reach Nielson Field, just outside Manila, about 11:30. The chief of staff of the Interceptor Command predicted that Clark Field, with its bombers, would be the prime target.[11]

Despite these advance notices the news of the invading force did not reach Clark Field. The radio messages did not get through; one source states that the radio operator had gone out to lunch, another attributes the failure to systematic jamming of radio frequencies by the Japanese. The only notice that apparently reached Clark Field was a phone call answered by a junior officer who failed for unknown reasons to make effective use of the information he had received.[12]

Consequently, the Japanese force arrived unheralded and unopposed. The bombers came first; a formation of twenty-seven planes flying at from 22,000 to 25,000 feet dropped their loads in a pattern across the field. Shortly afterward a second wave of bombers attacked. By this time antiaircraft fire had started from the field, but the shells fell short. Then Japanese fighters came in for a strafing attack of about an hour's duration. The bombers had caused heavy damage to installations and the field itself but had not destroyed too many planes. The Zeros, however, with their low-flying, continually repeated strafing runs were extremely effective in the attack on the grounded planes. As at Pearl Harbor, although caught completely off guard, the personnel fought back with the utmost courage.

The victory clearly lay with the Japanese. They attacked other fields and although they encountered some air resistance managed to inflict heavy damage with relatively few losses. At the end of a single day's fighting, the American bombers in the Philippines had been eliminated as a significant striking force. The unpreparedness at Clark Field is a fact that remains unexplained in the midst of conflicting testimony, charges and countercharges.

The Japanese continued the air attack. On December 9, they saturated Nichols Field and completed the destruction started the

[11] Morton, *The Fall of the Philippines,* pp. 84–85. The Japanese used naval land-based bombers. Their Army bombers did not have sufficient range, and their carriers were mainly involved in the Pearl Harbor attack. S. Woodburn Kirby, *The War Against Japan (History of the Second World War: United Kingdom Military Series)* (London, 1957), I, 100–102.

[12] Craven and Cate, *The A.A.F. in World War II,* I, 210; Morton, *The Fall of the Philippines,* p. 85.

previous day. Fog came temporarily to the aid of the Philippines and grounded the planes at Formosa. On the following day, the tenth, the enemy concentrated on the Manila Bay area.[13] The inadequacies of antiaircraft defense became tragically apparent as the bombers dropped their loads from twenty thousand feet, well above the range of the guns at Cavite. At this place the Navy Yard took a battering that convinced Admiral Hart, who watched from Manila, that the bay was no longer tenable as a naval base. One day later, Zeros caught and destroyed seven Navy PBY's at their moorings. It became apparent that Patrol Wing 10, the naval air force, would also have to move if it were to survive. Merchant vessels which had sought sanctuary in Manila Bay hastily left for more secure ports. The Japanese made one of their few blunders by permitting the bulk of these ships to make a safe departure.[14]

The attackers, however, continued with marked success toward their first aim and within the first few days of the war virtually eliminated the Far Eastern Air Force as a fighting arm of significance. Del Monte was the only airfield capable of servicing B-17's that yet remained undetected, and even there it became increasingly difficult to service planes. The command, consequently, decided to fly the heavy bombers to Australia. The B-17's left just in time, for two days later naval planes from the Japanese carrier *Ryujo* struck the Del Monte field a disastrous blow. The retreat of the bombers to Australia left only a small group of Army fighters on Luzon to represent the Far Eastern Air Force.[15]

Without waiting to complete the destruction of the American Air Force, the Japanese began their landing operations. They started with half a dozen small landings on small islands near Luzon and then on the northern part of Luzon itself. There was little more than token resistance. The defenders believed that the major thrust would be toward Manila and they decided not to weaken their forces by a minor military move to the north. The terrain was such that it was anticipated that the Japanese would attempt landings nearer the capital.

This estimate proved to be correct. The invaders made two main landings, a major thrust in Lingayen Gulf and a lesser operation at

[13] Craven and Cate, *The A.A.F. in World War II*, I, 213–218.
[14] Morison, *History*, III, 171–174, 193–202.
[15] Craven and Cate, *The A.A.F. in World War II*, I, 220–221.

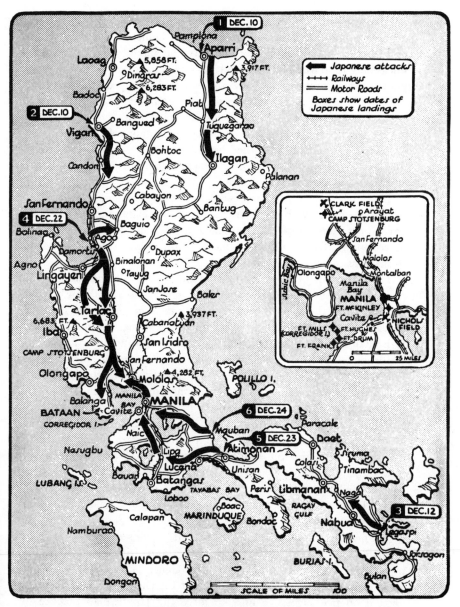

WAR IN THE PHILIPPINES

Lamon Bay, on the east coast of Luzon. In launching the former, one of their first major amphibious assaults, the Japanese experienced an uneasiness that was not borne out by the results. An American submarine attack and that of a few B-17's failed to impede progress, and even a heavy surf and land defenses were unable to prevent the landing force from securing its immediate objective. The Fourteenth Army, with supporting air force personnel, totaling 43,110 men, under General Homma established beachheads and then began its move southward. As a precaution, the Japanese took Baguio, the summer capital in the mountains to the east.[16]

Thus, by the end of three weeks of war, Japanese successes included the destruction of American air power, elimination of effective naval operations, important amphibious landings, and the severance of communications with Australia. General Homma was now ready to make his move on Manila.

The successful Japanese landings at Lingayen Gulf and Lamon Bay made it clear to MacArthur that his forces could not throw the invader back at the beaches and impelled him to make the key strategic decision in the campaign in the Philippines. This was to withdraw to Bataan and fight a delaying action against the Japanese, for, in the words of a contemporary, when MacArthur saw the North Luzon Force break under enemy attack he "realized that his cherished plan of defeating an enemy attempt to advance toward Manila from the north was not now possible."

Before declaring Manila an open city, MacArthur evacuated the High Commissioner and the Commonwealth government to the small island of Corregidor off Bataan on December 24 and that evening moved his headquarters to the same location. Quickly Corregidor was stocked with supplies for a six-months period, and in Manila a rear echelon worked to remove or destroy supplies, boats, and other equipment.

Meanwhile, Army leaders worked out a revised operations plan involving preparations for defense on Bataan, withdrawal from the north, and withdrawal from the south. General Jonathan M. Wainwright's North Luzon Force was to fight the enemy in the north long enough on five successive lines to force the Japanese to prepare to attack but not long enough to prevent the retreating force from

[16] For an account of early action, see Morton, *The Fall of the Philippines,* pp. 98–144, 161–215.

reaching Bataan intact. The South Luzon Force, which had been commanded by Major General George M. Parker, Jr., was to withdraw in similar fashion through successive defense lines past Manila, across the Pampanga River, to San Fernando and then Bataan. A key to the southern line of defense was the Calumpit Bridge, actually two bridges, across the Pampanga River, for it had to be held until all units from the south had crossed it. Turning over the South Luzon Force to Major General Albert M. Jones, Parker assumed command of the newly organized Bataan Defense Force, which began to prepare the peninsula for a last stand.

The withdrawal plans called for careful timing, use of rivers, swamps, and other features of the terrain as barriers, tank action to cover withdrawals and check enemy mechanized advance, and effective work by engineers to keep open roads and bridges for the retreating forces and destroy their usefulness to the advancing enemy. On the day before Christmas, the North Luzon Force made its first stand, along a line not far from Lingayen Gulf. During the night various units retreated toward the Agno River. Some made their way without encountering the enemy; others on Christmas Day lost a desperate struggle to hold the town of Urdanek and were forced back to the Agno. By evening on the twenty-seventh, the North Luzon Force was on its second line of defense, counting heavily on the Agno River as a natural barrier. It proved ineffective; consolidating their strength, the Japanese moved across the stream and forced the defenders to fall back. Infantry troops of the 11th Division were able to use a locomotive and freight cars in their retreat, and tanks of the 194th Tank Battalion staged a successful roadblock which surprised elements of the enemy, but later had to abandon their tanks when they reached a demolished bridge. Making only a brief pause at the third planned line of defense, which extended some forty miles across the Luzon central plain between Santa Ignacia and San José, the North Luzon Force retreated to the fourth line. In the meantime other units evacuated Fort Stotsenburg in the rear, trying either to take with them or destroy the fort's reserve supplies. Fortunately, many of the supplies which they had to leave behind were appropriated by the North Luzon Force as it passed through the area.

Although the Japanese knew of MacArthur's move to Corregidor and of the transfer of at least one division to Bataan, they did not change their plan of advancing directly toward Manila. The Americans, however, did make a shift; originally they had contemplated a brief stand at the fourth line of defense, or D-4, and a more determined fight on the fifth and last line. The Japanese advance was so strong that General Wainwright feared the enemy might push through this last obstacle and move from the north toward the Calumpit Bridge before the South Luzon Force completed its withdrawal to Bataan. Consequently, Wainright ordered, "D-4 will be held at all costs until ordered withdrawn. Maximum delay will be effected on each position. Withdrawal plan later."

On the morning of the twenty-eighth, Japanese forces struck the right flank of the D-4 line. The 92d Combat Team of the 91st Division destroyed two bridges across the Pampanga River but could not prevent the enemy from fording the river to the north. Outflanked, the combat team had to abandon Cabanatuan and retreat toward the fifth line of defense. The Japanese then made a flanking attack through Cabanatuan against the center of the D-4 line. Fighting desperately and incurring heavy losses, tank and infantry units of the 11th Division managed to delay Japanese advance for twenty-four hours and prevent these enemy forces from joining others who were attacking Tarlac on the western end of the defense line. In this area, fortunately for the defenders, a Japanese colonel displayed excessive caution until prodded by his superiors into moving from the Agno River. Tanks, artillery, and infantry joined in the fighting on the thirtieth until the 21st Division received orders to withdraw to the D-5 line. Determined artillery fire covered its retreat and helped it reach the line by dawn on the thirty-first.

In its retrograde action the North Luzon Force had withdrawn about fifty miles to its fifth defensive position. Considering the fact that the force consisted largely of poorly trained and equipped Philippine Army troops, the operation was conducted successfully.

The South Luzon Force, primarily Filipino and much smaller than Wainwright's force, had the same orders to harass the enemy and delay his advance. Because of the location of its landings on Lamon Bay, the Japanese force advanced in two columns to by-pass Mount Banahao, which blocked the way inland. Consequently, in the first contacts with the enemy, General Jones also had to divide his troops and guard against flanking attacks. Withdrawal of elements of the 1st Infantry of the 1st Regular Division of the Philippine Army in front of the Japanese column advancing north of the mountain fea-

tured confusion in orders, baptism by fire of green troops, the season-
ing influence of experienced Philippine Scouts, and a devastating
Japanese roadblock. Nevertheless, the force successfully completed its
retreat from Mauban on Lamon Bay to the south shore of Laguna
de Bay and was in a position to move past Manila on its way to
Bataan.

Farther south, by Christmas Day, the other Japanese column was
now facing the remaining South Luzon troops near Pagbilao, an important road junction some fifteen miles inland. Fighting a delaying
action, the 52d Infantry of the 51st Division pulled across the Pal-
sabangan River, demolished the bridge, but was unable to hold back
the enemy. As in other regions of this early campaign in the Philippines, green units became confused, found it difficult to evacuate
supplies and equipment, and encountered an aggressive foe. In the
mountains near Tiaong, General Jones prepared a strong position for
a defensive stand, only to be ordered to leave it and move his forces
across the Calumpit by early morning on the first of January. Then
early on the thirtieth, Jones received orders to stand on the defensive.
Without knowing the reason for the change in orders, probably issued
to give added time for the evacuation of Manila, Jones started to
make ready a second time for a strong defensive stand.

Fearing that Japanese troops advancing from the north might cut
off the retreat of the South Luzon Force into the Bataan Peninsula,
General MacArthur changed the orders again, and instead of making
a stand, Jones' forces started moving once more and by the end of
December had crossed the Calumpit Bridge. With few losses American and Filipino troops not only had reached their objectives, but
by blowing bridges and conducting other delaying action had slowed
down the advance of the pursuing foe.

In many ways Bataan was an ideal location for a last stand. Composed of mountains or jungle, it had in its restricted confines two
extinct volcanoes. In some places the mountains reached the sea;
where they did not, the land was often swampy. These same factors
complicated the problem of American withdrawal. Retreating troops
crowded the roads, and as a result much of the equipment went by
barge across the thirty miles or so of water from Manila to crude
docks on Bataan.

Food was a problem from the outset. As early as January 5, 1942,
General MacArthur placed the men on half-rations. Faced with this

inadequate diet, the men turned to other sources and used what they could get from the land. Rice was still standing in the lowlands, and mills were constructed to process it. The Philippine carabao, a large draft animal, found himself sacrificed to the cause. Fishermen operated until Japanese firing stopped them. Other supplies which soon entered the shortage list included clothing, blankets, sun helmets, oil, and drugs, especially quinine. These shortages, particularly of food, constituted the most important single factor affecting the course of the siege of Bataan.

On January 7, 1942, General MacArthur radioed the War Department, "I am on my main battle line, awaiting general attack."[17] Stretching across the peninsula, this line was broken in the middle by mountainous country, featured by Mount Natib and Mount Silanganan. Forces holding the eastern sector, known as the Abacay line, were headed by General Parker, who until this time had been in command of the entire Bataan Defense Force. General Jonathan W. Wainwright led forces in the western sector, or Mauban line. Over both forces General MacArthur, on Corregidor, had established a Bataan echelon under Brigadier General R. J. Marshall. The Americans planned a defense in depth on the Abacay-Mauban line and placed troops, including sailors and Marines, to guard the beaches of the peninsula against amphibious attacks. Some eight miles behind the main battle line, other forces were preparing a second, or Pilar-Bagac, line.

The Japanese launched their assault on January 9, with a barrage against the Abacay line followed by infantry attacks. Encouraged by what appeared to be satisfactory advances, General Homma sent a message to MacArthur advising surrender. This demand, which had been dropped from the air behind American lines, reached MacArthur when he was paying a visit to the peninsula. Increased artillery fire was the only American response. That night defending troops experienced a wild banzai attack, when, following an artillery and mortar barrage, shouting Japanese soldiers began the advance. The first troops threw themselves on the barbed-wire obstructions to form a quivering, tortured bridge over which succeeding Japanese soldiers poured. Forced at first to give way under the weight of the onslaught, the American unit in the path received reinforcements and after heavy fighting regained the ground lost. Other troops along the line

[17] Quoted in *ibid.*, p. 247.

that night became acquainted with enemy infiltrators who penetrated the lines and began sniping activities. When individual Scouts sent after the snipers ran into difficulties, sniping parties, consisting of riflemen and demolition engineers, carefully moved into the jungle, located, and eliminated the infiltrators.

As the fighting continued on the Abacay line, the eastern flank along the jungled slopes of the mountain started to give way, and the Japanese were in a position to turn the flank of the defenders and force them toward the beaches. Victory in this sector would also place Wainwright's troops in an untenable position and compel him to withdraw.

Although Homma had directed the major thrust against the Abacay line, he launched a second on Wainwright's forces. Initially, the defenders held, and then when obliged to withdraw found their way checked by a roadblock which the Japanese had slipped in and established behind the line to cut off retreat over the only main road. Consequently, elements of the 1st Division had to destroy their artillery and retreat along the beaches.

On January 22, the American high command ordered a withdrawal to the second line behind the Pilar-Bagac road. To the War Department, General MacArthur justified the move on the ground of heavy losses and the war of attrition which the Japanese, having command of the sea and the possibility of securing replacements, could conduct. Of the new line, MacArthur assured Washington, "I have personally selected and prepared this position, and it is strong." From this point there was to be no further retreat, except for the few who crossed to Corregidor. There was no place to go. MacArthur wrote of the new line: "With its occupation all maneuvering possibilities will cease. I intend to fight it out to complete destruction."[18]

During February, the American and Philippine forces appeared to be holding their line. They wiped out Japanese parties that attempted landings along the west shore. A feature of the heavy fighting along the line of defense was the isolation of large bodies of Japanese troops in pockets and virtual elimination of some in desperate jungle warfare. As a consequence, General Homma decided to withdraw slightly and request reinforcements.

While American morale was high because of this successful stand, General MacArthur received orders to leave the Philippines. The War

[18] MacArthur to Marshall, Jan. 23, 1942, quoted in *ibid.*, p. 290.

Department and the President had come to the opinion that Mac-Arthur should be removed from the danger of surrender to assume a position of high command in the Southwest Pacific.[19] On March 24, four PT boats left Corregidor carrying twenty-one persons—two naval officers, General MacArthur, members of his staff, his wife, son, and a Chinese nurse.

Although leaving, General MacArthur had no intention of relinquishing command, but planned to continue direction through Brigadier General Lewis C. Beebe. General Marshall and President Roosevelt were not aware of this fact and considered that Wainwright, who was promoted to lieutenant general, had succeeded MacArthur. MacArthur's protest produced a compromise. Wainwright remained in command in the Philippines, but under instructions from MacArthur in Australia. Wainwright removed to Corregidor, leaving Major General Edward P. King as commander of the forces on Luzon.

As the fighting continued, the food situation became increasingly critical. Rice became the basic commodity, and other foods were rationed as long as they lasted. Hospital patients received double the diet of others, but they could not be given the right food. One doctor wrote: "It was quite a sight to see . . . those who should have received adequate soft and liquid diet trying to eat a gob of sticky, gummy, half-cooked rice."[20]

The additional sources of food also gradually became exhausted. As long as the supply lasted, carabao were slaughtered. Then followed the 250 horses and 48 pack mules of the 26th Cavalry. Ingenious and hungry Filipinos and Americans tested other forms of protein diet. Colonel Mallonee wrote: "I can recommend mule. It is tasty, succulent and tender—all being phrases of comparison, of course. There is little to choose between calesa pony and carabao. The pony is tougher but better flavor than carabao. Iguana is fair. Monkey I do not recommend. I never had snake." Another person commented that "monkey meat is all right until the animal's hands turn up on the plate."[21]

[19] *Ibid.,* p. 353; Maurice Matloff and Edwin M. Snell, *Strategic Planning for Coalition Warfare, 1941–1942 (United States Army in World War II: The War Department)* (Washington, 1953), p. 165.

[20] Lieutenant Colonel Walter H. Waterous, Statement of Experiences and Observations Concerning the Bataan Campaign . . ., p. 51, quoted in Morton, *The Fall of the Philippines,* p. 368.

[21] Both statements are quoted in *ibid.,* p. 370. The first is from A. C. Tis-

The effect of the food situation on health was inevitable. Many suffered beriberi from malnutrition; vitamin deficiencies were widespread. Malaria found easy conquest in weakened bodies. The supply of quinine decreased until it could be used only as a cure and not a preventive. The increasing lack of proper sanitation facilities fostered dysentery and hookworm. One of the singular aspects of the campaign was that few persons went to the hospitals for psychotic disorders. One interpretation given for this fact was that there no longer remained any "possible retreat from reality."[22]

The effect of the lack of proper food was as inevitable on fighting ability as upon health. Men of one division, it was reported, were so weak that many could do no more than fire a rifle out of the trench. Attempts to send help to the 100,000 military and civilian personnel on Bataan on the whole were unsuccessful. Submarines made a few visits and took in ammunition and oil.

When General Wainwright assumed command toward the end of March, he reported that there was only food enough, "at one-third ration, poorly balanced and very deficient in vitamins," to last until April 15.[23] If further supplies did not arrive, he stated, the men would be starved into submission.

General MacArthur replied from Australia that when he left there had been food enough to last until May 1, and he issued Wainwright the following orders: "I am utterly opposed under any circumstances or conditions to the ultimate capitulation of this command. If food fails you will prepare and execute an attack upon the enemy."[24]

While the Americans were being debilitated by starvation and disease, the Japanese prepared to renew the attack. Although the Japanese had themselves not fared too well from the standpoint of food and disease, they received some reinforcements, and Homma started his new offensive on Good Friday, April 3, 1942. By the end of April 6, the attacking forces had driven a substantial wedge into the American line. In the next two days the defense fell completely apart.

General MacArthur had given his command, and at 11:30 P.M. on the fourth, General Wainwright had ordered General King to launch a counterattack at the base of the peninsula. The situation was

delle, Diary, entry of Mar. 14, 1942; the second, from Colonel R. C. Mallonee, Bataan Diary, II, 11.

[22] These are the words of a medical officer, quoted in *ibid.*, p. 380.
[23] Wainwright to Marshall, Mar. 26, 1942, quoted in *ibid.*, p. 402.
[24] MacArthur to Wainwright, Apr. 4, 1942, quoted in *ibid.*

desperate for commanders and men. The latter were in no condition to continue the fight. Wainwright was not only under orders from MacArthur not to surrender, but President Roosevelt on February 9 had said that there would be "no surrender." As the military historian of the campaign states the matter, "The only alternative remaining to King if he followed Wainwright's orders was to accept the whole-sale slaughter of his men without receiving any military advantage."[25] Under these circumstances, King chose to disobey orders and sur-render. After his return from prison camp at the conclusion of the war, General Wainwright explained why he could not authorize King to surrender and added that King "was on the ground and confronted by a situation in which he had either to surrender or have his people killed piecemeal. This would most certainly have happened to him within two or three days."[26]

King's surrender of April 9, 1942, was followed by one of the most infamous episodes of the war. Without food or water, clubbed, beaten, and bayoneted, the prisoners were forced to make what came to be called the "Death March," sixty-five miles from Mariveles to San Fernando.

Corregidor still remained. To complete the conquest and free Manila Bay for Japanese use, the invaders had to seize Corregidor and sister defenses across the mouth of the bay. Corregidor was three and a half miles long and a mile and a half across at the widest point. Originally strong, the harbor defenses had not been strength-ened to meet the rise of air power, because of the restrictions on armament imposed on the United States by the agreement resulting from the Washington Conference of 1921–22. The only changes made had been to create antiaircraft positions and dig an extensive tunnel system in Malinta Hill. The main tunnel was about fourteen hundred feet long and thirty feet wide. There were twenty-five laterals, each about four hundred feet in length. Connected to this system was a separate underground hospital system. Power and water were of course of prime importance.

Across the bay were three fortifications, the most spectacular of which was Fort Drum. This tiny island had been cut down to the

[25] Ibid., p. 456.
[26] Jonathan M. Wainwright, General Wainwright's Story (New York, 1946), p. 83.

waterline and upon it had been placed a concrete battleship with exterior walls twenty-five to thirty-six feet thick.

The siege of Corregidor began before the conquest of Bataan was completed. Air raids forced everyone into the tunnels. During the last week of March there were about sixty air raids lasting for a total of seventy-two hours. Actually not too much damage was done Corregidor by aerial bombing, but when Bataan fell the island fortress was doomed. The Japanese brought up heavy artillery and began to shell Corregidor. One day's damage was greater than that done by all the aerial bombing. One example will illustrate the terrific bombardment. A reinforced concrete slab, weighing about six tons, flew a thousand yards through the air, cut through a tree trunk about four feet in diameter, and came to a stop in a ravine.

The almost constant bombardment increased the difficulty of life in the tunnels. Nerves became taut, but only a few mental cases developed during the campaign. Again, it appears, there was no place to which to retreat. Food was on half-ration, and the water shortage became acute. The daily ration of water came to be one canteen. One officer wrote: "Many a night I washed myself with a cup of water and by standing in a basin saved the water to use over again on, first, my underwear, and then my socks. Order of laundering was very important. The dirtiest item always came last."[27]

By May 3, General Wainwright reported to General MacArthur, "Situation here is fast becoming desperate."[28] The Japanese guns outranged all but two American guns. That night an American submarine on the way back to Australia for torpedoes stopped outside the mine field. It picked up twenty-five passengers, of whom about half were Army nurses. With the submarine went a complete roster of those still alive on the island.[29]

The Japanese bombardment increased in intensity until the island lay "scorched, gaunt, and leafless, covered with the chocolate dust of countless explosions and pitted with shellholes."[30] At last the Japa-

[27] John McM. Gulick, Memoirs of Btry C, 91st CA (PS), p. 156, quoted in Morton, The Fall of the Philippines, p. 546.

[28] Wainwright to MacArthur, May 3, 1942, quoted in ibid., p. 548.

[29] Ibid., Morison states that twenty-seven persons left on the Nautilus. Morison, History, III, 206.

[30] Maude R. Williams, The Last Days of Corregidor, Supp., p. 1, quoted in Morton, The Fall of the Philippines, p. 550.

nese were ready for the attack, and the Americans were past the ability to withstand it. Chancing a moonlit night, Japanese troops in barges made their landings. Americans and Filipinos fought valiantly to check the assault, but the cause was hopeless. By midmorning of May 6, Wainwright was, like King, confronted with the choice of surrender or slaughter. Like King, he reluctantly came to the conclusion that nothing could be gained by further loss of life.

Unlike King, Wainwright was not disobeying orders by surrendering. His authorization to act was first sent from Washington by way of MacArthur, who did not forward it. President Roosevelt then sent the message directly to Wainwright. Before acting, Wainwright communicated with MacArthur, who told him that the decision was in Wainwright's hands.

General Wainwright made a last effort to save the other American forces scattered throughout the Philippines by releasing them to another general and retaining command only over the Manila Bay islands. The Japanese refused to accept this act and, to save the prisoners on Corregidor, Wainwright issued orders for the remaining American forces to surrender. When the commanding officers of these outlying forces realized why Wainwright acted as he did, most of them complied. Many of their men, however, deserted and later joined resistance movements.[31]

From one standpoint the campaign in the Philippines was of secondary importance in comparison with other advances of the Japanese. It was, however, significant in that for six months the Americans and Filipinos had deprived the enemy of the use of one of the best harbors in the Pacific. As a symbol of resistance, Bataan and Corregidor had shown that the Japanese could be checked, for the enemy had been forced to secure reinforcements to reach its objective. From this point of view, Luzon stood as a ray of hope in a dark picture of the Japanese armed forces sweeping all before them. At the time, it must be admitted, the ray seemed so slight as to be almost imaginary rather than real.

[31] *Ibid.*, pp. 552–584.

CHAPTER 5

The War in the Atlantic

W AR had burst on the Pacific with the Pearl Harbor attack. It arrived more gradually in the Atlantic and was preceded by an extended period of undeclared hostilities. When Britain and Germany went to war again in September, 1939, it was perhaps inevitable that they re-enact the struggle between surface and undersea craft, yet, despite the experience of World War I, neither side was especially well prepared to resume this type of warfare. Confronted by reduced naval appropriations and treaty limitations in the twenties and early thirties, the British had chosen to expend their funds on large rather than small ships. Consequently, at the outbreak of World War II they suffered from a shortage of escort vessels for convoy duty. In Germany's case the difficulty was also one of emphasis. Adolf Hitler and most of his advisers were air-minded and anticipated rapid Continental conquest rather than a protracted war of attrition at sea. Commodore Karl Doenitz, in command of the German undersea craft, was not in a position to influence the *Führer* and in September, 1939, had only forty-three submarines ready for combat.[1]

---

[1] Twenty-five of these submarines were so-called 250-tonners. The rest were 500- or 750-tonners, types which were the most effective in World War II. U.S. Strategic Bombing Survey, *German Submarine Industry Report* (1946), Exhibit B1, quoted in S. E. Morison, *History of United States Naval Operations in World War II* (Boston, 1951), I, 4. Admiral Karl Doenitz, without specifying types, places the number of submarines at the outbreak of war at fifty-six. The number of operational boats, he asserts, dropped to twenty-two in February, 1941. Karl Doenitz, *Memoirs: Ten Years and Twenty Days* (London, 1959), p. 47.

Although unprepared, the Germans quickly gave evidence of the nature if not the extent of the naval war they might fight. In 1936, the German government had adhered to the London Naval Treaty of 1930, which stated that submarines should not "sink or render incapable of navigation a merchant vessel without having first placed passengers, crew, and ship's papers in a place of safety." Only twelve hours after war had been declared, a German submarine torpedoed the unescorted and unarmed British passenger vessel, the *Athenia,* which sank, carrying to their death 112 men, women, and children.[2]

As it became apparent that Britain would rely heavily on the United States for supplies, the naval struggle in the Atlantic increased in proportion. Doenitz persuaded the German government to accelerate submarine construction and to concentrate as many of the operating craft as possible in the North Atlantic where chances for sinkings were the greatest, instead of weakening Germany's underwater striking power by diversionary attacks in other theaters of war.[3] The British at the same time sought to increase the supply of both convoys and escorts. At first, the British helped to balance losses by acquiring vessels of countries overrun by the enemy, especially France, Norway, Denmark, the Netherlands, and Greece. In addition, Britain obtained important but not decisive numbers of merchant vessels from the United States.[4] Advances in aviation resulted in extensive use of aircraft, both as defensive weapons by the British and their allies and as offensive instruments operating from Nazi-held bases in Northwestern Europe.

[2] Morison, *History,* I, 8–9. Hitler at first ordered submarines to fight according to Prize Regulations, in the hope that Britain and France might agree on peace after the fall of Poland. When he found that the democracies would not acquiesce, he withdrew the restrictions on German naval action. The Germans did not acknowledge responsibility for the sinking of the *Athenia.* S. W. Roskill, *The War at Sea, 1939–1945 (History of the Second World War: United Kingdom Military Series)* (London, 1954), I, 103–104. Admiral Doenitz, in command of Germany's U-boats, was satisfied that the commander of the U-boat which sank the *Athenia* thought that he was firing on an auxiliary cruiser, since the *Athenia* was steaming without lights and was zigzagging on an unusual course. Doenitz, *Memoirs,* p. 57.

[3] Hitler at first opposed the increase in submarines, and it was not until the end of 1941 that the number began to increase noticeably. Friedrich Ruge, *Sea Warfare, 1939–1945: A German Viewpoint* (London, 1957), pp. 37–38. Doenitz fought hard, and with limited success, for an air arm under naval control to aid the submarines. Doenitz, *Memoirs,* pp. 131–141.

[4] W. K. Hancock and M. M. Gowing, *British War Economy* (London, 1949), pp. 254–259.

It was in this increasingly dangerous arena that the United States Navy held its preliminary practice for participation in World War II. Prohibited by the neutrality legislation from entry into war zones around the belligerents, the Navy found itself assigned important duties in another area. As soon as war was declared between Germany and Great Britain, orders went to the United States Navy to patrol American waters and maintain our neutral rights. Less than a month later, the Act of Panama greatly expanded the obligations of our naval forces by creating a "safety belt" around the Western Hemisphere, extending from three hundred to one thousand miles offshore, and by warning belligerents against naval action in this region.

Although the Act of Panama was a joint statement of the American republics, the brunt of the task of policing the belt fell upon the United States, since most of the other American states lacked men or equipment for the work. The task was too great for one country alone, and in practice, instead of trying to patrol the entire area, the United States armed forces tended to limit their activities to belligerents who were interfering with neutral rights and trade. In September, 1939, soon after the Declaration of Panama was announced, units of the United States Navy began to patrol offshore from the Guianas to Newfoundland. A little later naval aviation and Coast Guard units joined in the coastal surveillance. In the first stages of the so-called Neutrality Patrol the aim was simply observation and reporting of belligerent craft. During the ensuing months there would be expanded duties and an altered objective.[5]

Administration leaders, notably President Roosevelt, Admiral H. R. ("Betty") Stark, Chief of Naval Operations, General George C. Marshall, Chief of Staff, Secretary of State Cordell Hull, Secretary of War Henry L. Stimson, and Secretary of the Navy Frank Knox, believed that the United States should be prepared for possible involvement in the war.[6] They felt that part of such preparation should be an understanding with England, the major nation with whom the United States would be confronting a common foe. Consequently, al-

[5] Morison, *History*, I, 14–16, 27–73; A. R. Buchanan (ed.), *The Navy's Air War: A Mission Completed* (New York [1946]), pp. 27–39.

[6] Two Republicans, Henry L. Stimson, Secretary of State under President Herbert Hoover, and Frank Knox, Republican candidate for Vice President in 1936, had joined Roosevelt's Cabinet in the summer of 1940. They had been invited and had accepted appointment largely as a result of their interventionist views. Robert E. Sherwood, *Roosevelt and Hopkins: An Intimate History* (New York, 1948), pp. 162–163.

though ranked as a neutral and long before it became openly a belligerent, the United States entered military conversations with the British government.

The first move came in the summer of 1940. Three high-ranking military officials, including Rear Admiral Robert L. Ghormley, went to England and held exploratory meetings with British officials. The German air assault on Britain was in full strength, and one of the objectives of the American contingent was to report on the chances of survival and on the British will to fight. Convinced that Englishmen would fight and that they would not be beaten easily, Admiral Ghormley next sought to determine how American military forces could be employed best if the United States should be drawn into the war. Obviously, such planning as this was beyond the powers of the three Americans in England; their function was to pave the way for a larger meeting.[7]

Such a gathering came into being early in the following year. High-ranking British staff officials went to Washington and on January 29, 1941, began a series of secret conferences with American staff officers. Out of these meetings, which lasted until March 27, 1941, came two important kinds of decisions. One dealt with American military action if the United States should become a belligerent. It should be noted that the conferences did not discuss plans designed to take the United States into war, but considered steps to be taken if such an eventuality occurred. The basic decision made was to defeat Hitler first.[8] There were impressive arguments for this decision. At that date Japan was fighting only China; Germany had conquered much of Europe and was threatening the existence of Britain and other free nations. Furthermore, in an extended war, Germany appeared to be potentially more dangerous than Japan, since, as Secretary of War Robert P. Patterson later expressed it, German scientists "might come up with new weapons of devastating destructiveness."[9]

Implementing the major policy decision, a staff agreement included the following points: continued collaboration in planning, enforcement

---

[7] Morison, *History*, I, 38–41; J. R. M. Butler, *Grand Strategy* (*History of the Second World War: United Kingdom Military Series*) (London, 1957), II (September, 1939—June, 1941), 341–343.

[8] Morison, *History*, I, 45–49; M. S. Watson, *Chief of Staff: Prewar Plans and Preparations* (*United States Army in World War II: The War Department*) (Washington, 1950), pp. 370–380.

[9] Quoted in J. P. Baxter, *Scientists Against Time* (Boston, 1950), p. 26.

1. President Franklin D. Roosevelt and Prime Minister Churchill on board the U.S.S. *Augusta* at the Atlantic Conference, August, 1941. General Marshall, Admiral King and Admiral Stark in rear

2. Shigenori Togo, Japanese Foreign Minister

3. Premier Hideki Tojo of Japan

4. The U.S.S. *West Virginia* and the U.S.S. *Tennessee* after the Japanese attack on Pearl Harbor, December 7, 1941

5. President Roosevelt with his War Cabinet in the White House, December 19, 1941. Left to right around table: Harry Hopkins, Lend-Lease Administrator; Frances Perkins, Secretary of Labor; Col. Philip B. Fleming, Federal Works Administrator; Vice President Henry A. Wallace; Fiorello LaGuardia, Civil Defense Administrator; Paul V. McNutt, Federal Security Administrator; Jesse Jones, Secretary of Commerce and Federal Loan Administrator; Secretary of Interior Harold Ickes; Postmaster General Frank C. Walker; Secretary of War Henry L. Stimson; Secretary of State Cordell Hull; President Roosevelt; Secretary of Treasury Henry Morgenthau; Attorney General Francis Biddle; Secretary of Navy Frank Knox and Secretary of Agriculture Claude R. Wickard

U.S. Navy P.

6. Navy reconnaissance plane (SOC) being catapulted from heavy cruiser

7. The infamous Death March from Bataan in 1942, showing thinning file of prisoners carrying comrades who dropped along the way

Wide World P

American soldiers fording a stream along the Munda Trail in New Georgia, July, 1943

9. Infantry reinforcements landing in New Georgia

Wounded American and Australian soldiers in New Guinea, December, 1942

Admiral Raymond Ames Spruance,
nmander of the Central Pacific Force

12. Admiral William F. Halsey,
Commander of the South Pacific Area

13. Secretary of the Navy Frank Knox (center) aboard the U.S.S. *Curtiss*
with Lt. Col. Carlson, U.S.M.C. (left) and Admiral Chester W. Nimitz

U.S. Army Pho

14. Infantrymen and tanks moving ahead on Bougainville

15. Carriers in the Pacific. The U.S.S. *Lexington* and U.S.S. *Saratoga* as seen from the flight deck of the U.S.S. *Ranger*

U.S. Navy Ph

16. A tank destroyer group on reconnaissance in the Kasserine Pass

17. Troops headed for landings in French Morocco

18. President Roosevelt and Prime Minister Winston Churchill with
their high-ranking Army and Navy officials at Casablanca, January, 1943

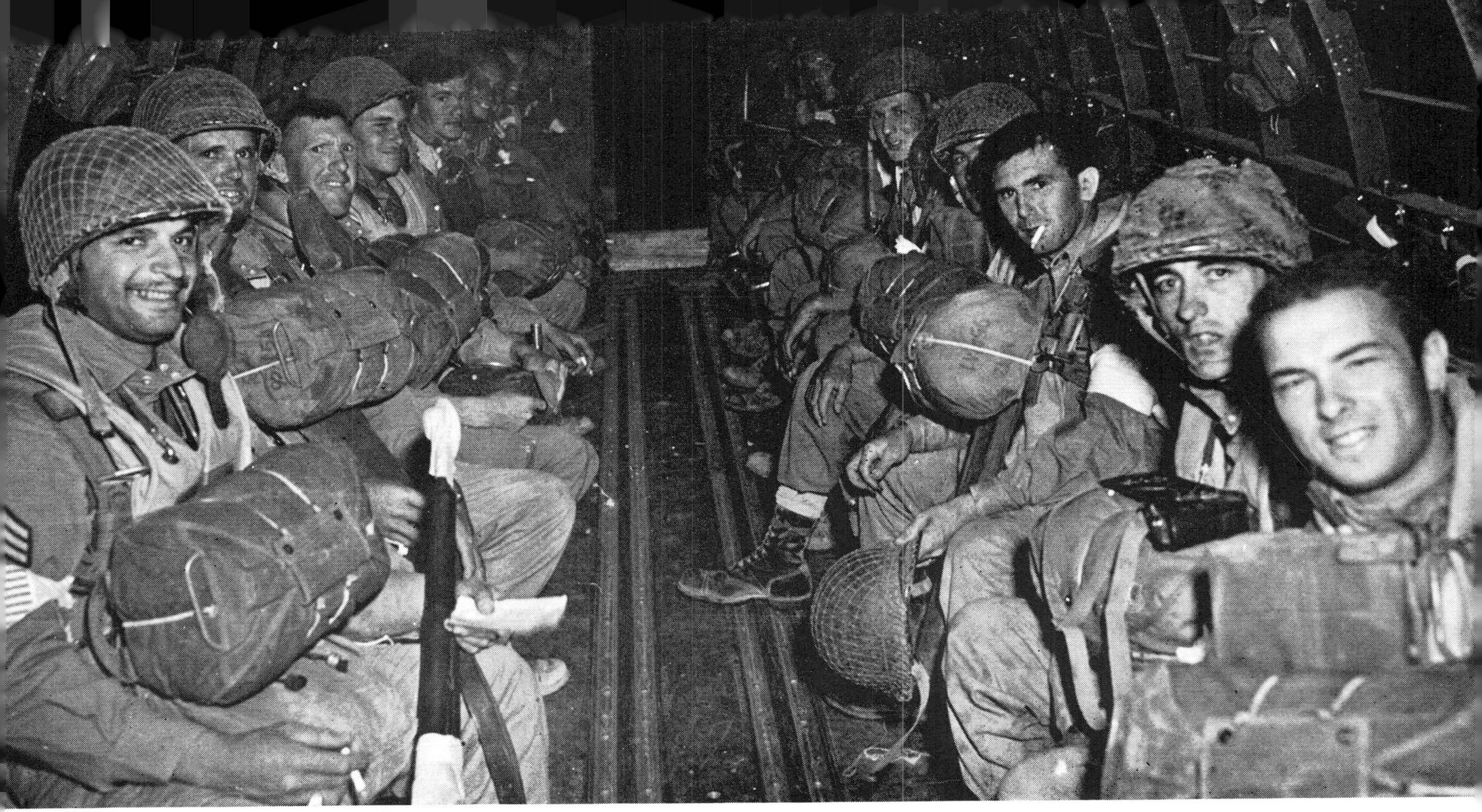

U.S. Air Force Photo

19. Paratroopers headed for Sicily

20. General Henri Honoré Giraud and General Charles de Gaulle agree to join forces at the time of the Casablanca conference. (President Roosevelt can be seen in background)

Wide World Photos

21. Wounded soldiers helping each other to the hospital area during the Italian campaign

U.S. Army Photo

U.S. Army Photo

22. Lt. Gen. Robert L. Eichelberger

23. General Mark Clark

24. Pinned to the beach by heavy bombing at Salerno

U.S. Coast Guard Photo

25. Half-track squeezing through narrow street in Gerami, Sicily

26. Getting firsthand report after bombing raid on Austrian aircraft factory are (right, back to camera) Lt. Gen. Carl Spaatz; (second from right, with cigarette) Maj. Gen. Nathan F. Twining; and (left of two men in background) Lt. Gen. Ira C. Eaker

27. General Gustaf Jodl, Nazi Chief
of Staff

28. Grand Admiral Karl Doenitz,
head of German submarine fleet
(shown here at the war crimes trial)

29. General Erwin Rommel

30. Field Marshal Gerd Von Runste

of the blockade against the Axis, with the United States assuming the main role in the Atlantic, development of naval striking power in the Mediterranean to eliminate Italy from the war, concentration of United States and British forces in the British Isles for an assault on the Continent.

The second type of decision centered on the role to be played by the United States "short of war." One of the most significant agreements was that the United States would assume responsibility for protection of transatlantic convoys as soon as the Atlantic Fleet was ready for the task. Such preparation involved many things. The United States had to accelerate its training program for escort duty. It needed to expand its bases both in the country and outside, especially to the north. The destroyers-for-bases deal gave an important start in this direction by making Newfoundland available. To aid the Americans in their training, the British passed on the experience they had gained in fighting the submarine, including the "very secret" antisubmarine warfare publications of the British Admiralty.[10]

If these were hardly the traditional actions of a neutral, it should be noted that Germany was not concerned with the niceties of international law. In May, 1941, a German submarine sank the S.S. *Robin Moor*, an American freighter, not in the war zone but in the South Atlantic, headed for Africa with general cargo. Fortunately, no lives were lost, but reaction was strong in the United States when it was learned that the crew had to make its way hundreds of miles in lifeboats to reach safety.[11]

The passage of Lend-Lease increased the pressure on the United States armed forces in the Atlantic. If we were to produce tremendous quantities of arms and supplies, we naturally were interested in seeing that they reached their objective. As the flow of goods across the North Atlantic increased, the United States acquired additional bases along the way. Shortly after Denmark fell, Greenland asked the United States for protection. By the spring of 1941 this protection had expanded from Coast Guard surveillance to the beginnings of military installations on the island. In time these included weather stations, air strips, and harbor facilities.[12] Early in July American Marines,

[10] Morison, *History*, I, 49–50.
[11] *Ibid.*, I, 63–64.
[12] *Ibid.*, I, 58–63. For diplomatic correspondence on the question of Greenland, see U.S. Department of State, *Foreign Relations of the United States, 1941* (Washington, 1959), II, 35–72.

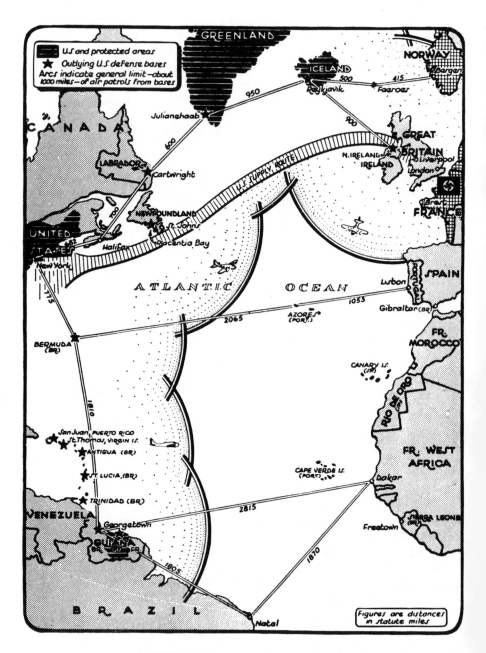

BATTLE OF THE ATLANTIC, 1939–41

who thought that they had been training for duty in the Caribbean, landed in Iceland to relieve the British, who had been protecting the island with the acquiescence of the local government. The aim of the American occupation was dual, to keep the Germans from seizing the region, and to establish bases for escort operations.[13]

The American forces at sea found themselves in a most difficult situation. In their orders for search and patrol, there was at first one important question unanswered. What should they do if they encountered German or Italian submarines or aircraft? Should they fire or wait to be fired upon? The experience of the U.S.S. *Greer* drew sharp attention to the dilemma that confronted the naval forces. On September 4, 1941, as this destroyer headed toward Iceland, it received word from a British plane that a submarine was in the area. The *Greer* immediately took defensive steps, general quarters, first increased speed and a zigzag course, and then reduced speed to permit maximum operation of sound gear. However, when the plane asked if the destroyer planned to attack, the reply was in the negative. The British plane dropped a few depth charges and left. A couple of hours later the submarine drew near the *Greer* and fired a torpedo which the destroyer managed to evade. Having let the Germans fire the first shot, the American destroyer responded with depth charges and avoided a second torpedo. No damage was done to either side; the submarine left, and the destroyer continued on its way to Iceland. The incident was significant, for it marked the beginning of *de facto* war between the United States and the Axis. It was still not open warfare. Germany restricted the activities of her submarines and sought to avoid encounters with the Americans. Neutrality legislation kept American merchant vessels unarmed and out of war zones.[14]

/ Actual escort duty by United States forces began with the sending of convoys to Iceland in the summer of 1941. Then, while Churchill and Roosevelt drafted the Atlantic Charter in their secret meeting at Argentia, Newfoundland, in August, their military advisers worked

[13] Morison, *History*, I, 66–67, 74–79. For diplomatic correspondence on Iceland, see *Foreign Relations of the United States, 1941,* II, 755–792.

[14] Morison, *History*, I, 79–81. Admiral Doenitz gives a different version of the *Greer* incident: "On September 4, 1941, U-652 was pursued by a destroyer, which dropped three depth charges. In self defence the U-boat fired two torpedoes, which the destroyer succeeded in evading. Not till the next day, when the captain of the U-boat received a wireless signal from the U-boat command, did he discover that the destroyer in question had been the USS *Greer*." Doenitz, *Memoirs*, p. 191.

out a project for American participation in transatlantic convoy protection. As a result, on September 1, Admiral King issued a new operational plan. The United States was to guard transatlantic convoys in the waters west of a mid-ocean meeting point, known as MOMP, on the meridian of Iceland. Ostensibly, American vessels were to be convoyed, but Allied merchantmen took advantage of the statement that "shipping of any nationality" might join the convoys. For the first time American vessels operated under war conditions and darkened ships at sea.[15] Operations orders of September 12, revised October 23, erased even more of the narrow line between peace and war. It stated that the mission of the United States Naval Air Detachment based at Argentia included not only escort but protection of "United States and foreign flag shipping other than German and Italian" by "destroying German and Italian naval, land, and air forces encountered."[16]

The first encounter came October 17. A few days earlier a pack of submarines had attacked a slow convoy about four hundred miles south of Iceland. Hard-pressed, the British escort issued a call for help that was answered by five American destroyers collected either from Iceland or from a westbound convoy. In the engagement that followed, the U.S.S. *Kearny* took a torpedo in the side. There were casualties but no loss of life, and the destroyer, escorted by the U.S.S. *Greer,* limped back to Iceland.

Toward the end of the month, the United States lost its first vessel in this *de facto* naval warfare. With four other destroyers, the U.S.S. *Reuben James* was escorting a convoy when, about six hundred miles west of Ireland, it was struck by a torpedo and sank in five minutes. Detonation of the vessel's own depth charges added to the loss of life, which amounted to more than a hundred persons. Like the *Kearny* and other destroyers at the time, the stricken vessel had not been equipped with radar.[17]

Even before these incidents occurred, President Roosevelt had

[15] Morison, *History,* I, 81–92.

[16] Buchanan, *The Navy's Air War,* p. 38.

[17] Morison, *History,* I, 92–98. On the significance of the change in U.S. naval operations, the British historian, Roskill, wrote: "From the British point of view the changes of September, 1941, made American participation in the Battle of the Atlantic a reality. . . . At the same time it brought an immediate sense of relief and a conviction that, though the road might yet be arduous and many setbacks suffered, the Battle of the Atlantic would finally be won." Roskill, *The War at Sea,* I, 472.

moved to secure repeal of some of the provisions of the Neutrality Law of 1939. News of the *Kearny* and *Reuben James* strengthened the hand of the so-called interventionists. On November 7, the Senate voted for repeal and on November 13, by a close vote of 212 to 194, the House followed its lead.[18] Three important sections of the Neutrality Act were deleted; these had prohibited trade with the belligerents, established war zones closed to entry by American citizens, surface vessels, or aircraft, and prevented the arming of merchant vessels. Little remained but formal declaration of war. This the Axis provided shortly after the attack on Pearl Harbor.

The so-called Neutrality Patrol was over, and the United States was now a full-fledged participant in the Battle of the Atlantic. Between December, 1941, and December, 1943, the antisubmarine warfare fell into two phases. During the first year, the United States and her allies were on the defensive, and shipping losses exceeded construction. German submarines sent to American shores concentrated on coastal shipping with devastating effect. In January, 1942, they sank fourteen ships off the Atlantic coast and twelve in Canadian waters. By February, nineteen vessels had been sunk in the Caribbean and Gulf of Mexico, with no effective retaliation. In March, twenty-eight more merchantmen were victims of U-boat attack along the Atlantic coast, and nineteen additional vessels went down in the Caribbean.[19] Many of the sinkings took place at night; it became common practice for a submarine to lie in shoal waters during the day and under cover of night seek its prey. Failure of residents of coastal cities to accept a black-out in the early months of the war caused more than one merchant vessel to be silhouetted as an inviting target for a submarine lying in wait a little farther offshore. For a time the hunting was so good that the German raiders waited for their pick, and let vessels in ballast go by to wait for a laden victim.[20]

Another disaster area in the first stages of the war was the north Russia run. Sorely pressed by the German invaders, the Soviets called

[18] W. L. Langer and S. E. Gleason, *The Undeclared War, 1940–1941* (New York, 1953), pp. 758–759. U.S. Congress, *Congressional Record,* Nov. 13, 1941, p. 8891.

[19] These and other statistics on sinkings are in Morison, *History,* I, 413–414; X (1956), 369.

[20] *Ibid.,* I, 129–130. On June 15, 1942, two freighters were sunk within sight of people on shore at Virginia Beach, Florida. *Ibid.,* I, 157.

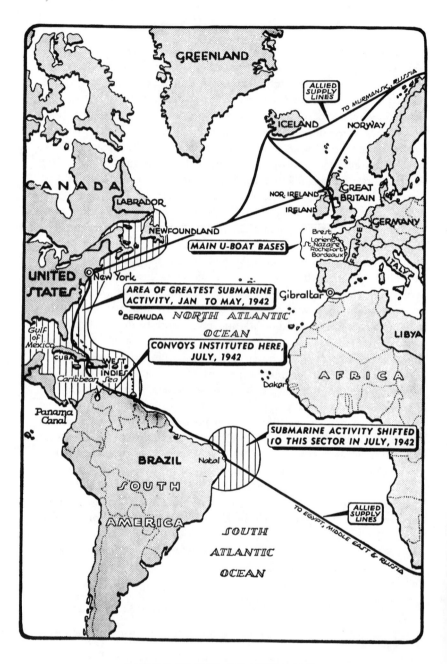

BATTLE OF THE ATLANTIC, 1942

on the United States for material aid. The route to the sian bases of Murmansk and Archangel was especially cause of the weather and because of the possibility of German-controlled bases. The conquest of Norway ga marked advantages, for the deeply indented fiords ar protected by offshore islands furnished well-located bases ѧѹ. marines, surface vessels, and aircraft. In the summer of 1942, for example, despite a heavy escort, a convoy of thirty-three merchantmen encountered both air and submarine attack and lost twenty-two ships, not counting losses by the escort vessels.[21]

Several factors helped to account for the initial successes of the Germans. The United States Navy, although it had gained some experience in the Neutrality Patrol, had not been prepared for antisubmarine warfare. Like the British Navy, it had concerned itself with heavier ships. Even the destroyer, when used independently, was of little use in antisubmarine warfare, particularly when it operated without radar. New devices, experience in using them, and teamwork were needed. These things took time, and meanwhile the submarine had its way.

Unprepared though it had been, the United States took two important steps to counteract the submarine assault. First, it introduced the system of convoying coastal shipping. All kinds of craft, air and sea, were pressed into service. The second step was administrative, the establishment of sea frontiers, in an endeavor to coordinate the efforts of all branches of the armed services that had been attempting to cope with the submarine menace. These included the Navy, Coast Guard, Army Air Force, and Civilian Air Patrol.[22] Meanwhile, all branches emphasized training.

/ Training was essential not only for the initial preparation of men to fight, but to keep them abreast of new scientific developments. Scientists played an important role in winning the Battle of the Atlantic. An essential of antisubmarine warfare, of course, is locating

[21] *Ibid.*, I, 191n. For importance of German bases in Norway, see Roskill, *The War at Sea*, I, 201.

[22] *Ibid.*, I, 205–209, 255–257. Doenitz describes the early German successes against American coastal shipping and notes the effectiveness of the convoy system. The number of German submarines in the area was never large, and their stay was limited by their oil supply. Gradually a few submarine tankers were sent to the region and lengthened the time submarines could stay on the attack. These tankers were especially helpful to submarines operating in the Gulf of Mexico. Doenitz, *Memoirs*, pp. 194–222.

the enemy. Detective devices, consequently, were extremely important. Scientists, both in and out of uniform, devised and improved these instruments. American industrial skill made possible their production in quantity, and training programs developed specialists to operate them. High on the list was radar, an electronic device that permitted the operator to pick up as an image on a screen objects that appeared above the surface of land or sea. Since radar did not reveal objects beneath the surface, it was necessary to develop other devices to attempt to locate the submerged submarine. The British had made the first start in radar development and passed that knowledge on to the Americans.[23] Similarly, they shared sound equipment with their ally. This sonar gear, as it was called, made use of the principle of counting the echoes from a U-boat's propellers to determine its speed and direction. Aircraft made use of a variant, the sonobuoy, an expendable buoy dropped in the water, which received the sonar impulses and automatically transmitted them to the aircraft by radio.[24] Ingenious though such instruments were, the human element was still very important, for one had to be an expert to distinguish between echoes made by submarine propellers and other noises picked up by the sonar devices.

Another detection device used with moderate success was magnetic equipment that enabled aircraft to locate metallic objects beneath the surface. The most effective use made of this gear was at the Strait of Gibraltar.[25]

Science also aided the armed services in the development of weapons. The Navy started the war with about the same type of depth charge that had been used in World War I. As the war progressed, it improved both the bomb and the means of ejecting it from the ship. Torpex replaced TNT as an explosive and had 50 percent more destructive power. The K-gun supplanted the old Y-gun and made possible a heavier concentration of depth charges, which as the name implies were set to detonate at a certain depth. Later, new firing

[23] The development of radar as an aircraft detection device began in 1935 as the by-product of an unsuccessful attempt to develop a "death ray" to destroy planes by electromagnetic radiation. Basil Collier, *The Defence of the United Kingdom* (London, 1957), pp. 36–40; Baxter, *Scientists Against Time*, pp. 136–157.

[24] Morison, *History*, X, 52–54; Buchanan (ed.), *The Navy's Air War*, pp. 376–380.

[25] *Ibid.*, pp. 68–69.

devices, popularly called "hedgehogs" and "mousetraps," discharged a contact-type projectile containing torpex. Aerial weapons also underwent significant experimentation and development.[26]

Germans met the scientific advances of their enemies with counter-devices. For a time, they rendered radar innocuous with search receivers which let the submarine know when it was being "floodlit" with radar, and enabled it to submerge before planes or ships could get within striking distance. The Allies countered this move effectively with a new microwave aircraft radar that could not be detected by the search receivers. The Germans had some success in confusing sonar operators with chemically produced bubbles that simulated propeller echoes. The Navy met this development with careful training of personnel to distinguish between true and false echoes. Toward the end of the war, the Germans employed a new type of acoustic torpedo that forced the Allies to take counterdefensive measures. One of the most significant German innovations was the Schnörkel, a breathing apparatus that enabled the submarine to use diesel engines underwater. With the Schnörkel, submarines could stay submerged for much longer periods of time, and they became correspondingly more difficult to locate and destroy.[27]

These developments were gradual and, as has been indicated, German submarine attacks along the Atlantic seaboard were extremely successful in the early months of American participation in the war. By May, 1942, antisubmarine efforts were increasing in effectiveness. The result was not a cessation of submarine attacks, merely a shift. The U-boats moved to the Caribbean and the Southern coasts of the United States and sank over seventy vessels in these waters. The United States cut down losses materially by introducing the convoy system, and the submarines then moved to the North Atlantic. It was in this area, incidentally, that one of the first definite kills by naval aircraft took place. A Catalina made a direct hit with a depth charge that lodged in the grating of the surfaced submarine. Zealous but inexperienced German seamen rolled the bomb overboard, and when it reached the proper depth it detonated and destroyed the U-boat.[28]

---

[26] Baxter, *Scientists Against Time,* pp. 253–259.

[27] *Ibid.,* pp. 158–169; Morison, *History,* X, 52–54, 317–319; Doenitz, *Memoirs,* pp. 265–271, 421–422.

[28] Buchanan (ed.), *The Navy's Air War,* pp. 42–43.

During the following year antisubmarine warfare became more effective as a result of improved devices, increased production of ships and planes, and an accelerated pilot-training program. Submarines, however, operating in wolf packs, pulled farther out to sea and operated out of reach of land-based planes. The Allies soon began to find the answer to this problem by forming hunter-killer teams, an important element of which was the escort carrier, or "baby flat-top." In these groups, carrier-based aircraft and various types of surface craft worked with increasing effectiveness to protect the widening flow of men and matériel to Europe.

Admiral Doenitz later admitted that the Battle of the Atlantic was lost by the end of May, 1943, and he noted especially, "Radar, and particularly radar locations by aircraft, had to all practical purposes robbed the U-boats of their power to fight on the surface."[29] Although he recognized defeat, Doenitz continued the undersea warfare as a defensive move to engage as many of the enemy's surface vessels and aircraft as possible in order to prevent their use in other action against Germany. Three basic improvements helped the Germans: improved radar and antiaircraft weapons for the submarines, and the production of acoustic torpedoes in August, 1943, instead of the fall of 1944 as earlier planned. For a time, in the summer of 1943, Admiral Doenitz ordered submarines to remain surfaced and fight it out with aircraft, but improvements in aircraft weapons and techniques caused a return to the policy of submerging to avoid air attack.[30] In the spring of 1945, two new types of submarines went into limited operation and demonstrated much faster underwater speed. They were introduced too late, however, for the war was already lost. German submarines fought to the last, although toward the end of the war they suffered heavy casualties in German coastal waters from air assault. When the collapse came, at least forty-nine U-boats were still at sea.

An important phase of the war in the Atlantic was cooperation with Latin America. United States forces established bases in Panama, Colombia, Dutch Guiana, and especially Brazil. West Indian and Bra-

---

[29] Doenitz, *Memoirs,* p. 341.

[30] Ruge, *Sea Warfare,* pp. 233–242 and *passim;* Morison, *History,* X, 108–129 and *passim.* The Germans had thought of wolf-pack or co-ordinated submarine attacks as early as 1935 and had been developing the techniques of joint attacks on convoys. The direction generally was from shore bases. Doenitz, *Memoirs,* pp. 18–22.

zilian bases were not only necessary for convoying surface craft; they were vital to the ferrying of aircraft to the Allies by way of South America and Africa. The establishment of an air base on Ascension Island in the summer of 1942 made possible a break in the eighteen-hundred-mile flight across the Atlantic.[31] The island of Trinidad became one of the most important bases for the escort of vessels from the Panama Canal. In addition to carrying on antisubmarine warfare, Allied forces sought to protect the approaches to the Canal.[32]

In summary of the naval warfare in the Atlantic, it may be said that the Allies won with a combination of many types of armed forces: surface craft, from the Canadian corvette to the United States destroyer escort and small carrier; and aircraft, from the blimp to the land-based patrol bombers and the carrier planes. All operated with growing effectiveness made possible by experience in combat, improved scientific equipment, and the cooperation of the various fighting units.

The significance of the Battle of the Atlantic is difficult to exaggerate, for it made possible the immense shipments of men and supplies that contributed so heavily to victory on land in North Africa, Italy, and Western Europe.

[31] W. F. Craven and J. L. Cate, *The Army Air Forces in World War II* (Chicago, 1948), I, 319–331.

[32] For the naval war in the Caribbean and South Atlantic, see Morison, *History*, I, 376–391; X, 188–228, 297–298.

CHAPTER 6

Democracy's Arsenal

THE recruitment and training of millions of men and the procurement of vast quantities of war materials formed a vital part of
America's war. The story of the preparation for conflict was not one
of easy, unimpeded progress. There were false starts, errors of judgment and execution, snarls of red tape, all sorts of friction, but as the
months passed the impression was one of cumulative achievement that
in time reached staggering proportions.

As far as military manpower was concerned, the United States had
a little more of a start than it had had in World War I. In 1917,
the government did not enact a Selective Service law until a month
after the war began; in December, 1941, Selective Service had been in
operation for more than a year, but still the number of men in uniform
was far below the requirements of a nation at war.

The first phase of the Army's expansion extended from July 1, 1939,
to the late spring of 1940 and was characterized by uncertainty as to
the influence the war would have on the United States. When General
George C. Marshall became Acting Chief of Staff on July 1, 1939, he
found an Army of about 174,000 enlisted men scattered among 130
posts or stations. Equipment had become obsolescent since the end of
World War I. Army organization was a mere framework, and funds
for training were inadequate. In his proclamation of limited emergency
on the outbreak of war in Europe in September, 1939, President Roosevelt authorized the expansion of the active Army to 227,000 and the
National Guard to 235,000. There was still strong resistance to any

sizable increase in the armed forces, and in March, 1940, the War Department found its request for replacement planes cut to fifty-seven and its estimate of a $12-million expenditure for a defense force in Alaska rejected. "The fundamental obstacle at the time," General Marshall explained, "was the fact that the American people were unable to visualize the dangerous possibilities of the situation."[1]

Then came the shift in Europe from the "phony" war to the *"Blitzkrieg"* as the Nazi forces rolled across the Lowlands and northern France. This inaugurated the second phase, the real beginning of the expansion of the armed forces. On May 16, 1940, President Roosevelt recommended to a special session of Congress an appropriation of about one billion dollars to increase the Army by 28,000 men, including 13,000 for the Air Corps. On May 31, Roosevelt followed with a request for an additional appropriation of approximately the same amount. Supplementary appropriations were designed to bring the Army to a total authorized strength of 375,000.

The fall of France and the peril in which Britain found itself precipitated action in the United States. Toward the end of the summer of 1940 came authorization to call the National Guard into service, and thousands of young men who had been drilling perhaps once a week found themselves at full military employment. Meanwhile, the battle for Selective Service was won, and on September 16, 1940, the President signed the Selective Service Act. As a result the United States could envisage an Army of 1,400,000, of which 500,000 would be in the Regular Army, 270,000 in the National Guard, and 630,000 selectees.

This sharp expansion inevitably brought problems of a varied nature, including housing, training, administration, and supply. Regular Army officers, aided by about 100,000 officers in the Reserves, began the task of training, first in basic centers and then in tactical units. In March, 1941, additional increases in the Army Air Corps were authorized, and plans developed for occupation of British bases acquired through the destroyers-for-bases deal. In the spring, also, the Army started a series

---

[1] General of the Army George C. Marshall, "Biennial Report . . . July 1, 1939 to June 30, 1941 . . ." *The War Reports of General of the Army George C. Marshall, Chief-of-Staff, General of the Army H. H. Arnold, Commanding General, Army Air Forces, Fleet Admiral Ernest J. King, Commander-in-Chief, United States Fleet and Chief of Naval Operations* (Philadelphia and New York, 1947), p. 20. Figures on the Army's growth are taken from the Marshall reports, *ibid.*, pp. 16, 18–21, 24, 64–69, 104, 264–266.

of officers' candidate schools to keep pace with the expanding military forces. By July 1, 1941, the Army had grown to 1,400,000 men.

The Army's growth moved into its third phase in the summer of 1941, as the European war increased in intensity with the German attack on Russia and as tension mounted between the United States and Japan. Congress extended the length of Selective Service, which originally had been twelve months, so that the new Army personnel could be retained on active duty. Training continued and included large battle rehearsals involving about 900,000 troops during the summer and early fall of 1941. The government took steps to strengthen overseas garrisons and, as has been noted elsewhere, made moves toward military preparedness in the Philippines.

December 7, 1941, marked the shift into a fourth phase, in which the Army became an offensive weapon of a nation at war. Within two years some five million men were added, and by the summer of 1943 it was decided to build the Army to an effective peak of 7,700,-000. By the end of the war in Europe the Army, including men who were hospitalized or enroute overseas as replacements, totaled approximately 8,300,000. Such expansion naturally required a tremendous enlargement of facilities in this country and, subsequently, in Britain, Australia, and elsewhere in the war theaters. By June, 1945, the Army Ground Forces Command had completed a cycle of its operations; it had trained divisions, deployed them overseas, sent them replacements, and finally was receiving them back under its control after the collapse of Germany.

During World War II the Air Force was an integral part of the Army. Confident of the importance of air power in modern warfare, the leaders in Army aviation worked aggressively for expansion and then for separate organization. Between 1935 and 1938 they made plans for a fighting air arm and in the latter year had about 1,300 officers and 18,000 men, with a Reserve of 2,800 officers and 400 men. The first real jump in size came with President Roosevelt's request on January 12, 1939, for money to increase plane production and provide primary flight training for 20,000 men. Since the Army Air Force did not have facilities to train one-tenth that number, it resorted to a temporary expedient and called into action civilian flying schools to give primary flight training until the Army could get its own program under way. The task was formidable; there was little training equipment, and at the outset even planes were lacking. As General H. H.

Arnold put it, "Instructors were somewhat in the position of a man teaching another to swim by showing him a glass of water."[2] To save time and money, the Army leased rather than constructed buildings. Meanwhile the Army Air Force expanded its air bases and by December 7, 1941, had completed 114 bases and had about 47 more in process of construction.[3] Gradually it developed a farflung but carefully organized system of advanced and special training, while tactical centers gave final training for combat.

Like the Army and Army Air Force, the Navy underwent rapid expansion of personnel as well as of physical equipment. During the twenties and early thirties, the naval limitation program naturally affected numbers of men as well as of ships. Outbreak of war in Europe led to the first significant change, for one effect of the President's proclamation of limited emergency was to fix the authorized strength of the Navy at 191,000 instead of 131,485. This was but a start. Until December 5, 1942, enlistment in the Navy was voluntary. After that date the Selective Service system provided the manpower needed, although the Navy continued to retain slightly more stringent physical requirements than those of the Army Ground Forces. During the period of recruiting, about 900,000 men volunteered for naval duty, and by the end of the war some 3,400,000 persons were in the Navy.[4] All varieties of training programs developed, from "boot training" for the neophyte bluejacket or "preflight" training for the would-be aviator to highly specialized courses in such subjects as underwater sound equipment, gunnery, or night flying.

The Marines, too, expanded. In September, 1939, the Marine Corps numbered 19,071; when Japan sued for peace there were 484,631 "Leathernecks."[5] Although under the Navy Department, the Marines had developed a separate tradition and identity; despite their growth they maintained a strong *esprit de corps*. Like the Navy, they developed an air arm with highly and specially trained personnel.

The Coast Guard, which is a separate branch of the armed forces

[2] General of the Army H. H. Arnold, "First Report . . . January 4, 1944 . . ." *ibid.*, p. 313. Figures on the growth of the Army Air Force are taken from the Arnold reports, *ibid.*, pp. 307–308.

[3] Wesley Frank Craven and James Lea Cate, *The Army Air Forces in World War II* (Chicago, 1955), VI, 145. For an extended treatment of recruitment and training, see *ibid.*, VI, 427–700.

[4] Fleet Admiral Ernest J. King reports in *War Reports*, pp. 478, 494–496, 706.

[5] Admiral King report, *ibid.*, pp. 494, 711.

in peacetime, went under the Navy's control in time of war and at the end of the conflict had increased to 170,480 persons. Unlike the other services, the Coast Guard had a "Temporary Reserve" of officers and men who served without pay but who had full military status while performing such duties as pilotage, port security, or the guarding of industrial plants. At its peak, in the spring of 1941, the Temporary Reserve totaled about seventy thousand members.

Volunteers augmented the huge flow of manpower created by Selective Service. The Navy, Marine Corps, and Army Air Force carried on active programs to get the men they needed. The Armed Forces worked closely with colleges and universities and created deferred programs to enable students to continue their college education for a time before assuming their military duties. The Navy, for example, had its V-1, V-5, and V-7 programs, which led to deck or flight officer training. Later it actually sent young men to college under the V-12 program.[6] The Marines offered a deferred program which led to a commission on graduation, to be followed by a course of "indoctrination" to prepare him for his Marine Corps duties. The Army had somewhat similar programs, although the period of deferment was usually shorter, especially for young men headed for pilot training. Both the volunteer system and Selective Service worked to the disadvantage of the Army Ground Forces and especially the infantry. The Army Air Forces, Navy, and Marine Corps, through direct commissioning or officer programs, drained away a disproportionate share of men with the highest physical and mental qualifications. Even the Army's own classification system worked against the ground forces. Men with occupational skills went into special services. Mental classification was based on the Army General Classification Test (AGCT), and selectees were placed in five grade levels. The different branches of the Army were to receive equal proportions of these five groups *after* men had been drawn out because of vocational abilities. In addition, the Army Air Force in February, 1942, was able to secure preferential treatment on the ground that many of the men previously assigned to them did not have the intelligence for the training given in the Air Force. The Army Ground Forces leaders were disturbed by the number of men in the lower classifications left for them and they feared especially that lack of leadership among junior officers

[6]Admiral King report, *ibid.*, pp. 497–498; A. R. Buchanan (ed.), *The Navy's Air War: A Mission Completed* (New York, 1946), pp. 307–329.

and noncommissioned officers might affect the Army's conduct on the battlefield. They tried without success to secure "fighting" pay for ground forces in combat comparable to "flight" pay for fliers.[7] In 1944, the Army introduced a "physical profile" system to screen out men who appeared best qualified for combat duty, but the plan came too late to have any marked effect upon the composition of the armed services.[8]

An important innovation of World War II was the widespread enlistment of women into the armed forces. In May, 1942, the Women's Army Auxiliary Corps [Wacs] came into being. Originally set for a complement of 25,000, the Corps so effectively demonstrated its worth that by the end of the war about 100,000 women were in Army uniform.[9] Correspondingly, the Navy had its Waves, the Coast Guard its Spars, and the Marine Corps a feminine contingent, for which the Marines strangely found no distinctive name. Originally the purpose of recruiting women had been to release men for combat duty, but many of the women demonstrated technical skill in their own right and became replacements rather than mere substitutes.

One of the most important phases of mobilization was the organization of scientists. Hitler blundered badly in dealing with this problem. Even before the war Nazi ideology and actions had forced some of the best minds out of Germany. Convinced that he could win a short war, Hitler neglected basic research and, leaving academic scientists out of war research, turned the problem over to industrial scientists who failed to gain the support of the military. After 1942, Germany realized its mistake and put its scientists to work. In certain fields, notably aerodynamics and ordnance, they gave a good account

[7] In October, 1943, the War Department authorized the titles, with appropriate badges, of "Expert Infantryman" and "Combat Infantryman." The first could be won by meeting certain standards of performance in training or in combat; the latter was awarded to infantrymen showing "exemplary conduct in action against the enemy." After June, 1944, holders of the badges received slight increases in base pay. Robert R. Palmer, Bell I. Wiley, and William R. Keast, *The Procurement and Training of Ground Combat Troops (United States Army in World War II: The Army Ground Forces)* (Washington, 1948), p. 62.

[8] In the "physical profile" plan each soldier was rated from 1 to 4 on six elements in physical condition: general stamina, upper extremities, lower extremities, hearing, vision, and emotional stability. His rating in each in this order constituted his "physical profile serial." Men with 211211 or better were considered qualified for rigorous combat duty. *Ibid.*, p. 67.

[9] Marshall report, *War Reports*, pp. 123, 272–273.

of themselves, but their effort came too late.[10] Japan, also, failed to make use of its scientific personnel and left its best scientists out of the war. The bitter rivalry that existed between the Japanese Army and Navy prevented coordinated scientific effort.

In comparison, Great Britain and the United States made wonderfully effective use of their scientific manpower. In 1915, before the United States entered World War I, Congress had created the National Advisory Committee for Aeronautics. It had continued to exist after the war, and in June, 1939, the President authorized it to become a consulting and research agency for the Joint Army and Navy Aeronautical Board in case of a national emergency. The head of the NACA was Dr. Vannevar Bush, president of the Carnegie Institution in Washington. This eminent scientist, feeling the need for similar coordination of scientists outside aviation, spearheaded the move for a new organization. The proposal gained the support of the administration and of Army and Navy leaders, and late in June, 1940, there came into being the National Defense Research Committee, with Bush as its chairman.

The problem confronting the organization was manpower, not money. Realizing that scientists in industry soon would be facing heavy tasks as a result of increased war production, the NDRC turned to the colleges and universities. By decentralizing and permitting scientists to work in their own laboratories, the committee mobilized research to a remarkable degree. As the work continued, it was found necessary to have central establishments for certain projects. The California Institute of Technology, for instance, laid heavy emphasis on rocket development and as another project built the world's largest torpedo tube. The Woods Hole Oceanographic Institution operated a laboratory to study underwater sound and underwater explosives. Princeton scientists worked on ballistics, and the Franklin Institute of Philadelphia on airborne fire control. Several factors help explain success. One was a streamlined system of contracts which facilitated completion of projects. More important was the fact that, after a period of mutual hesitation, civilian scientists and military officials generally worked well together.

[10] James Phinney Baxter III, *Scientists Against Time* (Boston, 1950), pp. 7-9; Lincoln R. Thiesmeyer and John E. Burchard, *Combat Scientists* (*Science in World War II: Office of Scientific Research and Development*) (Boston, 1947), p. 181.

In May, 1941, Dr. Bush became the head of an expanded organization which now bore the title of Office of Scientific Research and Development. The National Defense Research Committee and a newly created Committee on Medical Research became advisory to the OSRD, which grew in power and responsibility as the war progressed. One of the main administrative problems was not only to secure but to hold adequate scientific personnel. On the one hand, industry competed with research for scientists. On the other, there was the continuous possibility that young men engaged in research might be drafted into military service by Selective Service boards. Dr. Bush and other leaders of OSRD sought a solution of the difficulty with Paul V. McNutt, head of the War Manpower Commission. While they were unable to obtain blanket exemptions for scientists, they got the acceptance of a reserved list of scientists whose work was of such a character that local draft boards did not disturb them. Out of 9,755 men for whom deferment was requested by OSRD and its contractors, only sixty-four were drafted. Others no doubt went into the armed forces without protest, and still others failed to obtain positions as scientists because of their vulnerability to the draft. The United States was not so successful in placing its scientists in the right niche as was Great Britain, which had learned this lesson in World War I.

The most spectacular contribution of science to the winning of the war was, of course, the atomic bomb dropped on Hiroshima and Nagasaki. Scientists, however, aided the war in so many other ways that only a brief sampling of their work is possible in this study. One important field of endeavor has already been noted, antisubmarine warfare. Some of the new weapons and devices used at sea demonstrated their worth in other phases of warfare. Radar was used on the ground, in ships, and in the air. It aided night fighters in their air attacks in the Pacific; it helped fliers land when visibility was bad.[11] A high-power warning radar set up on the Devon coast on D-day enabled its operators "to control a patrol of Thunderbirds flying off the Brest peninsula, to dispatch fighter bombers over various targets and even to have a hand in air-sea rescue operations in the Channel."[12]

[11] One important development was a radar altimeter, which indicated the actual distance of a plane from the ground, rather than the elevation above sea level. George Raynor Thompson et al., The Signal Corps: The Test (December 1941 to July 1943) (United States Army in World War II: The Technical Services) (Washington, 1957), p. 85.

[12] Baxter, Scientists Against Time, p. 153.

A microwave navigational and bombing aid made it possible for men sitting in trucks in England to know within a few yards the precise location of American or British planes over Germany—in fact, to know the positions more accurately than did the crews of the planes. One of the most important navigational aids was a system known as Loran (Long Range Aid to Navigation). Using Loran charts with radio signals from certain shore radio stations as indicated by a special receiver, the navigator of a plane or ship could quickly and accurately plot his position without giving away the location to the enemy. Loran, incidentally, was one of a number of war developments that lent themselves easily to peacetime use.

The rocket appeared in World War II as an answer to the need for a weapon of great power but little recoil which could be fired from a plane or light vessel. Basically, the rocket is a tube, open at one end and closed at the other. When it is fired, the gas pressure rises and the gas goes out the open end but by exerting equal pressure on the closed end creates the thrust that propels the rocket. The principle had long been known, but the missile's inaccuracy of fire had resulted in its discard in favor of rifled ordnance. Belligerents in World War II, however, found that the right type of propellant fuel corrected inaccuracies and made the rocket a significant weapon with a variety of forms and uses. The largest and most devastating was the German V-2, which carried a ton of high explosives. The bazooka, using the rocket principle, enabled the infantryman to pierce a tank. By the end of the war rockets had become standard and powerful weapons on land, sea, and in the air.

It was not enough to create missiles of great explosive power. They had to be directed to the enemy and exploded at the proper time. Science made remarkable contributions in fire control, whether it was antiaircraft fire or bombsights for the Army Air Force. One of the most significant developments was that of the radio proximity fuze, which operated not on the principle of time, but on nearness to the target. It improved the effectiveness of fire against the V-1 rockets sent against England and, in the Pacific, enabled American forces to down many Japanese planes. For a time, so great was the fear that the enemy might obtain an unexploded fuze and learn the secret of construction that none could be fired except over water. This so-called VT-fuze later proved its effectiveness in land fighting in Western Europe. Among the other weapons and devices which illustrate science's role in the war were smoke generators used for screening purposes, amphibious vehicles such as the DUKW, an amphibious truck, and the flame throwers used with success on some of the Pacific islands.[13]

A vital part of science's role in the war was in the area of military medicine. In one aspect, science shared honors with the American people. Doctors and scientists developed the technique of using whole blood and plasma for the wounded or severely burned, but it was the citizen voluntarily giving his pint who helped create the great quantities needed for the lifesaving fluid. By the end of the war people had contributed thirteen million pints.[14]

The war in tropical areas of the Pacific and elsewhere dramatized the problem of malaria and forced its solution. In some places it was possible to conduct successful mosquito-control projects through draining, dusting, or spraying the water in which mosquito larvae normally developed. Such techniques were not feasible in many jungle areas. Consequently, scientists created repellents to make human beings unattractive to mosquitoes. Furthermore, since quinine, the customary remedy for malaria, was in short supply, scientists provided substitutes. Most widely used during the war was Atabrine, which when regularly administered in correct doses proved to be a satisfactory suppressive as well as cure.

The war hastened the development of what were popularly called "wonder drugs." The sulfonamides had been in clinical use for about five years before the war, but they had defects. They were ineffective against some bacteria, were so toxic that aviators taking treatment were not permitted to fly, and they were not uniformly effective in treating the same disease, because some bacteria acquired a resistance to the drugs. Penicillin, a nontoxic mold discovered by Sir Alexander Fleming in 1929 and developed during the war, avoided most of these disadvantages. It proved its worth in military hospitals in combination with transfusions and surgery in the treatment of wounds and was most effective in dealing with pneumonia.

Aviation brought with it numerous medical problems. High-altitude flying made necessary devices to furnish oxygen to the plane's occupants. At first, oxygen masks appeared to be the answer, and

[13] *Ibid.*, pp. 247–251; C. M. Green, H. C. Thompson, and P. C. Rootes, *The Ordnance Department: Planning Munitions for War (United States Army in World War II: The Technical Services)* (Washington, 1955), pp. 420–421.
[14] Baxter, *Scientists Against Time*, p. 324.

scientists struggled with the numerous problems these created. Before the end of the war, however, it was found that pressurized cabins, rather than masks for crew members, offered the better solution, and they came first into operational use in the B-29's. Another question centered about the centrifugal forces affecting men during sharp turns and "pull-outs" from dives. This force could cause a black-out, which often meant loss of control and a crash. The most satisfactory solution to this problem was the "anti-G suit," which by exerting pressure on the lower part of the body prevented the blood from leaving the brain during a dive. Although uncomfortable, these suits not only increased the safety factor but enabled fliers to engage in maneuvers that otherwise would not have been possible.[15]

The atomic bomb was far and away the most significant scientific achievement of the war. The study of atomic energy was not the work of any one race or nationality, and it had begun long before World War II. Albert Einstein's famous formula regarding energy, $E = mc^2$, quickened the thinking of other scientists, for Einstein held that energy (E) equaled mass (m) multiplied by the speed of light (c) squared. In 1938, two German scientists bombarded uranium with neutrons and produced barium. Two Jewish exiles in Denmark analyzed the significance of this experiment, and the great Danish physicist, Niels Bohr, passed on the interpretation to American scientists.[16] The importance of splitting the atom was the fact that according to Einstein's formula it would release almost infinite energy.

In the United States, Enrico Fermi, an Italian Nobel Prize winner teaching at Columbia, and Albert Einstein, at the Institute for Advanced Study at Princeton, both refugees from totalitarianism, sought government sponsorship of atomic research. These men realized that German scientists were aware of the potentialities of atomic fission and, indeed, might be farther advanced toward the solution of the problem. President Roosevelt had already made a very modest beginning of federal aid in 1939 by appointing an Advisory Committee on Uranium at a time when the interest was in peacetime utilization of atomic energy. By 1941, the military aspect had become predominant, and the President placed the committee under the control of

[15] For an account of the medical service in the A.A.F., see Craven and Cate, *The A.A.F. in World War II* (Chicago, 1958), VII, 365–430.

[16] Henry DeWolf Smyth, *Atomic Energy for Military Purposes: The Official Report on the Development of the Atomic Bomb under the Auspices of the United States Government, 1940–1945* (Princeton, 1945), p. 24.

the National Defense Research Committee. Later in the year, he appointed a "top policy group" consisting of Vice President Henry A. Wallace, Secretary of War Stimson, General Marshall, and two leaders of the NDRC, Dr. Vannevar Bush and President James B. Conant of Harvard University.[17]

The attack on Pearl Harbor intensified work on atomic energy and narrowed the objective to the construction of an atomic bomb to be ready for use as soon as possible. Scientists knew that the uranium atom had different species, or isotopes, practically identical chemically but differing in weight. They knew that in one of these isotypes, U-235, the atomic chain reaction had taken place. Consequently, scientists sought techniques of separating enough of these isotopes from the rest of the uranium isotopes to make possible the bomb they wanted. Different devices for this separation process emerged. Professor Ernest O. Lawrence, of the University of California, developed the electromagnetic method in the great cyclotron at Berkeley. Scientists at Columbia University, the Universities of Virginia and Minnesota concentrated on the gaseous diffusion method.

Because of the small quantities of U-235 available, scientists examined the possibility of starting a chain reaction in unseparated uranium. Dr. A. H. Compton and a group of scientists, including Dr. Fermi, began to study this problem at the University of Chicago. On December 2, 1942, they conducted their experiment successfully in a part of the stadium at Stagg Field. The importance of the venture was briefly as follows: Dr. Lawrence and his associates had been able with the cyclotron to separate uranium into two new elements, the more important of which was called plutonium. The chain reaction set in motion at Chicago showed that this process could produce plutonium much more rapidly. Furthermore, the Chicago experiment also demonstrated that scientists could measure and regulate the chain reaction.[18]

Significant though the step at Chicago was, it was but the beginning. As one scientist noted, "The technological gap between produc-

[17] *Ibid.,* pp. 45–54.

[18] For a description of the experiment by Dr. Compton, who was present, see Arthur Holly Compton, *Atomic Quest: A Personal Narrative* (New York, 1956), pp. 141–144. Dr. Compton wrote: "Atomic power! It had been produced, kept under control, and stopped. The power liberated was less than that needed to light an electric lamp, but that power marked a new era in man's history."

ing a controlled chain reaction and using it as a large scale power source or an explosive is comparable to the gap between the discovery of fire and the manufacture of a steam locomotive."[19] To shorten that gap required more than the continued effort of great scientists; it required also a government that would stake millions of dollars on an unknown and untested weapon and it needed, in addition, a superlative accomplishment of manufacturing skill.

For a time the Office of Scientific Research and Development and the Army conducted work on atomic energy as a joint project, but since the primary goal was the construction of a weapon of war it was perhaps inevitable that the Army assumed control. On May 1, 1943, the Army Corps of Engineers took over the contracts formerly held by the OSRD. A new administrative unit or district emerged within the corps, known as the Manhattan District, and for security reasons its work was designated "Development of Substitute Materials." In September, 1943, Secretary Stimson placed General L. R. Groves in charge of all Army activities in connection with the projected bombs and ordered him to report directly to the Secretary of War and to General Marshall. The "top policy group" then created a Military Policy Group to plan policies and report progress periodically to the top group.

Although the Army assumed control, liaison continued to be close with the scientists, and General Groves had as his scientific advisers Dr. Conant and Dr. Richard C. Tolman, Chairman and Vice Chairman of the National Defense Research Committee. The project was not that of the United States alone, for the British and Canadians joined representatives of the United States in a Combined Policy Committee. Since British scientists were engaged in other important war activities, the decision was made to produce the bomb in the United States.[20]

The heavy expenditures involved in the project posed a problem. Congress had been spending lavishly to finance the war, but in this case it was to be asked to vote hundreds of millions on a gamble

[19] Statement by Professor H. D. Smyth, Princeton University, quoted in Baxter, *Scientists Against Time*, p. 432.

[20] *Ibid.*, pp. 438–439; Henry L. Stimson and McGeorge Bundy, *On Active Service in Peace and War* (New York, 1948), p. 614. A Canadian, Dr. Alan Nunn May, and two members of the British team of physicists, Klaus Fuchs and Bruno Pontecorvo, gained information which was used for disloyal purposes. Compton, *Atomic Quest*, p. 117n.

without even knowing what the gamble was. When it became clear that the cost would be terrific, Secretary Stimson, General Marshall, and Dr. Bush met with Speaker of the House Samuel Rayburn and the two party leaders of that body, Congressmen Joseph Martin and John W. McCormack, and explained the program. Shortly afterward they conferred with key figures in the Senate. These political leaders pushed the necessary appropriations through Congress without debate and warded off several attempted Congressional investigations of phases of the project.[21]

Three important centers of activity developed.[22] One was in the mountains of eastern Tennessee where the city of Oak Ridge grew to 78,000. There several types of plants were constructed for the purpose of obtaining U-235 and plutonium. Then a large-scale plant was developed at Hanford above the great bend of the Columbia River in southeast Washington. Possibility of accidental explosion as well as security reasons led to the erection of a third center. Both at Oak Ridge and Hanford the aim was to produce and control atomic energy; at the third location the objective was to utilize the destructive power of atomic energy by making an atomic bomb.[23]

The site chosen was a relatively isolated area at Los Alamos, about twenty miles from Santa Fe, New Mexico. Under the leadership of the brilliant scientist, J. R. Oppenheimer, of the University of California at Berkeley, scientists and workers began their task.[24] The problem was to construct a bomb which would bring together enough fissionable material to create an explosion. Too little material would not explode; too much would not only be a waste of valuable material but might cause a premature blast that would destroy the Los

---

[21] Stimson and Bundy, *On Active Service*, pp. 614–615; Harry S. Truman, *Memoirs of Harry S. Truman* (New York, 1955), I, 10–11.

[22] While numerous companies participated in construction, the E. I. du Pont de Nemours Company assumed the heaviest responsibilities, construction of the intermediate plant in Tennessee and of the large-scale production plant in Washington. Already loaded with war contracts, the du Pont officials, when they became aware of the importance of the Manhattan project, undertook the task on the basis of cost plus a fixed fee of one dollar. Smyth, *Atomic Energy for Military Purposes*, pp. 110–111.

[23] For a description of these developments, see *ibid.*, pp. 141–153.

[24] After the war, Oppenheimer was declared a security risk, largely on the basis of earlier associations. Compton attests to Oppenheimer's loyalty and ability as a wartime leader of the Los Alamos Laboratory. Compton, *Atomic Quest*, p. 127. See also Robert Jungk, *Brighter Than a Thousand Suns: A Personal History of the Atomic Scientists* (New York, 1958), pp. 313–334.

Alamos Laboratory and the people in it. The scientists, therefore, had to determine what quantity was needed and what kind of casing would delay expansion of the reacting material. As explained in an official release, "Until detonation is desired, the bomb must consist of a number of separate pieces each one of which is below the critical size (either by reason of small size or unfavorable shape). To produce detonation, the parts of the bomb must be brought together rapidly."[25] Military experts, trained in ordnance, aided in the construction, and in July, 1945, the bomb was ready for trial.

The spot selected was another remote part of New Mexico, Alamagordo, about 120 miles southeast of Albuquerque, known to casual tourists for its famous white sands. The participants in the venture were understandably tense. Two billion dollars had been spent already. Everything had been planned with the utmost accuracy, but the planning was based on theoretical rather than actual knowledge. On Monday morning, July 16, after several delays caused by bad weather, from a vantage point ten thousand yards away from the steel tower on which the bomb had been placed, scientists put into operation an automatic mechanism that detonated the bomb.[26] As the steel tower evaporated under the terrific force of the blast, it became clear that the United States had a new weapon whose significance none could wholly foresee.

This brief case history of the making of the first atomic bomb illustrates the tremendous war production of the United States. To make possible such an increase in output, changes were required in peacetime economy. Production for military needs was primary and justified and required widespread intervention by government into business.

Such intervention came in almost every arena of the economy. The government sought to increase the supply of basic materials, such as metals, rubber, wood and fabrics, and to control their uses. Experience gained in World War I was of limited value here, and the government was rather slow in making effective moves. At first, the War Production Board made widespread use of priority ratings and tried to study their effects. The weakness of the Production Require-

[25] Smyth, *Atomic Energy for Military Purposes*, p. 211.

[26] For descriptions, see Baxter, *Scientists Against Time*, pp. 446–447; Jungk, *Brighter Than a Thousand Suns*, pp. 198–202.

ments Plan which went into operation in the summer of 1942 seems to have been that the total demands for critical materials exceeded the supply. In other words, industrial applicants could present valid claims to more material than was available. Some curb was necessary, too, on the various military procurement agencies. The Controlled Materials Plan, announced in the fall of 1942, but not made the basic material control system until July, 1943, attempted to solve this problem.[27]

The plan forced the various claimant agencies, such as the War and Navy departments, to convert their projected programs into common materials, which became the so-called controlled materials: carbon and alloy steel, brass, copper, and aluminum. Then after the total claims were balanced with total supply and with each other for relative need, each claimant agency received an allotment to an appropriate share of the whole. Each agency then reallocated its share to contractors so that they could produce the equipment needed.

Putting this relatively simple procedure into operation was a complex and at times confused experience. There was irritation at the heavy paper work involved, there were delays in passing allotments down through all production levels, and small business at times felt that it was unfairly submerged.[28]

In a war emphasizing metallic construction it is easy to forget the continuing importance of lumber. Wooden boxes and paper replaced burlap for agricultural packaging when the burlap supply from India was cut off; wooden barrels took the place of metal drums. Wood was used in the construction of small boats and as a substitute for light metals in gliders, transport planes, and trainers. Tremendous quantities of lumber went into packing boxes for the shipment of weapons and machines, especially when destined overseas. It took about fifty board feet a month to keep one overseas soldier supplied and five hundred board feet to ship his original equipment to him. Tremendous amounts of lumber also went for construction of military establishments at home and abroad. At first there were no restrictions

[27] David Novick, Melvin Anshen, and W. C. Trappner, *Wartime Production Controls* (New York, 1949), pp. 177–178; Donald M. Nelson, *Arsenal of Democracy: The Story of American War Production* (New York, 1946), pp. 364, 383–384.

[28] Novick, Anshen, and Trappner, *Wartime Production Controls*, pp. 178–193.

on military use of lumber; later, however, specific allocations were made to the agencies. Profiting by experience gained in control of metals, the government gradually developed a effective system of controlling the distribution of lumber.[29]

Attempts had been made to build a reserve supply of another important commodity, rubber, even before the United States entered the war. Unfortunately, although imports increased there was no check on consumption, and as a result when the nation went to war its rubber supply was only slightly above normal. Synthetic rubber could be and was made, but it took time to construct plants and cost over $700 million. Meanwhile, conservation became essential; gas rationing was designed to save rubber as well as fuel. Shortages developed in certain types of tires, especially for heavy trucks and buses. The effect on tires of the rough terrain of Pacific beaches, the roads of North Africa and Italy, and the countryside of France exceeded all expectations. By the end of the war, however, a Tire Allotment Plan was working satisfactorily.[30]

As the types of controls evolved during the war so did the agencies that devised and administered them. In August, 1939, a War Resources Board, with Edward R. Stettinius as its head, began a study of War Department plans for mobilizing the nation's resources for war. In May, 1940, the Office of Emergency Management was established as a liaison between the President and the defense agencies. Then came the Advisory Committee on National Defense, which had little authority and was less significant than the Office of Production Management, also created in 1940. Under its director, William S. Knudsen, president of General Motors Corporation, the OPM sought to coordinate defense activities. After war came to the United States, in January, 1942, Donald M. Nelson was appointed head of the new War Production Board, which became the dominant federal agency concerned with industrial mobilization.[31]

Closely associated with the problem of production was the matter

[29] *Ibid.*, pp. 205–224.

[30] *Ibid.*, pp. 225–241; Roland Young, *Congressional Politics in the Second World War* (New York, 1956), pp. 37–38; *Nelson, Arsenal of Democracy,* pp. 290–306.

[31] *Ibid.*, pp. 87–89, 116–154. For information on Nelson's appointment, see Robert E. Sherwood, *Roosevelt and Hopkins: An Intimate History* (New York, 1948), pp. 474–477.

of prices. In a total war, prices would be incidental. The nation in such circumstances would commandeer the materials needed and direct management and labor to produce without regard to price. But the United States was not fighting an all-out war, and although the government established controls of different sorts, it did not become a dictatorship. Price controls were considered necessary to maintain proper morale by protecting consumers and to prevent too inflationary a postwar period. In other words, price controls were designed to win the peace as well as the war. The move began even before American entrance into the war, as the Office of Price Administration started its work in April, 1940.

Like many other aspects of governmental control, price control has aroused controversy. The critics range from those who insist that a competitive economy uncontrolled by the government is the most efficient form of economic activity even in wartime to those who object not to the aims of price control but to its implementation. The latter point to the failures of administration, the rise of black markets, the unnecessary price-fixing, the alternating conservation and waste of the same product. No doubt such weaknesses existed. Unfortunately, the patriotic honesty of millions of citizens in living up to the rationing requirements was marred by the willingness and even eagerness of other persons to turn the war into sources of personal profit or convenience. People were urged to make gifts of items that in some cases were of no use to war production and that in others simply lined the pockets of profiteers. They contributed car floor mats made of rubber of too low quality for any other use. They donated kitchenware made of a type of aluminum that was valueless in aircraft production, and they saved toothpaste and shaving cream tubes for a lead that was of no strategic value. The OPA authorized bakers to reduce the size of a loaf of bread but not its price, despite the fact that there was a shortage of the smaller-size baking pans. Cuffs were eliminated from men's trousers, but often nothing was done with the cloth saved.[32]

On the other side were the defenders of price regulation as a necessary device to curb the cupidity of some individuals and protect the

[32] For a critical view, see Lawrence Sullivan, *Bureaucracy Runs Amuck* (Indianapolis, 1944), pp. 13–197. For a study of the black market, see Marshall B. Clinard, *The Black Market: A Study of White Collar Crime* (New York, 1952), pp. 115–186 and *passim*.

interests of the great mass of American consumers. And if a balance must be made, it seems clear that in the main price controls worked, that the average person abided by them, and that the controls contributed a fair share toward winning the war.

The tremendous productive record of the United States of course could not have been achieved without a substantial increase in industrial manpower. In the process one of the great domestic problems of the nation was solved, at least temporarily. As late as 1940, there were over eight million unemployed, but by 1943 unemployment had practically disappeared. As in the case of materials, the government did not fight a total war with manpower. It did not draft labor as did Great Britain. The administration endeavored successfully to maintain the gains made in labor's behalf by New Deal legislation. Attempts failed, for example, to abolish the forty-hour week, established in 1938 by the Wages and Hours Act. The worker was not prevented from working more than forty hours, but was guaranteed overtime pay for overtime work. The War Manpower Commission, established in April, 1942, tried to estimate the over-all needs for manpower and, although committing errors of judgment and execution, improved with experience.[33]

\ The reason for the great increase in productivity of American manpower was basically one of simple arithmetic. More people worked, and they worked longer hours than in peacetime. Between 1940 and 1944 the labor force rose about 36 percent. Part of this increase came from re-employment of the unemployed, but others joined the labor force. There was the normal expansion of young persons getting their first jobs. In addition, temporary workers swelled the ranks; boys and girls below the normal working age, married women, and retired persons entered one or another type of war work. As the number of war workers increased, the average work week also rose, from 37.7 to 46.6 hours.[34]

Shortly after the Pearl Harbor attack, representatives of management and labor conferred with President Roosevelt and pledged to refrain from action that would prevent maximum production. The

[33] Joel Seidman, *American Labor from Defense to Reconversion* (Chicago, 1953), p. 158.

[34] George A. Lincoln *et al., Economics of National Security* (New York, 1950), p. 100; Seymour Harris, *Inflation and the American Economy* (New York, 1945), pp. 120–131; Merle Fainsod and Lincoln Gordon, *Government and the American Economy* (New York, 1948) (rev. ed.), pp. 816–819.

administration set up a National War Labor Board which represented labor, management, and the government. In general, labor respected its promise not to impede the war, but there were periods of tension. As living costs increased, C.I.O. steel workers demanded a wage boost of a dollar a day to keep pace. The War Labor Board on July 16, 1942, granted them a 15 percent raise. This action came to be known as the "Little Steel Formula" and was applied to other wage controversies during the war.[35]

Probably the most serious labor controversy arose in the coal mines. In April, 1943, John L. Lewis threatened to take the United Mine Workers out on strike for more wages to meet the continuing increase in living costs. Friendly though he had shown himself to be toward labor, President Roosevelt was against this action and, using his war powers, had Secretary of the Interior Ickes take over the mines. Actually, Lewis won, for before the matter was over he had broken the Little Steel Formula in effect and had obtained premium pay and additional work for his men. Partly as a result of public sentiment aroused over this strike controversy, Congress passed the Smith-Connally Act in July, 1943. One feature of the act was the imposition of penalties on labor leaders who provoked strikes in plants working on government contracts.

An unexpected by-product of the act came in the following spring. In 1943, it was a labor leader, John L. Lewis, who had aroused the government to action; in April, 1944, it was a leader of management. Sewall Avery, head of Montgomery Ward & Company, had differed with the War Labor Board and refused to follow its instructions regarding a contract with a labor union. Using the Smith-Connally Act, despite Avery's insistence that his company had no war contracts, Roosevelt had the Secretary of Commerce take over the great mail-order house. After holding collective bargaining elections, the administration turned the company back to its managers. Avery still clashed with the War Labor Board and later in the year refused to comply with a board order to raise substandard wages. Toward the end of 1944 the President again intervened and this time placed the company under the control of the Army, which retained control until late in August, 1945.

Such labor-management disturbances were relatively incidental in

[35] Seidman, *American Labor*, pp. 109–130; Foster Rhea Dulles, *Labor in America* (New York, 1949), pp. 336–337.

comparison with the common effort to gear the nation's economy to war. The results were impressive, and the United States indeed became the arsenal for democracy. In the peak year of production, 1944, the United States produced over 50 percent more combat munitions than did the enemy and, in fact, had 45 percent of the total armament output of all the belligerent nations. A few examples illustrate the nation's production; 2,100 military planes were made in 1939. In 1942, 48,000 were built; in 1943, 86,000; in 1944, 96,359, including 16,078 heavy bombers. About 5,200 vessels were built with nearly 53 million dead-weight tonnage. Shipyard proficiency increased steadily. It took 244 days to build the first Liberty ship, a standard freighter built during the war; before the end of the conflict construction time had been reduced to forty-two days.[36]

In spite of the tremendous war output of the nation, it did not constitute total production for the period. In fact, only about half went toward war materials and the needs of the government. The rest was production for civilian needs.

The nation's production of food, although not so phenomenal as that of industrial products, was more than adequate. Although civilian food consumption in the United States during 1944 was the highest in history, almost a fourth of the agricultural goods went to the armed forces and to the Allies through Lend-Lease. Increased agricultural production was not the result of added workers as in the case of war industries, for the number of agricultural workers declined. It is accounted for only in part by increase in acreage, for this amounted to but 12 percent between 1941 and 1945, and the over-all acreage in 1945 was 5 percent less than it had been in 1932.[37] Economists point to other factors-in an effort to explain increased farm production. One was an extended period of good weather; another was greater efficiency resulting from mechanization and a heavy increase of fertilizers. Some experts feel that governmental planning and price controls were also instrumental in raising agricultural output.[38]

[36] Nelson, *Arsenal of Democracy*, pp. 245–246.

[37] Murray E. Benedict, *Farm Policies of the United States, 1790–1950: A Study of Their Origins and Development* (New York, 1953), p. 435.

[38] For discussions of agriculture during the war, see *ibid.*, pp. 431–459; Rainer Schickele, *Agricultural Policy: Farm Programs and National Welfare* (New York, 1954), pp. 241–252. Congress passed the Steagull Amendment (July, 1941, and subsequently amended) in an effort to protect from postwar slumps farmers who were being asked for all-out production. *Ibid.*, pp. 242–243.

Three factors kept farm labor from declining below the level of adequacy. First, draft boards which initially were uncooperative later made extensive deferments of farm workers. Second, women and children, stimulated by patriotic as well as economic motives, went into the fields and orchards to help with the crops. Third, the government sponsored temporary immigration. In August, 1942, the Mexican and United States governments signed an agreement for recruitment of Mexican labor to work in the United States. The conditions laid down showed a concern for both the temporary worker and other labor in the United States. Although there was some criticism of the administration of the program, Mexicans found work in twenty-one states and helped harvest every major agricultural crop. Additional temporary workers came from Jamaica, Bermuda, and other areas, and in 1944 and 1945 the government utilized upwards of 130,000 German and Italian prisoners of war.

The importance of ocean transportation has already been indicated. In internal transportation, which was equally important, the railroad was the basic means, and here again the results were remarkable. The United States learned much from its experience in World War I in this regard but did not take over the railroads as it had done during Wilson's administration. Instead, an Office of Defense Transportation cooperated with railroad management and labor to reach maximum efficiency. Between 1940 and 1944, the railroads nearly doubled their volume, rising from about 379 billion ton-miles to almost 747 billion.[39] They made this growth with a moderate increase in the number of freight cars and locomotives and made their gains primarily through maximum loading and use of equipment. The Office of Defense Transportation sought with general success to prevent freight congestion at ports and penalized shippers for holding freight cars. To a lesser extent, buses and trucks aided in the solution of the transportation problem. Great Lakes tonnage increased, but the submarine menace caused a decline in coastwise shipping. The airplane assumed some significance, especially in the transportation of personnel. Most passengers had to reconcile themselves to the possibility of being "bumped off" short of their destination to make room for someone with a higher priority rating.

The mobilization of the United States involved many other factors

[39] Charles B. Fowler et al., Economic Handbook: A Visual Survey (New York, 1955).

discussed elsewhere. Among these were the relationships of politics and government to the nation's economy, the problem of meeting the high cost of waging war, and the impact of war on American society. Nevertheless, the great war production of the United States gave its armed forces and to a considerable extent those of its allies the arms with which to fight and overpower the enemy.

CHAPTER 7

North Africa

T HE basic political decision underlying strategic military planning was that this war would be waged by a coalition. But a "strange alliance" it was, this collaboration of the United States, Britain, and Soviet Russia. The Russians had their own war to fight on the Eastern front and they had their own war aims of security and expansion. They wanted supplies from the other two allies and military action which would draw Germans away from the Russian front. Ideological and other factors made them suspicious of their allies, and only on a few significant occasions, as we shall see, did they meet at a high level with the leaders of Britain and the United States to consider war plans. In contrast, the British and the Americans, as already noted, began their collaboration even before the United States entered the war. Meeting from January 29 to March 27, 1941, military representatives of the two countries agreed that "The broad strategic objectives of the Associated Powers will be the defeat of Germany and her Allies."[1]

At the outset the British and the Americans held different views on the means toward this end. The British wished to defeat Germany by naval and air action. The immediate recollection of Dunkirk and the more remote memory of mass bloodletting on the Western front in World War I helped explain British reluctance to strike prema-

[1] "United States-British Staff Conversations Report. . . . Short Title ABC-1, March 27, 1941" in U.S. Congress, Joint Committee on the Investigation of the Pearl Harbor Attack, *Pearl Harbor Attack* (Washington, 1946), Part 15, p. 1489.

turely across the Channel or to reintroduce large-scale land warfare in Western Europe, and they did not favor launching a cross-Channel attack until Germany was on the verge of collapse.[2]

American military planners, on the other hand, felt that the most effective way of defeating Germany was by sustained air assault followed by mass landings and engagement with the enemy. Army strategic planners in the summer of 1941 declared that eventually "we must prepare to fight Germany by actually coming to grips with her and defeating her ground forces and definitely breaking her will to combat."[3]

Despite this fundamental cleavage of opinion, the British and Americans worked together. No "United Chiefs of Staff" of the three Allies came into being; there did develop a "Combined Chiefs of Staff," composed of top British and American military leaders whose task was to manage the war and develop military strategy for the two countries. The American half of this group consisted of the Joint Chiefs of Staff (JCS); these were Admiral William D. Leahy, Chief of Staff for the President; General George C. Marshall, Army Chief of Staff; Admiral Ernest J. King, Chief of Naval Operations; and General Henry H. Arnold, Commanding General, Army Air Forces. Above the Combined Chiefs of Staff were the political leaders, Prime Minister Churchill and President Roosevelt, both of whom took an intense and active interest in the military conduct of the war. Because of the nature of the British government the Prime Minister worked somewhat more closely with his military advisers than did the President with the Joint Chiefs of Staff.

Although the grand strategy was to consider Germany and not Japan as the primary foe and that presumably war in the West would take precedence over war in the East, events soon forced some modi-

[2] For discussions of strategy, see Maurice Matloff and Edwin M. Snell, *Strategic Planning for Coalition Warfare, 1941–1942* (*United States Army in World War II: The War Department*) (Washington, 1953), pp. 1–62 and *passim;* Mark S. Watson, *Chief of Staff: Prewar Plans and Preparations* (*United States Army in World War II: The War Department*) (Washington, 1950), pp. 367–410 and *passim;* Richard M. Leighton and Robert W. Coakley, *Global Logistics and Strategy, 1940–1943* (*United States Army in World War II: The War Department*) (Washington, 1955), pp. 46–75; G. A. Harrison, *Cross-Channel Attack* (*United States Army in World War II: European Theater of Operations*) (Washington, 1951), pp. 1–45. For a British view, see J. R. M. Butler, *Grand Strategy* (*History of the Second World War: United Kingdom Military Series*) (London, 1957), pp. 417–427 and *passim.*

[3] Quoted in Matloff and Snell, *Strategic Planning,* p. 61.

fication of the concept. It was the Japanese thrust that threatened most immediately American and British holdings. To keep Australia from going the way of nearly all that lay between it and Japan, the United States hurriedly sent reinforcements. Shipping available in the Atlantic was redeployed to help transport 79,000 troops to Australia and New Caledonia.[4]

The British first suggested military operations in French North Africa during staff talks held at the Atlantic Conference in August, 1941, and they referred again to the subject in Washington in December, 1941. Since the United States War Department raised objections, Churchill and Roosevelt, although interested in the project, delayed pushing the invasion of North Africa because of the critical military situation in the Far East.

Fearful of too much diversion, Army leaders continued to press for invasion of Western Europe,[5] and on April 2, 1942, the so-called Marshall Memorandum called for: (a) preparations (Bolero) for cross-Channel invasion, (b) preparations for a possible emergency offensive across the Channel in 1942 (Sledgehammer), and (c) actual invasion and building up of a beachhead for advance inland (Round-up).[6] Churchill and the British Chiefs of Staff accepted in principle the American proposal, and General Marshall announced the creation of a European Theater of Operations for the United States Army with General Eisenhower in command.

Against other pressures for military support, President Roosevelt gave reserved support to General Marshall's argument for continued planning to invade Western Europe, and on May 6, 1942, wrote: "I regard it essential that active operations be conducted in 1942."[7] However, by July, it was clear that the British would not launch Sledgehammer. Opposing the British counterproposal of a North African invasion, General Marshall and Admiral King recommended that "we should turn to the Pacific and strike decisively against Japan"

[4] Only about one-fourth this number of American forces went across the North Atlantic during this same period. *Ibid.*, p. 149; Leighton and Coakley, *Global Logistics and Strategy*, p. 165.

[5] Matloff and Snell, *Strategic Planning*, p. 156.

[6] *Ibid.*, pp. 184–186, and Appendix A; Leighton and Coakley, *Global Logistics and Strategy*, p. 359; Harrison, *Cross-Channel Attack*, pp. 13–21.

[7] Roosevelt's letter to Marshall is reproduced and extracts of his message to his military advisers are quoted in Matloff and Snell, *Strategic Planning*, pp. 220–221.

and assume the defensive against Germany, except for air operations.[8] On July 16, 1942, President Roosevelt rejected the Far Eastern proposal and optimistically predicted, "Defeat of Germany means defeat of Japan, probably without firing a shot or losing a life."[9]

On July 18, General Marshall, Admiral King, and Harry Hopkins arrived in London, as representatives of the President and with instructions to reach quick agreement with the British. There was little the Americans could do but go along with the North African proposal, especially since Roosevelt and Churchill favored it so strongly. The plan, formerly called Gymnast or at times Super-Gymnast, was renamed Torch. In retrospect, although Torch was pushed through by the political leaders over the objections of U.S. military leaders, it appears to have been preferable to a cross-Channel thrust in 1942, for the Allies had not yet developed sufficient resources for a direct attack on the European Continent. On the other hand, invasion of North Africa certainly postponed the assault on Europe.

There were inducements and dangers in the Torch project. The Russians, hard-pressed, wanted action that would divert Germans from the Eastern front. Nazi successes in North Africa were also startling; the "Desert Fox," Lieutenant General Erwin Rommel, and his Afrika Korps took the stronghold Tobruk in the summer of 1942 and pushing eastward threatened Egypt and the Suez Canal. To the Allies, opening a new front in North Africa west of the Germans seemed preferable to efforts to send forces to Egypt. Among the dangers involved in the Torch operation was uncertainty about Spain's reaction. Another question was whether or not the attackers could ward off submarine assaults; further, the western shore of Africa was known for its rugged surf, which alone might wreck landing efforts.[10]

In the slowly developing plans it was decided that most of the attacking forces would be American. Of the three parts of the invasion, one, about 35,000 Americans embarked from the United States, would invade the Atlantic coast of French Morocco and take Casablanca and Port Lyautey. The second, some 39,000 Americans embarked from England, would take Oran. The third, comprising

[8] Memorandum dated July 10, 1942, quoted in *ibid.*, p. 269.

[9] From instructions to Marshall, King, and Hopkins, July 16, 1942. Quoted in *ibid.*, pp. 272–273.

[10] Dwight D. Eisenhower, *Crusade in Europe* (New York, 1948), pp. 78–80.

about 10,000 Americans and 23,000 British, also sailing from Britain, would seize Algiers. The British and American navies shared the task of transporting and protecting the attack forces.[11]

Heavy use of Americans was partly the result of a desire to place these forces in the field against the enemy. In addition, it was hoped that the French would be more receptive to the Americans than to the British, against whom Frenchmen held bitter feelings; the British had been hostile toward the Vichy government and had raided French territory.[12]

General Eisenhower and his deputy commander, General Mark W. Clark, soon found themselves not only involved in planning and preparing the attack, but enmeshed in dealings with the French, who at best would join the invaders or at worst fight against them. Unlike the British, the United States government had maintained diplomatic relations with the Vichy government, and a blunt-speaking Admiral, William D. Leahy, had gone to Vichy as United States Ambassador. Robert D. Murphy, Counselor of the American Embassy at Vichy, visited the French possessions in Africa, worked out an agreement to supply food to North Africa, and arranged for American control officers to aid in its distribution. These men were able to secure information that was of value when the landings came.[13]

In secret discussions Murphy found that French leaders planned an insurrection in North Africa. General Charles Mast in Algiers was one of these, but it was expected that the real leader would be General Henri Giraud, captured by the Germans in the Battle for France, who had later escaped to Unoccupied France. The problem was difficult, since the Americans feared for security reasons to tell the French in detail about the invasion plans. General Clark went in a British submarine for a clandestine meeting in North Africa with General

[11] S. E. Morison, *History of United States Naval Operations in World War II* (Boston, 1951), II, 17, 190; Leighton and Coakley, *Global Logistics and Strategy*, pp. 424–439. For a careful study of the evolution of plans and preparations, see George F. Howe, *Northwest Africa: Seizing the Initiative in the West* (*United States Army in World War II: The Mediterranean Theater of Operations*) (Washington, 1957), pp. 15–85.

[12] Eisenhower, *Crusade in Europe*, pp. 71, 81. The French had been especially aroused by the British firing on French naval vessels in the port of Mers-el-Kebir, near Oran, on July 3, 1940. S. W. Roskill, *The War at Sea* (*History of the Second World War: United Kingdom Military Series*) (London, 1954), I, 242–245.

[13] Morison, *History*, II, 5–6, 9–10.

Mast and his colleagues.[14] Then General Giraud was taken to Gibraltar for a meeting with Eisenhower. At first Giraud demanded that he be head of the expedition, but when he realized that the invasion was already under way, he cast in his lot with the Americans in the hope that he would gain military command in French North Africa after the conquest.[15]

Late in October, the flotilla bound for French Morocco rendezvoused off the Atlantic coast; the fleet of 102 vessels was, for the time, impressive.[16] The test ahead was critical not only for the landing forces but for the Navy. The heavy percentage of the ships' companies consisted of naval reservists; half those aboard the escort carrier, U.S.S. *Sangamon,* for example, had never been to sea before in any capacity, and only five of the aviators aboard the U.S.S. *Santee* were experienced.[17] On Bermuda, their leaders had used three and a half tons of paper, maps, and photographs in briefing sessions, and had had time for but one practice rehearsal on the coast of Bermuda. The landing forces, too, were unevenly prepared; in contrast to those who had had training exercises were a number of men trained as machine gunners who were assigned as riflemen and did not know how to fire the M-1 rifles handed to them as they were about to embark. Bazookas were issued to men "without anybody knowing how to use them or even what they were for."[18]

The successful rendezvous and smooth sailing that followed did not lessen the concern of those in command. Sailing four thousand miles to land on a hostile shore was too new a venture to instill overconfidence. German submarines, African surf, and French resistance

[14] Mark W. Clark, *Calculated Risk* (New York, 1950), pp. 67–89; Howe, *Northwest Africa,* pp. 81–82.

[15] Clark, *Calculated Risk,* pp. 95–100; Eisenhower, *Crusade in Europe,* pp. 99–101. The British brought heavy pressure to bear on Giraud. A. B. Cunningham, *A Sailor's Odyssey* (London, 1951), pp. 486–487.

[16] Morison, *History,* II, 41–44; James Welland, *General George S. Patton, Jr., Man Under Mars* (New York, 1956), pp. 51–55.

[17] A. R. Buchanan (ed.), *The Navy's Air War: A Mission Completed* (New York [1946]), p. 50. The operation posed new and difficult problems of supply for the Army as well as the Navy. Leighton and Coakley, *Global Logistics and Strategy,* pp. 439–445.

[18] R. R. Palmer, B. I. Wiley, and W. R. Keast, *The Procurement and Training of Ground Combat Troops (United States Army in World War II: The Army Ground Forces)* (Washington, 1948), pp. 571–572; Howe, *Northwest Africa,* pp. 60–62. Training for the amphibious operations in the Mediterranean were also uneven and incomplete.

could be all too real. Careful planning and good luck reduced these hazards. Knowing probable submarine locations, Vice Admiral H. K. Hewitt took such a route that no submarines attacked on the trip across the Atlantic. Prize crews boarded one or two intercepted Spanish and Portuguese merchantmen to prevent broadcast of the task force's location. A surf up to fifteen feet in height was reported as the vessels neared their objective, but shortly thereafter the seas moderated.[19]

There were three main parts to the Moroccan landings.[20] On November 8, 1942, against little opposition American forces went ashore with medium tanks at Safi, about 140 miles southwest of Casablanca. The major landings were at Fedala, some sixteen miles east of Casablanca, which was well protected by coastal fortifications and the fifteen-inch guns of the partly constructed battleship *Jean Bart,* in the harbor. The leaders of the invasion hoped that the French would not resist, and some Frenchmen worked to the same end. Naval officers in Morocco, however, were loyal to Pétain, head of the Vichy government, and hesitated to throw themselves into the "dissident" camp of anti-Vichy Frenchmen, a category in which they placed General Giraud. Consequently, coastal batteries opened up, *Jean Bart*'s guns went into action, and French ground troops fought the invader. Despite opposition and landing mishaps, the American forces landed and moved toward Casablanca. Meanwhile a third landing farther east at Mehdia, also sharply opposed, resulted in seizure of the airport at nearby Port Lyautey.

In the late afternoon of November 10, General Auguste Paul Noguès, commanding the French forces, received word that Admiral Darlan, acting in the name of Marshal Pétain, had issued orders to halt useless fighting. Noguès could now move toward an armistice without being considered a "dissident." The armistice reached on November 11 meant the end of fighting in Morocco. There is an air of unreality about the whole episode, for it was not a case of friend against foe,

[19] Morison, *History,* II, 43–54; Howe, *Northwest Africa,* p. 69. The German Naval High Command had ordered no concentration of submarines in the area. On November 4, it had sent six boats to the Mediterranean to replace submarines lost since the previous January. Karl Doenitz, *Memoirs: Ten Years and Twenty Days* (London, 1959), p. 279.

[20] For accounts of the Moroccan landings, see Howe, *Northwest Africa,* pp. 89–181; Morison, *History,* II, 55–178; Walter Karig, Earl Burton, and Stephen L. Freeland, *Battle Report: The Atlantic War* (New York, 1946), II, 175–209.

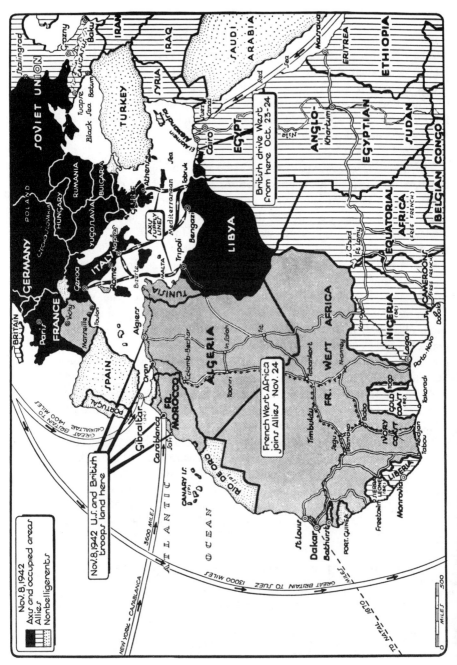

AFRICA LANDING

but of friend against friend. Not that this was a sham battle, for each side fought with all the skill at its command. The shells that landed on the *Murphy* and killed three men were real, and the 490 Frenchmen killed did not rise again when the play was over. But the Americans were in North Africa to fight Germans and Italians; they did not conquer Morocco or demand unconditional surrender. Instead, the tricolor still flew and the French still ruled the French, although it must be admitted that the invaders had some part in deciding which Frenchmen should rule.

The other two phases of Torch were aimed at French African ports in the Mediterranean. Like Morocco, Algeria was but a means to an end—first the conquest of Tunis to stop the flow of reinforcements from Sicily to the Afrika Korps and then the defeat of the Axis forces in North Africa. The force headed for Algiers consisted of 23,000 British and 10,000 American troops and was heavily escorted.[21] Hazards, potential and real, lay ahead. One which did not materialize was attack from Spain, for Franco decided to remain aloof; some think that American diplomacy, with overtones of oil and investments, helped produce this decision. The French Fleet remained in Toulon, and the Italian Fleet proved to be no deterrent.

While the Allies hoped for French cooperation or at least nonresistance, they chose three zones for amphibious attack if necessary.[22] At first the French did not contest the landings on November 8, and then a few hours later they began to check the Allied land advance. French resistance thwarted an effort by two destroyers to move directly into Algiers and take over the port, and the force which did land had to surrender to the French.[23] In another of the landings, troops seized the Maison Blanche airdrome.

French resistance in Algiers did not equal that offered in Morocco. As we have seen, General Eisenhower had reached agreement with General Giraud at Gibraltar. It soon became apparent that the French General did not have the authority he was thought to have, and it was highly doubtful that he could secure obedience in North

[21] Morison, *History*, II, 190.

[22] For accounts of the Algiers landings, see *ibid.*, II, 189–221; Howe, *Northwest Africa*, pp. 229–252. One of the transports, U.S.S. *Stone*, was badly damaged about 155 miles from Algiers. Morison (II, 195) asserts that the vessel was torpedoed by an enemy submarine. Howe (p. 187) indicates a belief that the vessel was attacked by an airplane.

[23] The men were released two days later. Howe, *Northwest Africa*, p. 244.

Africa to a cease-fire order. Instead, it seemed that aside from Marshal Pétain himself there was only one man whose orders would be obeyed. This was Admiral Jean-François Darlan, detested by the democratic world as a collaborationist with the Germans. Darlan was in Algiers visiting his son, who was seriously ill with infantile paralysis.[24]

The French government in the Franco-German treaty of 1940 had agreed to defend North Africa against Allied invasion, and if Pétain switched sides reprisals would be certain. In fact, Hitler was pressing the Vichy government to increase its collaboration by admitting German and Italian forces to Tunisia. Marshal Pétain attempted to steer a middle course by resisting this German pressure and voicing opposition to the Allied landings. On November 10–11, however, Hitler violated the armistice agreement by sending troops into hitherto unoccupied France, and Pétain became little more than a prisoner. A German attempt to seize French naval vessels at Toulon led to their scuttling by the French.

Meanwhile, General Clark arrived in Algiers to try to terminate hostilities and reach agreement among the various French leaders. After some four days of hectic meetings, he emerged with some results. Darlan, apparently acting on secret endorsement from Marshal Pétain, persuaded the French in North Africa to cease fighting the Allies and to join them against the Axis forces. The pro-Vichy and anti-Vichy elements agreed to work together, and appointments satisfied the main leaders; Darlan became High Commissioner and Commander in Chief of Naval Forces and Giraud, Commander in Chief of Ground and Air Forces.[25]

General Clark had reached this agreement on the basis of military exigencies, and the Allied-French understanding of November 13 had the approval of President Roosevelt, Prime Minister Churchill, and the Combined Chiefs of Staff. The Allied leaders soon found that there were political implications. Public opinion in Britain and the

[24] General Clark suggests that Darlan may have remained in Algiers to deal with the Americans. Clark, *Calculated Risk*, p. 107. Howe says that the evidence indicates that Darlan was surprised by the Allied landings. Howe, *Northwest Africa*, p. 250.

[25] For descriptions of the negotiations, see Clark, *Calculated Risk*, pp. 105–132; Howe, *Northwest Africa*, pp. 249–271; Morison, *History*, II, 208–209, 215–219. French West Africa also decided on collaboration with the Allies, and facilities at Dakar on the western bulge of Africa became available to the Allies. Howe, *Northwest Africa*, pp. 271–272.

United States criticized sharply the so-called deal with Darlan as collaboration with a collaborationist. The situation was further complicated by the fact that, instead of working with Vichy, the British government had been encouraging General Charles de Gaulle and the Free French. However, the Free French had made little headway in North Africa, and de Gaulle certainly could not have served Clark's purpose of persuading the French to cease their resistance.[26]

In the meantime, the third force in the Torch operation headed for Oran, a port about two hundred miles west of Algiers. The landing force, which consisted of 39,000 Americans, in general made successful landings, although hampered by inexperience and at times a heavy surf. The opposition was stiffer than at Algiers, and two British vessels which tried to run directly into the harbor were sunk. Within a few days the cease-fire order ended resistance, and salvage crews started to work on the scuttled vessels in the harbor.[27]

The planners of the invasions had considered landing farther east than Algiers and had concluded that German air opposition from Sicily would be too great a hazard. However, after taking Algiers, the invaders decided to move against the eastern ports, Bougie and Bône. By November 15, they had secured their objectives in the face of heavy German air attacks.[28]

Although surprised by the Allied landings in North Africa, the Germans reacted quickly with a counterinvasion of Tunisia. Troop-carrying planes took soldiers in at such a rate that most of the French leaders decided that collaboration was preferable to resistance, and Tunisia fell under the control of the Nazis and their Italian allies.[29]

The British and Americans also realized the strategic significance of Tunisia, the northern portion of which jutted into the Mediter-

[26] Eisenhower defended the dealings with Darlan, and Roosevelt issued a public statement accepting Eisenhower's actions as a temporary arrangement. He stated also that he did not favor a permanent arrangement with Darlan. Robert E. Sherwood, *Roosevelt and Hopkins: An Intimate History* (New York, 1948), pp. 651–653.

[27] For accounts of the Oran landings, see Morison, *History*, II, 222–238; Roskill, *The War at Sea*, II, 325–328: Howe, *Northwest Africa*, pp. 192–228; George F. Howe, *The Battle History of the 1st Armored Division "Old Ironsides"* (Washington, 1954), pp. 24–47.

[28] Howe, *Northwest Africa*, 334–335; Morison, *History*, II, 220–221.

[29] In contrast to widespread collaboration were the actions of General Georges Barre and Admiral Louis Derrien who sank vessels in the harbors of Tunis and Bizerte in an effort to delay use by the Germans. Howe, *Northwest Africa*, p. 258.

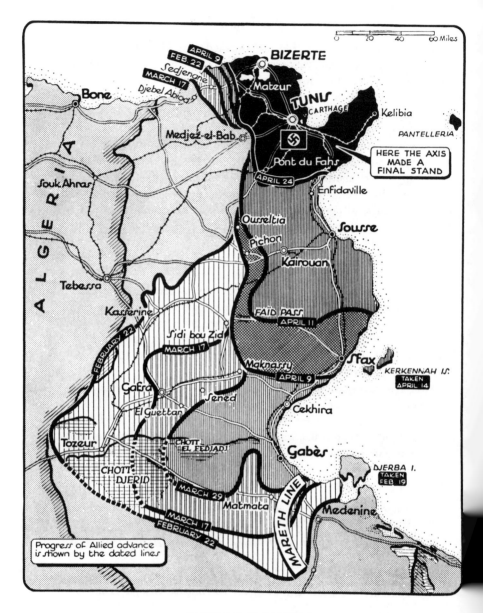

BATTLE FOR TUNISIA

ranean less than a hundred miles from Sicily, and once in North Africa, after seizing Bougie and Bône, the Allies started a quick overland move toward Tunisia.[30] The odds against success were heavy; German strength in Tunisia was mounting, Axis air strength was too near, the land was rugged, the attitude of the resident population was uncertain, and the rainy season was imminent. The prize was worth the gamble, for with Tunisia Eisenhower could bring his half of a great pincers movement to bear on the Axis forces in North Africa.[31] Farther east, the tide of war had turned, and General Sir Bernard L. Montgomery's Eighth Army was moving westward after a rapidly retreating foe.

General Eisenhower made the winter thrust into Tunisia primarily a British enterprise by assigning the task to Lieutenant General Sir Kenneth A. N. Anderson and the British First Army. Anderson was a Scot whose ability outweighed his blunt manners, which irritated many of his British and American associates.[32] Eisenhower detailed several American units to assist in the enterprise; elements of the 1st Armored Division ("Old Ironsides") and of the U.S. 1st Infantry Division were to participate in the invasion, and parts of the U.S. 34th Division guarded lines of communications, as did French troops.

Anderson's advance forces pushed across Tunisia to points within twenty or twenty-five miles of the seaport objectives, Bizerte and Tunis, but there the forward movement ended.[33] Among numerous restrictive factors perhaps the most important was the weather, for winter rains produced a mud that literally bogged down the attack.[34] Even air strips were affected, until later in the campaign the air forces thought to use isolated sand outcroppings for the construction of airfields.[35]

On November 23, Eisenhower transferred his headquarters from Gibraltar to Algiers. General Mark Clark was appointed head of a

[30] Morison, *History*, II, 182. Admiral Cunningham, Commander in Chief, Mediterranean, wanted to make initial landings farther east. *Ibid.*, II, 182–183; Cunningham, *A Sailor's Odyssey*, pp. 470, 501. General Clark expressed a similar view. Clark, *Calculated Risk*, pp. 134–135.

[31] Eisenhower, *Crusade in Europe*, pp. 115–119.

[32] Eisenhower praised Anderson highly. *Ibid.*, pp. 83, 118. Clark was not so complimentary. Clark, *Calculated Risk*, p. 41.

[33] Howe, *Northwest Africa*, pp. 299–344.

[34] Eisenhower, *Crusade in Europe*, pp. 116–117.

[35] W. F. Craven and J. L. Cate, *The Army Air Forces in World War II* (Chicago, 1949), II, 117.

newly activated army, the U.S. Fifth Army, whose immediate task was to hold against a Spanish thrust if it should come and, more important, to prepare for later invasion of Europe.[36] Visiting the front and impressed by the fighting qualities of the Allied troops, Eisenhower sought to strengthen the front even at the risk of weakening the rear.[37] As part of the move, he reorganized the functions and control of the Air Forces by calling the American airman, Lieutenant General Carl A. Spaatz, to Algiers, cutting administrative red tape, and making him Acting Deputy Commander for Air. Making the most of a rather vague authority, Spaatz sought not only to coordinate the activity of the U.S. Twelfth Air Force and the British Eastern Air Force, but to reconcile the conflict of strategic and tactical air warfare. Generally speaking, he solved the problem by assigning the British to tactical operations with the ground forces and by shifting the objectives of the U.S. heavy bombers to seaports.[38]

The Tunisian campaign was a testing ground for officers and men, and in the process of adjustment to battle experience both inevitably made errors. Early coordination between ground and air forces was poor; at a critical point P-38 fighters, mistaking a U.S. Tank Destroyer Battalion for the enemy, destroyed or damaged most of the vehicles and killed or wounded numbers of the men.[39] American foot soldiers, harassed by diving Stuka bombers, cared little for the strategic concept that the Air Force should strike seaports in preference to airfields.

The forward movement of the Allies halted in the face of counterattacks by the enemy, and a second visit to the front convinced Eisenhower that winter had thwarted his gamble and that he would have to wait to try again for his objective.[40]

Meanwhile U.S. paratroopers had landed at the interior airfield of Youks-les-Bains and joined by friendly French irregulars had made a flank move to the south and east toward the port of Sfax.[41] When reversals in the north threatened this minor operation, General Eisen-

[36] Clark, *Calculated Risk*, pp. 136–137.
[37] Eisenhower, *Crusade in Europe*, p. 121.
[38] Craven and Cate, *The A.A.F. in World War II*, II, 108.
[39] Howe, *The Battle History of the 1st Armored Division*, p. 69.
[40] Eisenhower, *Crusade in Europe*, pp. 123–124; Howe, *Northwest Africa*, pp. 352–354.
[41] Craven and Cate, *The A.A.F. in World War II*, II, 81; Howe, *Northwest Africa*, p. 279.

hower sent General L. R. Fredendall to command a flank sector with orders to defend the mountain passes and prepare an armored force to challenge any advance against communications by the enemy.[42] Assigned to his II Corps Headquarters were the U.S. 1st Armored Division, the U.S. 1st Infantry Division, the 36th Division, and most of the U.S. 9th Division.

Bitterness of the French toward the British and lack of understanding between the British and Americans for a time kept Eisenhower from creating a unified battle command. Continued German pressure made the move necessary, and in January Eisenhower placed General Anderson in command of the Allied forces in Tunisia.[43]

While the winter struggle continued at the front, high military planners met in the Casablanca Conference. Busy with his immediate problem, Eisenhower spent but one day at the conference, but the results of the conference tended to clarify the situation in North Africa. It became apparent that the struggle for Tunisia was a part of the wider struggle for North Africa, and to emphasize this point and provide unified control the conference leaders decided that when the British forces advancing through Tripoli reached Tunisia they would come under Eisenhower's command. The appointment of an American to top command came from American potentialities and not accomplishments to date. It was the British forces which were waging aggressive warfare from Egypt, and, in fact, Eisenhower soon concluded that the forces in Tunisia should hold their ground rather than attempt a major offensive.[44]

In February, somewhat reluctantly, General Rommel launched an offensive which became known as the Battle of Kasserine Pass.[45] This

[42] Eisenhower, *Crusade in Europe*, p. 126.

[43] *Ibid.*, p. 127. The French were extremely reluctant to serve under the British. General Juin, however, agreed to the reorganization of command. General Anderson received operational control over the French, but at the same time General Eisenhower directed him: "I know that you will be fully sympathetic with the efforts of General Juin to conserve the French forces and uphold the honor of France, and that you will always welcome him at your headquarters and at the front, and afford him every facility which will contribute to that end." Eisenhower to Anderson, Jan. 26, 1943, quoted in Howe, *Northwest Africa*, p. 384.

[44] Howe, *Northwest Africa*, pp. 383–386.

[45] For descriptions of the Battle of Kasserine Pass, see *ibid.*, pp. 438–441; Omar N. Bradley, *A Soldier's Story* (New York, 1951), pp. 25–27; Howe, *The Battle History of the 1st Armored Division*, pp. 180–198; Erwin Rommel, *The Rommel Papers* (ed. by B. H. Liddell Hart) (London, 1953), pp. 401–407.

was one of the passes being guarded by the U.S. II Corps; unfortunately, instead of defending adequately the shoulders of the pass, American troops spread thinly across the floor of the valley behind three lines of mines, some of which had been laid in the dark by men who had never seen the region in the daylight and who had simply placed the mines on top of the ground. The Allied forces nevertheless stubbornly held the pass on February 19, the first day of the attack. With additional forces the Germans pushed through the pass the following afternoon. Heavy fighting continued until February 22, when Rommel, realizing that he could not succeed against increasing Allied strength, withdrew his forces to direct them against the British Eighth Army assembling at the Mareth Line. The Battle of Kasserine Pass taught the American forces hard lessons in tactical warfare, although Rommel won at best a brief tactical victory which did not affect the strategy of the campaign. In some cases, American troops had shown inexperience and in other instances both stubborn courage and ability, which won the praise of the opposing general, Rommel.[46]

Feeling that not all officers were meeting the test of war, Eisenhower requested the assignment to the area of a man who would act as his "eyes and ears."[47] The man selected was Brigadier General Omar N. Bradley, a classmate of Eisenhower at West Point, who, however, had not served with him in the intervening years. Bradley, who became one of the ablest generals of the war, after thirty-two years' service in the Army received his initial battle experience in North Africa. Acting on Bradley's reports, Eisenhower replaced General Fredendall with General Patton, called from Morocco.[48]

Major General George S. Patton, Jr. was already one of the most colorful and controversial of American generals. His flamboyant attire, bloody speeches, and stern discipline over desert training in Arizona and California had attracted wide attention. His command in Morocco, aside from diplomatic and social maneuvering, had been inactive, and Patton was itching for a battle command. He blew into Tunisia like a cyclone, with the two stars of his commission painted on his steel helmet, on the command car, and on one of the flags flying by the motor's hood. He gave the men a fighting speech, punc-

[46] Ibid., p. 406.
[47] Eisenhower, Crusade in Europe, p. 215.
[48] Bradley, A Soldier's Story, pp. 39–42; Howe, Northwest Africa, p. 487.

tuated with expletives and dripping with the "blood and guts" for which his utterances were known, but this time Patton was not talking to raw recruits or even finished trainees. He was addressing men who had seen war firsthand, and to many the speech was raucous rather than inspiring. A wounded Ranger in an evacuation hospital commented, "We provide the blood, and he provides the guts."[49]

Patton produced further irritation and possibly helped create the fighting force he wanted by tightening discipline. As a symbol, he insisted that every soldier, whether in a combat post or repairing an engine, wear combat helmet, leggings, and tie as part of his uniform. He declared that officers should be leaders and he insisted that officers identify themselves clearly by painting their insignia on their helmets, despite the fact that some officers noted that they would also identify themselves to the enemy.[50]

In actual military leadership during the ensuing campaign, Patton was less spectacular and more solid than his theatrical ways might have indicated. Basically, Eisenhower's plan was for the eastern and western forces of the Allies to strike alternate blows at the enemy and force the Axis to move its mobile units back and forth from one front to another. Thus when Montgomery planned a heavy offensive against the Mareth Line between Tunisia and Tripoli, Patton received orders to make a diversionary thrust from Gafsa toward El Guettar in the southern Tunisian mountains.[51] There the Americans showed that they had learned the lesson of Kasserine Pass by gaining control of the sides of the pass before turning the defile into a trap for counterattacking Panzers. By March Rommel had returned to the European Continent, called back by Hitler for a long overdue sick leave.[52]

In mid-April II Army Corps received another commander, when Eisenhower relieved Patton and returned him to his old command over the I Armored Corps to prepare for the invasion of Sicily.[53]

[49] Quoted in Welland, *General George S. Patton, Jr.*, p. 76.

[50] William Bancroft Mellor, *Patton: Fighting Man* (New York, 1946), pp. 174–176; Bradley, *A Soldier's Story*, pp. 44–45.

[51] *Ibid.*, pp. 50–51. Before the war the French had constructed the system of defenses known as the Mareth Line to guard against the invasion of Tunisia from Italian Tripolitania. Howe, *The Battle History of the 1st Armored Division*, pp. 139–140.

[52] Rommel left March 9, 1943, and did not return to North Africa. Howe, *Northwest Africa*, p. 519; Rommel, *The Rommel Papers*, p. 418.

[53] Howe, *Northwest Africa*, p. 608.

Bradley earlier had become Patton's deputy corps commander and was a logical and excellent replacement. A leader rather than a driver of men, in North Africa Bradley gave a clear indication of the valuable service he would later give the Allied cause.

When the Germans and Italians retired for a last stand in the northeast corner of Tunisia, Bradley insisted that U.S. forces share in striking the final blow, lest the victory appear to be entirely British. Eisenhower and Alexander agreed to assign the II Army Corps the task of taking Bizerte, while the British moved toward Tunis. Bradley skillfully moved his forces across the lines of the British First Army to reach the jumping-off place for the attack.[54]

In the attack which began April 23, the forces under Bradley followed a tested formula as infantry and other ground troops struck at the hilly defenses of the enemy before using tanks. Then when the way was cleared, the tanks began a series of devastating attacks that brought the opposing enemy to collapse. On May 7, Bizerte fell, and a day later enemy forces in the area surrendered unconditionally. Meanwhile the British had blasted their way against Tunis with equal success. That city also fell on May 7, and British forces quickly cut across Cape Bon to prevent the Germans from retiring there for another last stand.[55]

Although the ground forces deserve full measure of credit for victory in North Africa, Allied naval and air arms contributed materially to success. Air Force leaders had opposed the North African operation as a wasteful sideshow, but once the decision had been made they gave strong support.[56] At first winter conditions and absence of usable airfields kept the Army Air Forces from active participation in air-ground operations, and aircraft with the British Eighth Army were more successful. At the same time, the U.S. IX Bomber Command, organized at Cairo in October, 1942, advanced to newly gained airports and concentrated on enemy-held seaports.[57] The Allied Air Forces not only were interested in bombing Axis-held North African

[54] Bradley, A Soldier's Story, pp. 56–59, 71–82.

[55] For accounts of the last Allied offensive in Tunisia, see Howe, Northwest Africa, pp. 595–668; Bradley, A Soldier's Story, pp. 71–101; Howe, The Battle History of the 1st Armored Division, pp. 222–251. A group of Germans held out for two days in the southern part of Cape Bon. Howe, Northwest Africa, p. 663.

[56] Craven and Cate, The A.A.F. in World War II, II, 205.

[57] Ibid., II, 33, 96, 100–103.

seaports, but they also sought to destroy shipping en route to these ports.[58] In January, their attacks on shipping led to increased defenses, including pontoon rafts carrying antiaircraft weapons.[59] As a result casualties increased on both sides.

In March, the Allies began an attack on Axis air strength in southern Tunisia. Gradually the technique of attacking airfields proved itself, and Axis planes found fewer and fewer fields from which to operate. The Stuka, which had been so destructive in the early stages of the Tunisian campaign, came to be an easy target for Allied planes; on April 3, 1943, for example, Allied fighters destroyed fourteen Stukas with the loss of only one Spitfire.[60] Other contributions of Allied aircraft included improved coordination of air-ground attack and raids on cities in Sicily and Italy.[61] Allied planes also successfully attacked the air transport of troops; on April 18 the destruction was so great that it was termed the Palm Sunday Massacre. Losses were so high that toward the end of the month the Germans stopped sending daylight convoys, although they still attempted to fly some planes in at night.

During the final assault on Bizerte and Tunis the Allied Air Forces conducted an around-the-clock bombing program; by April 22, the German Air Force gave up its part of the struggle and left control of the air to the Allies.[62] As the campaign neared its close, there was some thought that the enemy might escape to Sicily or Italy. Remembering Dunkirk, the British Navy prepared to intercept the troops, but they chose surrender on land to slaughter at sea.[63]

When the end came, the Allies were amazed at the size of the haul, for in the trap which had closed in northern Tunisia were more than a quarter of a million enemy troops. The five-month campaign, although it delayed an attack on the Continent, was a significant, even

[58] British submarines, in particular, had been successful in night attacks on shipping. *Ibid.*, II, 145–146; Roskill, *The War at Sea*, 439–440.

[59] These pontoon rafts, known as Siebel ferries, were of course designed mainly as transports, but in this case their firepower gave them added value. Craven and Cate, *The A.A.F. in World War II*, II, 149. The Germans had built the first of these ferries for the planned invasion of England in 1940. G. W. L. Nicholson, *Official History of the Canadian Army in the Second World War* (Ottawa, 1957), II, 172.

[60] Craven and Cate, *The A.A.F. in World War II*, II, 176.

[61] *Ibid.*, II, 178–181, 188.

[62] *Ibid.*, II, 200–201.

[63] Morison, *History*, II, 259–260; Roskill, *The War at Sea*, II, 441–442.

necessary stage in the war against the Axis forces. The Germans had lost many men, and the luster of the Desert Fox shone less brightly. The North African operation hurt the *Luftwaffe* and dealt a lethal blow to the Italian Army. Success of the operation reopened the Mediterranean to the Allies, made Malta, Suez, and the Near East more secure. Although there were periods of bitterness among the Allies, overbalancing these things was the gradually acquired sense of common purpose against a common foe.[64]

[64] For appraisals of the North African operations, see Bradley, *A Soldier's Story*, pp. 100–101; Eisenhower, *Crusade in Europe*, p. 158; Howe, *Northwest Africa*, pp. 669–677.

CHAPTER 8

Sicily and Italy

WHILE the North African conquest was still in progress, Allied leaders began planning their next moves. Stalin declined to attend a conference on the ground that he had pressing duties at home, but he indicated pointedly that what was needed was a second front against Hitler.[1] Although failing to secure Russian attendance, Roosevelt and Churchill decided to meet at Casablanca. The only reason for holding the conference in North Africa, states Harry Hopkins, was that Roosevelt "wanted to make a trip."[2] He was tired of having others travel for him as his representatives. As in the case of the Newfoundland meeting, elaborate provisions were made to keep Roosevelt's activities secret. On the train to Miami, for example, Filipino sailors replaced the regular Pullman porters, cooks, and waiters. The President and his party flew to their destination by way of Trinidad, Brazil, and West Africa.[3] Housed in villas outside Casablanca, Roosevelt, Churchill, and their advisers met from January 12 to 25, 1943, in nearby Anfa Hotel, from which came the official name, Anfa Conference.

Although the atmosphere was generally friendly, the Allies had to reconcile divergent views before reaching agreement. Churchill had advocated attacking Sicily, Italy, and possibly Sardinia in an effort to

[1] Message from Stalin to Roosevelt quoted in Winston Churchill, *The Second World War* (Boston, 1950), IV, 667.
[2] Robert E. Sherwood, *Roosevelt and Hopkins: An Intimate History* (New York, 1948), p. 669.
[3] *Ibid.*, pp. 668–674.

knock Italy out of the war, commit German troops to Southern Europe, and perhaps draw Turkey into the war on the Allied side. He envisaged attacks across the British Channel as coming only when German power had been weakened.[4] The Americans wished to reduce forces in the Mediterranean to a minimum at the end of the North African campaign and concentrate on preparations for a great cross-Channel invasion. Unlike the British, they wanted Far Eastern action to be more than a holding operation. Instead, they wanted aggressive movements to keep the Japanese from consolidating their holdings.[5]

Despite their differences, the leaders at Casablanca emerged with much agreement and some concessions. The basic compromise was to delay a cross-Channel invasion until after 1943 and, in return, permit the United States to retain the initiative in the Pacific, while the Americans accepted the British proposal to invade Sicily. Strategic bombing of Germany, which was gradually becoming a joint British-American enterprise, received the endorsement of the conference.[6]

In addition to making military decisions, Churchill and Roosevelt attempted to deal with political problems.[7] They failed in their effort

[4] Churchill as a result of Russian successes evidently anticipated that Germany would weaken. Churchill, *The Second World War*, II, 657; Richard M. Leighton and Robert W. Coakley, *Global Logistics and Strategy, 1940–1943* (*United States Army in World War II: The War Department*) (Washington, 1955), p. 664.

[5] *Ibid.*, pp. 665–666. There were some differences of opinion among the Americans, who as a result did not present a solid front at the conference. The Joint Chiefs of Staff had not agreed on the relationship any new action in the Mediterranean might have on a cross-Channel offensive and air operations in Europe, or on operations in the Pacific and the Far East. Admiral Ernest J. King, as always, was primarily concerned with the war in the Pacific. Maurice Matloff and Edwin M. Snell, *Strategic Planning for Coalition Warfare, 1941–1942* (*United States Army in World War II: The War Department*) (Washington, 1953), pp. 378–380; Gordon A. Harrison, *Cross-Channel Attack* (*United States Army in World War II: The European Theater of Operations*) (Washington, 1951), p. 38.

[6] For discussions of the Casablanca Conference, see *ibid.*, pp. 38–45; Leighton and Coakley, *Global Logistics and Strategy*, pp. 666–686; Sherwood, *Roosevelt and Hopkins*, pp. 674–697. British accounts include Churchill, *The Second World War*, IV, 674–695; John Slessor, *The Central Blue: The Autobiography of Sir John Slessor, Marshal of the RAF* (New York, 1957), pp. 433–463.

[7] Although political matters were considered, Roosevelt did not take Hull to Casablanca, and at Roosevelt's suggestion Churchill left Anthony Eden in England. Hull protested but was told that the meeting would deal with military matters. Cordell Hull, *The Memoirs of Cordell Hull* (New York, 1948), II, 1110. See also Sherwood, *Roosevelt and Hopkins*, pp. 661–662.

to bring together in real harmony General Giraud and General de Gaulle. Overshadowing this matter as the war continued was the policy of "unconditional surrender," which Hanson W. Baldwin lists as one of the "great mistakes" of the war. The British General J. F. C. Fuller, in an extreme statement, asserts that it turned the "soft underbelly" of Europe "into a crocodile's back; prolonged the war; wrecked Italy; and wasted thousands of American and British lives."[8]

The phrase "unconditional surrender" did not actually appear as a formal agreement at Casablanca; instead, it was part of a statement made by Roosevelt shortly after the termination of the conference. One of his purposes was to assure Stalin that we would fight to the end; ironically, the Russian leader was one of those who criticized the concept of "unconditional surrender." Critics of the phrase insist that it failed to distinguish between the enemy people and the enemy government and made the cause of the former common with that of their overlords. The immediate circumstances surrounding the Casablanca Conference help in part to explain the phrase. Charged with dealing with French collaborators, the President sought to make it clear that he would negotiate with no such persons emanating from Germany.[9]

It seems to this writer that the influence of "unconditional surrender" has been exaggerated. It doubtless made good grist for Goebbels' propagandist mill, and may have delayed briefly the Japanese decision to surrender. The German and Japanese military leaders, however, certainly were realists who knew that few surrenders are unconditional and who could have seen that the surrender of the Italians did not fall into that category.

---

[8] J. F. C. Fuller, *The Second World War, 1939–45; A Strategical and Tactical History* (New York, 1949), p. 265.

[9] The military historian Maurice Matloff suggests, "What the President appeared to be offering at the time was a simple formula of common and resolute purpose—a slogan that would rally the Allies for victory and drive home to friend and foe alike that this time there would be no negotiated peace and no 'escape clauses' offered by another Fourteen Points." He further asserts that "For the U. S. military staff, unconditional surrender was to serve essentially as a military objective, reinforcing their own notions of a concentrated, decisive war." Maurice Matloff, *Strategic Planning for Coalition Warfare, 1943–1944 (United States Army in World War II: The War Department)* (Washington, 1959), pp. 40–41. For discussions of "unconditional surrender" at Casablanca, see references in *ibid.,* p. 39n and Herbert Feis, *Churchill, Roosevelt, Stalin: The War They Waged and the Peace They Sought* (Princeton, 1957), pp. 100–113; Sherwood, *Roosevelt and Hopkins,* pp. 693–697; Churchill, *The Second World War,* IV, 688–695.

The Germans showed unexpected resistance and, as we have seen, it was not until early in May that fighting in Tunisia ended. Perhaps this delay intensified Allied realization that invasion of Sicily would not be easy. Although only ninety miles from Africa, much of the island was mountainous, it had half a dozen airfields, and could be reinforced easily from Italy.[10]

The Combined Chiefs of Staff appointed Eisenhower, now a full general, Supreme Commander of the project, which was named Husky.[11] In planning a British-American amphibious assault, ground and naval forces generally worked well together, but naval sources charged lack of cooperation by the Army Air Force in supplying air support over the landing beaches.[12] Air Force historians, on the other hand, while admitting that fighter support at times was lacking, insist that several factors, including distance from Malta or North African bases, explain the matter. They also assert that Army Air Force planes were performing the more valuable function of striking at distant airfields to reduce the air strength of the enemy.[13] Most writers agree on the effectiveness of air power in the early stages of the Husky operation. It secured air supremacy prior to the invasion and softened up the intervening island of Pantelleria, which surrendered without a land engagement and thus provided an airfield for about eighty planes.[14]

The task of invading Sicily fell to two armies, the United States Seventh Army, under General Patton, and the British Eighth Army, under General Montgomery. The forces left from ports extending from Algiers to Port Said. Some of Montgomery's troops made practice landings in the Red Sea.[15]

Attempting to mislead the enemy, the Allies floated a corpse ashore in Spain with letters indicating that an attack on Sicily would be a feint and that the real thrust would be at Greece or Sardinia. Hitler

---

[10] Samuel E. Morison, *History of United States Naval Operations in World War II* (Boston, 1954), IX, 12–13.

[11] *Ibid.,* IX, 10–11. A logical competitor for the assignment was General Alexander, who was senior to Eisenhower. Eisenhower received a promotion to general and the appointment to lead Husky. Sherwood, *Roosevelt and Hopkins,* p. 677.

[12] Morison, *History,* IX, 16.

[13] W. F. Craven and J. L. Cate, *The Army Air Forces in World War II* (Chicago, 1949), II, 418–419, 450–453.

[14] *Ibid.,* II, 419–434; Morison, *History,* II, 275–279.

[15] *Ibid.,* IX, 55–70; 148–150.

was misled and sent troops toward Greece, but Marshal Albert Kesselring, commanding German forces in southern Italy, was not and transferred the Hermann Göring Panzer Division across the Strait of Messina to bolster Sicily's defenses.[16]

According to Morison, the Allied force that headed for Sicily was the "greatest amphibious operation in recorded history, if measured by the strength of the initial assault." Vice Admiral H. K. Hewitt had under his command 580 ships and beaching craft in addition to 1,124 ship-borne landing craft. Vice Admiral Sir Bertram Ramsay, commanding the eastern naval task force, had 795 vessels and 715 ship-borne landing craft.[17]

The task force moving toward Sicily on the morning of July 9, 1943, encountered what Army writers call high winds and naval historians term a mistral. Whatever the name, it threatened the expedition, as men were made miserable by the wallowing of vessels and as there was danger that ships would miss their appointed places in the landing operations. Fortunately, the winds moderated and the seas began to subside. Foul weather actually may have served a useful purpose in curtailing enemy reconnaissance, and the higher surf in some places enabled landing craft to cross sand bars that normally obstructed access to many Sicilian beaches.[18]

Early the following morning the Americans made three landings along the southern coast, while the British landed in two operations farther east and north. The enemy was not surprised, but it was not ready, for information had not passed down the line to some of the shore defenses. The assault, against varied resistance, was of such a proportion that it could not be stopped, although this fact was not immediately apparent as heavy congestion on some beaches forced loaded craft to return to sea. Enemy use of tanks and temporary control of the air hampered landing operations; gradually, however, Sherman tanks began to get ashore.[19] Naval firepower was important as vessels offshore became virtually supporting artillery for the land forces.[20]

[16] *Ibid.*, IX, 45–47; Ewen Montagu, *The Man Who Never Was* (Philadelphia, 1954), *passim*. This was one of a number of cover plans for Allied landings.

[17] Morison, *History*, IX, 28–29.

[18] *Ibid.*, IX, 67–69; Omar N. Bradley, *A Soldier's Story* (New York, 1951), p. 126.

[19] Morison, *History*, IX, 71–147.

[20] *Ibid.*, IX, 88–89, 97, 103–104, 117.

The use of airborne troops was one of the less fortunate aspects of the campaign. High winds scattered the first waves of paratroopers throughout a wide area of Sicily. Even though their striking power was lessened, they helped weaken enemy morale by giving the impression of an airborne invasion that appeared larger than it was.[21] The poorest coordination between the air command and the other services came on the night of July 11. That afternoon Tactical Air Force Headquarters in Tunisia informed Admiral Hewitt that 144 transport planes would fly to Sicily in the evening to land paratroopers on an emergency air strip. Unfortunately, the planes flew through the battle area within range of Army and Navy guns, and there had not been time to pass the word to hold fire. Furthermore, shortly before the Allied transport planes arrived from one direction, enemy planes came in for a raid from the other. Consequently, Americans from vessels and from the beaches fired on their own aircraft. Twenty-three planes did not return, and many others were damaged; sixty pilots and crewmen and 20 percent of the airborne troops were killed. The costly experience increased interservice friction; in the Navy and ground forces it stimulated training in aircraft recognition, and it taught the Air Force that the safest guide was to avoid naval craft when transporting troops.[22]

By the end of the second day more than 80,000 men, 7,000 vehicles, and 300 tanks had been put ashore, and the next task was to overrun the island.[23] The Americans set out to conquer the western portion, and the British advanced toward a small but more difficult objective, the eastern part including Messina, just across the strait from Italy. Without too much difficulty, the Americans moved northward across the island and took the port of Palermo. By the end of the month, they joined the British to exert pressure on the enemy around Messina. At the time Allied leaders thought they were winning the campaign, for they were pushing the Germans and Italians ahead of

[21] *Ibid.*, IX, 120–121; Craven and Cate, *The A.A.F. in World War II*, II, 449.

[22] *Ibid.*, II, 453–455. Morison, *History*, IX, 120–121.

[23] George C. Marshall, "Biennial Report of the Chief of Staff of the United States Army July 1, 1943 to June 30, 1945, to the Secretary of War," *The War Reports of General of the Army George C. Marshall, Chief-of-Staff, General of the Army H. H. Arnold, Commanding General, Army Air Forces, Fleet Admiral Ernest J. King, Commander-in-Chief, United States Fleet and Chief of Naval Operations* (Philadelphia and New York, 1947), p. 162.

them.[24] Actually, the enemy was conducting a careful withdrawal with the purpose of evacuating as many German troops from Sicily as possible. While the Allies successfully conquered the island in a thirty-eight-day campaign, they let the bulk of the German forces and many Italian troops slip across the strait into Italy.[25]

Some experts, including commanders of the participating task forces, feel that the strait was too narrow to prevent the mass evacuation;[26] others suggest that properly directed fire from battleships could have silenced the heavy shore batteries and enabled cruisers and other craft to clear the shores of defenses and prevent the ferries from operating.[27] Army Air Force attacks hampered but did not prevent successful evacuation.[28]

It was August 17 when the Allied troops pushed their way into the rubble heap that had been Messina, only to find that the enemy had gone. The Sicilian conquest, however, had broken the power of one dictator. When, after the invasion of North Africa, Italians could see the possibility if not the certainty of defeat, opposition began to develop against the government. The Fascists themselves began to fall apart, military leaders began to turn against Mussolini, and anti-Fascists of all types increased their activity.[29] The first step toward

[24] *Ibid.*, pp. 162–163; Eisenhower, *Crusade in Europe*, pp. 174–179; Bradley, *A Soldier's Story*, pp. 134–164. In the Sicilian campaign General Patton became an increasingly controversial figure, for while going through field hospitals, he became enraged at two soldiers whom he considered malingerers and he abused them vocally and struck them until checked by hospital personnel. The news of the incident became known and strong pressure was brought to bear on Eisenhower to relieve Patton. Considering Patton too valuable a field commander to lose, Eisenhower retained him but instructed Patton to make a public apology to all concerned. Patton complied with the instruction. Eisenhower, *Crusade in Europe*, pp. 179–180; Bradley, *A Soldier's Story*, pp. 160–162.

[25] Morison, *History*, IX, 209–218. It is asserted that the Italians who crossed into Italy were of little fighting value. Not all escaped; a good many were captured.

[26] Eisenhower, *Crusade in Europe*, p. 177; A. B. Cunningham, *A Sailor's Odyssey* (London, 1951), p. 556.

[27] Morison, *History*, IX, pp. 216–218.

[28] Craven and Cate, *The A.A.F. in World War II*, II, 472–473. The Germans attempted to claim that the evacuation was more successful than Dunkirk. There is evidence that they suffered greater losses of men and equipment than they admitted. G. W. Nicholson, *Official History of the Canadian Army in the Second World War* (Ottawa, 1957), II, 173–174.

[29] Norman Kogan, *Italy and the Allies* (Cambridge, 1956), pp. 13–18.

the downfall of Mussolini was a series of strikes in March, 1943, in which the government was forced to negotiate with the strikers on the issue of wages. A second move was the organization of a Committee of Anti-Fascist Parties, headed by Ivanoe Bonomi, which decided to work with rather than against the monarchy in an effort to eliminate the Fascist dictatorship. At first the King resisted pressure, but when in July Italian military forces collapsed in Sicily, the end was in sight for Mussolini.[30] High military officers turned against him when it became apparent that he had neither the will nor the ability to take Italy out of the war, and then certain Fascist leaders, anxious to preserve or improve their own positions, took the actual steps leading to *Il Duce's* downfall. They persuaded the reluctant Mussolini to call the Fascist Grand Council into session and engineered a vote which the King interpreted as one of no confidence in Mussolini and he notified the dictator of his dismissal.[31]

The news of the collapse came as a general surprise, except, perhaps, to the unorganized combination that brought it about. The Allies had not realized the weakness of Mussolini's position, and even the Germans, who knew of the desperate situation of both Mussolini and Italy, were not prepared for the action and took no immediate steps against the new government.[32] There was no Fascist counterrevolution; no one rushed to the rescue when the police arrested Mussolini and took him as a prisoner first to small islands off Italy and Sardinia and then back to a mountain hotel in central Italy.[33]

The King appointed as head of the government Marshal Pietro Badoglio, former Chief of the General Staff, a man past his prime, who had taken no part in the plot against Mussolini.[34] Next came the difficult task of disengaging Italy from Germany and from the war. At first the Badoglio government asserted that it was continuing the war; taking advantage of this pretense, Hitler quickly poured troops

---

[30] *Ibid.*, pp. 18, 22.

[31] *Ibid.*, pp. 22–25; Arnold Toynbee and Veronica Toynbee (ed.), *Hitler's Europe (Survey of International Affairs, 1939–1946)* (London, 1954), pp. 313–315.

[32] Kogan, *Italy and the Allies*, pp. 26, 28–31; Toynbee and Toynbee (ed.), *Hitler's Europe*, pp. 315–316; Erwin Rommel,*The Rommel Papers* (ed. by B. H. Liddell Hart) (London, 1953), p. 431.

[33] Toynbee and Toynbee (ed.), *Hitler's Europe*, p. 315; Winston Churchill, *The Second World War* (Boston, 1955), V, 116.

[34] Toynbee and Toynbee (ed.), *Hitler's Europe*, p. 315.

into the Italian peninsula, partly to save the German troops already
there and partly to control Italy.[35]

While protesting friendship for Germany, the new government was
secretly trying to take itself out of the conflict. There had been peace
feelers before Mussolini's collapse,[36] but the first really significant
meetings came in Spain and Portugal. On August 19–20, 1943, General Giuseppe Castellano secretly met British and American military
representatives in Lisbon and startled them with an offer, not to make
peace, but to switch sides and become an ally against Germany.[37]
Unprepared for this proposal, the Allied representatives could only
reply with a proposed surrender document, whose harsh terms a note
from Churchill and Roosevelt softened sufficiently that Castellano
agreed to a further meeting.[38] In the negotiations there were inevitable mutual suspicions; the Italians wanted to surrender and have
Allied troops pour into the peninsula to afford protection from Italy's
former allies.[39] The Allies wanted any help they could get from the
Italians, but they doubted their intentions and their military potential.

After continued delaying action, which did not enhance their reputation with the Allies, the Italians agreed to an armistice on the terms
of surrender which the Allies had proposed, and Castellano signed
the document on the third of September.[40] General Eisenhower
planned that he and Badoglio would make simultaneous announcement of the surrender, and when Badoglio delayed Eisenhower forced
him to move by warning that if the Marshal did not make his announcement Italy would have no friends in the war. Having no other
recourse, Badoglio notified the Italian people of the surrender. He
ordered the Italian armies to cease fighting the British and the Americans, but instead of issuing a trenchant call to arms against the Germans he merely advised the Italians "to oppose attack from any
quarter." Aside from ordering the Italian Navy to sail for Allied
ports, the Italian leaders gave their military commanders no instruc-

[35] Kogan, *Italy and the Allies*, p. 27; Rommel, *The Rommel Papers*, pp.
432–435.

[36] Toynbee and Toynbee (ed.), *Hitler's Europe*, pp. 310–312.

[37] William Hardy McNeill, *America, Britain, and Russia: Their Co-operation
and Conflict (Survey of International Affairs, 1939–1946)* (London, 1953),
pp. 298–299.

[38] The document appears in Churchill, *The Second World War*, V, 105–106.

[39] Kogan, *Italy and the Allies*, pp. 35–41.

[40] McNeill, *America, Britain, and Russia*, p. 300.

tions.[41] Possibly in view of the heavy influx of German troops orders would have been useless; in any case, the Italian military forces disintegrated before the Nazi threat. A few days later, of the Italian Army of sixty-one divisions only seven remained for service with the Allies, and they were poorly equipped and low in morale.[42]

On September 3 General Montgomery's forces invaded the toe of the Italian peninsula after a heavy preliminary bombardment which some critics feel was unnecessary.[43] On September 8, the day that Eisenhower announced the peace with Italy, the U.S. Fifth Army under General Mark W. Clark neared the coast for landings at Salerno.[44]

In addition to fighting the Germans, who were determined to defend the peninsula, the Allies had to deal with the Italian people and government. The removal of Mussolini and the Italian shift of sides in the war led to vigorous efforts by some Italians to eliminate the monarchy. Churchill felt that, at least until Rome was taken, the King and his minister, Badoglio, might continue to be useful.[45] The Americans, on the other hand, had a traditional sympathy for democratic movements. During the winter of 1943–44, an economic commission headed by Adlai Stevenson visited Italy and noted little popular support for either the King or Badoglio and asserted that both stood in the way of economic rehabilitation.[46] For a time the Americans supported and the British opposed an ill-fated plan for the King to retain his crown but turn over authority to his son. Soviet Russia, in order to gain local support for Communism, complicated the picture by recognizing the Badoglio government.[47]

[41] Ibid., pp. 301–303; Eisenhower, Crusade in Europe, p. 186. For a description of the surrender of the Italian fleet which sailed to Malta, see Cunningham, A Sailor's Odyssey, pp. 562–565. An Italian naval officer's reaction is in M. A. Bragadin, The Italian Navy in World War II (Annapolis, 1957), pp. 312–315.

[42] Kogan, Italy and the Allies, p. 40. The royal family and the Italian government alienated public opinion in northern and central Italy by fleeing from Rome to a sanctuary in the Adriatic.

[43] Fuller, The Second World War, pp. 268–269; Morison, History, IX, 234.

[44] Mark W. Clark, Calculated Risk (New York, 1950), pp. 187–188.

[45] Churchill, The Second World War, V, 188.

[46] Kogan, Italy and the Allies, p. 56. Secretary of State Hull felt that the King and the Badoglio government might be useful and that no final decision on Italy's government should be made until the Germans were driven from the country. Hull, Memoirs, II, 1550–1551.

[47] Ibid., II, 1556–1557.

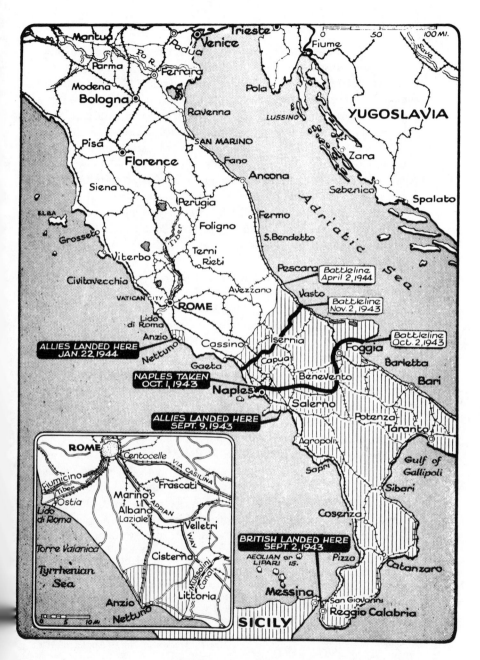

INVASION OF ITALY

Although ideologically the Americans preferred a democracy, practical factors caused them to swing to a support of the Badoglio government. Mainly, they wanted help in governing liberated parts of the area, and early in the invasion the Allies turned four southeastern provinces over to the King's rule. Outside this region, Allied Military Government (AMG) officers were in control. Their activities constituted an extension of a program instituted earlier for control of occupied territories, at the insistence of General Eisenhower. The Allied Military Government of Occupied Territory (AMGOT) during and after the invasion of Sicily was generally successful in maintaining law and order behind the fighting lines. Military government officials administered justice fairly, recruited labor, and tried to deal with such problems as divided command, looting of food, and black markets.

With the signing of the armistice and the conversion of the Italian government from enemy to cobelligerent, a new agency, the Allied Control Commission, came into being on November 10, 1943. Initially it attempted to enforce and execute the terms of the armistice and control the conduct of the Italian government to meet the requirements of an Allied base of operations, especially in matters of communication and transportation, and later it became an agency through which the United Nations conducted its policy in Italy. In general it performed its functions satisfactorily, although it suffered from unwieldiness, complicated procedures, and interminable delays in reaching decisions.[48]

In the early armistice negotiations, the Allies favored Italian military support, but when it became clear how weak this would be, they stated on September 20 that they would do without it. Allied military leaders felt that such aid would be a nuisance, yet in October they accepted the services of the 1st Italian Motorized Group, which went under control of the U.S. Fifth Army and after training went into

[48] G. C. Marshall, "Biennial Report of the Chief of Staff of the United States Army, July 1, 1941 to June 30, 1943 to the Secretary of War," *War Reports*, pp. 247–249. For a detailed study of Allied military government in Italy, see C. R. S. Harris, *Allied Military Administration of Italy (History of the Second World War: United Kingdom Military Series)* (London, 1957), *passim*. Authority was given to the Control Commission in the so-called "Long Armistice" signed by Badoglio and Eisenhower, September 29, 1943. This document may be found in Luigi Villari, *The Liberation of Italy* (Appleton, Wis., 1959), pp. 38–47.

action December 6, 1943, in the mountains east of Cassino.[49] Gradually opposition to the use of Italian forces shifted from military leaders in Italy to politicians in England, and the objectives became political rather than military, just as the interest of the Badoglio government was largely political. Both sides of the controversy saw that Italian military participation would strengthen Italy's position in postwar negotiations.

After the capture of Rome, the new government formed under Ivanoe Bonomi pressed with limited success for more extensive Italian participation, for by this time General Alexander wanted replacements for troops assigned to France. A small Italian army came into being; the first troops went into action in November, 1944, and five combat groups, totaling some 48,000 men, participated in the last drive against the Germans in the spring of 1945.[50]

The most significant Italian military contribution came from "partisans" who operated in German-occupied Italy. These were unofficial units, and many of them were soldiers from the disintegrated Italian military forces. Other partisan groups rallied around a political label, as did the Communist *Garibaldini* or the Party of Action's *Giustizia e Liberta* divisions. The military *maquis* developed their greatest strength around Rome, and the political bands centered in northern Italy. The differing political beliefs of the partisan groups at first held them apart, but by January, 1944, common hatred of the Germans brought even the Communists into a unified Committee of National Liberation of Upper Italy (CLNAI). Oriented toward the left, the committee opposed not only the Nazis but the Neo-Fascism which Hitler was attempting to foist on Italy. In March, 1944, the committee fostered a series of strikes in northern Italy which developed into the only general strike of the war in German-controlled Europe. In June, the committee created a military arm, the supreme headquarters of a Volunteers of Liberty Corps (CVL).[51]

When Allied forces began to advance into northern Italy, they met and welcomed the aid of the partisans. The partisans refused to take an oath of allegiance to the King and join the Italian Army; Allied leaders preferred them as they were since if they became a part of the

[49] C. G. Starr (ed.), *From Salerno to the Alps: A History of the Fifth Army, 1943–1945* (Washington, 1948), p. 54.
[50] Kogan, *Italy and the Allies,* pp. 70–75.
[51] *Ibid.,* p. 104.

Army they might spread left-wing ideas among other troops.[52]

During the early winter of 1944, the CLNAI tried to secure Allied recognition as the representative of the Italian government in northern Italy, but that government objected as did officials of the Allied Military Government (AMG), who did not want this complication of the administration of occupied territory. In late December, the Bonomi government and the CLNAI reached an agreement, and consequently at last the Allies agreed to attach partisan units to the Italian Army. These participated in the spring offensive and played an especially important role in retaking northern Italian cities.

Recognizing the value of partisans, the Allies gave them financial aid, supplies, and even leadership, when Allied officers parachuted behind German lines to help organize the partisans into fighting units. In return, partisans gave increasing aid, engaging in acts of sabotage, rescuing prisoners of war, carrying on reconnaissance, and fighting by the side of Allied troops. As the advance became more rapid, partisans protected cities from destruction by the retreating Germans, assumed temporary control, ferreted out Fascists and Germans who were attempting to escape detection. Partisan actions were swift and at times bloody, as evidenced by the seizure and assassination of Mussolini. Their numbers and their activities, nevertheless, contributed materially to Allied success.[53]

The Germans, like the Allies, made political as well as military moves in Italy. They located Mussolini in a ski hotel in the mountains of central Italy and made a spectacular glider-borne landing to rescue him from his captors.[54] Although it was apparent that Mussolini was sick and had lost any element of leadership which once he might have had, Hitler needed him as the head of a puppet state to oppose the Italian King and the Badoglio government, and in September, 1943, Hitler placed Mussolini at the head of a Neo-Fascist state. Mussolini took little part in the collaborationist government and remained most of the time in seclusion, emerging occasionally to let the world know

[52] *Ibid.,* p. 105; Clark, *Calculated Risk,* p. 381.

[53] Some accounts of partisan activity are in Starr, *From Salerno to the Alps,* pp. 275–276, 333, 379, 418, 423, 435–440; Nicholson, *History of the Canadian Army,* II, 449, 484–485, 621–622; Clark, *Calculated Risk,* pp. 381–382, 419, 430. For a violently critical account of partisan activity, see Villari, *The Liberation of Italy,* pp. 77–88 and *passim.*

[54] Rommel, *The Rommel Papers,* p. 441n. For descriptions of Mussolini's meetings with Hitler after his rescue, see Paul Joseph Goebbels, *The Goebbels Diaries* (London, 1948), pp. 360–371, 378–380.

that he still lived. The Germans, in real control, took no action toward Italians who laid down their arms, governed by force, exported Italians to work in Germany, and made anti-Semitism a reality in Italy. The Jewish population was small, only about 45,000 but of the 10,000 who were deported only 605 returned. Toward the end of the Italian campaign, Mussolini sought to make a separate peace, but the Germans checked his efforts, and when the collapse came he went to an inglorious death at the hands of partisans.[55]

Italy had tried to stop fighting the Allies; she could not avoid becoming a battleground. The struggle was two-pronged, with two immediate Allied objectives, a deep-water port at Naples and the Foggia airfields. The British Army without too much trouble landed and advanced up the foot of the peninsula,[56] but Clark's Fifth Army did not find the going as easy. The British landings were unopposed; at Salerno it was different. The U.S. Fifth Army violated one of the basic principles of assault when in the hope of making a surprise night landing it omitted preliminary bombardment. Since the Salerno beaches were the only logical landings south of Naples, which itself was heavily protected and out of easy air reach, the plan to catch the enemy off guard was visionary. Also, the landing schedule was dislocated when discovery of mines forced transfer of troops to landing craft farther offshore than anticipated. German coastal defenses, many of which preinvasion bombardment might have destroyed or disrupted, were intact, and the Germans were ready and waiting. Then heavy air raids strafed the beaches shortly after the landings started, but fortunately they were not sustained.[57]

Landings proceeded in the face of this enemy activity; Allied naval gunfire helped as an effective counterweapon to German tanks,[58] and air power cooperated with ground troops to avert disaster.[59] And "near disaster" it was, as General Clark called it, since the invaders had landed in what might well become a trap, for the Germans were ensconced in the surrounding hills.[60] By the end of the second day, the

[55] Toynbee and Toynbee (ed.), *Hitler's Europe*, pp. 324–326.

[56] Nicholson, *History of the Canadian Army*, II, 180–212; Eisenhower, *Crusade in Europe*, p. 184.

[57] Morison, *History*, IX, 259–265; Craven and Cate, *The A.A.F. in World War II*, II, 520–524.

[58] Morison, *History*, IX, 254–301.

[59] Craven and Cate, *The A.A.F. in World War II*, II, 520–541.

[60] The title of Chapter 9 in Clark's memoirs is "Salerno: A Near Disaster: September, 1943," Clark, *Calculated Risk*, pp. 183–215.

two components of the Fifth Army, the U.S. VI Corps and the British X Corps, had a beachhead extending inland four or five miles.[61] Paratroopers, originally scheduled for a drop on Rome which was canceled, rushed to the aid of the Fifth Army. Most reached their objectives, but others were widely scattered; 118 of the 600 men in the venture failed to arrive.[62]

It was soon evident that Field Marshal F. M. Albert Kesselring, commanding the German forces in southern Italy, planned to push a spearhead through the Fifth Army to divide and conquer. In view of the desperate straits of the ground troops, the Strategic Air Force turned to tactical operations and between September 12 and 15 dropped three thousand tons of bombs on a concentrated area, which, combined with naval gunfire and artillery bombardment, checked the German counterattack and saved the beachhead.[63] Realizing the serious position of the Fifth Army, General Alexander ordered his subordinate, General Montgomery, to advance to the aid of these forces, but Montgomery complied so slowly that his action cannot be counted as one of the factors saving the beachhead.[64]

By invading the boot of the Italian peninsula, the Allies were launching what became a secondary front, which was subject to all the frustrations of such an operation. The main aim, after Mussolini fell, was to keep pressure on Germany in order to make possible an invasion across the English Channel at a later date. The Allies might have selected Corsica or Sardinia as easier targets, but they would serve no useful purpose when taken and, indeed, might cause an unwanted concentration of German troops in southern France.[65] The

---

[61] Craven and Cate, *The A.A.F. in World War II*, II, 524. This source states that around Altaville and Roccadaspide the VI Corps' line penetrated eleven miles inland.

[62] *Ibid.*, II, 531–533; Clark, *Calculated Risk*, pp. 199, 203. All gunfire was ordered ceased at the expected time of arrival of the airborne troops. The enemy made an air raid during the "quiet" and was not fired on. Only elements of the U.S. 82d Airborne Division were flown in; the remainder went in as ground troops and fought until reassigned in November.

[63] Craven and Cate, *The A.A.F. in World War II*, II, 535.

[64] Nicholson, *History of the Canadian Army*, II, 218–223.

[65] John Ehrman, *Grand Strategy (History of the Second World War: United Kingdom Military Series)* (London, 1956), V, 60–61. After the Allied invasion of Italy, the Germans withdrew from Sardinia and Corsica. Local guerrilla leaders and, in Corsica, French forces from North Africa seized control of the islands. *Ibid.*, V, 67.

Balkans were tempting; their peoples were restive, and unlike Italy the region had no high mountains to block movement into Central Europe. On the other hand, the low mountains were relatively easy to defend, for the few lines of communication were in valleys which could be readily bombed. Furthermore, the Balkans lay out of range of Allied aircraft and under the protection of Nazi planes based on Crete and other nearby islands.[66] The Allied Mediterranean command could expect no aircraft carriers for amphibious asault; so Italy seemed to be the best choice, although it presented difficulties. The mountain spine down the center dictated an advance along two coastal plains which in places were narrow and at times were flooded by swollen streams. The relief from a frontal asault against a well-supplied and reinforced army would be a risky flank assault by sea.

Having established a beachhead, Clark's forces pressed toward Naples against a stubborn and resourceful foe, and by early October hammered its way into the city, securing a port which with quick rehabilitation handled twenty thousand tons of cargo daily.[67] Toward the end of September, the British Eighth Army seized the enemy air bases around Foggia, across the peninsula from Naples.[68] The capture not only placed Allied fighters within easier range of the fronts, but provided an extremely important base from which the Air Force later launched strategic bombing raids on the Ploesti oil fields in Rumania and other vital Nazi holdings. The bases competed with the Fifth Army for cargo space, and during a period in which Clark could have used reinforcements, some 300,000 tons of shipping went to build up Foggia for the Strategic Air Force.[69]

At first the Germans planned to withdraw to the Apennines and defend only Rome on the way, but by the middle of October they decided to try to hold the enemy at the middle of Italy at least during the approaching winter. Rommel, who had been in command in the

[66] The Germans anticipated an attack on the Balkans and had heavier defenses there than in Italy. In July, 1943, there were six German divisions and one brigade in Italy and Sicily in contrast to twelve German divisions and two brigades in Southeast Europe and the Greek islands. *Ibid.*, V, 61. Churchill was, of course, deeply interested in the Balkans. Churchill, *The Second World War*, V, 128–129.

[67] Clark, *Calculated Risk*, pp. 216–217.

[68] Craven and Cate, *The A.A.F. in World War II*, II, 506.

[69] Marshall, "Biennial Report . . . July 1, 1943 to June 30, 1945 . . ." *War Reports*, p. 167; Fuller, *The Second World War*, p. 270.

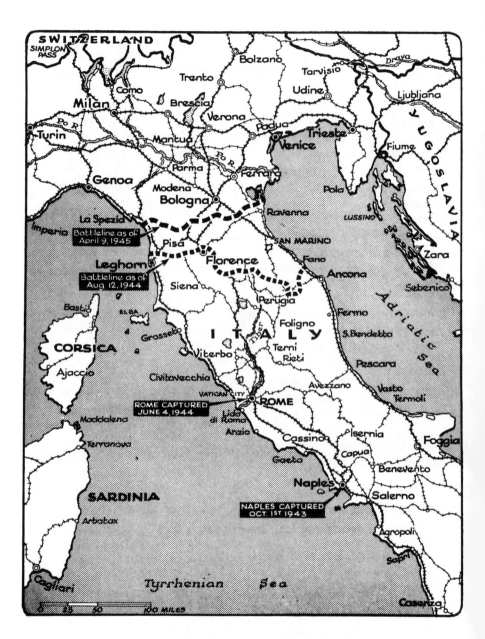

THE ITALIAN CAMPAIGN

north, left for Western Europe, and Kesselring assumed full charge of the Italian campaign.[70] He established a defensive line along the Volturno River, which was to be replaced by other lines as the Allies slowly beat their way north.

The Allied purpose to engage German troops succeeded almost beyond expectation. In the middle of September there were in Italy about eighteen German and thirteen Allied divisions; by the end of October the Allied forces had dropped to eleven and the German divisions had increased to about twenty-five. Alexander stressed the importance of maintaining continuous pressure to prevent a German counterattack; according to Alexander's plan, which Eisenhower approved, the British would advance far enough up the Adriatic coast to be able to move southwest toward Rome over established transportation routes. At the same time the Fifth Army would drive north on the other coast directly toward Rome.[71]

Other commitments made difficult the accomplishment of these objectives. Seven divisions, including one airborne and one armored, were scheduled to leave for cross-Channel preparations, bomber groups going into Foggia needed supplies, and starting in mid-October the Mediterranean Theater was slated to lose from two-thirds to four-fifths of its landing craft to other areas. On receiving Eisenhower's protest, the Chiefs of Staff agreed to a short delay in the removal of these craft.[72]

On his return to the United States after the Cairo and Teheran conferences, President Roosevelt announced the selection of Eisenhower to head the cross-Channel invasion, and General Sir Henry Maitland Wilson replaced Eisenhower as Allied commander in the Mediterranean.[73] Wilson, experienced in both diplomatic and military matters, received the appointment over the very able General Alexander, whose continued presence in Italy at a critical military juncture the combined Chiefs of Staff considered essential.[74]

While the high command considered strategy and leaders, the Fifth Army moved against the Volturno Line. Gaining recognition for ad-

[70] Siegfried Westphal, *The German Army in the West* (London, 1951), pp. 153–154; Rommel, *The Rommel Papers,* pp. 446–447.

[71] Ehrman, *Grand Strategy,* V, 69–70.

[72] The seven divisions (four American and three British) were scheduled to leave by the end of November. *Ibid.,* V, 71–75.

[73] Eisenhower, *Crusade in Europe,* pp. 207–211.

[74] Ehrman, *Grand Strategy,* V, 203–204.

vances in the face of heavy losses was the 100th Battalion of the 34th Regiment, composed of Americans of Japanese ancestry recruited in Hawaii.[75] After hard fighting, the Fifth Army pushed its way across the river but came to a halt against the German Winter Line, a part of the larger Gustav Line. The enemy made skillful use of the terrain, fortified the mountains, diverted the Rapido River into lowlands to check motorized vehicles, and built Cassino into a veritable fortress. For a time the fighting settled down to a dreary, muddy stalemate.[76]

Next followed an attempted "end run" around the Gustav Line to move toward Rome, which appeared as a desirable political rather than military objective. The Allies actually planned the move before they knew they would be bogged down in front of the Gustav Line, and the spot selected for amphibious assault was Anzio, not far from the Alban Hills which might control entrance into Rome.[77] When he realized that his army was not advancing as anticipated, Clark recommended that the Anzio operation, known as Shingle, be canceled,[78] and on December 22, with Eisenhower concurring, Alexander canceled the plan.[79] Unfortunately, some experts believe, the idea was revived at the political level by Churchill, who met with military leaders, including Eisenhower, in Tunis. Desirous of seizing Rome and arguing that a thrust at Anzio would draw German troops away from the Gustav Line, Churchill reinstated the Shingle operation in spite of Eisenhower's reluctance and raised it from a one-division to a two-division venture. Much of the difference of opinion centered on availability of landing craft and the question of supply.[80]

In their unopposed landings, which started in the predawn hours of January 22, 1944, for once the Allies surprised the enemy, who had defended the area lightly in the belief that if attack came it would be nearer the mouth of the Tiber River.[81] Control of the Alban Hills

[75] Thomas D. Murphy, *Ambassadors in Arms* (Honolulu, 1954), *passim;* Clark, *Calculated Risk,* pp. 220–221.

[76] *Ibid.*, pp. 216–261.

[77] Morison, *History,* IX, 317–318.

[78] Clark, *Calculated Risk,* pp. 250–251.

[79] Morison, *History,* IX, 324.

[80] Churchill, *The Second World War,* V, 426–437; Eisenhower, *Crusade in Europe,* pp. 212–213; Clark, *Calculated Risk,* pp. 254–255. Eisenhower, having been appointed Supreme Commander, Allied Expeditionary Forces, was concerned lest landing craft used at Anzio might not be available in time for the cross-Channel attack.

[81] Morison, *History,* IX, 335–350; *Anzio Beachhead (22 January—25 May, 1944)* (Historical Division, Department of the Army) (Washington, 1947), pp. 1–26.

was vital to the Germans, and once over their surprise they struck at the invader. The result was for the Allies one of the most frustrating experiences of the war. Instead of moving quickly to interior positions, perhaps because of an overcautious commanding general, the landing forces paused to consolidate their beachhead. Determined to eliminate the Anzio forces, rather than weaken the Rapido-Garigliano front, Hitler threw in reinforcements from more distant areas, northern Italy, France, and Yugoslavia, and within two weeks had seventy thousand men on the Anzio front. As a result, Allied troops were pinned down and remained a heavily beleaguered isolated pocket which was not taken only because of the men's dogged will for freedom and the unceasing fire of naval vessels in the roadstead. In retrospect, Anzio appears to have been a case of attempting too much with too little.[82]

Associated with the Anzio operation was another controversial military venture in which, to relieve pressure on Anzio when the landings came, General Clark decided to attempt a crossing on the Rapido River, although he noted in his diary that he expected heavy losses. On the day of the Anzio landings the 36th Infantry secured a temporary foothold across the river but was forced to retire. In the process the 141st Infantry Regiment was practically wiped out. Later, Secretary of War Robert P. Patterson supported Clark's contention that the Rapido crossing, although costly, justified itself by withdrawing German troops at a critical time from Anzio.[83]

Another military move came rather generally to be looked upon as a blunder. This was the destruction of the Abbey of St. Benedict, on a hill overlooking Cassino. Fearing that the Germans were making use of the abbey, the Allies determined to destroy it and, not wishing to injure the monks, gave warning. Apparently there were no Germans in the abbey, but the warning would have given them a chance to leave. On the following day 229 bombers turned the abbey into ruins. Aside from the fact that the move was unnecessary, it was tactically unsuccessful because the bombing made the stone structure more defensible if the Germans had been inclined to use it.[84]

---

[82] *Ibid.*, pp. 27–104. The Germans were amazed at Allied failure to move quickly from the beachhead. Westphal, *The German Army in the West*, p. 158. For a strong indictment of overcautious leadership at Anzio and an equally strong defense of air support of landing operations, see Slessor, *The Central Blue*, pp. 562–566. Morison is critical of the Air Force. *History*, IX, 351.

[83] Clark, *Calculated Risk*, pp. 271–282.

[84] Craven and Cate, *The A.A.F. in World War II*, III, 363–364. General

The force opposing the Germans along the Gustav Line was truly an Allied army and included not only British and American forces but French, Polish, Brazilian, and Italian troops. On May 11, they opened an attack which was so successful, especially on the part of the French Expeditionary Force, that the enemy fell back to a new defensive position, the Adolf Hitler Line, which also failed to hold back the advancing Allies. By the end of the month the Germans were definitely retreating; fortunately, Kesselring decided not to defend Rome, and it escaped the fate of Monte Cassino or Naples.[85]

The Germans continued their retreat until they reached the Apennines about 175 miles north of Rome, where they stood on the defensive again, this time along the Gothic Line, which with Italian labor they had been constructing for almost a year, mostly in rugged, mountainous country.[86] The British managed to break through a part of the eastern portion of the line along the Adriatic coast,[87] and on September 10 the Americans started an attack in the west. The heavily fortified and mountainous nature of the area reduced the actual number of belligerents who came in contact with each other. The Americans had a force of 262,000 troops, yet the break-through came after several days of intense fighting by relatively few men, never more than two rifle companies of 350 men and more often a single platoon. The attack started with a feint at the less rugged but more strongly fortified Futa Pass to conceal the main effort, which was

---

Clark places the responsibility for the bombing of the abbey on General Bernard Freyberg, commanding a New Zealand division recently shifted from the Eighth to the Fifth Army. Clark and General Alfred M. Gruenther, in charge of air operation, objected, but General Alexander supported Freyberg. Clark, *Calculated Risk*, pp. 315–320; Slessor, *The Central Blue*, p. 577. An historian of the Fifth Army states of the abbey: "Enemy activity around the famous structure had been observed for some time. Ammunition dumps were dangerously close to the Abbey; observers used it constantly to direct artillery fire; snipers had fired from it; and gun emplacements were numerous around the building. The hallowed Benedictine monastery, thus far spared by the Fifth Army, was definitely a military objective." Starr, *From Salerno to the Alps*, p. 114.

[85] Clark, *Calculated Risk*, pp. 334–366. Extremely helpful were the Air Force's blows against German communications in central Italy. Craven and Cate, *The A.A.F. in World War II*, III, 373-407.

[86] Charles B. MacDonald and Sidney T. Mathews, *Three Battles: Arnaville, Altuzzo, and Schmidt* (*United States Army in World War II*) (Washington, 1952), pp. 103–107.

[87] For a detailed account of the advance of the Canadians with the British Eighth Army, see Nicholson, *History of the Canadian Army*, II, pp. 487–525 and *passim*.

to break through Giogo Pass and outflank the enemy. Elements of the 338th Infantry Regiment, 85th Infantry Division spearheaded the attack with rifle, grenade, and mortar. More than once advanced groups had to turn back; effective support, however, came from artillery, chemical mortars to lay down smoke screens, and the tactical air force. Once they had secured Giogo Pass, the Americans outflanked Futa Pass, took it with little difficulty, and moved on toward the Po Valley.[88]

The enemy was on the retreat, but the pursuers were exhausted and depleted in number, for by this time the Italian campaign had become of minor importance. These factors, enemy reinforcements, and heavy rain prevented the Allies from reaching the Po River by winter, and they carried on indecisive skirmishes until spring.[89] The Germans were heavily engaged elsewhere, and the task of the Allies was to move in swiftly before the remaining German troops could retire to almost impregnable defenses in the Alps. Allied air attacks p. ved the way by knocking out German lines of communications. Gradually water drained from land which the Germans had flooded as a protective measure, and the Allies began the ground attack. Heavy fighting recommenced April 14, 1945, and after a few days of intense warfare, the Allies were clearly in the ascendancy. Coordinated air strikes, mobile spearheads to surround segments of the enemy forces, and effective infantry tactics combined to bring the enemy to a state of collapse by the first of May. The formal ending came four days later when the German commander signed unconditional surrender papers.[90]

The war in Italy had been long and hard. Parts of it, like any war, had been ugly: Mussolini and his mistress hanged head down by vindictive partisans, German soldiers using a white flag as a cover to move a machine-gun nest, enemy troops booby-trapping an entire section of Leghorn before evacuating it. Parts of the war in Italy have

[88] For a careful account of the break-through spearheaded by the 338th Infantry Regiment, 85th Infantry Division, see MacDonald and Mathews, *Three Battles*, pp. 103–247.

[89] On November 25, 1944 (Thanksgiving Day), General Clark received word of his appointment to replace General Alexander as head of the Allied Forces in Italy (Fifteenth Army Group). Alexander became Allied Commander in Chief, Mediterranean, when General Sir Henry Maitland Wilson left to join the Staff Mission in Washington after the death of Field Marshal Sir John Dill. Clark, *Calculated Risk*, pp. 404–405.

[90] *Ibid.*, pp. 431–442.

produced controversy not yet ended. In addition to those already noted were others: criticism of excessive preliminary air bombardment that killed too few Germans but turned Italian cities into rubble heaps that obstructed the Allied Army's advance; charges that instead of pushing the Germans north of Rome against the Apennines, the Allies could have stood on the defensive and actually engaged more troops than by attacking;[91] assertions that the armies in Italy should have been increased rather than decreased to make possible advance beyond Italy into Central Europe.

In the face of such controversy, one hesitates to make more than a tentative appraisal. One is inclined to agree with those who say that if the primary aim of the invasion of Sicily and Italy was to divert German troops from action elsewhere, that purpose was accomplished. It is a sobering thought, however, to note that after the war Kesselring argued that the German campaign in Italy had been successful because it had engaged Allied troops and prevented their use in other parts of Europe.

[91] In contrast, a German view is that the Allies should have struck at Leghorn, north of Rome, instead of at Anzio. Westphal, *The German Army in the West,* pp. 166–167. It might be noted that through 1944–45 the Germans never had fewer than twenty-four and as many as twenty-eight good divisions in Italy, in addition to fifteen divisions of uneven quality in Yugoslavia.

CHAPTER 9

Strategic Air Warfare

BEHIND the invasion of the Normandy beaches lay months of Allied effort. Essentially, the preparations followed two main lines. One was strategic air bombing of Germany and the lands under her control; the other was the complex task of making ready for the actual cross-Channel invasion.

Since air warfare was both new and powerful it was also controversial. Its leaders in many instances were zealots who viewed the established services with the disdain of youth toward age. Regular Army and Navy officers, on the other hand, often grumbled about the "bomber barons" who wished to fight their own private war with the enemy. The basic difference of opinion was over the role of aviation in war. The leaders of the older services tended to believe that air power should be primarily a tactical weapon, which would aid the ground forces in a variety of ways, including support for amphibious landings, bombing attacks on the opposing forces, and strafing of enemy troops. Air Force leaders, on the other hand, while agreeing that planes could give tactical support to the other branches, believed that primarily air power should develop into a strategic rather than a tactical weapon. In other words, it was the function of aviation to win wars, not merely battles.

The air leaders had established this point prior to our entrance into World War II. One of the provisions of the joint British-American staff report of March, 1941, was that if the United States should become involved in the war, American air bombardment forces would collaborate offensively with British air forces "primarily against German Military Power at its source."[1]

At the outbreak of war the Air Force not only was a part of the Army, but even in this dependent status lacked unified control. In June, 1941, it had made an important stride toward independence and parity when the Assistant Secretary of War for Air, Robert A. Lovett, sponsored a reorganization which created the Army Air Forces.[2] When work on planning revision started in the following August, the Army Air Forces made the most of the restricted autonomy that had accompanied its creation and submitted plans as if it were on a par with the older services. The heart of its proposal was that Allied air power should strike at Germany's industrial strength, and even before entry into the war the Army Air Forces indicated what its role should be in this campaign. This was to conduct daylight high-level precision bombing raids instead of night attacks. Recognizing the dangers to the bombers involved, the planners recommended the development of long-range fighters to escort the raiders. Never ones to underestimate the potentialities of air power, the planners predicted the possibility that by 1944 strategic air bombardment of the enemy might make a land attack unnecessary. However, they did not recommend that the armies cease preparations for a cross-Channel assault.[3]

In their meeting in Washington shortly after the entrance of the United States into the war, Allied leaders reiterated their agreement that Germany constituted the principal enemy. At that time, however, actual participation by U.S. ground forces against the Nazis seemed remote, for extensive preparations must precede European landings, and, furthermore, the immediate pressures were in the Far East. It seemed probable, therefore, that the first contacts with the Germans, aside from antisubmarine operations, would be by air. To this end, although delayed by the need for aircraft and crews for the Pacific and for training purposes, an A.A.F. bombardment force went to England to join the Royal Air Force in its assaults on the enemy.[4]

---

[1] W. F. Craven and J. L. Cate, *The Army Air Forces in World War II* (Chicago, 1948), I, 138.

[2] *Ibid.*, I, 115; Mark Skinner Watson, *Chief of Staff: Prewar Plans and Preparations (United States Army in World War II: The War Department* (Washington, 1950), pp. 293–297.

[3] Craven and Cate, *The A.A.F. in World War II*, I, 146–149.

[4] *Ibid.*, I, 557–558. For an account of the German daylight offensive against

The German Air Force had started a heavy daytime assault of Britain on August 12, 1940, which continued until early in October. A determined Royal Air Force stood off the enemy until in October the *Luftwaffe* abandoned its daytime attacks in favor of night raids. Gradually the Royal Air Force was able to move from the defensive to a bombing offensive against German-controlled Western Europe.

Ambitious though they were for independent status, Army Air Force leaders deferred their struggle for this position during the war. Instead they sought and secured increasing autonomy within the Army. The significant role of air power in the conflict and the encouragement of General Marshall helped make such developments possible.[5] General H. H. Arnold in his dual role as Deputy Chief of Staff and Chief of the Air Corps not only was one of the top military figures in the nation, but his high position added stature to the service he represented. Furthermore, a directive of March 2, 1942, reorganized the Army and gave the Army Air Forces added autonomy.[6]

The shifting plans for cross-Channel invasion sharply affected Air Force planning, and Major General Carl Spaatz in May, 1942, wryly noted to Secretary of War Stimson that European strategy, which originally anticipated the use of air power supported by ground forces, had altered to a utilization of air power to support the ground forces.[7] By June, however, the current had shifted again, and directives from Generals Arnold and Eisenhower definitely set the role of the Army Air Force in England. All its units merged into the Eighth Air Force, whose commander, General Spaatz, had his own headquarters, with staff and provision for bomber, fighter, ground-air support, and air service commands. The Force's basic function was to conduct bomber operations in conjunction with the Royal Air Force on a basis of equality. Their combined objective was to secure "air supremacy over Western Continental Europe in preparation for and in support of a combined land, sea, and air movement across the Channel into Continental Europe."[8] In short, as part of its own conceived mission of striking at the heart of Germany, the Army Air Force would contribute materially to the preparation for cross-Channel invasion.

Britain, see Denis Richards, *Royal Air Force, 1939–1945* (London, 1953), I, 164–188.

[5] Watson, *Chief of Staff*, p. 291.
[6] Craven and Cate, *The A.A.F. in World War II*, I, 264–265.
[7] *Ibid.*, I, 565.
[8] *Ibid.*, I, 590.

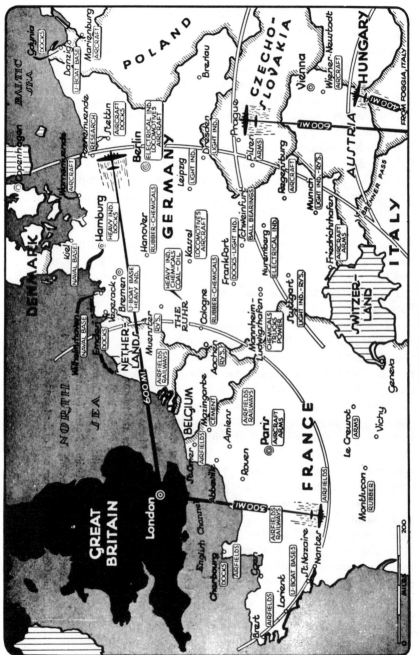

WAR IN THE AIR

The next task for the Army Air Force was to reconcile its difference with the Royal Air Force over daylight and night bombings. Weakened by the early successes of the enemy, the British had developed the concept of strategic bombing prior to American entrance into the war. Lacking other weapons, they viewed bombers as one offensive instrument which might wage a war of attrition while the British rebuilt their strength in other ways. In their combat experience the Royal Air Force had come to feel that night bombing was preferable to daytime attacks, from the standpoint of both economy of operation and percentage of losses. During peacetime years, on the contrary, the U.S. Army Air Force leaders had developed a liking for daytime bombing, since they believed that high-altitude daytime precision bombing could be more selective and thus avoid hitting non-military targets. In 1931 they had been impressed by naval air tests with the Norden bombsight, and starting in 1933 they had contracted with the Sperry Gyroscope Company for the production of improved models. The introduction of the B-17 in 1935 gave the Army Air Forces the requisite long-range aircraft for its daylight bombing. The B-17 was the first of the big bombers used by the Army Air Forces in World War II. First produced in 1935, this four-engine, Boeing-built plane went through a number of modifications before and after the United States entered the war. By 1945, the plane had an operating ceiling of 30,000 feet and a maximum speed of about 300 miles an hour; it could carry a bombload of 4,000 pounds for a combat range in excess of 2,000 miles. Although used in practically every area of the war, the B-17's were concentrated in the European Theater. Between January, 1940, and August, 1945, the Army Air Forces accepted from the producers a total of 12,692 B-17's.

In the spring of 1941, the Royal Air Force received some B-17 Flying Fortresses and in July made a series of trial daylight raids. The results were disappointing, for in the twenty-two raids only half the planes reached their objectives, and eight planes were lost from enemy action or faulty operation. Consequently, the R.A.F. returned to night bombing and was dubious of the possibilities for success of daytime action. The British were also dissatisfied with the early performance of the B-24 and considered their own aircraft superior to the two new American products.[9] The B-24 came into being as a result of a request from General Arnold to Consolidated Aircraft Company

[9] *Ibid.*, I, 591–602; VI, 203–208.

for a four-engine bomber with a 3,000-mile range, 35,000-foot ceiling, and speed in excess of 300 miles an hour. Like the B-17, the B-24, or Liberator, underwent numerous modifications. With the same-sized crew, the B-24 could carry a larger bombload farther than could the B-17; its range was 2,850 miles with a bombload of 2,500 pounds. Against Germany it was found wanting in armament and armor, and when these were added, the plane weight was increased and made the aircraft less stable. As a result, the B-17, especially after it increased its range, was preferred in the war against Germany. The Army Air Forces, however, between January, 1940, and August, 1945, accepted 18,190 B-24's, considerably more than the number of B-17's it secured.

Possible keys to successful daytime bombing lay in increasing the defenses of the bombers and in providing long-range fighter escorts. The Army Air Force began modifications which added significant armament to the Flying Fortresses, but for reasons that are not clear was much slower in developing the desired fighter aircraft.

The decision to send U.S. air forces to the British Isles created the need for careful planning, for Britain had been at war for some time, and the Royal Air Force was using existing airdromes and facilities. Major General Ira C. Eaker, who would head the VIII Bomber Command, proceeded to England with a small staff to prepare for the arrival of the Eighth Air Force, scheduled to conduct U.S. air operations against Germany. Setting up headquarters, April 15, 1942, in an evacuated girls' school at High Wycombe, some thirty miles west of London, he began the complicated preparations for the arrival of the American forces.[10] Relations with the Royal Air Force from the outset were excellent, and although there were occasional differences, the two air services proved to be friendly and effective partners.

In addition to attacking the problems of logistics and physical arrangements, the Air Force leaders concerned themselves with a division of labor in the air war. The R.A.F. at first suggested that American fighters should join the British in defensive operations against German air attacks, but General Spaatz, head of the Eighth Air Force, insisted that although they might aid in an emergency, the primary function of the A.A.F. fighters was to support U.S. bombers "in an effort to secure air *Supremacy* and not for the defense of Britain."[11] Spaatz won his point, and the R.A.F. assumed the full

[10] *Ibid.*, I, 620.
[11] Quoted in *ibid.*, I, 623.

responsibility for defense, even of airdromes used by the American forces. In 1943, the Eighth Air Force relaxed its position to the extent of furnishing a share of the ground antiaircraft protection for its air facilities.[12]

Since they were joining experienced forces already long engaged with the enemy, the U.S. Air Force leaders drew heavily upon British experience in such matters as combat intelligence and communications. They conducted their training program in the light of the joint war the A.A.F. and R.A.F. would be waging.[13]

Army Air Force leaders anticipated the need for repair facilities and selected sites which ultimately became great depots. These included Langford Lodge in North Ireland, Warton, north of Liverpool and near the industrial facilities of Lancashire, and especially Burton-wood, a huge British repair depot between Liverpool and Manchester. American air operations came to be centered in the Huntingdon and East Anglia areas north of London.[14]

On April 22, 1942, advance units of the Eighth Air Force left Boston on the transport *Andes* bound for Liverpool. Since the British for some time had been ferrying planes by air across the Atlantic, the Eighth Air Force logically determined to transport its planes in the same manner. The operation encountered numerous obstacles. Pilots had to take special training in ferrying procedures, and since it was felt that fighters should not attempt the flight alone, groups of fighters (P-38's and P-39's) included a B-17 escort. The Battle of Midway threw these plans off schedule, for as A.A.F. bombers moved from Hawaii to Midway and from the West Coast to Hawaii, in anticipation of the engagement, B-17's of the VIII Bomber Command had to fly to the West Coast to stand guard until planes returned from the Pacific areas. As a result, fighter crews went by sea to England and, lacking their own planes, began training in British Spitfires.[15]

---

[12] *Ibid.*, I, 622–623. For other antiaircraft contributions of U.S. forces, see Basil Collier, *The Defence of the United Kingdom* (London, 1957), p. 322n.

[13] Craven and Cate, *The A.A.F. in World War II*, I, 623–627.

[14] *Ibid.*, I, 628–639.

[15] *Ibid.*, I, 639–642. The Lockheed P-38 (Lightning) was a high-flying twin-engine fighter, which had a high rate of climb and with top speed of about 414 miles an hour could match the speed of the German Messerschmitt 109 and the British Spitfire. When used as a fighter-bomber the P-38's combat range averaged between 600 and 700 miles. On escort duty, later models had a range of 1,500 and even 2,000 miles. The Bell P-39 (Airacobra) was a single-engine

Gradually, however, the ferrying operations got under way. The course lay from Presque Isle in Maine to Goose Bay in Labrador, some 567 miles away. The next leg to Bluie West 8 in western Greenland was the longest (1,002 miles) and most strenuous part of the trip. From Greenland the planes flew 847 miles to Reykjavik in Iceland and then the remaining 846 miles to Prestwick in Scotland. Fliers encountered adverse weather conditions and occasional misleading directional broadcasts by the enemy, but by the end of August 386 aircraft (164 P-38's, 119 B-17's, and 103 C-47's) had made the trip. The A.A.F. had predicted a possible loss of 10 percent, but the actual accident ratio amounted to but 5.2 percent loss in planes and no serious injury to personnel.[16]

American pilots and crews arrived in England with insufficient training in combat operations to go into immediate action. The first American participation in the air war was, therefore, more a harbinger

---

plane whose engine was mounted behind the cockpit. Its maximum elevation was about 13,000 feet and its top speed was 368 miles an hour. The single-engine British Spitfire was termed the best fighter of the war by U.S. Army Air Force historians. The modified Spitfire could reach an altitude of 42,000 feet. Hilary St. George Saunders, *Royal Air Force, 1939–1945* (London, 1954), III, 72.

[16] For map of the route and alternate landing fields, see Craven and Cate, *The A.A.F. in World War II*, I, 643. Another important ferrying route was developed to deliver planes and supplies to the Middle East and Southeast Asia. In the spring of 1941, the British had started shipping aircraft by sea to West Africa, assembling them, and flying them across Africa, stopping at airfields built for the purpose. Flights to West Africa from the United States began in June, 1941, when a subsidiary of Pan American Airways delivered twenty transport-type aircraft, under the Lend-Lease Act, to the British. Once the United States entered the war, service developed rapidly by way of bases in Florida, the Caribbean, and Brazil, and by the end of 1942 about 464 planes had been sent across this route destined for the Middle or Far East. There developed also a passenger service, using four-engine flying boats, or Clippers (Boeing B-314A). Like the British, the Americans took fighter craft by sea to the West Coast of Africa, and on at least one occasion delivered them by carrier. The South Atlantic route became important for the shipment of Lend-Lease planes and supplies to the Allies, including Soviet Russia and China, and also to United States forces in the Middle and Near East. *Ibid.*, I, 319–342; VI, 416. For aircraft deliveries to Soviet Russia, see T. H. Vail Motter, *The Persian Corridor and Aid to Russia (United States Army in World War II: The Middle East Theater)* (Washington, 1952), pp. 124–138. The Douglas C-47 was the military cargo version of the standard DC-3 used by commercial airlines. The A.A.F. used more than 10,000 DC-3-type planes before the end of the war.

of the American will to fight than of the nature or extent of U.S. participation in strategic air warfare. The 15th Bombardment Squadron had arrived in May and had been training in American light bombers (Bostons) used by the R.A.F. On July 4, 1942, six of its crews joined an equal number of R.A.F. crews in a raid on four airdromes in Holland. The venture was hardly a success, for only two of the U.S. planes dropped bombs on the target. Two planes were shot down, and one was badly damaged by unusually heavy anti-aircraft fire sent up by the Germans who evidently had received warning of the approaching raid. One pilot, Captain Charles C. Kegelman, demonstrated skill and courage under fire. With one of his two engines knocked out, Kegelman literally bounced his plane off the ground to turn against a ground battery and then fly safely at sea level to England and a Distinguished Service Cross. Disappointing though the results of the mission were, American morale rose at this first taste of combat.[17]

The heavy bomber groups continued their training and on August 17, 1942, staged their first raid. In comparison with current R.A.F. activity or later A.A.F. operations the venture was modest, for it included only eighteen bombers. Twelve struck at the Sotteville freight or marshaling yard at Rouen while the remainder made diversionary thrusts along the coast. Protected by R.A.F. Spitfires, the bombers gave a good account of themselves and could report reasonably accurate high-altitude, daylight bombing on the rail center. The conditions for attack, it should be noted, were favorable; the weather was good, and enemy opposition, both from the air and ground, was negligible. Nevertheless, this raid had an importance greater than its physical results. American production could not satisfy all war needs; there had to be allocations on a priority basis. The A.A.F. still had to prove that daylight, high-altitude bombing could be sufficiently effective to outweigh the needs of ground or naval forces. The small bomber mission headed by General Eaker, consequently, attracted far above average interest.[18]

On September 8, 1942, the R.A.F. and the A.A.F. agreed on their respective roles in the air war against Germany. The British would continue night bombardment, and the Americans would develop day

[17] Craven and Cate, *The A.A.F. in World War II*, I, 658–660.
[18] *Ibid.*, I, 661–668.

bombing "to achieve continuity in the bombing offensive against the Axis."[19] The plan envisaged a start with U.S. bombers escorted by British fighters and the gradual emergence of a full-fledged American bomber offensive.

The VIII Bomber Command followed its initial raid with a series of thirteen additional bombing missions. The first nine, against relatively accessible targets, met little opposition and resulted in fairly accurate bombing. Then the Germans began to send up strong fighter resistance, and again the results were encouraging to the Bomber Command, for although they suffered some casualties, the B-17's demonstrated strong defensive power. The claims of extensive destruction of German planes later proved greatly exaggerated, and it appears that the early B-17's could protect themselves but could not inflict heavy damage to enemy aircraft.[20] Their primary purpose, of course, was to drop a bombload, not to fight enemy aircraft in the air.

Pleased though they were with early bombing accomplishments, the Eighth Air Force leaders encountered several discouraging checks to the expansion of their operations. The generally inclement weather reduced the number of bombing raids across the Channel. In addition, an American fighter force developed very slowly in England, for mechanical failures combined with bad weather to delay the introduction of the P-38 (Lightning) into combat operations.[21] The decision to invade North Africa affected the strategic bombing program in several ways. The Eighth Air Force had to divert considerable effort to the training of the Twelfth Air Force for its role in that campaign.[22] Then, toward the end of October, General Eisenhower, acting in his capacity as theater commander and speaking for the Combined Chiefs of Staff, issued new directives to the Eighth Air Force which delayed its direct air assault on Germany. He instructed it to strike at enemy submarine pens and at airfields to help safeguard the North

[19] Quoted in *ibid.*, I, 608.

[20] *Ibid.*, II, 216–229.

[21] *Ibid.*, II, 229–231.

[22] The Eighth Air Force lost about half its planes (1,100) and important personnel to the Twelfth Air Force. General Spaatz went to the new command, and General Eaker replaced him as head of the Eighth Air Force. Gordon A. Harrison, *Cross-Channel Attack (United States Army in World War II: The European Theater of Operations)* (Washington, 1951), p. 47. This source states that the transfers delayed the bomber offensive against Germany eight or nine months.

African invasion forces from attack. The order to strike at French airfields complicated an already difficult problem, for although the French welcomed attacks upon the German occupation forces, they were concerned about damages to nonmilitary objects and casualties to civilians resulting from inaccurate bombing. Anxious to protect the French people, the Army Air Force issued radio warnings to French citizens to leave the vicinity of military targets. Meanwhile, German authorities assiduously sought to arouse French opinion against the Allies.[23]

In response to Eisenhower's directive, the Eighth Air Force on October 21, 1942, began the first of a number of raids against submarine bases in the Bay of Biscay. The distances involved and the lack of available fighter aircraft forced the B-17's to make unescorted attacks. Dropping their bombs from an elevation of 17,500 feet instead of the customary 22,000 to 25,000 feet, the bombers inflicted considerable damage on buildings around the submarine pens. Bad weather, however, seriously reduced the effectiveness of the mission, for of the ninety planes which left England only fifteen reached the objective. The restricted nature of the targets prompted General Spaatz to direct the bombers to try low-level attacks, and in a raid on Saint-Nazaire on November 9 the Bomber Command complied with the order. A dozen B-24's bombing from altitudes of 17,500 to 18,300 feet suffered little damage, but thirty-one B-17's attacking at 7,500 to 10,000 feet ran into a curtain of flak and sustained heavy damage, including three planes crashed. After this experience the bombers returned to 17,500-to-20,000-foot levels in half a dozen subsequent attacks prior to January 3, 1943.

It proved extremely difficult to evaluate the results. The Bomber Command had struck at the submarine bases rather than at the industries producing the submarines as a temporary device to prevent repair and servicing of existing craft. According to postwar statements of Admiral Karl Doenitz, head of U-Boat warfare, the concrete pens proved impervious to air attack, and since these installations contained the essentials for servicing and repair, the Allied attacks must be viewed as unsuccessful, although they caused irritation and minor damage.[24] The best target was the water in front of the pens, for the

[23] Craven and Cate, *The A.A.F. in World War II*, II, 237–241.
[24] *Ibid.*, II, 246–254. The historians of the Royal Air Force place a somewhat higher appraisal of the damage inflicted on the submarine pens, although they contend that the British and American bomber attacks should have been

compacted water resulting from the explosion squeezed into the pens and caused damage.

On December 20, the Bomber Command received its most serious test to date. A mission of one hundred B-17's left England to bomb aircraft facilities at Romilly-sur-Seine, about sixty-five miles southwest of Paris. An Allied fighter escort accompanied the bombers across the Channel and anticipated picking them up again on their return trip. Shortly after the fighters left, between fifty and sixty enemy fighters attacked the B-17's, and later another force of about the same number relieved the first group. As a result the bombers had to fight their way to and from the target. The bombing runs were satisfactory, but the mission lost six bombers to enemy action. Although first reports of enemy losses were gratifyingly high, German sources later revealed that the enemy loss of fighters was less than that of U.S. bombers. The success of the Germans came largely from the fact that they had discovered the B-17's vulnerability to a frontal attack.[25]

Continued enemy concentration on this weakness caused the A.A.F. to correct the defect. One answer was to install armament to eliminate the blind spot in the front of the plane. At first crewmen used hand-held .50-caliber machine guns in the nose, but in August and September, 1943, modified B-17's and B-24's with power-driven nose turrets reached England. Furthermore, the A.A.F. helped solve this defensive problem by improving its combat formations. A trial-and-error procedure produced a combat wing, consisting of two or three combat boxes, which proved to be the most satisfactory formation.[26]

Another problem was that of bombing accuracy. It was one thing to drop a bomb with no opposition; it was something else again to hit the target when the flak was heavy or when enemy planes were making a nose attack just at the time of the bombing run. Other factors contributing to bombing inaccuracy were ineffective use of delicate instruments by inexperienced personnel, severe cold, and

made earlier, while the pens were in process of construction. Denis Richards and Hilary St. George Saunders, *Royal Air Force*, Volume II, *The Fight Avails* (London, 1954), pp. 282–283.

[25] Craven and Cate, *The A.A.F. in World War II*, II, 256–258. The "blind" spot was a point in front which neither upper turret nor ball turret guns could reach. *Ibid.*, II, 264–265. In 1943 the B-24 was modified by the addition of a belly turret, and flak suits were introduced.

[26] The combat box consisted of eighteen to twenty-one bombers "stacked" so that they could bring maximum forward fire on enemy aircraft making a frontal attack. *Ibid.*, II, 266–267.

bulky oxygen apparatus. Some mistakes were errors of identification. In a raid on Lille twenty-five or thirty bombs landed on the wrong factory three miles from the intended target. On another occasion bombs which fell on Saint-Nazaire were intended for a spot one hundred miles away. Clearly the bombsight was not in error in this instance.[27]

While the Eighth Air Force seemed to be making little progress toward its strategic goals during the first months of its operations, it was, nevertheless, gaining valuable tactical experience. Combat crews in mounting numbers became veterans of the air war; their experiences directly and continuously resulted in modifications in aircraft armament and equipment. The hard realities of combat, furthermore, forced Air Force leaders to test and refine flight formations, and they found that close-flying units offered greater protection, although at some loss of maneuverability. They demonstrated that escort was better than no escort and they developed a division of labor with that escort. They discovered that chances of driving off enemy attacks improved if fighters concentrated on frontal attackers and left the bombers to direct their heavy fire to the rear without having to identify planes approaching from that direction.[28]

Late in January, 1943, a group of ninety-one U.S. bombers headed for their first really German objective, instead of one in occupied territory. Fifty-three planes reached the target and dropped bombs on the port of Wilhelmshaven without incurring excessive losses from the hundred or more German fighters that rose to challenge them.[29] Not all the missions were so successful, for the A.A.F. was fighting a determined and resourceful foe. German fighters tried varying techniques and experimented with different types of armament; they attacked from different angles and in prepared formations. They knew the most vulnerable parts of the bombers and of the box formations

[27] *Ibid.*, II, 270–273. The Germans sought with considerable success to improve fighting techniques and tactics. *Royal Air Force*, III (1954), 1–3. To acquaint German airmen with enemy planes the Nazi Air Force leaders developed what they called the "Rosarius Traveling Circus," consisting of captured aircraft restored to working order. Adolf Galland, *The First and the Last: The Rise and Fall of the German Fighter Forces, 1938–1945* (New York, 1954), p. 198.

[28] Craven and Cate, *The A.A.F. in World War II*, II, 321–347.

[29] *Ibid.*, II, 323. A German Air Force officer, Adolf Galland, notes this raid and asserts that the German high command failed to take the Americans seriously at this time. Galland, *The First and the Last*, p. 190.

which the bombers flew; they concentrated their attacks as the force reached the target and centered their attention on lead planes, not only in the hope of destroying them, but in an effort to disrupt the bombing run, for the lead bomber's drop was the signal for others to drop their bombs. They attempted air-to-air bombing, trailed ropes with bombs attached, and modified their fighters to add heavier armament.[30] As a result, although they checked frontal assaults by improved defenses, the U.S. bomber crews still found the German fighter to be their worst enemy. Flak was annoying and caused varying damage to aircraft, but by itself it downed few planes. Its real effectiveness lay in disabling an aircraft so that, forced out of formation, it became prey to fighter attack.[31]

For a time Air Force leaders felt that medium bombers might play a role in ground-level bombing of coastal and other short-range objectives. A successful raid made on May 14, 1943, against a generating station in Holland gave rise to optimism which a subsequent mission quickly shattered. On May 17, eleven B-26's left for another raid on the same target; one plane turned back as a result of mechanical difficulty and was the only plane to return to base, for the remaining ten were lost to enemy action. As a consequence, General Eaker concluded that the medium bombers belonged to tactical warfare and he ordered them to train for operations in connection with the anticipated cross-Channel attack.[32] Another lesson learned from bitter experience was that small bombing forces suffered more heavily than large groups. Time would enable American production and an expanded training program to correct this weakness.

The air war during the first half of 1943, to summarize, showed that although the Germans could check strategic bombing they could not stop it. It also demonstrated that the principal obstacle to successful strategic air warfare was the German Air Force.

In addition to experience and size, the A.A.F. needed a comprehensive plan if it expected to take a significant part in strategic air warfare. American air leaders could rely on British information to a certain point only, for the British concentrated on area bombing, and the Americans believed that their daylight bombers should seek out

[30] The mass production of standard fighters to meet the bomber menace helped materially to delay the development of German jet planes. *Ibid.*, p. 201.
[31] Craven and Cate, *The A.A.F. in World War II*, II, 341–342.
[32] *Ibid.*, II, 339–341. The medium bombers were B-26's.

specific targets. A.A.F. planners sought to develop a program that would strike at the enemy's vital areas with as little waste effort as possible. By the spring of 1943, a Committee of Operations Analysts, including civilians, government officials, and military personnel, had made studies of nineteen German war industries.[33] At the head of the list was the aircraft industry, although the experts differed on the relative importance of aircraft assembly and aircraft engine plants.

Second priority went to ball bearings; both British and American planners believed that Germany had failed to stockpile ball bearings and that destruction of plants producing these essential industrial items would deal a serious blow to German plane, tank, and other war production.

The analysts placed petroleum third on the list and estimated that two-thirds of the German supply came from crude oil, of which the Ploesti fields in Rumania contributed about 60 percent, and the remainder came from synthetic production. Later evidence indicates that the analysts underestimated the potential effects of a concentrated attack on the petroleum industry. Apparently, lack of intelligence data gave them an exaggerated view of Germany's ability to absorb losses in this area of production; they failed also to realize the close connection of synthetic oil plants with the production of nitrogen. A blow at the oil industries, therefore, would have struck indirectly at the munitions industry as well.

Other industries on the list included those producing grinding wheels and crude abrasives, nonferrous metals, such as copper and aluminum, and synthetic rubber. Farther down the list came submarines and transportation systems. Curiously, experiences of the British in the "Blitz" led them to think that electric power was too decentralized to present an attractive target. As a result, A.A.F. planners did not include German electric power as a major objective, although it appears that the Germans were greatly concerned over the possibilities of such an attack.[34]

The A.A.F. discussed the reports of the experts with the R.A.F. and the two agreed upon a priority list of some seventy-six targets in

[33] Security reasons prevented actual priority ratings, but the order of listing indicated by the committee implied priorities. *Ibid.*, II, 356.

[34] After the war the U.S. Strategic Bombing Survey corroborated the belief of the Germans that curtailment of electric power would have had a serious effect on German war industry. *Ibid.*, II, 362. Ball bearings, which had high priority, could be secured from Sweden.

the following areas, listed in order of importance: submarine construction yards and bases, German aircraft production, ball bearings, synthetic rubber and tires, and military transport vehicles. The serious nature of the Battle of the Atlantic gave submarines top priority.[35]

Next, General Eaker appointed a British-American committee, which developed a plan of operations against the seventy-six targets which had been selected. This Combined Bomber Offensive (CBO) Plan made a temporary shift in priority. German fighter strength became the first target, since it jeopardized the entire bomber offensive. The CBO Plan contemplated an offensive developing through four phases. By the end of the first phase, June 30, 1943, there should be 944 heavy and 200 medium bombers in the theater. Lack of size and experience would limit the raids to escorted attacks on submarine pens or airfields. There would be two long-range attacks, one on oil facilities at Ploesti and the other on the Schweinfurt ball-bearing industry. During the next period the plane totals should reach 1,192 and the range of the missions should extend to 400 miles. By the third phase, toward the end of the year, the Air Force should have sufficient strength to assume its full role in the strategic air war. There should be 1,746 bombers in the area by January, 1944, and the number should increase to 2,702 by the end of the following March. The plan anticipated corresponding development of medium bombers for strikes at enemy airfields and of fighters to escort the heavy bombers.[36]

General Eaker took the Combined Bomber Offensive Plan to the Combined Chiefs of Staff, who accepted it after detailed discussion.[37]

[35] *Ibid.*, II, 364–365.

[36] The Joint Chiefs of Staff approved the CBO Plan on May 4, 1943. *Ibid.*, II, 372. The North American B-25 (Mitchell) and the Martin B-26 (Marauder) were the main medium bombers used by the Army Air Forces in World War II. The B-25, with combat weight in 1945 of 35,000 pounds, had a maximum speed of about 285 miles an hour, which was roughly the same as that of the somewhat larger B-26 (37,000 pounds). The range by 1945 was 1,200 miles for a B-25 with a 3,200-pound load and 1,200 miles for the B-26 carrying a 4,000-pound load. Pilots liked the B-25 but at first dubbed the B-26 as the "Widow Maker" or worse, because of its high accident rate. After careful training, pilots came to like the B-26, with its "hot" performance and high landing speed. Entering the field late was the Douglas A-26 (Invader), which was heavily armed and carried a bomb load of 4,000 pounds to a maximum range of 1,000 miles. Redesignated after the war as the B-26, this aircraft became the standard tactical bomber in the Korean war.

[37] The Combined Chiefs of Staff approved the plan May 18, 1943, at the

They also noted a second great purpose of the offensive. Not only would the plan further strategic air warfare, so close to the heart of Air Force leaders, but in addition it would help materially to prepare the way for cross-Channel invasion of Europe, currently anticipated for May 1, 1944.[38]

The tremendous increase of combat aircraft naturally involved similar expansion of airdromes, facilities, and supporting ground personnel. The build-up of U.S. Army Air Forces in England began in earnest in May, 1943. The combat units expanded in satisfying fashion, but by midsummer General Arnold became aware that the serious lag in expansion of service units spelled difficulty for the bomber offensive. Attempts to solve this problem led to the shipment of so many men to England that the movement became known in Air Force circles as the "Gold Rush." Unfortunately, large numbers of the men were inadequately prepared for service positions and had to undergo further training before they could be useful.[39]

During this expansion period, the region north of London became a huge, complex American airfield, vitally affecting the towns and countryside in which it mushroomed. The matter of oil supply, of course, was critical; tankers entered the Thames and unloaded their liquid cargo into a pipeline which the British constructed to the East Anglia airfields.[40] Bomber crews continued their practice of flying their own planes across the Atlantic under the guidance of experienced ferry pilots. Fighter craft reached England mainly by sea; some were boxed and stowed below, but the bulk went partly assembled and deck-loaded on tankers or escort carriers. Workers in plants in England removed the protective grease and completed the assembly of the planes.[41]

The pressing need for long-range fighter craft made the jettisonable gas tank a critical item of supply. Both Americans and British experimented with different types. The British developed a paper tank

Washington Conference. Air Marshal Sir Charles Portal, British Chief of Air Staff, who had strategic direction over combined air operations, on June 10 issued the order to start the offensive. Harrison, *Cross-Channel Attack*, p. 209.

[38] Craven and Cate, *The A.A.F. in World War II*, II, 373.

[39] *Ibid.*, II, 640–641.

[40] *Ibid.*, II, 652. Good maps of A.A.F. installations in Great Britain are in *ibid.*, 647, 650.

[41] *Ibid.*, II, 651, 660–661. The final assembly consisted mainly in attaching the wings to the planes.

which proved quite satisfactory, but at first production was disappointingly slow. The Americans made metal tanks, but tried various sizes. Fighter pilots preferred a 125-gallon tank to the 200-gallon type they first received, and later U.S. plants sent over large quantities of 75-gallon steel tanks. Never in excess supply, British and American tank production nevertheless produced enough tanks to make possible fighter escort of bombing raids on Berlin.[42]

Beginning in the summer of 1943, the modification of aircraft became an increasingly heavy responsibility. Repair units in the British Isles made most of these changes, although in time it became possible for factories in the United States to incorporate some of them in initial production. Modifications were time-consuming; during the last half of 1943, the average time for a heavy bomber was twelve days. A type of maintenance, the extent of which A.A.F. leaders had not anticipated, was repair of battle damage. During the latter half of 1943, about 30 percent of the bombers participating in bombing operations received battle damage. Gradually, repair facilities were able to cope with the situation, and such repairs became routine.[43]

The Combined Bomber Offensive began to get under way in June, 1943, and until the following spring, although the Eighth Air Force struck at land targets, its principal objective was to eliminate the German Air Force. The *Luftwaffe* rose to the bait and stubbornly resisted the strategic air offensive. Each side had already tested its pattern of fighting, and there were few innovations in the bitter struggle for air supremacy. It soon became apparent that bomber missions beyond the range of fighter escorts were expensive ventures. On June 13, sixty B-17's reached Kiel and dropped their bombs, but the heaviest German air attack launched to date against an Eighth Air Force mission struck down twenty-two of the bombers. The successful approach to the target, the courage of the crews in the fierce action, and the destruction of some thirty-nine enemy aircraft only modified an American defeat. The concentration of German fighters against the Kiel mission, however, diverted enemy attention from an even larger force of B-17's which a few moments after the Kiel attack struck at Bremen. In this instance only four of 102 bombers crashed.[44]

[42] *Ibid.*, II, 654–655.
[43] *Ibid.*, II, 661–664.
[44] *Ibid.*, II, 670–671.

A little later in the month U.S. daylight bombers struck the industrialized Ruhr area for the first time. The target was the Hüls synthetic rubber plant, the second largest in Germany, which had escaped Allied air attention since the R.A.F. had made a few light raids in 1941. On June 22, 183 B-17's sought out this plant and achieved both tactical and strategic success in their mission. They demonstrated a high degree of accuracy in dropping 88.6 percent of their bombs in the plant area, and as a result the Buna plant closed a month for repairs and did not return to full production for half a year. Unfortunately, although several more raids might have destroyed the plant completely, the U.S. Air Force did not return to the attack. The Hüls bombing caused more than normal reaction in worker morale, for the employees had enjoyed freedom from air attack so long that they considered themselves immune. They even watched the bombers approach in the belief that they were German planes.[45]

Bad weather intervened to postpone further attacks on Germany, and the Eighth Air Force planes turned to new assaults on aircraft industries and submarine bases on the French coast. They demonstrated high precision in their bombing, but the concrete submarine lairs remained undestroyed.[46]

Toward the end of July the weather cleared, and the R.A.F. and the A.A.F. launched a heavy campaign against Germany, during which Hamburg, second largest city in the Reich, became the particular object of attention. Utilizing the new "H2S" radar screen on the night of July 24–25, some 740 R.A.F. bombers found the target and dropped 2,396 tons of bombs. For the first time, on an extensive scale at any rate, the bombers used "window," or metallic strips, which so fogged German radar screens that they became temporarily useless as warning devices. This raid was the first of four night attacks on

[45] The attack killed 186 persons and injured 1,000. *Ibid.*, II, 671–672.

[46] *Ibid.*, II, 673–674. At Nantes 61 planes dropped 145 tons on the objective and made 18 direct hits from 25,000 feet on a target only 650 feet square. Much more effective against the submarines were British air-surface hunter groups operating in the Bay of Biscay during the summer. John Slessor, *The Central Blue: The Autobiography of Sir John Slessor, Marshal of the RAF* (New York, 1957), pp. 519–520. Admiral Doenitz suggests that the pens should have been attacked from the air while under construction, but that it was too late when they were completed. Karl Doenitz, *Memoirs: Ten Years and Twenty Days* (London, 1959), p. 409.

Hamburg, in which 3,095 bombers dropped 8,621 tons of bombs. Of the eighty-seven bombers lost, thirty crashed on the last raid as a result more of foul weather than enemy action.[47]

While the R.A.F. was making nightly assaults, the A.A.F. made the campaign an around-the-clock affair by conducting daytime raids. B-17's struck sharp blows especially at tire plants at Hannover, although German opposition made the effort a costly one by destroying twenty-four of the ninety-two bombers on the mission. On July 28 a force of 120 bombers drove deep into Germany at aircraft production facilities ninety miles from Berlin. Only twenty-eight bombers reached the target, and the Germans struck down twenty-two planes. In this defense the rocket, a new weapon, proved its devastating power. A German fighter pilot made a phenomenal if lucky hit, when his rocket struck one B-17, which crashed into two others and caused the loss of all three. The raid also featured an innovation by the Eighth Air Force; 105 P-47's (Thunderbolt fighters) bore jettisonable gas tanks and, penetrating some thirty miles farther than usual, caught sixty German fighters by surprise and dispersed them with a loss of nine German planes to one U.S. fighter. The American conversion of some of the B-17's into fighting escorts, however, proved unsatisfactory, for the overweight, modified planes, known as YB-40's, were still vulnerable to enemy attack and were so slow that they disorganized flight formations.[48]

In August, 1943, B-24's carried out one of the principal air attacks of the war. The Ploesti oil refineries in Rumania long had offered a tempting target, but one that was out of range of planes based in Britain. After the conquest of North Africa, the Army Air Forces decided on a long-range attack from this area. General L. H. Brereton, commander of the Ninth Air Force, which had been established in the Middle East in November, 1942, was in charge of the operation and put a special staff in his advanced headquarters to work planning it. Crews located near Bengasi trained in low-level attack and practiced on dummy targets in remote desert locations. Early in the morning of August 1, 1943, 177 planes left Libya, crossed the Mediterranean, and headed northeast across Albania and Yugoslavia. In Bulgaria, before

---

[47] Saunders, *Royal Air Force*, III, 6–8. German sources attest to the serious effect of the raids on German morale. Galland, *The First and the Last,* pp. 202–205.

[48] Craven and Cate, *The A.A.F. in World War II,* II, 677–681.

reaching the Danube the attacking force ran into high clouds which, with radio silence imposed to gain surprise, destroyed its unity and marred execution of the raid. The leading squadron missed its way and before it realized its error had alerted the enemy. Consequently, the bulk of the planes encountered stiff opposition from antiaircraft fire. Late arrivals also had to run the gantlet of fires and exploding bombs from the first bombings, and the entire force on the return had to fight off persistent air attack. As a result fifty-four planes were lost, and with them 532 airmen were killed, imprisoned, missing, or interned. On the other hand the damage, although not so high as expected, was severe. About 42 percent of Ploesti's total refining capacity was destroyed, and roughly 42 percent of its cracking capacity was knocked out for a period of from four to six months. No other raids on Ploesti followed until late in the spring of 1944.[49]

Shortly after the Ploesti raid, the Army Air Forces made their first attempt to coordinate attacks from Britain and the Mediterranean. The Ninth Air Force led off from North Africa on August 13 with a raid on Messerschmitt factories in Wiener-Neustadt. Although the bombers failed to hit many of the projected targets, including the principal plant, they inflicted enough damage to reduce total production of single-engine fighter aircraft by this production complex from 270 in July, 1943, to 184 in August.

On August 17, the Eighth Air Force from England struck a spectacular but costly blow at enemy production. The double mission, totaling 516 B-17's, against Regensburg and Schweinfurt was the largest A.A.F. force yet sent against Germany. Bad weather in England altered original plans, and the Regensburg mission left first. Squadrons of fighters escorted the bombers to the limit of their gas supply, and medium bombers hit airfields in France in an effort to keep German planes down, but despite these actions the German fighters rose to challenge the bombers in one of the most intense air battles of the war. The Germans used all the tactics they had developed and attacked from every direction in varied formations, using rockets, cannons, and parachute bombs, in addition to more conventional weapons. The bombers pressed on, however, and inflicted a heavy strike on the Messerschmitt plants. Then, instead of returning to England, they surprised the Germans by flying on to North African bases. The Schweinfurt mission encountered similar dogged resistance to and

[49] *Ibid.*, II, 477–484.

from the target, but it also carried the bulk of its bombloads to the appointed objective. Plane losses were heavy on both sides; the A.A.F. lost sixty heavy bombers, a loss of 16 percent of those starting on the mission and 19 percent of those under attack by the enemy. Eighth Air Force claims of 288 enemy planes destroyed appear excessive, but German losses were at least extensive.[50] General Arnold had hoped to develop shuttle bombing between British and North African bases, but although the Regensburg experiment probably cut down the loss of planes on that particular raid, Arnold dropped the idea of this type of shuttle operation. North African bases were not equipped to handle large numbers of bombers, and crew morale seemed higher when planes could return to their home base.[51]

Since cloudy and otherwise adverse weather constituted a serious deterrent to strategic air war on Germany, A.A.F. leaders sought to develop blind or radar bombing as a means of surmounting this problem. The British had made a start in this direction, and in the fall of 1942 U.S. leaders tried installing the British H2S radar in American planes. The British, however, could not supply their own demand, and the A.A.F. turned to American science and production. The Radiation Laboratory, at the Massachusetts Institute of Technology, began production of the H2X, an American version of the British radar. A dozen planes with H2X installation and specially trained navigators reached England in the fall of 1943 and soon afterward participated in test raids. At about the same time the Americans used radar-jamming techniques similar to British "window."[52]

The second week of October, 1943, was especially tense for the Eighth Air Force. Its bombers made extensive raids against the enemy, showed increasing marksmanship in its bombing runs, but also lost heavily in air battles to and from the targets. In six days the Eighth Air Force lost 148 bombers and crews, primarily from air action. Clearly, the B-17's needed long-range fighter escorts to secure control of the air and ultimate victory in the strategic air war. Jettison-

[50] *Ibid.*, II, 682–686. Galland claims that the Germans lost only 25 fighters, and not 228 as claimed by the A.A.F. Galland, *The First and the Last*, p. 229.

[51] Craven and Cate, *The A.A.F. in World War II*, II, 687. The R.A.F. tried shuttle flights to North Africa and abandoned them for similar reasons. Saunders, *Royal Air Force*, III, 5.

[52] Craven and Cate, *The A.A.F. in World War II*, II, 689–696. The A.A.F. called the tinfoil strips "chaff" and estimated that electrically two thousand strips about one-sixteenth of an inch wide and eleven inches long were equivalent to one B-17. The A.A.F. also began to use "carpet," an airborne transmitter used to jam German radar.

able gas tanks pointed the way, but they were slow in arriving in satisfactory numbers. P-38's by October, 1943, with two 75-gallon wing tanks could escort a maximum radius of 520 miles and by February, 1944, with larger tanks (108 gallons) could go 585 miles. The P-47's, on the other hand, could not travel over 375 miles and often not over 300 miles. The P-51's were not available for combat until December, 1943, and it was not until the following March that they secured additional tanks which made it possible to accompany bombers all the way.[53]

The heavy losses of unescorted daytime bombers led to a reconsideration of this form of attack. For a time Allied leaders thought of diverting forces to expand greatly the Air Force in Italy. General Arnold was interested in an over-all command of strategic air warfare which could shift bombers between England and Italy as indicated by weather conditions and the choice of targets. Bases in northern Italy, it was contended, would be in closer range of industrial targets in southern Germany, and German air forces would have to be divided to meet the new threat. Major General Ira C. Eaker, head of the Eighth Air Force in England, objected strenuously, and he was joined by the British Air Staff, which initially had favored the idea but came to feel that it was premature. These persons asserted that the creation of a strategic air force in Italy would result in a drain on the air forces in England and hamper the build-up of daylight strategic air forces in Britain. They also questioned the validity of the argument that weather generally was better in Italy than in England on the ground and that it was the weather over the German targets that was the critical point. They further argued that planes returning to Italy would have to fly a circuitous route to avoid the Alps and Swiss neutrality. In addition, they claimed that base facilities in England could provide better services than could bases in Italy. In spite of these protests, General Arnold secured the support of the Combined Chiefs of Staff, and on November 1, 1943, the Fifteenth Air Force, to operate from Italian bases, came into being.[54] Although this Air Force engaged in important strikes, the main Allied air bases in

[53] *Ibid.*, II, 696–706.

[54] Under General Spaatz, Brigadier General H. J. Knerr served as Deputy Commander for Administration, U. S. Strategic Air Forces, while at the same time he was Commanding General, Air Service Command. This dual role of General Knerr raised logistics to parity with operations. *Ibid.*, 755–756. For R.A.F. opposition to the increase of the strength of the A.A.F. in Italy at the expense of air power in England, see Saunders, *Royal Air Force*, III, 14–16.

the strategic air war remained in the British Isles, and they continued to grow in size and strength. As a result, by December, 1943, the Eighth Air Force could send three raids of over seven hundred bombers each, in contrast to the maximum of four hundred reached in mid-October.[55]

With this rapid increase of air forces went administrative reorganization. Numerous factors complicated the matter; the R.A.F. leaders, intent on their strategic war against Germany, resisted any move toward over-all control that might threaten their autonomy. They zealously watched powers considered for the new Supreme Commander of Overlord, or cross-Channel invasion, and they fought single control of strategic air operations in the Western European and Mediterranean theaters. Reluctantly, and after much discussion, they agreed to such unification of U.S. Army Air Forces. Accordingly, on December 8, 1943, General Arnold informed General Spaatz that he would command the combined U.S. Strategic Air Forces in Europe. The choice of Spaatz was inevitable; he was senior to General Eaker, who commanded the Eighth Air Force, and he had worked well with Eisenhower in the North African and Mediterranean campaigns. Spaatz took most of his staff to England with him, and a disappointed Eaker, who had led his forces to the edge of the promised land, left them to go to the Mediterranean as head of the U.S. Air Forces in that area.[56]

Bad weather plagued the bomber offensive during January, 1944. The Eighth Air Force continued and expanded its experiments with radar bombing, primarily as a device to keep the pressure on Germany. Blind bombing lacked the precision of visual bombing and approached in its nature the RAF's night bombing of areas rather than specific objects. The P-51 was proving its worth as an escort fighter, but its conversion to a long-range escort was still slow.[57] Determined enemy air attacks on A.A.F. missions deep into Germany made it increasingly apparent that the *Luftwaffe* was a menace that the A.A.F. must remove before it could proceed to its basic task of destroying the economy of Germany. Although they disagreed on procedures, the R.A.F. leaders came to the same conclusion, and on February 13 a

[55] Craven and Cate, *The A.A.F. in World War II*, II, 729.

[56] *Ibid.*, II, 733–756; Forrest C. Pogue, *The Supreme Command (United States Army in World War II: The European Theatre of Operations)* (Washington, 1954), pp. 48–49.

[57] Craven and Cate, *The A.A.F. in World War II* (1951), III, 21–26.

new directive underlined the necessity of striking at German air power, both in production and in action. This directive resulted in a major Allied bombing offensive known as the "Big Week." On February 20, under heavy escort, one thousand bombers, the largest unit which the Eighth Air Force had yet dispatched, raided fighter aircraft factories in central Germany. A heavy R.A.F. raid on Leipzig the previous night contributed to unusually light enemy air opposition, and the mission lost only twenty-one planes, instead of the two hundred which A.A.F. leaders feared they might lose. The Eighth Air Force followed this attack with a series of heavy blows at German aircraft industries, while the Fifteenth Air Force dispatched smaller missions from its Foggia air bases. After the fortunate raid on February 20, the A.A.F. planes encountered fierce resistance. Bad weather closed in on February 26 and terminated the operation, appropriately called "Argument."

During "Big Week," more than 3,300 bombers from the Eighth Air Force and 500 from the Fifteenth Air Force had struck at the heart of Germany. While the damage was not so devastating as Allied leaders thought at the time, it was nonetheless considerable. In dropping almost ten thousand tons of bombs, about as many as the Eighth Air Force had dropped during its first year of operation, the A.A.F. inflicted heavy damage to aircraft and associated industries, as well as to nearby transportation facilities. Perhaps more significant was the fact that Operation Argument forced the Germans into a dispersal of aircraft production. At an important juncture of the air war, also, the Germans had lost a significant number of aircraft and an even more significant number of pilots. The *Luftwaffe* could ill afford this loss of over five hundred planes and those who flew them, and "Big Week" marked a change in enemy tactics. Thereafter, in an effort to conserve its strength, the German Air Force ceased to challenge every Allied thrust but concentrated on the larger missions.[58]

Having gained this measure of air superiority, the Allied air leaders moved to their primary targets in the air war. At the same time, instead of selecting routes to avoid contact with the enemy, the Allies deliberately moved to draw out German fighters. When on March 4 the Eighth Air Force bombed Berlin for the first time, its primary purpose was not to destroy the city or weaken civilian morale but to compel the German Air Force to act. Just as the Germans in World

[58] *Ibid.*, III, 26–48; Galland, *The First and the Last*, pp. 245–246.

War I struck at Verdun because it was a fort every Frenchman would fight to defend, so in 1944 did the A.A.F. hit Berlin in the belief that this was one target the *Luftwaffe* would rise to protect.[59]

The decision to bomb Berlin also indicated that the P-51 had met the test as a long-range fighter, for with two extra 108-gallon tanks it could escort planes 850 miles from base. The supply of these fighters was still short, but there were enough to justify the start of escorted daytime raids on the enemy's capital. The attack of March 4 was little more than a harbinger; of the fourteen combat wings only one reached the target and, forced to bomb by radar, it did little damage. Aside from one skirmish with thirty or thirty-five fighters, the long-range fighter escorts encountered no opposition. Two days later, when the A.A.F. tried again, it achieved more substantial results, as 660 bombers dropped 1,626.2 tons of bombs. This time the *Luftwaffe* rose in force and engaged the attackers in a running battle. While the P-51's gave a good account of themselves, they could not provide complete protection, and the mission lost sixty-nine bombers and eleven fighters. A.A.F. claims of *Luftwaffe* losses were too high (ninety-seven claimed by bomber crews and eighty-two by escort fighter pilots)', but the Germans could ill afford their losses in this war of attrition. Significant was the fact that the Germans had called on their night fighters to battle the daytime marauders. The A.A.F. returned to the attack on March 6, in which for the first time bomber crews were able to bomb visually, and they knocked the Erkner bearing plant out of operation for some time. The P-51 escort was the largest yet, and the Germans apparently had not recovered sufficiently from previous encounters to offer much resistance. When the A.A.F. made the fourth raid of the month on Berlin, German fighters showed a reluctance to challenge the P-51's.[60]

Meanwhile, the Fifteenth Air Force was increasing in effectiveness, and by the end of January, as a result of strikes at airfields and repair facilities in the Po Valley, had practically eliminated the German Air Force's effectiveness in the area.[61]

As the air war continued and the *Luftwaffe* declined in strength,

[59] The R.A.F. had begun night attacks on Berlin much earlier. Isolated raids earlier in 1943 gave way in November and December to a series of heavy blows at the capital which continued into 1944. Saunders, *Royal Air Force*, III, 11–13; Galland, *The First and the Last*, pp. 244–245.

[60] Craven and Cate, *The A.A.F. in World War II*, III, 48–53.

[61] *Ibid.*, III, 54.

German leaders sought with some success to improve antiaircraft operations, and by late spring flak was more destructive than enemy fighters. To meet this danger, A.A.F. units changed their flight formations and tried antiradar devices to check automatic antiaircraft fire.[62]

In April, 1944, the A.A.F. advanced to a new phase in its air war. The submarines faced defeat, though not as a result of air blows at their bases. The German Air Force was also beaten, and the A.A.F. had contributed heavily to this defeat. The victory served a dual purpose; the Allies could wage their strategic war against primary objectives, and the Allies also had control of the air as they readied for cross-Channel invasion.

Curiously, although the German Air Force had lost its war by March, 1944, the production of German aircraft actually increased during the remainder of the year. The real shortage was not in planes, which a diversified industry continued to produce, but in trained pilots. German air leaders, who minimized pilot training to conserve oil, did not have experienced pilots to protect that oil when Allied bombers turned to its destruction. In view of this paradox, it is possible that the Allied Air Forces should have concentrated first on oil instead of on aircraft production.[63]

[62] *Ibid.,* III, 60.

[63] *Ibid.,* III, 56–66; Galland, *The First and the Last,* p. 255. For a critical appraisal of strategic bombing in World War II, see Bernard Brodie, *Strategy in the Missile Age* (Princeton, 1959), pp. 107–127, 131–138.

CHAPTER 10

The Pacific War: Plans and Objectives

RESPONDING to the attack on Pearl Harbor, General Marshall notified commanders of defense garrisons that war had started and instructed them to govern their operations by Rainbow 5 as far as it related to Japan.[1] With limited resources available, he sought to strengthen defenses in Hawaii, Panama, and on the West Coast. Feeling that the Philippines would soon fall, military leaders ordered a convoy already on its way to stop in the Fijis and await further orders.[2] Stimson and others were convinced that the United States should not abandon the Far East; they won their point, and instead of returning to Hawaii, the convoy received orders to proceed, not directly to Manila and almost certain destruction, but to Brisbane, Australia, and the senior officer aboard was made responsible to General MacArthur. Meanwhile, MacArthur was insisting that "if the western Pacific is to be saved it will have to be saved here and now."[3] Marshall responded: "The strategic importance of the Philippines is fully recognized and there has been and will be no repeat no wavering in the determination to support you."[4]

Determination to send reinforcements to the Philippines represented

[1] Maurice Matloff and Edwin M. Snell, *Strategic Planning for Coalition Warfare, 1941–1942 (United States Army in World War II: The War Department)* (Washington, 1953), pp. 80–81.

[2] Louis Morton, *The Fall of the Philippines (United States Army in World War II: The War in the Pacific)* (Washington, 1953), pp. 145–146.

[3] Message, MacArthur to Marshall, quoted in Matloff and Snell, *Strategic Planning*, p. 84.

[4] Marshall to MacArthur, December 15, 1941, quoted in *ibid.*, p. 85.

not so much a belief that these islands could be held as a move toward defining American strategy in the Pacific. Since the United States was beginning a coalition war, not singlehanded opposition to the enemy, at President Roosevelt's suggestion two conferences were held concurrently by military leaders in the Far East, one in Chungking on December 17 and 23 and the other in Singapore on December 18 and 20, the most important result of which was realization that the United States did not intend to retire from war in the Far East.

The United States early made an important strategic decision to establish an advanced military base at Port Darwin in northern Australia.[5] From the military standpoint, the Philippines were lost, but from the political point of view the United States should try to retain the islands or if they were lost to retake them. Such reconquest would necessarily be slow, since American leaders had already made their primary strategic decision, to concentrate on the war against Germany.

Despite this grand strategy, President Roosevelt and Prime Minister Churchill, under extreme Japanese pressure in the Pacific, endorsed allocation of shipments to Australia, which, in view of the shortage of ships, inevitably delayed plans for a North African operation, troop shipments in the North Atlantic, and even reinforcement of Hawaii. As a case in point, on January 2, 1942, seven vessels with about 20,500 troops and two months' supplies, originally intended for North Atlantic transit, left New York for the Pacific.[6] Vessels like the *Queen Mary* and the *Aquitania* began carrying troops in the Pacific. During the first three months of the war the bulk of the Army's deployment went toward an effort to create a base in Australia and protect the lines of communication with that continent. Correspondingly, shipments to Hawaii almost ceased, and even the North Atlantic secured only 12 percent of all troop and 9 percent of all cargo shipments. Nevertheless the supply did not meet the demand in the Pacific.

On March 16, 1942, the Joint Chiefs of Staff decided to provide additional forces for the Pacific considered as "the minimum required for the defensive position and simultaneously build up the United Kingdom forces intended for offense at the earliest practicable time."[7]

---

[5] *Ibid.*, p. 87.
[6] Richard M. Leighton and Robert W. Coakley, *Global Logistics and Strategy, 1940–1943 (United States Army in World War II: The War Department)* (Washington, 1955), p. 157.
[7] Memo, WPD for CofS, 28 Feb 42. This memorandum is described and parts are quoted in Matloff and Snell, *Strategic Planning,* pp. 157–159.

They also accepted the view that as long as naval forces were adequate, minimum ground troops only would be needed for Hawaii.

Collapse of the defense in the Netherlands East Indies spelled early death for the unified command created by the Arcadia Conference in Washington, and at the suggestion of President Roosevelt, Britain and the United States divided responsibilities; the former took Burma, and the latter "because of our geographical position" was assigned the Pacific Theater on March 24, 1942, by the Combined Chiefs of Staff.[8] Anticipating this development, the Joint Chiefs of Staff created a "Southwest Pacific Area," consisting of Australia and the regions to the north, including the Philippines, and placed this area under control of the Army. They gave the Navy direction of the "Pacific Ocean Area," which comprised the remainder of the Pacific Theater with the exception of a small "Southeast Pacific Area," for which no command was selected at the time. In a formal directive dated March 30, 1942, the Joint Chiefs of Staff named General MacArthur Supreme Commander of the Southwest Pacific Area and designated Admiral Chester W. Nimitz to head forces in the Pacific Ocean Area. Operational strategy rested with the Joint Chiefs of Staff; the Combined Chiefs of Staff had general jurisdiction over grand strategic policy and such related matters as the allocation of forces and of war materials. The War Department soon made it clear that for the time MacArthur's role would be defensive.[9] Similarly, Admiral Nimitz received orders to hold island positions between the Southwest Pacific and the United States, support operations in the Southwest Pacific area, protect sea and air communications and "prepare for the execution of major amphibious offensives to be launched from the South Pacific Area and the Southwest Pacific Area."[10]

Both Admiral King and General MacArthur urged a diversion of greater support to the Pacific.[11] Early in May, President Roosevelt explained to the General that the simple fact was that Russian armies

[8] Message, Roosevelt to Churchill, 18 Feb 42, No. 106, with JPS 11 in ABC 323.31 POA (1-29-42), 1-A, quoted in *ibid.*, p. 165; CCS 57/2, Strategic Responsibility of the U.K. and the U.S., 24 Mar 42, in ABC 323.31, POA (1-29-42), Sec. 2 cited in *ibid.*, p. 20 *n.*

[9] Message (originator WPD), Marshall to MacArthur (CG USAFFE, Melbourne), 18 Mar 42, No. 739, WPD Msg. File 13, 1885, quoted in *ibid.*, p. 172.

[10] JCS Directive to the CinC Pacific Ocean Area, 30 Mar 42, in CCS 57/1, quoted in Samuel Milner, *Victory in Papua* (*United States Army in World War II: The War in the Pacific*) (Washington, 1957), p. 22.

[11] Memo, King for CofS, 29 Mar 42, sub: Strategic Deployment in Pacific

were "killing more Axis personnel and destroying more Axis matériel than all the other twenty-five United Nations put together." Consequently, stated the President, it seemed "wholly logical" to aid the Russians in 1942 by sending all munitions possible to them and "also to develop plans aimed at diverting German land and air forces from the Russian front."[12] In reply, MacArthur urged that the place for the "second front" was in the Pacific, for "nowhere else can it be so successfully launched and nowhere else will it so assist the Russians."[13]

For a time Pacific plans appeared to be competing with the "Bolero" plans for build-up in England, but Roosevelt made it clear that he did not want Bolero slowed down, and the War Department took Roosevelt's letter as authorization to bring forces in the Pacific merely to authorized strength.[14] General Marshall resisted heavy pressure from Admiral King to increase the priorities of heavy bombers to the Pacific in view of intercepted messages in a broken Japanese code which predicted a massed naval and air attack in the Pacific. The War Department could and did use planes and forces already in the area.

As we shall see, the Japanese made their attack and were checked at Midway. The victory strengthened the United States Navy's belief in its tactics of naval air attack on surface vessels and in the protection land-based planes could give a fleet. More important, the Battle of Midway made possible the start of a limited offensive, and discussion began of a move into the Solomons.[15]

On July 8, 1942, the British government decided not to continue with the plan to invade Western Europe in 1942 (Operation Sledgehammer) and instead urged the United States to agree to North African invasion. General Marshall suggested as an alternative that "the U.S. should turn to the Pacific for decisive action against Japan."[16] It

---

Against Japan, Navy File A 16-3 (1), quoted in Matloff and Snell, *Strategic Planning*, p. 211.

[12] In Memo, CofS for President, 6 May 42, no sub, Items 7a and 53, Exec. 10, quoted in *ibid.*, pp. 214–215.

[13] Message, MacArthur to Marshall, 8 May 42, CM-IN 2333, quoted in *ibid.*, pp. 215–216.

[14] Memo, CofS for President, 6 May 42, sub: Pacific Theater versus Bolero, and three incls, with JCS 48 in ABC 381 Pacific Bases (1-22-42) 2, quoted in *ibid.*, pp. 218–219.

[15] John Miller, Jr., *Guadalcanal: The First Offensive (United States Army in World War II: The War in the Pacific)* (Washington, 1949), p. 9.

[16] Min. 24th mtg JCS, 10 Jul 42, quoted in Matloff and Snell, *Strategic Planning*, p. 268.

is clear that Marshall saw the alternative mainly as a weapon to force the British to continue with plans to attack Western Europe.[17] President Roosevelt made the key decision; he would not even present the alternative to the British. He sent King, Marshall, and Harry Hopkins to London with instructions that he was "opposed to an American all-out effort in the Pacific" to defeat Japan as quickly as possible. Such action would delay defeat of Germany and increase the chance of "German domination of Europe and Africa." On the other hand, predicted the President, "Defeat of Germany means the defeat of Japan, probably without firing a shot or losing a life."[18]

Logistical problems differed in marked respects from those in the Atlantic or Mediterranean. Distances, for example, were greater and mainly over water. It was 3,500 nautical miles from New York to Liverpool or Casablanca; from San Francisco it was 6,400 to Nouméa in New Caledonia and 7,200 to Brisbane. In July, 1942, Marshall and King estimated that it would take as much shipping to transport 40,000 troops to Australia as it would to send 100,000 to the British Isles.[19] Since it was difficult to establish central points in the Pacific area for distribution of supplies, most shipping went directly to all types of island bases. There was a heavy drain on shipping space for construction materials and labor for creating storage, base, port, and transportation facilities. Tropical living conditions and jungle obstacles further complicated the problem as they debilitated the men and wreaked havoc with materials. In addition, parallel lines of separate Army and Navy organizations often led to duplication and waste. In spite of obstacles, support of the Pacific war was considerable; by the end of June, 1942, almost half (245,000) of the U.S. Army troops stationed outside the country (505,000) were protecting the line from Hawaii to Australia. Toward the end of the year a little over half of the divisions overseas and about one-third of air-combat groups overseas were in the war against Japan. Despite the main strategy to concentrate on

[17] Stimson agreed with Marshall at the time and later regretted his position. Henry L. Stimson and McGeorge Bundy, *On Active Service in Peace and War* (New York, 1947, 1948), pp. 424–425.

[18] Memo, President for Hopkins, Marshall, and King, 16 Jul 42, sub: Instns for London Conf—July 1942, WDCSA 381, 1 (SS), quoted in Matloff and Snell, *Strategic Planning*, pp. 272–273.

[19] Memo, Marshall, King, and Arnold for President, 12 Jul 42, sub: Pac Opns, OPD 381 Gen. 73, cited in Leighton and Coakley, *Global Logistics and Strategy*, p. 386.

Germany and the Bolero plan, the Pacific during the year got considerably more support than originally planned, not only in manpower
but in planes and supplies.[20]

While the top command coped with plans and logistics, forces in the
Pacific were attempting to check Japanese advances. Encouraged by
their startling early successes, instead of pausing to establish themselves
in their newly gained lands, the Japanese developed plans for a new
three-part offensive.[21] First would be seizure of Tulagi in the Solomons
and Port Moresby in Papua on the southeastern shore of New Guinea
as a means of gaining air control of the Coral Sea and the lands
around it. The second objective was to take Midway Atoll and the
Western Aleutian Islands in order to force the U.S. Pacific Fleet into
a decisive engagement. A secondary purpose was to help guard Japan
from attacks from the sea. After April 18, 1942, the Japanese were a
little sensitive to attacks from this direction, for on that day sixteen
U.S. Army bombers, B-25's, suddenly appeared over Japan and began
to bomb military targets, mainly in the Tokyo area. The famous Tokyo
raid was apparently conceived as a stimulus to the morale of a nation
hard hit and reeling in the Pacific from the blows of the enemy.[22] The
risks were too great for a carrier raid by carrier planes, but an attack
on Tokyo from carriers by Army bombers flying on to Chinese airfields
would not only damage Japan but provide planes for the Chinese
national defenses.

After practicing take-offs from spaces the size of a carrier top on a
Florida airfield, Lieutenant Colonel James H. Doolittle's squadron of
volunteer bomber crews left San Francisco with their planes loaded on
the open deck of the carrier, *Hornet*, which rendezvoused between the
western Aleutians and Midway with Task Force 16, under command
of Vice Admiral William F. Halsey, Jr. About a thousand miles from
Tokyo, on April 17, the carriers and cruisers left destroyers and oilers
behind in a dash toward Japan. Sighted earlier than they had hoped,
Halsey and Doolittle knew that the element of surprise was lost and
although the 650 miles instead of the 450 or 500 miles hoped for from

[20] Matloff and Snell, *Strategic Planning*, pp. 357–360; Leighton and Coakley, *Global Logistics and Strategy*, pp. 388–416.
[21] Morison, *History of United States Naval Operations in World War II*
(Boston, 1949), IV, 5–6.
[22] W. F. Craven and J. L. Cate, *The Army Air Forces in World War II*
(Chicago, 1948), I, 438–444.

Japan made arrival in China problematical, they decided to send the bombers on a daylight attack.[23]

Although the bombers had never flown from a carrier before, the pilots managed without mishap to take their heavy planes into the air. Thirteen headed for Tokyo and the other three for Nagoya, Osaka, and Kobe. When the planes reached Tokyo, by a curious coincidence that city was undergoing a test air raid with simulated attacks by Japanese aircraft. Aside from those affected by the actual bombing, probably few citizens realized that they were experiencing the real thing. The test raid aided the Americans in that the real alarm was slow in sounding, and with minor damage the bombers moved on toward China. There their luck ran out, word did not reach darkened Chinese airfields of their coming, and most flew until out of fuel and crash-landed or the crews parachuted. One man died in a parachute drop; eight men landed in enemy territory and of these, three were executed for bombing errors which had resulted in hits on Japanese residential areas. The only plane to land safely was seized by the Russians and interned. Physically, the results of the raid were slight, the effect on enemy morale was negligible, and usable planes had failed to reach China. There was a certain bolstering of morale among the Allies when there was little other cause for rejoicing.[24] The Japanese officials knew of the raid, but did not know the bombers had flown from carriers, and some even suspected that they had come from Midway.

As a third phase of conquest, the Japanese contemplated seizure of New Caledonia, Fiji, and Samoa to cut communications between Australasia and the United States.

Meanwhile, the United States was slowly adding to its strength in Australia and beginning substantial defense installations on New Caledonia.[25] The U.S. Joint Chiefs of Staff assigned the Pacific Ocean Area to Admiral Nimitz, but broke the tremendous expanse into three administrative regions, two controlled directly by Nimitz and the third, the South, indirectly through a deputy, Vice Admiral R. L. Ghormley. Early efforts at shipment encountered mishaps through inexperience as, for example, when ships arrived expecting to unload by means of

[23] For an account stressing the Navy's part in the raid, see Morison, *History,* III, 389–398.

[24] For appraisals of the raid, see *ibid.,* III, p. 398; Craven and Cate, *The A.A.F. in World War II,* I, 442, 444.

[25] Milner, *Victory in Papua,* pp. 14–15; Craven and Cate, *The A.A.F. in World War II,* I, 431.

floating equipment which could not be reached without first unloading the rest of the cargo.[26] Fortunately, such experiences prevented more serious difficulties in later landings.

The Japanese continued their moves, establishing a major base at Rabaul early in 1942, and in March moving across to Lae and Salamaua on New Guinea, north of Port Moresby, which was on the south shore separated by the lofty Owen Stanley Range.[27] Then they established a fighter strip on Buna, most northerly of the Solomons and on nearby Bougainville.[28]

Although not prepared to mount a major offensive, United States naval forces early in 1942 undertook a series of nuisance raids, which were not particularly successful but which gave valuable experience both in the air and afloat.[29] In one of these the *Enterprise* in a small task force made a raid on Wake Island and then in a daring move struck at Marcus Island, less than twelve hundred miles from Japan. The action stimulated morale but inflicted relatively minor damage. A little later, with a force including two carriers, Vice Admiral Wilson Brown sent carrier planes in a spectacular raid over the Owen Stanley Mountains against Lae and Salamaua.

While these carrier raids may have raised American morale, they probably had little effect as a deterrent to the Japanese, who continued their plans to advance. Their next objective in the Southwest Pacific was Port Moresby. Postwar analysis indicates that the complexity of the plan contributed to its failure. The Allied forces, having broken the enemy's code, were forewarned and tried to muster what forces they had.[30] The Japanese thought their carriers were sufficient and were unaware that the *Lexington* had gone to join the *Yorktown* in the Coral Sea.[31]

The Japanese had several objectives. One invasion group headed for Tulagi to seize it and establish a seaplane base. A much larger force,

[26] Leighton and Coakley, *Global, Logistics and Strategy*, pp. 176–177, 179–185.

[27] Milner, *Victory in Papua*, pp. 10–11.

[28] John N. Rentz, *Marines in the Central Solomons* (Marine Corps Monographs [11]) ([Washington] 1952), p. 4.

[29] An account of these early raids will be found in Morison, *History*, III, 261–268, 387–389; IV, 13.

[30] E. B. Potter (ed.), *The United States and World Sea Power* (Englewood Cliffs, N.J., 1955), p. 674.

[31] This account of the Battle of the Coral Sea is drawn primarily from Morison, *History*, IV, 10–63.

consisting of eleven transports supported by destroyers, planned an amphibious assault on Port Moresby. Covering it was a group of one light carrier, the *Shoho,* four heavy cruisers, and a destroyer which intended to continue south and act as one part of a pincers movement against Allied sea and air power in the Coral Sea. Another larger striking force, consisting of two large carriers, two heavy cruisers, and six destroyers, planned to move south as the other part of the pincers to close in on the enemy. This division of forces placed a heavy premium on close coordination.

On the *Yorktown,* Admiral Fletcher, who was in tactical command, heard of the Japanese move toward Tulagi and made a daring and perhaps reckless air raid on the Japanese which sank three mine sweepers and forced one destroyer to beach itself. Luckily he avoided detection and met the *Lexington* at the rendezvous on May 5, one day late. On the seventh, Japanese planes located a destroyer (*Sims*) and an oiler (*Neosho*), sank the former, and damaged the other so badly that it later had to be scuttled. On the same day, American planes located the carrier *Shoho* and sank it, leaving the U.S. carriers open to attack. Japanese planes, however, were so preoccupied with the oiler and the destroyer that they did not discover the carriers.

Toward evening some of the opposing planes met and fought, but night intervened and neither tried a night attack. On the following day came the climax of the Battle of the Coral Sea. The aircraft were about equal in number, 121 Japanese and 122 American. The battle ended shortly before noon, and at that time the American forces had won a victory. They had lost thirty-three planes to the enemy's forty-three. They had destroyed a light carrier, a destroyer, and several mine craft and knocked a heavy carrier, *Shokaku,* temporarily out of action. Both the *Lexington* and the *Yorktown* had been hit, however, and about an hour after the fighting, on the *Lexington* there suddenly occurred a terrific explosion followed by even more severe internal blasts. Apparently a motor generator left running had ignited gasoline vapors. Fires started, and about two hours later another explosion doomed the vessel. The men were removed to safety on other vessels, and the destroyer *Phelps* sank the flaming hulk with torpedoes.

This loss reversed the decision and gave the tactical victory to the Japanese; strategically, the victory still went to the Americans. The Port Moresby invasion force returned to Rabaul without attempting to land, and the battle marked the most distant advance of the Japanese in the Southwest Pacific. In addition, both enemy carriers were out of action for the Battle of Midway, which followed. The Battle of the Coral Sea was the first naval engagement in history in which surface craft had not fired at each other. There were numerous errors made by each side through inexperience, but news of heroism aboard the *Lexington* and elsewhere during the battle gave a needed boost to American morale.[32]

Even before the Battle of the Coral Sea, Admiral Nimitz became aware that the Japanese were planning a great offensive in the Central Pacific, and he became convinced that a principal target would be strategically located Midway, situated about eleven hundred miles from Hawaii.[33]

Admiral Yamamoto had a dual purpose, to take Midway and locations in the Aleutians as key points in an expanded perimeter of defense and to draw out enemy naval forces. According to his plans, an advance force of submarines would precede a striking force centering about four carriers. In addition, there would be a landing force to occupy Midway and a main force of three battleships and a light carrier. Another task force including two carriers and an occupation force would head for the Aleutians. He planned to start with a feint at Dutch Harbor in the Aleutians, a softening up of Midway, and a strike at the U.S. Fleet if it interfered. At night the occupation force would land on Midway, and the northern force would fall back and stand on guard halfway between the Aleutians and Midway.

Aided greatly by intelligence reports, Admiral Nimitz believed these reports instead of assuming as did some officers that this was a great Japanese hoax. In retrospect, it can be seen that Yamamoto made a basic error in planning. Having strongly superior forces in all important categories of vessels, he dissipated their strength by dividing and separating them. He also misjudged the probable actions of the enemy. Underestimating the number of carriers which the United States would have available and knowing that Nimitz had no fast battleships, he evidently anticipated easy conquest of Midway and expected that the enemy would then be forced to counterattack.

[32] For appraisals of the Battle of the Coral Sea, see *ibid.*, IV, 63–64; Craven and Cate, *The A.A.F. in World II*, I, 450–451; A. R. Buchanan (ed.), *The Navy's Air War: A Mission Completed* (New York [1946]), p. 147; E. B. Potter and Chester W. Nimitz (ed.), *The Great Sea War: The Story of Naval Action in World War II* (Englewood Cliffs, N.J., 1960), pp. 219–220.

[33] Morison, *History*, IV, 69–74.

Nimitz was able to send three carriers out of Hawaii, the *Enterprise* and *Hornet,* as well as the *Yorktown,* which had been restored to fighting trim in three days by fourteen hundred men working around the clock in Pearl Harbor. Halsey, who had brought in the *Enterprise* and *Hornet,* was temporarily on the sick list with a skin ailment and was replaced by Rear Admiral Raymond A. Spruance, who although not so colorful as Halsey possessed ability and strength.[34] The United States battleships in the Pacific were too slow for the carriers, and Nimitz declined to use them. However, he had the advantage over the Japanese of shorter distance from base to area of hostilities, and he had *Midway,* which in effect was an unsinkable carrier, satisfactorily equipped with radar. On it the Marines, preparing to resist invasion, mined the surrounding beaches and installed sturdy defenses. Their weakness was in the air, for their planes were obsolescent and many of the pilots inexperienced.[35] The Army Air Forces sent in B-17's and B-26's to bolster the defenses.[36]

By the end of May, opposing forces were moving toward their objectives. The Japanese advance submarines arrived late and did not sight the American carriers; a Navy PBY pilot located the Japanese transports, but, as a result of good intelligence, the U.S. task force leader was not misled into thinking this was the main Japanese force. Instead, planes from Midway attacked the transports, with reported successes that were not borne out in later estimates. The major engagements took place on the following day, June 4. Japanese planes left their carriers about four-thirty in the morning from a point about 240 miles distant from Midway. Marine planes met them about thirty miles out, but were outnumbered and outmaneuvered by the superior Zero-type Japanese fighter planes and failed to check the bombers, which from fourteen thousand feet dropped their loads, causing a good deal of damage to property but not to life. The first round went to the Japanese, for the Marine fighters had been hard hit. Marine and Army bombers flew from Midway against the carriers; without fighter protection they suffered heavy loss without compensating damage to the enemy.

Meanwhile, *Yorktown* scouts had located the Japanese carriers. Knowing of the carrier attack on Midway, Admiral Spruance took one

---

[34] *Ibid.,* IV, 74–85.

[35] Robert D. Heinl, Jr., *Marines at Midway* (Marine Corps Monographs [3]) ([Washington] 1948), pp. 24–30.

[36] Craven and Cate, *The A.A.F. in World War II,* I, 455–456.

of the big risks of the war and sent the planes from the *Hornet* and *Enterprise* early, and he sent all that were operable, even though they might run out of gas, in the hope that he could catch the enemy carriers in the process of refueling and rearming.[37] While the carrier planes were heading toward their objective, more land-based planes made unsuccessful attempts to reach and destroy the target. A U.S. submarine discovered the Japanese vessels and missed with a torpedo; it then managed to exist through a heavy concentration of depth charges.

So ineffectual were these assaults that the Japanese did not let them interfere with the recovery of planes from the attack on Midway. A little past eight-thirty in the morning, these planes began to return and by 0917 all bombers were on board, refueling or rearming. Knowing that U.S. carrier planes were headed toward him, the Japanese striking force commander, Vice Admiral C. Nagumo, planned to counterattack as soon as he could get his planes into the air, and he ordered his force to shift directions. This turn caused the first group of dive bombers from the *Hornet* to miss the target and the battle. Torpedo Squadron 8 sighted the enemy and having been separated from its fighter escorts decided to attack without them. The slow, vulnerable planes did not have a chance, and all fifteen were shot down before they could inflict any injury on the enemy; one pilot, Ensign George H. Gay, survived by floating in the water and hiding under a rubber seat cushion. Other torpedo planes arrived and were almost as ineffective; of the forty-six which participated only six returned, and none reached the enemy carriers with their torpedoes. Actually, however, the courageous men who flew these planes against seemingly hopeless odds made a real contribution to victory. Their attacks forced the carriers into so much maneuvering that they could not launch their planes, and in addition the torpedo bombers drew down from their high altitude Japanese fighters who consequently were not prepared to deal with U.S. dive bombers which arrived for the attack.

Thirty-seven dive bombers from the *Enterprise* and *Yorktown*, carrying five-hundred- and thousand-pound bombs, went into their dives. The *Akagi*, with forty planes being serviced on deck, took three bomb hits, had to be abandoned, and later sunk. Two other carriers, *Kaga* and *Soryu*, received hits and sank, one with further assistance from a U.S. submarine. The fourth carrier, *Hiryu*, was also doomed, but it

[37] This account of the Battle of Midway is drawn primarily from Morison, *History*, IV, 69–159.

wreaked vengeance in advance when its planes made two attacks on the *Yorktown* and left it in a helpless condition. B-17's from Midway first found the *Hiryu* and knocked out an antiaircraft battery. U.S. dive bombers then located the ship, damaged it severely, and started fires which led to its destruction. A Japanese submarine fatally hit the *Yorktown* and a destroyer, *Hammann,* which was attempting salvage operations. The Battle of Midway ended rather slowly. Dive bombers, on the sixth, located two Japanese cruisers which had collided with each other while attempting to avoid being hit by a U.S. submarine, sank one and damaged the other so badly that it was out of action for two years.

The Japanese had been somewhat more successful in their attack on the Aleutians, in which their plan had been to occupy a few of the westernmost islands. Aided by bad weather, an American force too far east to be able to interfere, and a couple of air raids on Dutch Harbor, the Japanese on June 7 landed with insignificant opposition on Kiska and Attu.[38]

The Battle of Midway was a major victory and may well have been the turning point in the Pacific war. It demonstrated that carrier air power properly utilized could defeat a superior surface force. It marked the end of the Japanese advance, insured the retention of both Midway and the Hawaiian Islands. The Allies would find the road back through the Pacific hard but they had started in the right direction. Statistics emphasized the victory. In losing a carrier and a destroyer, the U.S. forces had sunk four carriers and a cruiser. The American loss in planes was 150 to 253 for the enemy. The disparity was greater in loss of life; 307 Americans died in contrast to 3,500 Japanese, including a hundred pilots. This loss of naval aviators was a critical one for the Japanese.[39]

Potentially, the occupation of Kiska and Attu constituted a menace to the United States, just as American military movement in the region posed a danger to the Japanese homeland. Actually, largely as a result of the generally bad weather in the North Pacific and the emphasis on war elsewhere, the Aleutians became a minor theater of operations. There was a stalemate for about nine months, during which weather made what air and naval engagements there were hard, frustrating, and indecisive. Unaware that the Japanese were conducting merely a holding operation, American public opinion demanded that U.S. forces

[38] *Ibid.,* IV, 170–172.
[39] Potter (ed.), *U.S. and World Sea Power,* p. 701.

retake Kiska and Attu. The American government also wanted to dislodge the Japanese to clear the way for Lend-Lease support to Soviet Russia by way of Vladivostok, and American commanders in the North Pacific area were anxious to move against the Japanese. General Marshall and his staff planners on the other hand felt that little would be gained from such action unless Soviet Russia entered the war and unless greater use was made of the northern route to Japan. They wished also to fit operations in the Aleutians into over-all planning for the Pacific. At the Casablanca Conference of January, 1943, Allied planners merely stated that the objective was to make the Aleutians secure. In the Trident Conference, held in Washington the following May, the Joint Chiefs of Staff, with the assent of the British Chiefs of Staff, proposed to eject the Japanese from the Aleutians. A move in this direction had already begun, for plans were developing for an attack on Attu, which though farther west than Kiska was considered a better initial target.[40] Late in March, as a result of a long-range surface battle, an American force turned back Japanese transports headed for reinforcement of Attu.[41] Preparations for the American assault were completed, and on May 11, U.S. 7th Division troops began landings on the treeless and mountainous island of Attu. The conquest was largely a foot soldier's battle, for the unpredictable weather made air and naval support equally unpredictable, and the Aleutian mud imprisoned tanks and other vehicles. Hard fighting continued throughout May until the Japanese were forced into a flat area around the Chicagof Harbor base. On the night of May 29, about a thousand Japanese failed in a fierce banzai attack, and half committed suicide. The remainder held out for about a day and a half and then either killed themselves or were killed. The landing force of some 11,000 men had lost about 600 of their number to take an island with 2,351 dead Japanese and 28 prisoners.[42]

On August 13, an expeditionary force of some 34,426 troops, including 5,000 Canadians, left Adak and began landings on Kiska two days later. Groping through the fog on the island friend fired on friend, and other soldiers were killed or wounded by booby traps. For five days the

[40] Maurice Matloff, *Strategic Planning for Coalition Warfare, 1943–1944* (*United States Army in World War II: The War Department*) (Washington, 1959), pp. 100, 138, 144.

[41] Morison, *History,* VII, 22–36.

[42] Accounts of the conquest of Attu include *ibid.,* VII, 37–51; Craven and Cate, *The A.A.F. in World War II,* IV, 377–386.

Americans searched for Japanese and found only two or three mongrel dogs. Offshore, a Japanese mine broke loose, struck a vessel, and cost seventy lives.[43] The Japanese, unnoticed, had evacuated the island some time before the attack, and when news came of the occupation, exulted in the trick they had played. They had, indeed, extricated a garrison from a dangerously exposed position. On the other hand, U.S. forces thereafter controlled the Aleutians.

After conclusion of the Aleutian campaign, the theater became a minor one, although in Washington planning continued for a northern approach to Japan in case Soviet Russia entered the war. Plans, which never materialized, also included establishing B-29 bases in the Alaskan Department.[44] Although the U.S. forces made no moves on Japan from the northern route, aside from light raids, it should be noted that the Japanese immobilized sizable ground troops and over four hundred aircraft to ward off the attack that never came.[45]

[43] Morison, *History*, VII, 52–66.

[44] In November, 1943, the War Department created an Alaskan Department, as a separate theater of operations. Matloff, *Strategic Planning, 1943–1944*, pp. 316–317.

[45] Craven and Cate, *The A.A.F. in World War II*, IV, 401.

CHAPTER 11

Guadalcanal and Papua

AS A RESULT of the defeat at Midway the Japanese canceled their plans to invade New Caledonia, Fiji, and Samoa, and instead turned to strengthen some of the areas already occupied. The local commander of the new seaplane base on Tulagi, possibly on his own initiative, had ordered the construction of an airfield on Guadalcanal, another island in the Solomons about twenty miles away. Coastwatchers forwarded information of these activities to Australian Intelligence, and this knowledge affected Allied action.[1]

The most important Japanese stronghold in this part of the South-west Pacific was Rabaul, on the northeastern end of New Britain. Warships and planes from Rabaul threatened the line of communications between the United States and Australia. It was also a strong point in what came to be called the Bismarck barrier, which blocked Allied advance along the north coast of New Guinea or toward the Philippines.

The victory at Midway made it possible for the American high command to plan a limited initiative, although the strategic purpose still remained defensive, to check the Japanese advance and protect the line of communications to Australia. After a debate arose between the Army and Navy over command, Admiral King and General Marshall worked out a compromise, embodied in a directive by the Joint Chiefs

[1] John Miller, Jr., *Guadalcanal: The First Offensive* (*United States Army in World War II: The War in the Pacific*) (Washington, 1949), pp. 5–8.

of Staff, July 2, 1942. They assigned three tasks, the first of which was occupation of the Santa Cruz Islands, Tulagi, and "adjacent positions." Admiral Nimitz would designate the officer in command, and General MacArthur would furnish necessary assistance and prevent enemy attack from the west. Task Two charged MacArthur with the seizure of Lae and Salamaua and the rest of the northwest coast of New Guinea. MacArthur would also head Task Three, which was the conquest of Rabaul and adjoining positions. To simplify command relations, the Joint Chiefs of Staff shifted the boundary between the South Pacific and Southwest Pacific so that Tulagi and Guadalcanal fell in Vice Admiral Robert R. Ghormley's area.[2]

Since the beginning of the twentieth century the United States Marine Corps had been developing a doctrine of amphibious assault. In 1934, the Fleet Marine Force came into being as a part of the fleet, and the following year, the Marine Corps issued a tentative manual of landing instructions. The Navy adopted the manual with revisions in 1938, and in 1941 the Army used it extensively in preparing its first basic field manual for landings on hostile shores. The doctrine applied to amphibious assault against determined and strong opposition rather than to amphibious landings against little or no resistance. Basically, this doctrine broke amphibious assault into six parts:

1. *Command relationships.* Command relationships of the various services involved are essential. The Gallipoli offensive in World War I, for example, had failed in part because of jurisdictional controversy.

2. *Naval gunfire.* Artillery support is essential just before and during the ship-to-shore movement. The doctrine on this point was clear; the need was to develop techniques to implement it.

3. *Aerial support.* Aircraft plays a triple role in amphibious assault, preinvasion reconnaissance flights, protection of the ship-to-shore movement, and participation in the attack.

4. *Ship-to-shore movement.* This is a tactical movement rather than a mere ferrying operation and is designed to transport troops as rapidly and safely as possible to designated locations on the beach.

5. *Securing the beachhead.* It is necessary to secure a zone contiguous to the beach which will permit the continuous landing of troops and supplies without serious interference from the enemy and provide ample space to maneuver for further advance.

[2] Maurice Matloff and Edwin M. Snell, *Strategic Planning for Coalition Warfare, 1941–1942* (*United States Army in World War II: The War Department*) (Washington, 1953), pp. 258–265.

6. *Logistics.* An essential condition for successful landing operations is proper loading of vessels.[3]

This amphibious assault doctrine played an important role in the Pacific war.

Although Admiral Nimitz had started planning the invasion of the Solomons some time before the July 2 directive set the target date at August 1, the time for preparation was still short. Nimitz assigned to Ghormley strategic control, to Vice Admiral Frank J. Fletcher command of the entire sea-borne invasion, to Rear Admiral Richmond Kelly Turner direction of the amphibious force, to Major General Alexander A. Vandegrift command of the Marines who would lead the assault, and to Rear Admiral John S. McCain control of land-based aircraft. General MacArthur was also expected to provide land-based planes. News of Japanese activity on Guadalcanal caused it to be added to Tulagi as one of the first objectives.

While Nimitz, Fletcher, and Turner discussed plans in Honolulu, Ghormley flew from New Zealand to Australia to confer with Mac-Arthur. They urged delay in launching Task One until all three tasks could be attempted at once, but the Joint Chiefs of Staff rejected the recommendation, feeling that Japanese concentration in New Guinea might increase the chances of a surprise Allied attack in the Solomons.[4] Several factors made the effort a definite risk. The invaders knew little about the terrain they were approaching or the sea around it, since charts were inadequate and often inaccurate. Tulagi and Guadalcanal lay about twenty miles apart, separated by a strip of water which Americans soon came to call Iron Bottom Sound. To the south was Guadalcanal, about ninety miles long and twenty-five wide. Much of it was mountainous, steaming jungle, infested with malaria-bearing mosquitoes, and drenched with excessive rainfall. Where there were no trees there were plains covered with high, tough, sharp-bladed *kunai* grass. Only in scattered places along the shore had men replaced jungle with coconut plantations, and even there swollen streams impeded progress. Tulagi, an islet adjacent to Florida Island across the sound, was the center of British government in the Solomons and was somewhat more highly developed than Guadalcanal.[5]

[3] Jeter A. Isely and Philip A. Crowl, *The U. S. Marines and Amphibious War: Its Theory and Its Practice in the Pacific* (Princeton, 1951), pp. 37–44.

[4] John L. Zimmerman, *The Guadalcanal Campaign* (Marine Corps Monographs [V]) ([Washington] 1949), p. 9.

[5] Samuel E. Morison, *History of United States Naval Operations in World War II* (Boston, 1949), V, 4–11.

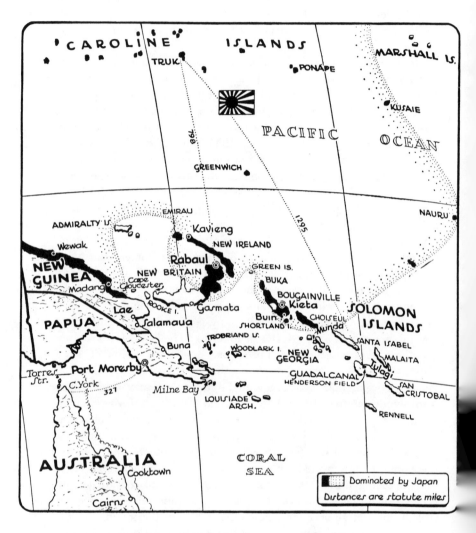

NEW GUINEA AND THE SOLOMONS

Although there were about 32,000 Army ground troops in the South Pacific, they could not be used easily as replacements on Guadalcanal, for Ghormley felt they could not be released from garrison duty.[6] Consequently, the men of the 1st Marine Division who landed as assault troops stayed for months as combat troops instead of being released for further amphibious operations.

Major General Vandegrift, in command of this division, was a veteran of Marine duty in the Caribbean and China. His division had been organized around two infantry regiments, the 1st Marines and the 5th Marines, with some training in North Carolina and Maryland. While the division was on its way to New Zealand, Vandegrift found to his consternation that he would have to take his men into action in August without further training; he proceeded on the assumption that the Allies would have control of sea and air routes to the Solomons.[7] Combat reloading of vessels took place in New Zealand with limited facilities and under adverse weather conditions. Longshoremen, unaware of the purpose of the reloading and jealous of their hard-won labor rights, declined to work overtime, and the Marines themselves had to perform most of the manual labor involved.[8] When the reinforced 7th Marines were detached for garrison duty in Samoa, the reinforced 2d Marines of the 2d Marine Division sailed from San Diego to become the landing force reserve. The addition of the 1st Raider Division and the 3d Defense Battalion raised the division strength to over nineteen thousand.

By the time of the invasion, Admiral McCain had 291 land-based planes, including Army heavy and medium bombers and Naval patrol craft, for preliminary bombing and interdiction of enemy attacks after the landings were made. Planes of three carriers, *Wasp, Enterprise,* and *Saratoga,* were to cover the amphibious assault.[9]

Command relations were poor; Admiral Ghormley moved his headquarters from New Zealand to Nouméa but never saw the force which he technically controlled and did not get into the combat area. Actually he had little authority over Admiral Fletcher and no advance consultation with him. In turn Fletcher did not collaborate effectively with Admiral Turner, who reported directly to Ghormley.[10]

[6] Miller, *Guadalcanal,* p. 24.
[7] *Ibid.,* p. 41.
[8] Zimmerman, *Guadalcanal Campaign,* p. 21.
[9] Morison, *History,* V, 14.
[10] Isely and Crowl, *The U.S. Marines and Amphibious War,* pp. 105–109.

Delays caused Ghormley to postpone the attack to August 7, and toward the end of July the combined forces met in the Fijis for rehearsal. Practice landings were unsatisfactory, but at least they brought the leaders of the attack force together. At this time Fletcher, who should have welded the component parts into a fighting unit, declined to assume this responsibility, and Vandegrift and Turner had to work out their own problems. The task force commander also made it evident that he looked on the attack more as a raid than as a permanent landing. Somewhat defense-minded from his months of warfare to date, he refused to risk his carriers and announced that his planes would not cover the operations later than the fourth day after landing. He had reason for caution, for the Japanese had fast battleships and at least five carriers at Rabaul or Truk, but it was only in the Fijis on the eve of attack that Fletcher relayed to Turner and Vandegrift this news of Japanese naval superiority in the area. For the first time the Marine Commander, who had anticipated conditions of land, sea, and air control, found that he was taking nineteen thousand men to a region 550 miles beyond the nearest friendly air base. Since for security reasons radio silence was in effect, Vandegrift could not appeal to Ghormley; he could only argue with Fletcher. At last Turner promised that surface craft would remain in the region as long as possible, and it was agreed that land-based planes would be ferried into Guadalcanal probably the morning after the departure of the carriers. Of course, these could not function unless the Japanese had virtually completed the airfield and the Americans could capture it intact.[11]

Seven days before the landings, B-17's flying from primitive fields in the New Hebrides began preliminary bombardments of the target areas, while other land planes watched enemy movements and helped chart this little-known area.[12] The invading forces left the Fijis on July 31, and in their approach, helped by poor weather, did not come in contact with the enemy. In clearing weather the forces entered the sound on August 7, and as Marines moved from transports to landing barges about nine thousand yards offshore, cruisers and destroyers opened fire, destroying the only Japanese craft in sight, a small gasoline schooner. Marines under Brigadier General William H. Rupertus made unopposed landings on Tulagi and adjacent islets and found that the Jap-

11 *Ibid.*, pp. 116–117.
12 Wesley Frank Craven and James Lea Cate, *The Army Air Forces in World War II* (Chicago, 1950), IV, 35–36.

anese had retired to hill tunnels and emplacements. Not yet using flame throwers, the Marines had to blast the enemy out with grenades and high explosives placed by hand against the defenses. By the end of the day, with heavy casualties, the Marines had wiped out a tenacious foe almost to the man.[13]

Landings were virtually unopposed on Guadalcanal, and by eight in the evening ten thousand men were ashore. These were the reinforced 5th Marines (less the 2d Battalion) and the reinforced 1st Marines. Tactically, the operation was succeeding well, and on the next day a Marine battalion took the airfield, left practically intact by the rapidly retreating enemy. Logistically, the situation was less favorable. Unloading parties were exhausted from having to lift everything over the sides of old-fashioned landing craft, there were not enough of the versatile amphibious tractors, and early in the afternoon the air raids began. Fortunately advance warning by coastwatchers enabled vessels to scatter and avoid heavy damage, but the air raids produced delays in discharging cargo.[14]

Then late in the afternoon of August 8, Admiral Turner received word that a Japanese naval force was approaching the northern Solomons through a passage soon to be known as the Slot, and he posted destroyers and cruisers on watch or patrol. At about the same time Admiral Fletcher made a significant and, some critics feel, unfortunate decision. Concerned because his carriers were within reach of land-based planes and because his fuel was running low, he decided to withdraw them earlier than he had indicated in the Fijis. Securing permission from Ghormley, he left the morning of the ninth. It is true that his planes had been depleted by attacks on Japanese air raiders, but he still had seventy-eight planes, and he could have sent his carriers out one at a time for refueling.

Admiral Turner not only received news of Fletcher's decision but he heard through MacArthur's headquarters that an Australian pilot had sighted the Japanese vessels headed down the Slot. This report had tragic consequences. In the first place, instead of breaking radio silence with this significant information, the pilot completed his patrol, had tea, and then turned in his report, which reached Guadalcanal about eight hours after the sighting. More important, he mistakenly identified

13 Zimmerman, *Guadalcanal Campaign*, pp. 27–33; Miller, *Guadalcanal*, pp. 61–67.

14 Zimmerman, *Guadalcanal Campaign*, pp. 41–49.

two of the vessels as seaplane tenders, although actually there were five heavy cruisers, two light cruisers, and a destroyer. Turner reasoned from the report that the enemy was planning to establish a seaplane base near the invading forces. Since he was losing his carrier support, the commander of the amphibious forces decided that he would have to leave the following morning, and he and Rear Admiral V. A. C. Crutchley, the screen commander, had a long talk with General Vandegrift. It was near dawn when Crutchley returned to his flagship, the cruiser *Australia,* and he ordered the vessel to patrol seven miles west of the transports.

The Japanese force was not headed to establish a seaplane base; with crews carefully trained for night action, they hoped to make a surprise attack against American warships and transports. Their good luck continued as they neared their target. One of the Allied pickets saw an observation plane fly overhead about eleven at night, August 8, and issued a warning which for some reason was ignored by other ships and did not reach Admiral Turner's flagship only twenty miles away. Sighted by other lookouts, the plane unaccountably was viewed as friendly as it flew over the American vessels for an hour and a half, sending vital information back to the Japanese force commander, Vice Admiral G. Mikawa.

The Japanese force's amazing luck continued, for it passed the pickets without being seen, and effected complete surprise. The Japanese retired as quickly as they had come after inflicting on the U.S. Navy one of the worst defeats in its history. Four cruisers had gone down in what was now appropriately called Iron Bottom Sound, and over a thousand men had lost their lives in this Battle of Savo Island. Mikawa decided against returning to attack the transports, possibly because he feared the American carriers, which unknown to him had left. A Navy report on the causes of the defeat listed among the reasons inadequate condition of readiness, failure to recognize the implications of Japanese planes in the area, and early departure of the carriers. Admiral Nimitz added to the list a lack of battle-mindedness. The Japanese had contributed to their own victory; in addition to careful training, they had developed a superior torpedo which was most effective in the initial attack.[15]

The defeat left Turner no recourse but to withdraw; even the hard-

---

[15] For details on the Battle of Savo Island, see Morison, *History,* V, 17–64.

préssed Marines, who felt that they were being left stranded, understood this fact as they made ready for their own ordeal. Until relieved, they were in as desperate a situation as the defenders on Wake or Bataan. Their main tasks were to ward off enemy attacks, keep alive, and complete the airfield; they might expect help from the air and later by sea. Most of the Marines had landed, but some of their supplies had not.[16]

It was the Japanese turn to blunder. Admiral Mikawa had been too cautious in not following up his victory at Savo Island, Japanese leaders at first did not sense the significance of Guadalcanal and concentrated on their New Guinea operations, and planes attacking Guadalcanal struck at the airfield and bivouac areas instead of the supplies piled high near the beaches.

The Marines set up a coastal defense which discouraged amphibious attacks but could not stop enemy naval gunfire. Coping with air raids and mud, 1st Marine Engineer Battalion had Henderson Field, named in memory of a Marine pilot killed in the Battle of Midway, ready for limited operation by August 20. Five days earlier Navy destroyer-transports began to take in a few supplies.

The responsibility for the Japanese campaign for Guadalcanal had shifted from Navy to Army leaders, who underestimated the size of the Marine force on the island and sent a thousand men to retake it. They landed unopposed, but were practically wiped out several days later in the Battle of the Tenaru River. Meanwhile, a larger force under command of Major General Kiyotake Kawaguchi was building up on the island. Cutting their way through the jungle behind the airfield, his forces began a fierce engagement featured by the successful stand of Colonel Merritt A. Edson and B Company of the Marine Raiders on Bloody Ridge against a dozen attacks during the night of September 13. By mid-September, living on short rations and neither relieved nor strengthened, the Marines on Guadalcanal had stood off the enemy in numerous engagements. On the eighteenth, under Admiral Turner, Task Force 65 arrived with the 7th Marines from Samoa and took out the 1st Parachute Battalion, some wounded, and a few prisoners. On this day also troops on the island returned to full rations.[17]

Air defenses were gradually improving. The first Naval Construction

---

[16] Isely and Crowl, *The U.S. Marines and Amphibious War*, p. 130.

[17] For accounts of action through September, see Zimmerman, *Guadalcanal Campaign*, pp. 55–101; Miller, *Guadalcanal*, pp. 59–134.

Battalion to reach a fighting front arrived on Guadalcanal and assumed charge of maintenance and repair of Henderson Field.[18] On August 22, part of the Army's 67th Fighter Squadron joined the Marines, and carrier planes arrived on August 24 from the carrier *Enterprise,* which had been damaged in the Battle of the Eastern Solomons, a battle resulting from a Japanese effort to land an expeditionary force on Guadalcanal.[19] A carrier engagement took place in which the Japanese lost ninety planes while seriously but not fatally damaging the *Enterprise,* and U.S. planes sank the light carrier *Chokai.* More important, the Battle of the Eastern Solomons prevented the landing of the expeditionary force. However, after failing in daytime ventures to strengthen their forces, the Japanese began sending men in by night and put practically an entire division ashore. So many vessels came down the Slot from Rabaul and Truk that Americans spoke of the Tokyo Express.

Toward the end of October, the Japanese made a concerted attempt to retake Guadalcanal. They were a month or two late, for American defenses were becoming stronger in the air and on the ground. The war of attrition continued; the Americans had lost three carriers and other craft, but the Japanese had suffered a significant weakening of air strength through the loss of trained pilots, a blow they would feel increasingly as the war progressed. The war on the island continued; the Japanese were hard fighters who used every trick conceivable, and the Marines developed a perimeter defense with artillery that could lay down a murderous fire at every possible point of attack. Their losses were heavy, but for every fallen Marine about six of the enemy died.[20] Losses went on at sea; submarine attacks sank the carrier *Wasp* and the destroyer *O'Brien* and seriously damaged the battleship *North Carolina.*[21]

On October 11, Task Force 64, clearing the way for a convoy headed for Guadalcanal, surprised the Japanese in what was called the Battle of Cape Esperance and sank a cruiser and three destroyers in return for the loss of a destroyer, even though the Americans made ineffective

---

[18] Morison, *History,* V, 75–77; A. R. Buchanan (ed.), *The Navy's Air War: A Mission Completed* (New York [1946]), p. 157.

[19] For details of this battle, see Morison, *History,* V, 79–107.

[20] See Zimmerman, *Guadalcanal Campaign,* pp. 168–169, for summary of casualties.

[21] Morison, *History,* V, 130–138.

use of the radar which they had and the Japanese lacked.[22] This battle made possible the arrival of the 164th Regiment of the Americal Division, a force of almost three thousand men, on Guadalcanal on October 13. That day Henderson Field came in for heavy attack, first from high-altitude bombers which pitted the field, and then from "Pistol Pete," heavy artillery which the Japanese had taken ashore a few days before and placed in concealed positions to the west. That evening two Japanese battleships, *Kongo* and *Haruna,* came down the Slot, lay out of range, and began to fire shells from sixteen 14-inch guns into Henderson Field.

The attack was devastating. Over half the planes were either destroyed or made nonoperational, practically all the gasoline supply was gone, and the field was so full of holes that it was necessary to resort to an emergency grass strip which could be used only in dry weather and by light planes. Other raids and continued firing by Pistol Pete added to the damage; the Marines fought back, but were unable to prevent the Japanese from landing an additional force of from three to four thousand men.[23]

Allied morale was low, not only on the island, but in the higher echelons of command, and one result was a change of leadership. Perhaps no one could have done more, but Admiral Nimitz decided that the situation required a "more aggressive commander" and on October 16 replaced Admiral Ghormley with Vice Admiral William F. Halsey, who had a distinguished naval record dating back to World War I, and whose personal popularity with the fleet made his appointment a stimulus to morale.[24] Halsey was convinced that control of Guadalcanal was essential, and fortunately for him Washington was reaching the same opinion.[25] Consequently, Halsey found that he had more with which to work than had Ghormley.

The Japanese also were paying more attention to Guadalcanal, and a Tokyo order of mid-September made its capture a joint Army-Navy venture. About a month later the Japanese had some twenty thousand men on Guadalcanal, and they began to move toward the Marine per-

[22] *Ibid.,* V, 147–171.
[23] Miller, *Guadalcanal,* pp. 149–152.
[24] Morison, *History,* V, 183.
[25] Robert E. Sherwood, *Roosevelt and Hopkins: An Intimate History* (New York, 1948), pp. 622–625.

imeter of defense. Throughout, they underestimated the strength of the enemy, as for example when Marines, losing only twenty-five casualties, slaughtered more than six hundred Japanese in a region thereafter known as "Hell's Corner."[26]

The main Japanese attacks came during the nights of October 24 and 25. They made minor breaks in the defenses, but after hard fighting the Japanese were driven back and then began a gradual withdrawal from the area. Several factors accounted for American success. The infantryman and Marine had stood fast against the enemy's violent and often reckless advance. The perimeter of defense was generally considered outdated by defense in depth, but on Guadalcanal it proved successful, for heavy fire could be laid down whenever attempts were made to rush American positions. The Japanese showed skill in traversing jungles but they had to leave heavy weapons behind to do it, and the result was a case of frontal assaults by infantry against prepared positions well supported by artillery and heavy guns.[27]

Meanwhile, at sea an engagement north of the Santa Cruz Islands cost the Americans the carrier *Hornet* and the Japanese a loss of a hundred planes to seventy-four for the Americans.[28] The Japanese could ill afford this attrition, for American plane production and pilot training were increasing.

In early November, the situation on the island looked more hopeful as numerous reinforcements arrived.[29] Part of the task force accompanying elements of the Americal Division which landed on the eleventh attempted to prevent a Japanese force, including two battleships, from bombarding Guadalcanal. The result, the "Naval Battle of Guadalcanal," was one of the most confused engagements in modern history.[30] In the night fight and subsequent day encounter, which featured surface engagements and air and submarine attacks, the Japanese lost two destroyers and a battleship badly damaged by gunfire and later sunk by plane attacks. The United States had lost two cruisers and four destroyers and all but one of its vessels nad been hit. Casualties ran much higher among the Americans; the cruiser *Juneau*, for ex-

[26] Zimmerman, *Guadalcanal Campaign*, pp. 115–116; Miller, *Guadalcanal*, 156–158.

[27] *Ibid.*, pp. 165–167; Zimmerman, *Guadalcanal Campaign*, 123–125.

[28] Morison, *History*, V, 199–224.

[29] Miller, *Guadalcanal*, p. 180.

[30] For details of the Naval Battle of Guadalcanal, see Morison, *History*, V, 225–287.

ample, took to their death about seven hundred men, including the
five Sullivan brothers. Rear Admiral Daniel J. Callaghan, in command of the force, lost his life. The strategic advantage went to the
Americans, for they had turned back temporarily a bombardment force
that would have given Henderson Field a terrific pounding.

The Japanese then blundered by sending a convoy of ten thousand
soldiers to Guadalcanal with only destroyer support. Air attacks struck
nine transports and sank seven. The remainder continued moving
through the night, and four reached their destination only to come
under heavy air and ground fire. Although some four thousand soldiers
may have reached shore, their vessels and supplies were destroyed.
Earlier that night a battleship engagement, one of the few of the war,
took place; the *South Dakota* was damaged but the Japanese battleship
Kirishima was so hard hit that it had to be scuttled. On November 30,
in the Battle of Tassafaronga, an American cruiser force took a terrific
beating from effective Japanese action and use of torpedoes.[31] Nevertheless the Japanese attempt to retake the island had failed. There still
remained hard fighting before the Americans could expand their perimeter of defense to control of the entire island, but they were ready
to take the offensive.

In December, General Vandegrift turned over command on Guadalcanal to Major General Alexander M. Patch, Commanding General
of the Americal Division, and the 1st Marines finally got well-earned
evacuation from the island. Patch, a West Pointer, had seen active duty
in World War I. Early in January, American forces on Guadalcanal
totaled a little over fifty thousand.[32] Air power had grown correspondingly; Henderson Field was bigger and free from heavy bombing, although individual Japanese planes, known to the men on the island
as "Louie the Louse" or "Washingmachine Charlie," conducted frequent nuisance raids. Toward the end of November, 1942, there were
188 aircraft of all types on Guadalcanal, representing U.S. Army,
Navy, and Marine Corps, and the Royal New Zealand Air Force.[33]
With the arrival of Army bombers, the clumsy PBY's, vulnerable and
slow, found new and valuable roles. As "Black Cats" equipped with
radar they operated effectively at night for reconnaissance and raids.[34]

[31] *Ibid.,* V, 313–315.
[32] Miller, *Guadalcanal,* p. 219.
[33] Craven and Cate, *The A.A.F. in World War II,* IV, 79–91; Miller, *Guadalcanal,* pp. 220–222.
[34] Buchanan, *The Navy's Air War,* pp. 181–183.

As "Dumbos" they fished more than one sailor or airman out of the sea in daring rescue operations. PT boats harassed the enemy and often took on opposition that outclassed it in firepower but not in courage. On the island, malaria continued to be an important debilitating factor; from November 1, 1942, to February 13, 1943, the hospital admission rate for this disease averaged 420 admissions per thousand men.[35]

The Japanese position became increasingly worse. They suffered from malaria, other diseases, and malnutrition, and troop strength declined from a peak of 30,000 to about 25,000.[36] In their weakened condition, they could only dig in and assume the defensive. There were about fifty thousand men in Rabaul waiting to go down the Slot and reinforce the island, but memory of the transport debacle of November and knowledge of American air power made the Japanese leaders decide not to take the risk. To facilitate their raids on Henderson Field, the Japanese secretly began construction of an emergency air strip at Munda, about 175 miles north of Guadalcanal on New Georgia Island. U.S. fliers discovered it and a naval force subsequently bombarded it, but it became apparent that the only way to close the field was to attack it. The Americans were in no position at this time to make such a move.

Toward the end of January, Halsey sent in reinforcements to Guadalcanal, with heavy naval and air protection. The Japanese dispatched land-based bombers, which struck the cruiser *Chicago* one day and sank it the next. One feature of the engagement was the introduction of the proximity fuze in antiaircraft fire.[37]

After the naval Battle of Guadalcanal, the Japanese leaders favored abandoning Guadalcanal, and on January 4, 1943, Tokyo ordered evacuation within a month. The decision was an amazingly well-kept secret as far as the Americans were concerned. Even when destroyers were rushing down the Slot to evacuate the soldiers, the Americans thought they were taking in more men. On the island, fighting continued to be hard. The Japanese completed their plans and on three nights early in February evacuated eleven thousand men from Guadalcanal in a masterly operation which completely fooled the enemy. The operation also left Guadalcanal in the hands of the enemy, and a bitter

---

[35] Miller, *Guadalcanal*, p. 227.
[36] *Ibid.*, p. 228.
[37] Morison, *History*, V, 356.

campaign of half a year had come to an end.[38] Losses on the American side had been high but not excessive; the Japanese had lost two-thirds of the forces they had put on the island and had suffered costly attrition of air and naval power.

While opposing forces were contending for possession of Guadalcanal, other Japanese and Allied forces were fighting in New Guinea. This huge island, one of the largest in the world, is over thirteen hundred miles long and in places four hundred miles wide, and its terrain and climate are among the most inhospitable known to man. Dense tropical forests and swamps stifle its lowlands, and high mountains, largely covered with moss forests, restrict travel and communications. The native populations vary widely in customs and in speech, and in remote areas head-hunting persisted until recent times. European penetration of the island was late and relatively slight. The Dutch acquired the western portion as part of their colonial empire, and Australians moved into Papua, the southern section of the eastern portion of the island. Germans at first colonized the area to the north, but after World War I it became an Australian mandate, which also included the adjacent islands, New Britain and New Ireland. On New Guinea European or Australian economic activity and, for that matter, political control penetrated little beyond the coastal plantations and a gold mining center in the eastern interior of the island. The capital of the northern Territory of New Guinea was Rabaul on the northeastern tip of New Britain, and the Australians had developed Port Moresby as the leading city of Papua.[39]

The initial Japanese advance in this area had been the occupation of Lae and Salamaua on the northeast coast of New Guinea in March, 1942. In May, Japanese forces sought to take Port Moresby but had turned back as a result of the Battle of the Coral Sea. Next they planned a two-pronged approach. Late in July, 1942, they seized Buna, a small

---

[38] For operations on Guadalcanal from December, 1942, to the end of the campaign, see Miller, *Guadalcanal*, pp. 232–350; Zimmerman, *Guadalcanal Campaign*, pp. 156–167; Frank O. Hough, Verle E. Ludwig, Henry I. Shaw, Jr., *Pearl Harbor to Guadalcanal: History of U.S. Marine Corps Operations in World War II* (Washington [1958]), pp. 359–374.

[39] Linden A. Mander, *Some Dependent Peoples of the South Pacific* (New York, 1954), pp. 199–258; W. E. H. Stanner, *The South Seas in Transition* (Sydney, Wellington, London, 1953), pp. 1–16; Kenneth B. Cumberland, *Southwest Pacific* (New York, 1956), pp. 134–149.

town on the north coast of New Guinea, and planned a march on the Kokoda trail through a 6,500-foot pass across the Owen Stanley Range to Port Moresby a hundred miles to the north. Slowly they worked their way, and by September 17, 1942, their advance forces were only thirty-two miles from Port Moresby and twenty from its airfield. The Australians held, and gradually forced the Japanese to retreat. In this withdrawal the enemy leader drowned, and his troops were decimated by starvation and disease.[40]

Meanwhile, the Japanese had begun the second line of attack. Splitting the eastern end of New Guinea is Milne Bay, twenty-six miles long and five to seven miles wide. Its strategic location and available flat land made it desirable for both an airfield and a naval base. General MacArthur's forces got there first and on a Lever Brothers coconut plantation at the head of the bay began construction of an airfield. Overconfident, the Japanese tried to take Milne Bay with inadequate naval or air support, as late in July a convoy with invasion troops arrived and made unopposed landings. Allied air and ground attack then repulsed the enemy, and Milne Bay remained in the hands of the Allies.[41]

Buna and other Japanese holdings on the north shore of New Guinea still constituted a threat to Port Moresby and a barrier to Allied advance. The effort to remove the Japanese from these little holdings consumed six months and cost many lives in some of the most difficult fighting of the war. In October, 1942, General MacArthur issued a plan for an overland approach from Port Moresby.[42] The sea route was hazardous, for a shoal-ridden, poorly charted, and little-known coastline made travel dangerous by night, and Japanese planes increased the risk by day.

The coastal region of the Buna area is low swamp or jungle, heavily covered with trees and underbrush. Here and there were groves of coconut palms, patches of *kunai* grass, and shrub-covered areas. The humidity averaged 85 percent and the daily temperature 96°F. Among the diseases and ailments that racked people in the region were ma-

[40] For the U.S. Army's military history of the Papuan campaign, see Samuel Milner, *Victory in Papua* (*United States Army in World War II: The War in the Pacific*) (Washington, 1957), *passim*.

[41] *Ibid.*, pp. 77–88; S. E. Morison, *History of United States Naval Operations in World War II* (Boston, 1950), VI, 34–39.

[42] Parts of the plan are quoted in Milner, *Victory in Papua,* p. 102.

laria, dengue fever, scrub typhus, bacillary and amoebic dysentery. The Japanese had built a series of strong defenses on an eleven-mile front from Gona to Cape Endaiadere. The three principal positions were Gona, along the Sanananda track, and the Buna area from the Girua River to Cape Endaiadere. Some of the fortifications were on dry ground in the midst of swamps. The Japanese had constructed strongly fortified pillboxes in relatively open ground and in jungle locations had built bunkers of coconut logs, strengthened with steel rails, steel oil drums filled with sand, and similar materials. They had then covered the bunkers with dirt and planted fast-growing vegetation on them so that in a short time they were naturally covered and well concealed. From these positions the Japanese could emerge to fire trenches which, again, were not easily visible. Approaching Allied troops, therefore, found their way blocked not only by almost impenetrable swamp and jungle, but by a honeycomb of strong fortifications carefully situated to cover such localities as river crossings, egress from swamps, or jungle tracks.

The 7th Australian Division under Major General George A. Vasey had gradually pushed the Japanese back across the mountains to the Gona area.[43] Other units secured the coast from Milne Bay to Cape Nelson, east of the Buna-Gona area, and still other Allied forces had taken Goodenough Island off the coast. The 2d Battalion, 126th Infantry, marched across the mountains, encountering impossible terrain and atrocious weather. Fortunately, the discovery of airfield sites made it possible to fly in remaining units of the 126th Infantry.[44] Orders for an over-all attack, dated November 14, called for the 7th Australian Division and the 32d U.S. Division to destroy the enemy in the Buna-Gona area. The offensive started with the Australians on the left and the Americans on the right and almost immediately ran into trouble against a well-entrenched foe. On the nineteenth, over the protests of Major General Edwin F. Harding, who commanded the Americans, the 126th Infantry was assigned to General Vasey. With great effort,

[43] Earlier in the war the 7th Australian Division had fought in North Africa. Robert L. Eichelberger, *Our Jungle Road to Tokyo* (New York, 1950), p. 11.

[44] On August 4, 1942, Major General George C. Kenney assumed command of the Allied Air Forces in the Southwest Pacific Area. Kenney had made an enviable record as commander of the Fourth Air Force. Craven and Cate, *The A.A.F. in World War II*, IV, 26; George C. Kenney, *General Kenney Reports: A Personal History of the Pacific War* (New York, 1949), p. 51.

elements of this regiment established a roadblock at a track junction south of Japanese defenses. Then the campaign on the left reached a stalemate until toward the end of November the Australians started moving again. Bitter fighting ensued, and after suffering heavy losses the Australians took Buna village on December 9. An Australian journalist with the troops described the grisly sight in the captured stronghold: "Rotting bodies, sometimes weeks old, formed part of the fortifications. The living fired over the bodies of the dead, slept side by side with them."[45]

On the east, the 128th Infantry launched an offensive on November 16, but was badly handicapped as Japanese planes destroyed luggers and barges loaded with supplies. The loss of military matériel, as well as other supplies, seriously affected attack plans, and drenching rains further complicated operations so that for two weeks the attack continued without success on two fronts (Urbana and Warren) against the Japanese in the Buna area. General Harding requested tanks to break enemy defensive positions, but could get only a promise of some lightly armored reconnaissance vehicles, known as Bren carriers.

By the end of November, morale was low on the Buna fronts. The men had gone into battle unprepared; they were short of rations, wet, and disease-ridden. Their weapons functioned poorly because of the weather and the lack of gun oil and other cleaning aids. There were no tanks, and attempts to use flame throwers failed miserably. Harding pleaded for more artillery and for more men, but Major General Richard K. Sutherland, General MacArthur's Chief of Staff, who visited the front late in November, evidently concluded that what was needed was a change in leadership. MacArthur called to his headquarters Lieutenant General Robert L. Eichelberger, who had been training the 41st Division in Australia. Eichelberger, a graduate of West Point, had been with the American forces in Siberia at the conclusion of World War I and in 1941 was superintendent of the Military Academy at West Point. MacArthur said that he was humiliated by reports of a lack of fighting spirit among the Americans on the Papuan front and he stated that since the Japanese might land reinforcements at any time, "time was of the essence." MacArthur then told Eichelberger that

---

[45] Quoted in Milner, *Victory in Papua*, p. 217. For a British account of the campaign, see S. Woodburn Kirby, *The War Against Japan* (*History of the Second World War: United Kingdom Military Series*) (London, 1958), II, 286–289.

he was putting him in command and he said, "Bob, I want you to take Buna, or not come back alive."[46]

As Commander of I Corps, Eichelberger reviewed the front and, dissatisfied with conditions as he saw them, relieved General Harding and the task force commanders under him. Eichelberger proved to be a hard-driving leader. He regrouped the forces, and they launched a new attack. The Bren carriers arrived and lasted only twenty or thirty minutes in action; the men, however, convinced Eichelberger of their valor, and he informed General MacArthur that there was no longer need for concern over American conduct in battle.

The only piece that was effective against the Japanese bunker defenses was a 105-mm. howitzer, which unfortunately soon ran out of ammunition. The American forces made limited gains; on December 14 they took Buna village and a few days later a Japanese stronghold in a coconut grove. By mid-December morale was on the upswing, for the troops were learning their business, food was more plentiful, the mail was coming in, and the men were getting more rest. On December 15, the first handful of tanks arrived; they were American M3 tanks (General Stuart) or Matildas, as they were called by the Australian units which operated them. General Eichelberger soon could write General Sutherland that with tanks they had taken concrete pillboxes with steel doors that it would "have been almost impossible" for unassisted infantry to reduce.[47]

On the Warren front an Allied attack started which made slow, hard progress as a twenty-five-pounder using armor-piercing projectiles with supercharge broke the defenses in an Old Strip section, and infantrymen moving in had to wipe out the defenders almost literally to the man.

On the Urbana front, the problem was to move against several points of strength, an island separated from the mainland by a tidal stream, a track junction known as the Triangle, south of the mission, the nearby Government Gardens, and the mission itself. When the first attacks failed, General Eichelberger decided to by-pass the Triangle, and at his insistence Colonel John E. Grose ordered Company K, 127th Infantry, to cross an "unfordable stream under fire at night."[48] Suffering

[46] Eichelberger, *Our Jungle Road to Tokyo*, p. 21.

[47] Eichelberger to Sutherland, Dec. 18, 1942, quoted in Milner, *Victory in Papua*, p. 264.

[48] Eichelberger, *Our Jungle Road to Tokyo*, p. 46.

fifty-four casualties, the company accomplished its task. With heavy fighting, the Americans took the island, the Government Gardens, and by outflanking them forced evacuation of the Japanese from the Triangle. The remaining Japanese in the mission resisted furiously, but the limit of their endurance was near. Soon it became apparent that they were trying to escape, and they were shot down near landing barges or in the sea. Their military leaders committed hara-kiri, and by late afternoon of January 2, 1943, Buna Mission was in Allied hands.[49]

The Sanananda area still remained; the fresh, well-trained 163d Infantry went into action, and the weary 126th Infantry finally got relief. In a command shift, General Eichelberger became Commander, Advance New Guinea Force, and after one unsuccessful assault agreed to General Vasey's plan of surrounding the area, harassing it, and keeping supplies from reaching it. The Japanese situation was more desperate than the Allies realized, and on January 13, Japanese Imperial Headquarters ordered withdrawal of the force of some five thousand men facing death by starvation. Hearing of the order from a captured, sick Japanese soldier, General Vasey immediately launched an offensive and tried to close off escape routes. By the nineteenth the Allies had pretty well broken up the resistance; clean-up operations took a couple of days more, and the six months' campaign at last came to an end.

The cost was heavy, 5,698 casualties for the Australians and 2,848 for the Americans, and among 14,646 American troops committed to the area, for example, there had been 8,659 cases of infectious disease. Japanese losses were greater, for although they successfully evacuated about 4,500 men, they lost 12,000. Of these 350 became prisoners; the others were buried by either the Japanese or the Allies. Starvation was a definite factor in causing the Japanese defeat, and in some cases was so extreme that its victims resorted to cannibalism.

A principal Allied shortage in the campaign had been the right kind of artillery. The American forces had had only one piece, the 105-mm. howitzer, capable of knocking out a bunker with one shell, and its supply of ammunition had been inadequate. The Air Force had played an important role; it had taken troops to and from the front, provided excellent logistical support under trying circumstances, had attacked enemy convoys, spotted for artillery, and carried on reconnaissance along the coast. It had been less successful in direct support of ground

---

[49] Milner, *Victory in Papua,* pp. 316–318.

forces, and occasional errors resulting in the bombing or shooting of American troops did little for morale. The naval role in the Papuan campaign had been relatively small, aside from the work of torpedo boats and the transport on one occasion of troops from Goodenough Island.[50]

In both the Guadalcanal and Papuan campaigns, relatively evenly matched forces faced each other on narrow fronts. The results hinged on actions of regiments or smaller units, and the principal lessons learned were tactical.[51] This experience was reflected in later engagements in the Pacific, just as strategically each of these campaigns was a steppingstone toward the reduction of Rabaul.

[50] For a description of the cost and an appraisal of the results of the campaign, see *ibid.*, pp. 369-378. For other appraisals, see Eichelberger, *Our Jungle Road to Tokyo*, pp. 61-62; Craven and Cate, *The A.A.F. in World War II*, IV, 127-128.

[51] John Miller, Jr., *Cartwheel: The Reduction of Rabaul* (*United States Army in World War II: The War in the Pacific*) (Washington, 1959), p. ix.

CHAPTER 12

The Pacific War—1943

A T CASABLANCA there had been agreement on taking the initiative to keep the pressure on Japan.[1] The U.S. Staff was concerned primarily with reducing Rabaul after completing the preliminary campaigns in New Guinea and Guadalcanal. Unfortunately, the question of command was involved in the problems of operational strategy and policy. The views of the Army and Navy conflicted, neither would accept an over-all solution, and the result was a series of compromises to meet changing conditions.

Faced with various plans from the Pacific, the Joint Chiefs of Staff arranged for a meeting in Washington of representatives of the Pacific commanders. This Pacific Military Conference began March 12, 1943, after the end of the Papuan and Guadalcanal campaigns, and after Admiral Halsey's forces had also occupied the Russell Islands, about sixty miles northwest of Guadalcanal. Some sort of agreement for operations in the Pacific was certainly in order, for by February, 1943, there were deployed in the Pacific (excluding Alaska) 374,000 troops, in contrast to 298,000 in the Mediterranean and about 107,000 in the European theater.[2]

In the Pacific Military Conference Washington planners, Brigadier General Albert O. Wedemeyer, Rear Admiral Charles M. Cooke, Jr., and Brigadier General Orville A. Anderson (Air Force), met with the

[1] Maurice Matloff, *Strategic Planning for Coalition Warfare, 1943–1944* (*United States Army in World War II*) (Washington, 1959), p. 36.
[2] *Ibid.*, p. 92 *n.*

leading staff officers of the Pacific theaters.[3] At the first meeting General Sutherland, General MacArthur's Chief of Staff, presented MacArthur's plan (Elkton) for the seizure and occupation of the New Britain–New Ireland–New Guinea area. On the western axis Southwest Pacific forces would seize operating air bases on the Huon Peninsula to cover the approaches to New Britain. South Pacific forces would seize and set up bases on New Georgia to cover an advance to Bougainville, and then take Kavieng, isolating Rabaul, which then would be taken by assault. These plans called for more strength than Washington Operations had projected for the area. Admiral Cooke, chief Navy planner, introduced the matter of allocation of aircraft to the European Theater into the discussion, and out of the conference came an increase in air allotments to the Pacific. With some modifications the plan was approved by the conference and then by the Joint Chiefs of Staff. Much more difficult was the question of command. From the proposals and the discussions which followed them came a directive sent to the Pacific commanders on March 29, which stated that the operations against Rabaul would be under MacArthur's direction, and that Halsey, under MacArthur's general direction, would be in direct command of operations in the Solomons.[4] All naval units, with the exception of those assigned by the Joint Chiefs of Staff to task forces, would be under Nimitz' control. MacArthur would submit to the Joint Chiefs of Staff his general plans on the composition of task forces and the sequence and timing of the operations.

From the Pacific Military Conference the Pacific commanders had failed to secure all the aircraft allocations they had wanted, since granting the request would have reduced severely the allotment to the United Kingdom for the Allied Bomber Offensive and since, also, there was not enough available shipping to handle the request. The Pacific did get some additional planes, but at the expense of ground forces already planned for the area and at some cost to the Allied Bomber Offensive. The compromise on command was perhaps the best that could be reached at the time, and it became workable because of the excellent relationship between the two men principally involved, Gen-

[3] Accounts of the Pacific Military Conference include John Miller, Jr., *Cartwheel: The Reduction of Rabaul* (*United States Army in World War II*) (Washington, 1959), pp. 11–15; Matloff, *Strategic Planning*, pp. 91–98; George C. Kenney, *General Kenney Reports: A Personal History of the Pacific War* (New York, 1949), pp. 211–218.

[4] The directive is cited and summarized in Miller, *Cartwheel*, p. 19.

eral MacArthur and Admiral Halsey. There was still no long-range plan for the Pacific, and there was still no major ultimate military objective.

On April 20, 1943, the Joint Chiefs of Staff made some advance toward interservice cooperation by agreeing on principles governing future operations.[5] The Joint Chiefs of Staff would designate a single commander on the basis of the particular operation to be carried out, and his command prerogatives would apply to all the forces under him as if the Army and Navy were one. A joint staff would aid him, and normally he would not command directly any of the component parts of the force. This agreement expedited individual operations in the Pacific. The Army and the Navy, on the other hand, were not in a position to decide the questions of over-all strategy and deployment in the war against Japan, for these were inextricably involved with the war in Europe and had to await agreement of the coalition forces fighting the war. The Pacific war, therefore, would have to be planned and fought on a contingent basis until firm decisions and a commitment of men and resources were made for the war in Europe.

This situation continued through the Trident Conference held in Washington in May, 1943,[6] even though the U.S. Chiefs of Staff had gone to the meeting with a concept of long-range strategy for war in the Pacific, which was that pressure should be maintained on Japan while the war against Germany continued. The British contended, however, that the war in the Pacific should be coordinated with that in Europe to make sure that it not endanger the chance to beat Germany or unduly prolong the war. The Joint Chiefs of Staff considered the final objective in the Pacific to be the unconditional surrender of Japan, and they presented a six-phase, unscheduled program leading to this end. It involved operations in the Philippines and China, an air offensive against Japan from bases in China, and invasion of Japan. The Combined Chiefs of Staff accepted these proposals as a basis for study by Combined Staff planners. After the conference, both Washington and Pacific Theater planners began work on half a dozen projects for the war against Japan.

Most important of these during the summer of 1943 was the firm

[5] Matloff, *Strategic Planning for Coalition Warfare*, pp. 104–105.

[6] For accounts of the Trident Conference, see William D. Leahy, *I Was There* (New York, London, Toronto, 1950), pp. 158–164; Matloff, *Strategic Planning*, pp. 126–145; Robert E. Sherwood, *Roosevelt and Hopkins: An Intimate History* (New York, 1948), pp. 728–733.

decision to start a campaign through the Central Pacific islands. Concerned by the idleness of the fleet after the conquest of Guadalcanal, Admiral King on June 11 recommended an attack on the Marshall Islands, starting about the first of November. The Joint Chiefs of Staff on June 15 told General MacArthur of the tentative plans and informed him that for these operations the 1st Marine Division would be withdrawn from the Southwest Pacific Area and the 2d Marines, combat loaders, and most of Halsey's naval forces would be taken from the South Pacific Area. If the plans proved unfeasible, other plans were presented for seizure of the less heavily defended Gilbert Islands.

MacArthur immediately protested against the proposed Marshalls operation, arguing that the best line of advance was through New Guinea to Mindanao, since land-based planes would offer protection for this route.[7] Amphibious attacks through the mandated islands, on the other hand, would pit carrier-based planes against the land-based air forces of the enemy. He also insisted that withdrawal of the two Marine divisions would prevent capture of Rabaul. MacArthur then listed his own timetable of operations. Two regimental teams would take Kiriwina and Woodlark islands between June 30 and the middle of August. Australian and American forces would start a campaign on the northeastern coast of New Guinea, extending from September 1 to the end of the year. Other forces on December 1 would assault western New Britain, planning to complete the operation by February, 1944. Meanwhile, on the eastern axis, Halsey would invade New Georgia on June 30 with hopes of controlling the situation by September 15. Finally, regions on or near Bougainville would be taken between December 1 and the middle of January, 1944.

As a result of MacArthur's vigorous protest, Marshall turned down King's request for the two Marine divisions, and MacArthur's objections also prevented diversion of a heavy and a medium bomber group from either the South Pacific or the Southwest Pacific to the Central Pacific. Later the Central Pacific received bomber groups directly from the United States. Army planners also claimed that the Marshalls and Gilberts operations would be subsidiary without achieving a worthwhile strategic objective. The Navy, however, viewed the projected operations as the beginning of a new phase of the war which would hasten its end. A Joint Strategic Survey Committee, which had just reviewed

[7] Message, MacArthur to Marshall, June 20, 1943, cited and summarized in Matloff, *Strategic Planning*, pp. 188–189.

U.S. strategy in the Pacific, supported the Navy's views on the grounds that the slowness of advance in New Guinea and Guadalcanal dictated a change in strategy to give first priority to the Central Pacific project. Army planners then suggested going ahead with the operations against Rabaul, which would be coordinated with an attack against the Gilberts instead of the Marshalls. The Joint Chiefs of Staff accepted the Army's counterproposal but kept Admiral King's date of November 15 and applied it to the Gilberts operation. The offensive forces would be the 2d Marine Division and an Army division. On July 20, Admiral Nimitz received a directive to prepare for operations against the Ellice and Gilbert Islands and Nauru with a target date of November 15.[8] The directive also looked forward to an attack on the Marshalls about January 1, 1944.

While these discussions had been going on at a high level, planning and preparations had been continuing in the theaters of operation.[9] It will be remembered that the July 2, 1942, directive had set forth three tasks. The first was the seizure of Tulagi and Guadalcanal in the Solomons and the Santa Cruz Islands. The last proved unnecessary, and the Santa Cruz Islands were not taken.

MacArthur's plan for Task Two envisaged an advance along two lines converging on Rabaul, and was restated in January, 1943, but MacArthur could not move until the completion of the Guadalcanal and Papuan campaigns made troops and air forces available. In February, 1943, the General and his staff were looking beyond Rabaul to the Philippines and feeling that the advance should be along the northern coast of New Guinea and then north through the intervening islands to the Philippines. This plan increased the need for reducing Rabaul, for from it the Japanese could send ships and planes to block Allied progress.

Admiral Halsey, studying his part in Task Two, considered his first objectives to be Munda Point on New Georgia and a second airfield at Vila, 180 nautical miles away on Kolombangara Island. Also, in American hands these airfields would aid Allied advance toward Bougainville, which was needed for use by Allied planes striking at Rabaul. On March 28, 1943, the Joint Chiefs of Staff canceled their directive

[8] Samuel E. Morison, *History of United States Naval Operations in World War II* (Boston, 1951), VII, 83–84, 201; Philip A. Crowl and Edmund G. Love, *Seizure of the Gilberts and Marshalls (United States Army in World War II: The War in the Pacific)* (Washington, 1955), pp. 23–25.

[9] For a discussion of the shifts in plans, see Miller, *Cartwheel,* pp. 9–19.

of July 2, 1942, and issued a new one ordering MacArthur and Halsey to establish airfields on Woodlark and Kiriwina islands, to occupy the Lae-Salamaua, Finschhafen-Madang section of New Guinea, and conquer the southern Solomons as far as southern Bougainville.[10]

As Allied Commander in Chief, General MacArthur had organized his General Headquarters (GHQ), Southwest Pacific Area, along U.S. Army lines. Under General Sutherland, Chief of Staff, were the usual general staff sections, and under GHQ in Australia were also three special staff sections, Allied Land Forces, Allied Naval Forces, and Allied Air Forces. An Australian, General Sir Thomas Blamey, commanded Allied Land Forces and theoretically was responsible for tactical direction of land forces, with the exception of some antiaircraft units. In February, 1943, the U.S. Sixth Army had been established in the area under Lieutenant General Walter Krueger. Included in this army were Lieutenant General Robert L. Eichelberger's I Corps, the 2d Engineer Special Brigade, and the 503d Parachute Infantry Regiment. The 1st Marine Division was also under Krueger's operational control. The First and Second Australian Armies, parts of which were still in training, were in addition parts of the Allied Land Forces. Vice Admiral Arthur S. Carpender, U.S. Navy, commanded Allied Naval Forces, including the U.S. Seventh Fleet, which Carpender commanded, and large segments of the Australian and Netherlands navies. Lieutenant General George C. Kenney headed the Allied Air Forces, consisting of the U.S. Fifth Air Force and the Royal Australian Air Command.[11]

Conferring in Brisbane, General MacArthur and Admiral Halsey agreed to launch the invasions of New Georgia, Woodlark, and Kiriwina at the same time. The latter two islands were outside the bad-weather belt and would be useful as staging bases for an interchange of planes between the South and Southwest Pacific areas. The operations planned were placed under the code name Cartwheel and included some thirteen actions in about eight months with as much mutual support as possible between the two areas. Although generally using the headquarters already existing in his area, MacArthur added a new task force, at first called New Britain Force and later Alamo Force, which was commanded by General Krueger and consisted mainly of

---

[10] *Ibid.*, p. 19; Morison, *History*, VI, 95–96.

[11] Miller, *Cartwheel*, pp. 20–22; for a description of naval organization and planners, see Morison, *History*, VI, 9–15.

his Sixth Army. One effect of this action was to remove these American troops from General Blamey's control.[12] In general the New Guinea Force was to conduct operations in New Guinea, and the Alamo Force would operate in Woodlark, Kiriwina, and New Britain. The date set for the attacks on New Georgia, Woodlark, and Kiriwina was June 30.

Recognizing the strategic significance of Rabaul, the Japanese by the end of 1942 had developed it into the principal air and naval base of the Japanese Southeast Asia Area and the location of the highest headquarters of the area. The Japanese did not have unified command; Army and Navy officials cooperated with each other but reported to different higher authorities.[13] General Hitoshi Imamura commanded the Eighth Area Army with headquarters in Rabaul, and Vice Admiral Jinichi Kusaka commanded the Southeast Area Fleet. After deciding to evacuate Guadalcanal, the Japanese planned to conduct an active offensive in New Guinea and stand on the defensive in the Solomons. Consequently, they took steps to strengthen holdings in New Guinea, for they were as anxious to block a route to the Philippines as the Allies were to develop it.

During the first half of 1943 the Japanese launched an offensive in New Guinea against Wau, in the Bulolo Valley gold fields south of the Huon Peninsula, inland from Salamaua. The small Australian contingent held, and, with reinforcements flown in, by early April had forced the enemy back toward Salamaua.[14] A Japanese attempt to send additional reinforcements resulted in what is known as the Battle of the Bismarck Sea.[15] Late in February, hoping to take advantage of a weather front and fighter air protection, the Japanese sent a convoy carrying 6,912 soldiers from Rabaul down the Bismarck Sea north of

[12] Miller, *Cartwheel*, p. 29; the British military history states that MacArthur divided his forces into their national components; Woodburn Kirby, *The War Against Japan (History of the Second World War: United Kingdom Military Series)* (London, 1958), pp. 410–411.

[13] For a discussion of Japanese organization, see Miller, *Cartwheel*, pp. 32–36.

[14] Accounts of the engagements between Wau and Salamaua include, *ibid.*, pp. 36–39; George Odgers, *Air War Against Japan, 1943–1945 (Australia in the War of 1939–1945,* Series 3, Volume II) (Canberra, 1957), pp. 24–29.

[15] For descriptions of the Battle of the Bismarck Sea, see Kenney, *General Kenney Reports,* pp. 197–206; Wesley Frank Craven and J. L. Cate, *The Army Air Forces in World War II* (Chicago, 1950), IV, 129–162; Morison, *History,* VI, 54–65.

New Britain and around the end of that island into the Solomon Sea toward its objective. Several factors contributed to the subsequent troubles of this convoy of eight transports and eight destroyers; the weather front disappeared, the fighter support ran low on gas, and the U.S. Fifth Air Force had been practicing low-level masthead attacks, using delayed fuses to enable the plane to pass beyond the blast area.

A B-24 on March 1 sighted the convoy north of New Britain, some time later B-17's inflicted damage as the vessels turned into Vitiaz Strait, and in the Solomon Sea many types of planes made a concerted attack which sank all the transports and most of the destroyers. The next day planes and torpedo boats picked off survivors trying to reach shore. As a result of this victory, the Japanese made no further efforts to dispatch convoys to New Guinea but sent such reinforcements as it could by barge from Cape Gloucester at the western end of New Britain or by submarine.

Failing to send reinforcements by sea to Lae, the Japanese began to construct a road from Madang to Lae.[16] The Allies reasoned that the Japanese would make such an attempt, but predicted accurately that they could not finish in time to be helpful. Difficult terrain, adverse weather, and inadequate equipment prevented completion of the road. At the same time, the Japanese Navy launched an air campaign, called I Operation, with a raid on the Russells on April 1 and six days later a major attack on Guadalcanal.[17] In a fierce air battle the enemy lost thirty-nine planes to seven fighter planes for the Allies; the Japanese sank a New Zealand corvette, and an American oiler and a destroyer. The Japanese followed with an attack in New Guinea and concluded their operation thinking that it had been successful, although actually it had not been especially damaging.

Toward the middle of April, American Intelligence officers not only learned that Admiral Yamamoto planned to visit bases in the upper Solomons, but discovered his time schedule. Realizing the Admiral's great ability, the American command sought to strike him down. A squadron of eighteen long-range P-38's, flying a circuitous route practically at sea level to avoid detection, arrived just in time to shoot down the plane bearing Admiral Yamamoto as it came in for a landing.

---

[16] Miller, *Cartwheel: The Reduction of Rabaul*, pp. 41–42.

[17] Descriptions of I Operation include Morison, *History*, VI, 117–127; Craven and Cate, *The A.A.F. in World War II*, IV, 211–213; Miller, *Cartwheel*, pp. 42–44.

Losing only one aircraft in the ensuing struggle with Zeros, the squadron returned from a successfully completed mission, for Yamamoto had died in the crash.[18]

As planning continued, an additional operation was added to the projected invasions of Woodlark, Kiriwina, and New Georgia. This was a landing at Nassau Bay in New Guinea to prepare for later Lae-Salamaua operations. General Krueger and the Alamo Force were responsible for the invasion of the Trobriands (Woodlark and Kiriwina). Since this was the first real amphibious operation in MacArthur's area, planning and preparations were thorough, so thorough, in fact, that they became standard procedure for later landings. As there were no Japanese on the Trobriands, the landings turned out to be training exercises, and by July 23 an air garrison arrived to use a newly constructed airstrip on Woodlark.[19] Bad weather delayed completion of a strip on Kiriwina for almost a month.

The purpose of invading Nassau Bay was to facilitate supply of troops which would later attack Lae and Salamaua and also to mislead the Japanese into thinking that Salamaua was the principal objective instead of Lae, which the Allies really wanted.[20] The attack on Nassau was a shore-to-shore approach from Morobe farther along the coast. Heavy surf made night landings hectic, and there was some opposition ashore in the next few days, but by July 2 enough elements had landed to make the position secure.

Meanwhile, Admiral Halsey made ready for the New Georgia landings. His immediate superior in the chain of command, Admiral Nimitz, was to provide him with the means of making war. On the other hand, his strategic directions came from MacArthur. The naval forces were designated the Third Fleet, and were mainly from the U.S. and New Zealand navies. Task Force 32 (the South Pacific Amphibious Force), commanded by Admiral Richmond K. Turner, was a permanent organization to which landing forces were added for amphibious operations. Task Force 33 consisted of land-based air units from all the Allied services in the area and was under command of Vice Admiral Aubrey W. Fitch. Tactical operations were under direc-

[18] Morison, *History*, VI, 128–129; Craven and Cate, *The A.A.F. in World War II*, IV, 213–214.

[19] For a description of the invasion of the Trobriands, see Miller, *Cartwheel*, pp. 49–59.

[20] Descriptions of Nassau Bay landings include *ibid.*, pp. 59–66; Morison, *History*, VI, 136–137.

tion of an interservice and interallied Air-Command, Solomons, headed until July, 1943, by Rear Admiral Marc A. Mitscher. Under Lieutenant General Millard F. Harmon, commanding general of the U.S. Army forces in the South Pacific Area, were four infantry divisions and the Thirteenth Air Force. Although his duties were mainly administrative and logistical, Harmon was called on frequently by Halsey for advice on operations. In the Marine Corps, holding a position somewhat comparable to that of Harmon, Major General Clayton B. Vogel commanded the I Marine Amphibious Corps. These disparate organizations seemed to work effectively together as a result of the ability and cooperation of the senior officers, who were strongly loyal to Admiral Halsey.

New Georgia in the central Solomons is really a cluster of islands, of which one, the largest, is called New Georgia.[21] Others in the group include Rendova, Vella Lavella, Kolombangara, and Vangunu. Small islands, narrow channels, coral reefs, and other obstacles made access difficult in many places. Munda Point, one of the ultimate targets, could not be reached by large vessels. Halsey's plan for invasion involved several simultaneous landings preliminary to main landings on Rendova. Operations started successfully as some six thousand troops in a convoy made their way peacefully to Rendova from Guadalcanal on the night of June 29–30, thanks to air and naval action which had isolated the area by bombardments and mine-laying. The Japanese had not anticipated the move, and as soon as they realized what was happening began to turn their heavy coastal guns emplaced on or near Munda Point against the landing forces. This firing and Japanese air raids slowed down but did not stop landings on Rendova, or the coming of reinforcements. Admiral Turner reorganized his force into five units, an air force, assault flotillas, a naval base group, and Northern and Southern Landing Groups. The Northern Landing Group was to land at Rice Anchorage and move from Enogai Inlet to Bairoko Harbor; the Southern Landing Group would move across the lagoon from Rendova to Zanana Beach on New Georgia and march across to Munda Point, five air-miles away. Between July 2 and 6, the 172d and 169th Regiments were established in a beachhead at Zanana; when

---

[21] Principal accounts of the landings in New Georgia include John N. Rentz, *Marines in the Central Solomons* (Marine Corps Monographs [11]) ([Washington] 1952), pp. 36–121; Miller, *Cartwheel*, pp. 67–97; Morison, *History*, VI, 138–159.

they started to advance through the jungle they met determined opposition, and even though reinforced, the attack bogged down. In addition to battle casualties and persons ill of tropical diseases, a disproportionate number of men suffered from "war neurosis," apparently brought on by unfamiliarity with the jungle and by extreme exhaustion. In the middle of July, Major General Oscar W. Griswold took command of the New Georgia Occupation Force, and he made ready to bring in reinforcements and launch a major attack on Munda Point.

On July 5, the Northern Landing Group, under Colonel Harry B. Liversedge, had made landings at Rice Anchorage. His forces took Enogai Inlet but were kept away from Bairoko Harbor by heavy mortar fire and for a time settled down to patrols.

On the other front the Southern Landing Group established a new beachhead at Laiana and used tanks with some success against Japanese pillboxes and other defensive positions. Elsewhere in the area fighting continued, and such names as Reincke Hill, Kelley Hill, and Horseshoe Hill became etched in fighting men's memories. The supply picture improved, and air support of various types increased in quantity and effectiveness.[22] On July 25, General Griswold and his XIV Corps launched an attack. Despite heavy preliminary bombardment, the corps made little progress except for a slight gain in the center of the 43d Division's line. On July 29, Major General John R. Hodge, capable and experienced commander of the Americal Division, became commander of the 43d Division. The 37th Division launched attacks against Japanese-held ridges and encountered heavy opposition; American tanks were disabled, and flame-thrower operators, weighed down with their equipment, were picked off and killed. On the twenty-eighth, the attack progressed more successfully as the Americans used a variety of weapons to knock out one pillbox after another, and by August 1 the ridge positions had been taken. The Japanese withdrew to a new defensive position, about 3,800 yards from Munda Point.

Although weary, the invading soldiers by this time had become veterans, proficient in jungle warfare, in the use of tanks, and the employment of flame throwers. Because of the difficulty of carrying out reconnaissance in the dense jungle, the Americans developed a system of attack to determine the centers of resistance. First they employed

[22] For accounts of air operations, see Craven and Cate, *The A.A.F. in World War II*, IV, 219–237; Miller, *Cartwheel*, pp. 140–142.

artillery fire to tear away trees and shrubbery and expose enemy positions. Then mortars, especially 81-mm. mortars firing heavy shells with delayed fuses, attempted to force Japanese soldiers into the open to come under assault by a company or platoon using BAR's, M1's, grenades, and when available flame throwers. The procedure was of course wasteful when the enemy did not happen to be present; it was effective when they were. Advance through jungle was difficult to keep uniform, and there was the danger that a unit might get so far ahead of other units that it might be exposed to flanking attacks or the friendly mortar of adjoining forces.

In spite of the difficulties, the Americans developed flexible variations of tactics until on August 5 the 43d Division flushed out the last of the enemy on the point. General Griswold radioed Admiral Halsey: "Our ground forces today wrested Munda from the Japs and present it to you . . . as the sole owner."[23] There was still clean-up to be done, although the bulk of the Japanese force had evacuated the island. By mid-October, a six-thousand-foot runway was ready for bomber use.

While the ground forces were mired in the six weeks' struggle to take Munda, air and naval engagements resulted from the Japanese efforts first to relieve and then to evacuate its besieged garrisons. In one respect the Japanese had a technical advantage in their "long lance" torpedo, which was superior to anything yet developed by the Allies. This torpedo, twice as powerful as the average underwater missile and capable of traveling eleven miles at forty-nine knots, resulted in sinkings that were as baffling as they were damaging to the Americans. Also, unknown to the enemy, the Japanese had developed a torpedo-loading device which enabled their vessels to carry a larger supply than the Americans thought possible.[24] On the other hand, in what was essentially a war of attrition, the Japanese could ill afford the losses in manpower and equipment which accompanied what at the time seemed to be successful operations.

Anticipating that the enemy would next invade Kolombangara, the Japanese placed on this island some ten thousand men, including those who had just evacuated New Georgia Island. Admiral Halsey, instead, turned to the island-skipping technique which the Americans had first used in the Pacific by by-passing Kiska to strike at Attu in the Aleu-

[23] Radio, Griswold to Halsey, Aug. 5, 1943, quoted in *ibid.*, p. 164.
[24] Morison, *History*, VI, 194–197.

tians. Skipping Kolombangara, Halsey's forces took lightly defended Vella Lavella in the middle of August.[25] This by-passing procedure frustrated the Japanese intention of wearing down the foe by contesting every island across the Pacific and according to General Tojo was a major cause of Allied victory.

Having by-passed Kolombangara, the Allies next attempted to make it untenable for the enemy by blasting it from the air and blockading it by sea. Although not completely successful in either effort, the Allies gradually wore the Japanese down so that after about a month they decided that they had endured enough on the island, and despite American efforts made a successful evacuation. Attempts to evacuate a force of Japanese that had landed on Vella Lavella led to a naval engagement in which the Japanese sank a destroyer, damaged two others, and removed their garrison. Both Kolombangara and Vella Lavella, however, were in Allied hands.

While the New Georgia campaign was in progress, General MacArthur's Southwest Pacific forces started Operation II of the Elkton Plan, which involved taking the Markham Valley and the Huon Peninsula of New Guinea in order to increase control over Vitiaz and Dampier straits. The operation was a continuation of the defense of Wau starting in January, 1943, and of the landings in Nassau Bay on June 30. Lacking enough ships for a full amphibious attack or enough planes for a complete airborne attack, MacArthur used a variety of means to bring a substantial force to bear on the enemy; these included amphibious assault, shore-to-shore movement, attack by paratroopers, and airlift.

Cutting off the Huon Peninsula was a trough consisting of the Markham and Ramu valleys between two mountain ranges. These valleys, because they contained excellent sites for air bases, became valuable military objectives. Lae, with its harbor and airfield, was more significant than Salamaua as a port through which supplies could go to inland airfields.[26] Consequently, the Allies decided to strike first at Salamaua in the hope that the Japanese would concentrate their

[25] Accounts of the Vella Lavella landings include *ibid.*, VI, 225–253; Rentz, *Marines in the Central Solomons,* pp. 131 139; Miller, *Cartwheel,* pp. 172–184.

[26] Accounts of the Lae-Salamaua operations include *ibid.*, pp. 189–221; Craven and Cate, *The A.A.F. in World War II,* IV, 168–200; Kenney, *General Kenney Reports,* pp. 262–311; Morison, *History,* VI, 254–268; Odgers, *Air War Against Japan,* 1943–45, pp. 68–87.

strength there rather than at Lae. Preliminary air and sea operations included development of two inland grass air strips as staging bases for fighter protection, which made possible bomber and naval raids on Japanese installations farther along the coast. In July, troops began a diversionary attack toward Salamaua and by the end of August had fought their way near Salamaua. On September 11, Australians crossed the Francisco River, a natural barrier made more difficult by Japanese defensive positions, and the next day Salamaua fell. Although the cost had been heavy in casualties, the diversion had succeeded, for of about ten thousand troops in the Lae-Salamaua area the majority had centered on Salamaua.

The sea-borne invasion of Lae began on September 4, and was made by the 9th Australian Division, which had left Milne Bay on ships of Task Force 76 and had been joined by fifty-seven landing craft of the 2d Engineer Special Brigade at Morobe. They landed on two beaches east of Lae, protected ably from an eighty-plane enemy air attack by some sixty Allied planes. Japanese resistance, heavy rains, and river barriers impeded but did not prevent Allied progress toward the objective.

While these landings were taking place, the 503d Parachute Infantry Regiment left Port Moresby in planes and took Nadzeb in a parachute drop. This was an excellent site in the Markham Valley on which the Australians had built an air strip before the war. Australian forces came in by river, and by the end of two weeks the Allies had finished two parallel air strips six thousand feet in length and were working on six others.

Australian forces continued their advance toward Lae, and although encountering some resistance entered Lae early on September 16. The majority of the Japanese had evacuated, and instead of trying to go through the Markham-Ramu trough, the retreating troops made their way across the mountains. Of about nine thousand men who made the difficult march toward Madang some six hundred died en route.[27]

As a result of the loss of the Lae-Salamaua area, the Japanese leaders altered their strategic plans and decided to pull back their perimeter to strengthen their defenses and also prepare for an offensive. More specifically, they determined to hold Bougainville, strengthen Wewak and Madang in New Guinea, and keep control of Vitiaz and Dampier

[27] Miller, *Cartwheel*, p. 212. The Japanese loss in life for the campaign and retreat was about 2,600.

straits. Lieutenant General Hatazo Adachi, commander of the Eighteenth Army in charge of eastern New Guinea, thought Finschhafen soon would be attacked and ordered the bulk of the 20th Division to start a two-hundred-mile march to this port on the Huon Peninsula. The move came too late, for the Allies struck before these reinforcements could arrive.

The rapid conquest of Lae and Salamaua and the move of the Japanese 20th Division dictated an advance in the date of the Allied attack on Finschhafen. After a meeting of top leaders, General MacArthur on September 15 ordered General Blamey's New Guinea Force, with air support from General Kenney's forces, to seize Kaipit at the head of the Markham Valley and Dumpu in the Ramu Valley. On the seventeenth he also ordered the New Guinea Force, with naval aid, to seize Finschhafen. On the other hand, he postponed the attack on Madang, which was strongly defended.

The notice to attack Finschhafen was short, but Rear Admiral Daniel E. Barbey's amphibious forces were experienced by this time, and on September 21 Australian soldiers and American sailors left Lae for an attack on Finschhafen, eighty-two miles away.[28] After destroyer bombardment the next day, the Australians landed and established a beachhead; the Japanese contested the action, but kept the bulk of their force near the port. Fighting continued for the rest of the month, and on October 1 three Australian battalions took Finschhafen. There remained the problem of the advancing Japanese 20th Division. Luckily, its commanding general did not concentrate his forces after advancing inland and committed them piecemeal. The Australian 9th Division held out until reinforcements arrived and then started an offensive, which by January 15 had progressed around the north coast of the peninsula to Sio. The Japanese 20th Division, which in September had had 12,526 men, had only 6,949 by December. There was still fighting to do, but the Allies had captured their strategic objectives, the airfields and the coast along Vitiaz Strait.

While the campaigns in New Guinea and the Solomons were continuing, in Washington the view was changing toward seizure of Rabaul. The Joint Strategic Survey Committee in June, 1943, expressed the opinion that it would be more economical to neutralize Rabaul than to capture it. They also felt that the Allied drive north in the area was simply a reversal of the earlier Japanese offensive and did not give

---

[28] For details of the Finschhafen operation, see *ibid.*, pp. 217–221; Morison, *History*, VI, 269–271.

indication of early success. By July, General Marshall was convinced, and he radioed General MacArthur suggesting that he follow Cartwheel with the seizure of Manus in the Admiralties and Kavieng in New Britain in order to isolate Rabaul. He also suggested capture of Wewak. In spite of MacArthur's insistence that Rabaul must be taken, the Joint Chiefs of Staff recommended neutralization rather than seizure of Rabaul, and the Combined Chiefs of Staff approved the recommendation at the Quadrant meeting in Quebec in August, 1943.[29] MacArthur raised no further protest when he found that after moving west on the New Guinea coast to Vogelkop Peninsula his forces would move north toward the Philippines.

While top military leaders were considering the question of Rabaul, General MacArthur and Admiral Halsey were planning the invasion of Bougainville, the largest island in the Solomons. This island had been a German possession until the end of World War I, and some of the German missionaries who remained in the area welcomed the Japanese and sought to win native support for them. In March, 1943, the Japanese made a concerted and generally successful attempt to eliminate coastwatchers from the island. So desperate did the position of such persons become that a U.S. submarine, by prearrangement, slipped in and evacuated them, together with a number of women and children.[30] Thereafter, the Allies had no inside information on conditions on Bougainville.

By November, 1943, Allied estimates placed between 37,500 and 40,000 Japanese military and some 20,000 naval personnel on the island.[31] About 130 miles in length and 30 to 50 miles wide, Bougainville has two active volcanoes and mountains over 10,000 feet high. The region is densely tropical, and around Empress Augusta Bay on the west coast was a marshy area sparsely settled and little known. In the southern plains, plantations had replaced jungle, and it was in this region that the Japanese had the bulk of their men. Some five thousand were thought to be along the east coast, a comparable number at Buka and Bona in the north, and only two or three thousand in the Empress Augusta Bay area.

This disposition of Japanese forces affected Halsey's plans, for it was

[29] Miller, *Cartwheel,* pp. 222–225; Matloff, *Strategic Planning,* pp. 194–235.
[30] Morison, *History,* VI, 280–281.
[31] Morison says there were 40,000 troops (*ibid.,* VI, 281); Miller gives the figure 37,500 as the estimate of Allied Intelligence agencies. Miller, *Cartwheel,* p. 235.

estimated that it would take four divisions to conquer the strongly defended southern part of the island, and there were just four divisions
in the area ready for action. Campaigning after the seizure of this objective, therefore, might be delayed for months. Halsey, on advice of
his subordinates and with MacArthur's approval, decided to try to
neutralize southern Bougainville without seizing it. There were two possible courses toward this objective. One was to seize Choiseul Island,
southeast of Bougainville, in preparation for an attack on Kieta, on
the eastern coast of Bougainville; the other was to take the Treasury
Islands, south of Bougainville and then advance to Empress Augusta
Bay on the west coast of Bougainville. Kieta had a protected harbor;
Empress Augusta Bay was on the exposed side of the island in the
approaching monsoon season. However, it would be easier to take the
Treasury Islands than Choiseul, and Empress Augusta Bay was so isolated that it would take months for the Japanese to send in substantial
reinforcements.

Cape Torokina on Empress Augusta Bay was only sixty-five miles
from Japanese airfields on Bougainville and 215 from bases around
Rabaul; neutralization of these fields, therefore, would be essential to
landings. Aware of these risks and of the fact that invasion would pro-
voke strong Japanese reaction on sea and in the air, Halsey decided on
Empress Augusta Bay as the target. MacArthur approved and promised
full air support from the Southwest Pacific. The landing date was set
at November 1, 1943. During October the Fifth Air Force carried the
air attack to Rabaul. Dobodura was the main staging base for heavy
bombers, and Nadzeb was preparing for a similar role in future operations. P-38's could stage through Kiriwina from New Guinea and escort heavy bombers all the way to Rabaul. The first large raid, with
349 planes involved, took place on October 12, and others followed
as weather permitted. Although not as devastating as claimed at the
time, the punishment inflicted on a sharply resisting foe was real, and
the Fifth Air Force performed well its role of preparing for the Bougainville invasion.[32] To Air Command, Solomons, went the task of
neutralizing the airfields on Bougainville. General Nathan F. Twining
had about six hundred planes in his composite force and began a campaign on October 18. Although the Japanese showed remarkable in-

---

[32] For air operations in the Bougainville campaign, see Craven and Cate,
The A.A.F. in World War II, IV, 246–280; Kenney, *General Kenney Reports,*
pp. 312–325.

genuity in using the badly damaged fields, the Allies continued their punishing attacks until by the day of the landings in Empress Augusta Bay the Japanese airfields on Bougainville were inoperative.

On October 12, Admiral Halsey issued basic orders for the invasion.[33] There were five task forces, similar to those used in the New Georgia campaign. A submarine task force would engage in offensive reconnaissance, and a force of cruisers and destroyers would deal with enemy ships and bombard Buka in the north and the Shortland Islands south of Bougainville. Another task force, centering around the carrier *Saratoga* and the light carrier *Princeton,* would raid Buka and Bona. A land-based air force would carry out the customary missions of reconnaissance, attacks on enemy ships and planes, and air cover and support of the landing force. The invasion force itself, under Rear Admiral Theodore S. Wilkinson, would transport the ground troops under the commanding general, I Marine Amphibious Corps.

General Vandegrift, who had won experience and reputation at Guadalcanal, was the ground commander during the first phase of the operation. Wilkinson divided the task force into the Northern Force, command of which he retained, which would make the major landings at Empress Augusta Bay, and the Southern Force, which would seize the Treasury Islands and make a diversionary raid on Choiseul to convince the Japanese that the main thrust would be on the east coast of Bougainville. The 3d Marine Division reinforced, as the initial landing force, was to land, establish a strong perimeter, and withdraw after the Army had arrived to defend the area. By this device a trained amphibious assault force would be ready for further advances.

The invaders made their preliminary moves with skill. New Zealand troops, starting on October 27, took the Treasury Islands, and made possible establishment of advance naval supply bases and installation of long-range radar to give advance warning of planes from Rabaul. Marine raiders carried out a blustering attack on Choiseul Island as if it were a preliminary to mass landings on that or the nearby Shortland Islands.

The real amphibious assault on Empress Augusta Bay began on November 1, and was aided greatly by the earlier air campaigns which had temporarily neutralized enemy air strength. The Northern Force,

---

[33] Accounts of the Bougainville operation include Miller, *Cartwheel,* pp. 222–271; John N. Rentz, *Bougainville and the Northern Solomons* (Marine Corps Monographs [4]) ([Washington] 1948), *passim;* Morison, *History,* VI, 279–365.

organized into three divisions, made a night run to Empress Augusta Bay after shifting course as a ruse. Destroyers poured in their preliminary bombardment, and torpedo bombers from New Georgia strafed the coastline before the assault waves reached shore. There were relatively few Japanese, but some of them were well ensconced, and before they were eliminated inflicted casualties of 78 dead and 104 wounded. The invaders, however, landed, seized a beachhead, and cleared out the defenders. Little had been known of the region; the vessels encountered uncharted reefs, and the Marines discovered that behind most of the beach lay a swamp extending some two miles inland.

The real battle for Bougainville took place in the air and on the sea and began as soon as the Japanese heard of the landings. Planes speeding down from Rabaul on November 1 were able to inflict only minor damage, for radar warnings gave time for the ships to put out to sea and the air defenses to form. On the same day a Japanese task force of two heavy and two light cruisers and six destroyers started for Empress Augusta Bay to attack the transports and cargo ships. Rear Admiral A. S. Merrill's Task Force 39, which had just finished successful bombardment of Japanese positions on Bougainville, intercepted the Japanese off Cape Torokina in an engagement known as the Battle of Empress Augusta Bay and sank a light cruiser and a destroyer in return for heavy damage to one destroyer and light damage to other vessels. Merrill's force was then subjected to an air attack; by steaming clockwise and firing everything up to six-inch guns, the surface craft avoided damage to all ships but one, which received two bomb hits. The Japanese lost a number of planes in air battles on their way to and from the target.

When Admiral Halsey learned that a force of cruisers had been transferred from Truk to Rabaul, he ordered Admiral Sherman's carriers to attack them. The move was risky, for to date carriers had been used only sparingly against land bases. On the other hand, Halsey could not wait for Japanese cruisers to bombard Empress Augusta Bay. In the strike which followed, land-based Navy planes from New Georgia flew to cover the ships of Task Force 38 while its planes flew against Rabaul. There was no doubt about the success of the raid, which was followed by an attack by planes of the Fifth Air Force, for the Japanese pulled their cruisers, a number of which had been damaged, away from Rabaul to Truk. This ended the threat by sea to the Marine beachhead, and no heavy ships went thereafter to Rabaul.

The air struggle went on as the Japanese continued to attack Cape Torokina and as Allied planes sought both to thwart this immediate objective and to eliminate Rabaul's air strength. New carriers of the Fifth Fleet joined Task Force 38 in a strike against Rabaul on November 11. Meanwhile, the Japanese launched a sustained air attack of their own, called Operation RO, combining land- and carrier-based planes, against Allied positions. Between November 1 and 11, 1943, they reported great successes; actually the claims were exaggerated, and theirs was the real loss, for they suffered heavy attrition of planes and men. Of the 173 planes and 192 men who went from Truk to Rabaul, by the end of the operation 121 planes had been destroyed and 86 men killed.[34] After November 12, Rabaul was no longer an offensive threat, although it remained a sturdy point of defense. Japanese air losses in this area affected Japanese actions in the Central Pacific as well and aided Allied actions in this area toward the end of the year.

While these significant developments were occurring in the sea and air around Bougainville, the Marines at Empress Augusta Bay went slowly ahead, establishing their beachhead, expanding it, and surrounding it with a strong defensive perimeter. Reinforcements arrived, and Admiral Wilkinson, who had headed the amphibious phase, turned over command to Major General Roy S. Geiger, a veteran of Guadalcanal, who came in to relieve General Vandegrift. On November 7, about 475 Japanese soldiers landed unnoticed near the perimeter, but were wiped out with a twenty-minute concentration from five field batteries when they attacked. This fiasco made it clear that the Japanese would have to come overland if they wished to dislodge the Marines.

During November and December heavy fighting took place on the perimeter. One of the most stubborn positions established by the Japanese was on Hellsapoppin Ridge, a natural fortress which overlooked the beachhead. The final perimeter which the Americans reached in mid-December extended for about 22,500 yards on the inland side and contained over 44,000 men. The Marines protected the perimeter with everything from machine guns to heavy artillery.

Halsey had other plans for the Marines who had established this strong position on Bougainville, and on December 15, General Griswold, with his XIV Corps, relieved General Geiger, and the Americal Division came in to replace the 3d Marine Division. There was little

---

[34] Miller, *Cartwheel,* p. 255.

fighting, and Griswold's main task was logistical development. A fighter strip was ready for use on December 9, and fighters began making sweeps against Rabaul or escorting long-range bombers in their attacks on the same target. Neither these nor General Kenney's heavy bombers could knock out Rabaul, and work progressed on fields in Bougainville that would handle medium, dive, and torpedo bombers. Two such fields were ready by January 9, 1944.

Operation II of Elkton III had been planned when it was assumed that the Allies would try to seize Rabaul. When it was thought to by-pass Rabaul, General Kenney argued against the necessity of seizing Cape Gloucester at the other end of New Britain, on the ground that it would take too much time to turn it into a satisfactory air base.[35] General MacArthur's headquarters insisted that there was time to take Cape Gloucester, and that it would be useful for control of Vitiaz Strait. On November 21, 1943, it was agreed to seize Cape Gloucester and also Arawe, a harbor in New Britain. General Krueger and the Alamo Force had charge of planning and carrying out the operations.

Anticipating invasion, the Japanese had been reinforcing western New Britain between October and mid-December, but Japanese air defenses had been weakened not only by battle losses but by transfer of an air division to another area. In contrast, the Allies began the most extensive air preparations to date in the Southwest Pacific and their air attacks increased in intensity during November, concentrating on Cape Gloucester and Gasmata on the south coast. Planes avoided Arawe until mid-December to mislead the Japanese.

The Arawe force left Goodenough Island on December 13, and an hour before dawn of the fifteenth, 150 men of A Troop, 112th Cavalry, attempting a surprise landing ran into machine-gun fire which sank all but three of the fifteen rubber boats.[36] Destroyer fire eliminated the machine gunners, and later landings were successful, forcing the few Japanese in the area to retreat to the west. The Japanese in January came in with a land attack, for which the Allies were well prepared, and a combined tank-infantry attack knocked out the enemy. As it

---

[35] Craven and Cate, The A.A.F. in World War II, IV, 330; Miller, Cartwheel, pp. 273–274.

[36] For accounts of the Arawe operation, see ibid., pp. 282–289; Frank O. Hough and John A. Crown, The Campaign on New Britain (Marine Corps Monographs [10]) ([Washington] 1952), pp. 140–151; Morison, History, VI, 373–377.

turned out, Arawe was not worth the effort; it became neither a PT base nor an important air base.

In the meantime a more important struggle had begun for Cape Gloucester.[37] The 1st Marine Division and the 7th Marines in a convoy escorted by a task force of American and Australian cruisers arrived offshore and in the early morning of December 26, 1943, after a ninety-minute naval bombardment, began landings on beaches east of Cape Gloucester. As at Empress Augusta Bay, the assault troops found the narrow beach backed by swamp. The Japanese did not contest the landings but fought a detachment attempting to move along the shore and sent air raids which failed to destroy the beachhead. West of Cape Gloucester the reinforced 2d Battalion, 1st Marines, landed and established a smaller foothold at Tauali. The next day, despite monsoon rains, Marines began to advance from the major beachhead toward the airfield and, using heavy air and artillery bombardment followed by tank attacks, gradually broke the strong block which the Japanese had constructed for the protection of the field. When his reserves, the reinforced 5th Marines arrived, Major General William H. Rupertus advanced with his force and took the principal objective, the airfield. There was still hard fighting to do; by difficult ridge fighting and by the use of jungle patrols, sometimes provisioned by airdrops, the Marines gradually gained control of western New Britain. The Japanese were on the eastern end around Rabaul, and the central part of the island became a sort of no-man's land.

Although the campaign in western New Britain proved to be relatively unimportant strategically, as a source of future bases, tactically the invaders added greatly to their renown as jungle fighters as they improved techniques of fighting acquired in New Guinea and the Solomons. One of the most important developments was the adaption of medium and light tanks to jungle warfare, and amphibian tractors and bulldozers again showed their versatility and effectiveness. On the other hand, the bazooka, which proved so serviceable elsewhere, was a disappointment in New Britain since its rockets often refused to detonate in the mud and its battery system failed in the prevailing wetness.

Two days after the landings at Arawe, General MacArthur decided

[37] Principal accounts of the Cape Gloucester operations include *ibid.*, VI, 378–389; Miller, *Cartwheel*, pp. 289–294; Hough and Crown, *The Campaign on New Britain*, pp. 48–139; Craven and Cate, *The A.A.F. in World War II*, IV, 337–345.

to make another advance along the coast of New Guinea, and he ordered General Krueger to prepare to seize Saidor with an operation from Goodenough Island.[38] Possession of Saidor, 110 nautical miles from Finschhafen and 52 from Madang, would not only strengthen the Allied position but would divide the Japanese, for it lay between the two points of concentration of the Japanese Eighteenth Army. Instead of using the New Guinea Force which had been handling operations on that island, MacArthur called on Krueger and the Alamo Force. Although the notice was short, preparations went ahead smoothly, and on January 2, 1944, 6,779 men landed with little or no opposition and few casualties. By February 15th, about fifteen thousand men were in the garrison and construction of air and other facilities was under way. The move prompted the Japanese to abandon Sio to the Australians approaching from the other direction and march inland in an attempt to by-pass Saidor and reach Madang some two hundred miles away. Only about half the twenty thousand men who had been in the two Japanese divisions in December reached their destination. Unable to secure reinforcements in time to stop the march, General Clarence A. Martin, head of the task force at Saidor, sent elements of the 126th Infantry to attack toward the west, and the Australians were also pushing toward Madang from the Markham-Ramu trough. Imperial Headquarters decided not to defend Madang and pulled its forces west to Wewak, leaving the Australians to enter an abandoned Madang on April 24, 1944.

The Saidor landing completed the seizure of the Huon Peninsula and the Markham-Ramu trough, aside from inevitable mopping-up procedures. At Saidor the Allies soon had another airfield to support further operations. Cartwheel had been completed; Rabaul had been isolated but not yet completely neutralized.

---

[38] For details on the Saidor operation, see Miller, *Cartwheel*, pp. 295–305; Craven and Cate, *The A.A.F. in World War II*, IV, 345–350.

CHAPTER 13

The Pacific War, November, 1943–May, 1944

D URING 1943, military planners in Washington became more interested in a long-range strategic plan for the defeat of Japan,
for without such a plan it was difficult to determine which operations
against Japan merited priority in men and materials. Consequently,
in the summer of 1943, the planners outlined specific objectives for
1944 and worked on an over-all plan for war against Japan on the
assumption that Italy would be defeated in 1943 and Germany in the
fall of 1944. They also assumed that Soviet Russia would enter the war
against Japan only if the cost of such a venture became slight.

The tentative schedule which the Joint Planners drew on August 6,
1943, called for invasion of the Gilberts on November 15, western New
Britain and Kieta, on Bougainville, in December, 1943. On the first of
January, 1944, would come invasion of the Marshalls, and by the first
of February South and Southwest Pacific forces would neutralize Rabaul and take Wewak in New Guinea. Seizure of Kavieng, on New
Ireland, would come on May 1, 1944, and that of Manus, in the Admiralties, on June 1. The advance westward along the coast of New
Guinea had a timetable extending from August 1 for Hollandia to
November 30 for the Vogelkop Peninsula. After the seizure of the
Marshalls the schedule for the Central Pacific was Ponape, in the Carolines, on June 1, 1944, Truk, also in the Carolines, on September 1,
and Palau on December 31.[1] Central Pacific and Southwest Pacific

[1] This tentative schedule is reproduced in Maurice Matloff, *Strategic Plan-
ning for Coalition Warfare, 1943–1944 (United States Army in World War
II: The War Department)* (Washington, 1959), p. 207. The schedule is from
JCS 446, 6 Aug 43, "Specific Operations in the Pacific and Far East."

forces would support each other in their advances. The planners also noted the possibility that the capture of Kiska in the Aleutians might lead to an attack on the Kuriles.

Meanwhile, in a report dated August 8, 1943, Combined Staff Planners attempted an overview of the war against Japan, in which they expressed the belief that the Allies should defeat Japan by bombardment, encirclement, and blockade.[2] Predicting that actual invasion of Japan might be necessary to break the Japanese will and ability to resist, they stated that the Allies should make every effort to destroy the Japanese Fleet, the air forces, industry, and shipping. The Allies should expect little help from Soviet Russia or, for that matter, China, although aid should be extended to that country. The Combined Planners agreed with the U.S. Navy's contention that the main approach to Japan should be through the Central Pacific, and that campaigns in the Aleutians and the Southwest Pacific should be secondary. Burma should be retaken, and China kept in the war. Although they differed on timing, American and British planners agreed that Asiatic and Pacific drives should be coordinated as much as possible to be mutually supporting and to converge in the Hong Kong–Formosa area. If Hong Kong were seized first, the Allies could use it as a base of operations against Formosa. The planners cited Luzon, Hainan, and one of the Ryukyus as alternatives for Hong Kong if these became impracticable targets. The report also noted the possibility of long-range bombing of Japan. Anticipating conquest of the Palaus by the end of 1944, the planners looked ahead to the Philippines, Formosa, the Ryukyus, and Malaya as targets for 1945 and 1946. The attack on Japan itself would start in 1947 and extend into 1948.

Dissatisfied with this over-all plan, Admiral Cooke, main U.S. Navy planner, suggested an alternative to the defeat of Germany in 1944 and of Japan in 1948. This was to reassign forces and defeat both countries in 1946. Cooke's reasoning was that under the Combined Planners' plan the Allied will to continue fighting would decline after the defeat of Germany. However, choice between such alternatives was not the prerogative of the planners and rested with top American and British officials, who were not ready to make such a policy decision.

Between the Trident Conference in May, 1943, and the Quadrant

[2] CPS 83, 8 Aug 43, "Appreciation and Plan for the defeat of Japan." Summarized in *ibid.*, pp. 207–208.

Conference in August, 1943, work went ahead on the major projects against Japan. The South-Southwest Pacific campaign, under way, and the Central Pacific drive, in the making, were still on an equal footing. The Japanese had evacuated the Aleutians; in the China-Burma-India (CBI) Theater an airlift, after difficult preparations, was beginning to look promising, but in Burma the outlook for the Allies was still dim. In the two months after the Trident Conference, the U.S. War Department sent 87,000 men to the Pacific, 3,600 to the CBI Theater, and 19,000 to Alaska.[3] In general, the purpose of the campaigns continued to be maintenance of the initiative, further attrition of the enemy, and seizure of strategic positions for later offensives.

At the Quadrant Conference, held in Quebec in August, the United States representatives, fearing a long war of attrition against Japan, wanted to outline both the course and timing of operations. Britain still shrank from too great commitment to the Pacific war for fear of delaying Germany's defeat.[4] Admiral King, as in the other midwar conferences, was the chief protagonist of the American point of view. General Marshall supported him but was also concerned with protecting General MacArthur's views toward strategy in the Pacific war. At Quebec the basis for discussion was the Combined Planning Staff's over-all plan, to which, as we have seen, the Navy had taken exception. Both King and Marshall opposed the idea that the war should last until 1948 or 1949. Marshall insisted that "no time should be lost in agreeing on a general plan for the defeat of Japan," for, he asserted, Germany's collapse would raise the problem of partial demobilization "and a growing impatience would ensue throughout the United States for the rapid defeat of Japan."[5] Thinking also of the possibility of demobilization, the British were willing to see early completion of a plan to defeat Japan. They wanted to contribute naval and air support and agreed that for planning purposes an invasion of Japan by land forces must be envisaged. Americans and British at Quebec did agree that forth-

[3] *Ibid.*, p. 209.

[4] For British accounts, see S. Woodburn Kirby, *The War Against Japan* (*History of the Second World War: United Kingdom Military Series*) (London, 1958), II, 421–423; Arthur Bryant, *The Turn of the Tide: A History of the War Years Based on the Diaries of Field-Marshal Lord Alanbrooke, Chief of the Imperial General Staff* (New York, 1957), pp. 575–579.

[5] From the minutes of the Combined Chiefs of Staff, 107th Meeting, August 14, 1943, quoted in Matloff, *Strategic Planning*, p. 231.

coming operations would include American advance through both the Central and Southwest Pacific, and a British drive through the Strait of Malacca and the South China Sea, and the development through Burma of an American supply line to China. There was lack of accord on operations around South Burma and Singapore.

At Quebec, the U.S. Joint Chiefs of Staff urged acceptance of the twelve-month deadline for conclusion of the war after the collapse of Germany and added a new argument. This was the projected use of the very long-range bomber, the B-29 Superfortress, which had a cruising tactical radius of fifteen hundred miles and which, consequently, might operate from Chinese bases. The idea was so new that it required further study. The British assented to the use of the twelve-month target date for planning purposes but insisted that reorientation of troop movements should depend on the situation in Europe. It was at this conference that the decision was made to neutralize rather than seize Rabaul. Perhaps more important than some of the specific agreements reached at Quebec was a growing sense of urgency to speed up the war against Japan. There was still much that was tentative; there was no decision on the necessity for actual invasion of Japan, and the main route of approach to Japan was still undetermined.[6]

In the months after the Quadrant Conference, increasing demands from commanders in the various theaters underlined the need for a systematic deployment of forces in accord with an over-all plan, rather than a haphazard parceling out of men and resources in the Pacific. American planners began to think, among other things, of short cuts that would speed up the collapse of Japan. There was still a long way to go, for Japan's perimeter had hardly been breached, and Japan was strengthening its defensive rings. Washington planners wanted to make faster and deeper thrusts into enemy territory; they did not want British or French help in fighting the Pacific war. The U.S. Navy was not enthusiastic over suggestions that large segments of the British Fleet go to the Pacific and cited lack of facilities, logistics, and appropriate targets. The U.S. Army was equally cold to the idea of French forces going to the Pacific and asserted that they would add too much strain to American production and shipping.[7]

[6] Accounts of the Quebec Conference include *ibid.*, pp. 211–243; Albert C. Wedemeyer, *Wedemeyer Reports!* (New York, 1958), pp. 243–246; H. H. Arnold, *Global Mission* (New York, 1949), pp. 442–444; Winston S. Churchill, *The Second World War* (Boston, 1954), V, 80–97.

[7] Matloff, *Strategic Planning*, p. 309. Churchill made such a suggestion for

Efforts to outline an actual plan that would lead to Japan's defeat twelve months after Germany's anticipated collapse in October, 1944, resulted in differences among planners. U.S. Army planners suggested an approach from Hawaii and the Aleutians culminating in an assault on Hokkaido, a large northern island of Japan. The combined (British and American) planning teams felt the deadline could not be met since the approach must be through China and would take a longer period of time. The Joint Strategic Survey Committee, on the other hand, believed that such planning was too conservative and did not assess real Allied strength in the Pacific. Rejecting Hokkaido as a target, this committee's report of November 8, 1943, insisted that the way to Japan's defeat lay in "all-out operations through the Central Pacific with supporting operations on the northern and southern flanks."[8]

The needs of the war in Europe, the competing demands of the Central Pacific and the South-Southwest Pacific, and the great distances involved continued to complicate the problem of supply. The demand for long-range fighter planes in Europe, for example, caused the War Department to deny requested increases for the South-Southwest Pacific. As in Europe, there was a shortage of landing craft in the Pacific, and in October, 1943, the Army and Navy agreed to interchange of these craft between the South Pacific and the Southwest Pacific.

In order to prepare for larger movements to the Pacific as soon as conditions were favorable, the Army turned Hawaii into a training ground for the Pacific war. The troops in training at the same time furnished protection for the islands, much as troops in Britain building up for invasion also provided a protective force for the British Isles.

Despite the numerous bottlenecks and shortages, by the end of September, 1943, the Army had 578,278 men in the Pacific Theaters, 131,670 in Alaska, and 61,198 in the CBI Theater. This total of 771,146 was considerably under the total of 1,032,296 for Europe and the Middle East. There were, however, thirteen U.S. divisions against Germany and an equal number against Japan. There were seventy-five air groups opposing Germany, in contrast to thirty-five against Japan, but the

---

British naval aid in the Pacific war in a memorandum to President Roosevelt, dated September 9, 1943. Churchill, *The Second World War,* V, 134.

[8] JCS 533/5, 8 Nov. 43, "Recommended Line of Action at Next U.S.-Br Staff Conf," quoted in Matloff, *Strategic Planning,* p. 312.

bulk of the Navy's fleet and air force and of the Marines were in the Pacific.[9]

At the Cairo-Teheran conferences, held toward the end of 1943, the main interest in the war against Japan was in China's role, and there was little discussion of either an over-all plan or specific operations for 1944. From the conferences came authorization for the Joint Chiefs of Staff to go ahead with the war against Japan. The principal effort would be in the Pacific; flexibility would be the main theme and would make it possible for the Joint Chiefs of Staff, according to General Marshall, "to take advantage of the situation as it develops."[10] He also noted that deciding the merits of the Central Pacific and the Southwest Pacific lay with the Joint Chiefs of Staff. Aside from the problems of Southeast Asia, the conference leaders accepted the schedule of operations presented to them.

This schedule of December 3, 1943, was a revision of that of August 6, and provided for a continuance of the drive against Japanese forces along both axes, in the Central Pacific and the Southwest Pacific.[11] On the former route, forces would take the Marshalls during January, attack Ponape on May 1, the eastern Carolines, including Truk, July 20, and Guam and the Japanese Marianas, October 1. Then, as an important addition to the schedule, initial bombings of Japan by B-29's would start at the end of the year. In the Southwest Pacific MacArthur's forces would seize New Britain and finish neutralization of Rabaul in January, 1944. They would attack Hansa Bay February 1, Kavieng March 20, and Manus on April 20. Advancing along New Guinea, they would attack Hollandia June 1 and be on the Vogelkop Peninsula by the middle of August. B-29's would start to bomb targets in the Netherlands East Indies in mid-July. The schedule noted factors which might make short cuts possible, including early defeat of the Japanese Fleet, sudden withdrawal of Japanese forces, as from Kiska, increased production of assault shipping, collapse of Germany earlier

[9] *Ibid.*, p. 319.

[10] Marshall was actually reading from a memorandum to him by Major General Thomas T. Handy, Assistant Chief of Staff, OPD, quoted in *ibid.*, p. 375. See also, Ray S. Cline, *Washington Command Post: The Operations Division (United States Army in World War II: The War Department)* (Washington, 1951), p. 335.

[11] CCS 397 (rev), 3 Dec 43, "Specific Operations for the Defeat of Japan." This schedule is reproduced in Matloff, *Strategic Planning*, p. 377.

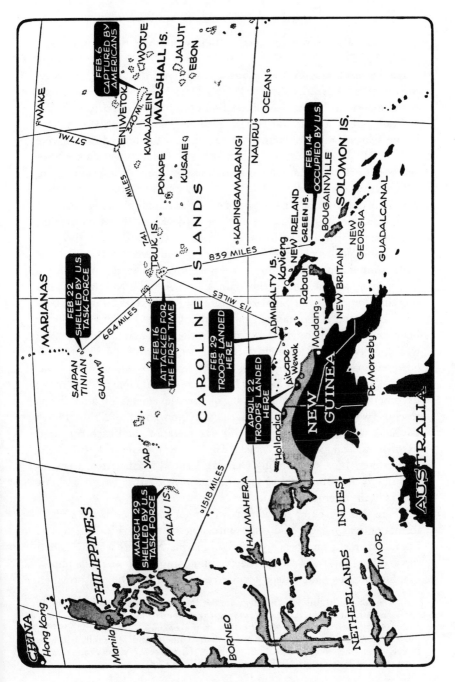

ADVANCE IN THE CENTRAL PACIFIC

than anticipated, and early collaboration with Soviet Russia in the war against Japan.

Having examined over-all plans and top-level discussions, let us return to actual operations in the Pacific. During preparations for operations against the Ellice and Gilbert Islands and Nauru, the Joint Chiefs of Staff agreed to Admiral Nimitz' recommendation that Makin Atoll in the Gilberts replace Nauru as a target, and the revised orders were to seize Makin, Tarawa, and Apamama, on a final target date of November 20, 1943.[12] The planners saw these actions as the beginning of Allied advance across the Pacific, a new phase of the Pacific war, mainly a naval phase, made possible by the mobility of new fast carriers, and one which was featured by large naval forces cutting off Japanese forward positions.

The complexity of amphibious assault is indicated by the fact that half a dozen separate headquarters were involved in the preparation and training for the Gilberts invasion. Under Admiral Nimitz, who had supreme command and final responsibility for the task, was Vice Admiral Raymond A. Spruance, Commander, Central Pacific Forces, who held the highest operational command in the area, and under Spruance was Rear Admiral Richmond Kelly Turner, Head of the V Amphibious Force, established August 24, 1943. Created a week or so later was the V Amphibious Corps, headed by Major General Holland M. Smith; its function was to train and control the movements of amphibious forces. Two divisions, the 2d Marine Division and the 27th Infantry Division, were available for the Gilberts operation, and each prepared its own tactical plans for attack. To Lieutenant General Robert A. Richardson, Jr., Commanding General, Central Pacific Area, went responsibility for training and logistical supply of Army troops and Air Forces in the operation.

There was a lack of specific knowledge of the target areas, and information was meager and often unreliable on such critical matters as tides, surf, reefs, and beaches. The submarine *Nautilus* secretly visited the area and returned with periscopic photographs, planes made photographic missions, and sixteen former residents of the Gilberts provided

---

[12] JCS 386/2, 20 Jul 43, "Strategy in the Pacific," summarized in Philip A. Crowl and Edmund G. Love, *Seizure of the Gilberts and Marshalls (United States Army in World War II: The War in the Pacific)* (Washington, 1955), pp. 23–24. The account of the invasion of the Gilberts and Marshalls is drawn largely from this source and S. E. Morison, *History of United States Naval Operations in World War II* (Boston, 1951), VII, 69–281.

as much information as they could. The 2d Marine Raider Battalion under Lieutenant Colonel Evans Carlson had raided Makin August 2, 1942, and one of the leaders of that group, Lieutenant Colonel James Roosevelt, conferred with leaders of the Gilberts expedition shortly before it left.[13]

The two major objectives, Makin and Tarawa, are small atolls consisting of coral reefs and low strips of land. Reefs guarded the beach approaches, but some of the planners thought landing craft could get across them at high tide, although a British officer, long resident in the area, warned of neap and "dodging" tides which might ruin these calculations. One man listened; Major General Julian Smith, of the 2d Marine Division, warned his men that they might have to walk in across the reefs.

The invaders knew that Betio Island in the Tarawa Atoll was most heavily fortified; on this strip of land three miles long and less than six hundred yards wide the Japanese had amassed a formidable array of coastal defense guns, antiaircraft and antitank guns manned by almost three thousand persons. Makin had upwards of eight hundred men and was less heavily fortified.[14] Major General Ralph Smith commanded the Makin force, which was drawn largely from the 27th Infantry Division. Major General Julian Smith commanded the Tarawa force, composed of the 2d Marine Division and elements from the 2d and 8th Marine Defense Battalions, which was also to take supposedly unoccupied Apamama. Included in the Makin force were four old battleships, four heavy cruisers, thirteen destroyers, and three escort carriers (CVE's), and for the Tarawa venture there were three battleships, three heavy cruisers, three light cruisers, twenty-one destroyers, and five escort carriers.[15]

The 27th Infantry Division had been in Hawaii training for amphibious assault for about eight months. The Marines trained at Wellington, New Zealand; some units had had experience on Guadalcanal.

---

[13] General Holland M. Smith later criticized this raid as premature and inadvisable. *Ibid.*, VII, 77. For another critical account, see Crowl and Love, *Gilberts and Marshalls,* p. 62. A Marine Corps history states that the raid was of little military significance, but asserts that it raised public morale at home. F. O. Hough, V. E. Ludwig, H. I. Shaw, *Pearl Harbor to Guadalcanal: History of U.S. Marine Corps Operations in World War II* (Washington [1958]), pp. 285–286.

[14] Robert D. Heinl and John A. Crown, *The Marshalls: Increasing the Tempo* (Marine Corps Monographs [14]) ([Washington] 1954), pp. 28–29.

[15] Morison, *History,* VII, 114–118.

A critical logistical shortage was in amphibian tractors; the LVT (Alligator) could carry about twenty men across water and coral reefs not normally passable for other landing craft. For the Tarawa assault, the 2d Marines secured 125 LVT's, many of which were unarmored and mechanically erratic. The Northern Force obtained about forty-eight, but so late that few persons had experience in using them. The Gilberts invasion saw the introduction of the pallet, a sledlike structure for dragging supplies across beaches or ground. The Army was somewhat ahead of the Marines in improving the delivery of packaged goods.[16]

Bombing raids on the Gilberts had begun well in advance of the invasion, as B-24's flew from Canton, Funafuti, and other islands in the Ellice group on which air strips had been built.[17] The first strike of the actual operation began on November 13, and between that date and November 17 heavy bombers of the Seventh Air Force flew 141 bombing sorties against the Gilberts and Marshalls and dropped 173 tons of bombs. Earlier a fast carrier task force and bombers from Guadalcanal made a joint raid which caused damage and also brought back additional photographic information. There were other bomber and task force raids, which if they did nothing else seriously reduced the Japanese supply of antiaircraft ammunition.

Early on November 20, the two forces arrived at their separate destinations and in the early dawn began their landings. The strong defenses in the Gilberts were the result in part of the Carlson Marine raid of August, 1942, which led to larger garrisons and concrete bomb shelters. As a consequence of the Bougainville operations which were in progress and of air engagements with American task carrier forces 38 and 50.3, the Japanese had few planes to send to the Gilberts.

The principal defense feature on Makin was a tank barrier system, made of ditches, coconut logs, and gun positions. The initial landings were assigned to the 165th Regimental Combat Team of the 27th Infantry Division, whose strength with attached units was 6,470 men. General Ralph Smith, Commanding General, 27th Division, devised the plan of attack, and General Holland Smith, commander of the V Amphibious Corps, approved it with reluctance.[18] Two battalions, followed by tanks and artillery pieces, would land on the west coast

---

[16] Crowl and Love, *Gilberts and Marshalls,* pp. 48–49.

[17] W. F. Craven and J. L. Cate, *The Army Air Forces in World War II* (Chicago, 1950), IV, 284.

[18] Crowl and Love, *Gilberts and Marshalls,* pp. 40–41.

(Red Beaches) of Butaritari, one of the two largest islands on the atoll. Two hours after the first landings a third battalion would land on the north, lagoon side (Yellow Beach). The two groups would close toward each other to eliminate intervening Japanese and tank traps and seize the western end of the island. Then they would turn eastward against the strongest Japanese position, known as the Citadel.

Preliminary bombings which neutralized many of the defenses facilitated landings on the Red Beaches, although some beach conditions were treacherous. Landings on Yellow Beach were more orderly at first but encountered heavy fire; eleven of the fifteen medium tanks reached shore, however, and effectively ran down isolated groups of the enemy, although coordination of tanks with infantry was poor. Joining, the forces turned toward the strong tank barriers of the Citadel. Snipers in trees checked the advance as tanks and infantry with grenades and TNT pole charges carried on the slow work of eliminating the enemy from concealed and protected shelters. Flame-throwing devices had become so soaked in the landings that they were useless. Another glaring defect in landing operations was that radio gear became water-soaked and so seriously affected ground communications that for a time contacts were lacking between the two landing forces. Ship-to-shore communications, on the other hand, worked well. The slow advance continued and shortly before noon on November 23, General Smith radioed Admiral Turner the euphonious news, "Makin Taken."[19]

Casualties on the American side were 218, of whom 58 were dead. Considering the number of Japanese in opposition, about 300 fighting men in a total of 798 enemy personnel, the losses were relatively high. Furthermore, while waiting to escort the attack force back to Hawaii, the *Liscombe Bay* was sunk by an enemy submarine with a loss of over six hundred lives.[20]

Tarawa presented a much more formidable obstacle than Makin. Of about five thousand persons on the island probably three thousand were effective combat soldiers. Beach obstructions had been created to channel landing craft into murderous lines of fire. Wire, logs, and concrete combined to make Tarawa the most heavily protected island attacked in the Pacific, with the possible exception of Iwo Jima. To win, the Americans would have to knock out the strongest part of the

---

[19] *Ibid.*, pp. 124–126.
[20] Morison, *History,* VII, 140–141.

enemy's defenses, which were on Betio Island, a part of Tarawa Atoll.[21]

For the landings on Tarawa, General Julian Smith planned to use two reinforced regiments of the 2d Marine Division, the 2d and 8th Regimental Combat Teams. The 6th Regimental Combat Team was held in reserve to be landed at Tarawa, Makin, or Apamama if needed. Smith planned initial landings on three adjoining beaches (Red Beaches 1, 2, 3) on the lagoon side of Betio, which was on the south side of the atoll near the entrance to the lagoon. The first three waves would be of amphibious tractors, the fourth would carry tanks, and the fifth more troops. Colonel David M. Shoup, commander of the 2d Marine Regimental Combat Team, was in command of the three battalion landing teams.

Early in the morning of November 19, the transports assumed their stations off Betio. Unfortunately, they were too far south and within range of Japanese naval guns emplaced on shore, which opened fire. They did little damage and in turn drew the fire of American naval guns. The next hitch in landing operations came when Navy planes, for highly debatable reasons, failed to arrive on schedule for their share in the preliminary bombardment. Although there was exchange of fire between ships and guns on shore, the unexpectedly slow approach of landing craft to the beach area caused a lag between the end of the preliminary bombardment and the landings which enabled the Japanese to strengthen their defenses and continue firing. At least five machine guns, for example, were operative against the unprotected troops landing on the Red Beaches. Sea walls of coconut logs on two of the beaches, 1 and 2, impeded the progress of amphibious tractors, many of which were turned aside and wrecked. The first companies had to walk in from their disabled craft and were pinned down by enemy fire behind the sea walls and received 50 percent casualties. At the end of the first day on these two beaches the beachhead was but a tenuous thread along a thin coral strip behind coconut logs. The situation was slightly better on the third beach, Red Beach 3, from which the Marines had been able to push a short distance inland. The reserves had been thrown into the battle, but they encountered the same difficulties; Japanese fire disabled landing craft and exacted casualties from men who had to swim or walk to shore.

Intercepting the news that Shoup was committing his reserve, Gen-

[21] James R. Stockman, *The Battle for Tarawa* (Marine Corps Monographs [2]) ([Washington] 1947), pp. 7–8, 80.

eral Smith dispatched another reserve battalion, the 3d Battalion, 8th Marines, which also lost heavily while landing. Thus, by early afternoon, five Marine battalions had taken a terrific beating in attempting to land on Tarawa. By nightfall the situation was a little better, but the beachhead was still a desperately held, unorganized line. The difficulties in landings naturally hampered efforts to land supplies, and communications also broke down badly. Ship-to-shore communications became so confused that General Smith could secure no clear picture of what was transpiring on the beaches, and when he sent Brigadier General Leo D. Hermle ashore, the latter could not get his messages back to Smith. A few tanks and a section of a pack howitzer battalion landed toward nightfall.

Luckily, the Japanese commander also suffered from a breakdown in communications and could not exercise direction outside his own command post. One important consequence was the lack of a concerted counterattack by the enemy during the first critical night. The next day, although the Japanese were able to score heavily on reinforcements attempting to land, the Marines moved ahead, grimly eliminated pockets of Japanese, and cut across the island in several places. After heavy fighting, helped by naval gunfire and air support, the Marines by the end of the third day had pushed the remaining Japanese into the narrow end of the island, from which they dissipated their strength in reckless countercharges. By the end of the fourth day, the Marines had eliminated Japanese resistance and the Japanese from Betio. The hard work was done; a Marine battalion followed the remaining Japanese around the other islands in the atoll and destroyed them.[22]

In sharp contrast to the bloodletting on Tarawa, the conquest of Apamama, or Abamama, was a simple, inexpensive operation. The only mishap occurred at the start, when a U.S. destroyer, mistaking the *Nautilus* for an enemy submarine, put a five-inch shell through her conning tower. Controlling the damage, the *Nautilus* took the small invading force to the attractive island, on which with native help the Marines rounded up the few Japanese who were there. Cooperative fire from the submarine killed about half the pocketed Japanese, and the remainder committed suicide.[23]

At a cost of 3,301 Marines, killed, wounded, or missing, the Southern Attack Force had secured its objective. General Holland Smith

[22] *Ibid.*, pp. 29–69.
[23] Morison, *History*, VII, 154, 179–181.

later asserted that Tarawa should have been by-passed and isolated.[24] The heavy majority of opinion is in opposition to the Marine Corps General's views. Strategically, Tarawa needed to be taken, if for no other reason than to provide bases for land-based planes. By about the end of the year, planes were operating from Tarawa, Makin, and Apamama. Cutting the distance in half meant that bombers could carry heavier loads with less risk, and land-based fighters and medium bombers could engage in bombing strikes and photographic missions. Clearly, it was a marked advantage in the move across the Central Pacific to have American not Japanese planes flying out of the Gilberts.

In this first great test of amphibious assault against a strongly held shore, amphibious doctrine had proven itself to be sound; the invader had gained his objectives, and the losses, although they shocked the public, were under 20 percent. Tarawa showed numerous weaknesses in the implementation of the doctrine, many of which centered around communications. The battleship *Maryland* proved inadequate as an amphibious command ship since firing from her own main batteries knocked out her communications. Portable radios became wet and were useless until dry. Radio between tanks and infantry was needed; no crew member was killed in a tank on Tarawa, but some were wounded or killed trying to get out to communicate with other ground troops. Part of the weakness of air support came from faulty communications, but inexperience and inadequate training were also responsible. General Holland Smith recommended the assignment of a Marine aircraft wing to give air support to amphibious landings, but during World War II his suggestion was not followed.

One result of the struggle for Tarawa was a reassessment of the role of naval gunfire. There had not been enough firepower at Tarawa to obliterate the target; fire had been too rapid, had shifted too quickly from one target to another, and had been of too short duration. The experience showed that a naval task force could stay in the area to give much more effective gunfire support, in which fire would be slow, careful, and sustained. Tarawa also showed that concrete emplacements needed armor-piercing shells for their destruction, not five-inch antiaircraft or six-inch bombardment shells. The light tank proved to be an inadequate offensive weapon, but since one of the worst short-

[24] Cited in *ibid.*, VII, 183 *n.* Morison disagreed with Smith, and stated that Vice Admiral R. A. Spruance and Rear Admiral R. K. Turner also differed with Smith's views.

ages was of flame-throwing weapons, some critics felt that light tanks might redeem themselves if equipped with such devices. The amphibious tractor proved its worth but also showed that it should be armed and more plentiful. An insufficient number of the amphtracs slowed down the entire operation and forced Marines to take the wet and bloody walk in from stalled landing craft. Tarawa was costly, but many of its lessons were learned and saved American lives in the advance across the Pacific. Furthermore, American conquests in the Gilberts caused the Japanese to abandon plans for a campaign against the Ellice, Fiji, and Samoan Islands.[25]

The best demonstration that all branches of the service profited from the Tarawa experience came a few months later in the invasion of the Marshalls. The first problem was the selection of targets, for the Marshalls consist of thirty-two atolls or island groups and more than eight hundred reefs scattered over 400,000 square miles of ocean. All the islands are small, and the highest elevation in the archipelago is twenty-one feet above sea level; but they were strategically located, and some of the coral strips were ideal for quick conversion into airfields.

The Japanese, having obtained the Marshalls as mandates after World War I, had secretly fortified some of the atolls before December, 1941, and later had increased their defenses. By the time of the invasion of the Marshalls, however, the Japanese had already classed them as impossible to defend successfully. Japanese resistance to American assault, therefore, was a delaying action designed to raise the cost of the archipelago as high as possible, and to this end the Japanese sent Army replacements to the area.[26]

The Americans knew that virtually all the Japanese air strength in the Marshalls was distributed among half a dozen atolls. Knowing that little had been done on Eniwetok and believing that they would by-pass Jaluit and Mille, the Joint Chiefs of Staff issued a directive for an operation beginning January 1, 1944, to seize the other three islands, Kwajalein, Maloelap, and Wotje. Admiral Nimitz, to whom the directive was issued, acting against the advice of most of his commanders, recommended skipping not two but four atolls and striking at only one, Kwajalein.[27] Defended atolls could be extremely hard to take,

[25] For appraisals of the Gilberts operation, see *ibid.*, VII, 182-186; Crowl and Love, *Gilberts and Marshalls*, pp. 157-165; Stockman, *Tarawa*, pp. 66-69
[26] Crowl and Love, *Gilberts and Marshalls*, p. 210.
[27] J. A. Isely and Philip A. Crowl, *The U.S. Marines and Amphibious War: Its Theory and Its Practice in the Pacific* (Princeton, 1951), pp. 254-255.

and Nimitz made the correct decision to by-pass and neutralize as many as possible. In selecting Kwajalein he gained an element of surprise, for although it was the administrative center for control of the archipelago, it was not so strongly defended as some of the other atolls.

Kwajalein has been called the world's largest atoll; shaped like a roughly flattened triangle, it is about sixty miles long and twenty miles across at its widest point. Planners concentrated on the two strongest points of the triangle and planned two operations, one in the north against two adjacent islands, Roi and Namur, and one against Kwajalein in the southeast. Unoccupied Majuro in the southeastern Marshalls would be picked up to serve as a fleet base.

The Army Air Force had first struck at the Marshalls during the Gilberts operation and as far as it was concerned the two campaigns blended into each other. At first bombers had to fly two thousand miles or farther on their missions, but during January facilities constructed in the Gilberts permitted staging heavier bombardments over shorter routes. Land-based planes concentrated first on the nearer targets, Mille, Jaluit, and Maloelap, and later in January turned their attention more to Wotje and Kwajalein.[28] Carrier attacks had begun the preceding November. A succession of raids in December, in which land-based bombers had the protection of land-based fighters, gradually reduced Mille to impotence; its structures were pulverized into coral dust, its planes either were destroyed or flew away, and surface craft no longer dared appear in the area. Maloelap was farther away, but a succession of raids, especially on January 26 and 28, practically eliminated it as a significant Japanese air base. Air power had removed Maloelap as a menace just in time, for the carrier task force arrived in the Marshalls on January 28. Jaluit was a naval base and since it lacked air installations needed much less attention. American forces struck enough, however, to level the Japanese establishment and render its occupants incapable of action. Raids on Wotje during December and January placed it also on the inactive list.[29]

Kwajalein itself was too far away to be reached adequately by Seventh Air Force bombers, and the main task of bombing it rested with the carrier task force.[30] Early in December two task groups centering

[28] Craven and Cate, *The A.A.F. in World War II*, IV, 303–306.
[29] Crowl and Love, *Gilberts and Marshalls*, pp. 197–199.
[30] For details of the invasion of Kwajalein, see *ibid.,* pp. 199–301; Heinl and

about six fast carriers moved within range and launched 246 planes against Kwajalein and Wotje. They caused considerable damage to enemy ships and aircraft, but missed numerous planes parked in camouflaged positions. The task groups withdrew and left it to the forces that would precede actual invasion to complete the destruction of air power on Kwajalein.

Each of the invasion forces, one Army and one Marine, faced a formidable problem, since besides assaulting the main objective it had to secure adjacent islets in the atoll. A third force was to seize Majuro, stand by in case it was needed at Roi-Namur or Kwajalein, and if not move on to the capture of Eniwetok.

In the imposing armada advancing against the Marshalls were four fast carrier task forces under command of Admiral Marc A. Mitscher. Their twelve carriers, protected by battleships, cruisers, and other naval craft, sent aloft planes which eliminated Japanese air and naval power in the archipelago and thereby created the control of sea and air so essential to amphibious assault. In addition to the fast carrier task forces nearly three hundred vessels bore the invaders toward their objective; they varied from escort carriers for air support in the landings to landing craft.

It was the task of the 4th Marine Division to seize Roi and Namur islands. Unfortunately, both this division and the transports which landed them were inexperienced in amphibious assault, although under their commander, Major General Harry Schmidt, the Marines had had some training. The Northern Attack Force began its landings on small islands flanking Roi and Namur. Heavy surf and choppy water even within the lagoon checked but did not prevent landings and the establishment of artillery on shore to aid in the assault of the principal islands. Meanwhile, naval vessels and planes concluded an extensive bombardment of Roi-Namur, concentrating more on Namur since it was thought to contain more Japanese and more defenses than Roi, which was little more than an extended airfield, connected to Namur by a sandy strip and an artificial causeway.

To a considerable extent the bombardment was successful, as many Japanese were killed and others pounded into a state of shock. Consequently, on February 1, 1944, the Marines went ashore against little

Crown, *The Marshalls*, pp. 100–116; Morison, *History*, VII, 230–281; Isely and Crowl, *The U.S. Marines and Amphibious War*, pp. 252–291.

opposition. The destruction was not complete; the main enemy posts were intact, and the Japanese within, although temporarily dazed, were very much alive and dangerous. Despite the fact that they escaped enemy fire, the landing troops encountered many difficulties, mainly arising from adverse winds, rough water, and inexperienced personnel. Once ashore, there remained the task of rooting the Japanese from their concrete and steel structures. Roi proved easier, and demolition squads finished its conquest in another day. As anticipated, there were more Japanese on Namur and, offering bitter resistance, they fired from undamaged blockhouses and pillboxes or conducted harassing sniper attacks from piles of rubble. Early in the afternoon a demolition squad placed a charge against what it thought was a pillbox. Instead, it was a Japanese torpedo warhead magazine, and the resultant explosion killed twenty Marines and wounded many others. The catastrophe interrupted communications and slowed down coordination of attack. Advance infantry and tanks at times failed to work closely together; in one instance Japanese approached a lost tank and dropping a grenade into an open vent killed the tank captain and the driver.

On the next day, moving more effectively and using 75-mm. half-tracks, flame throwers, and demolition squads, the Marines secured control of Namur by noon. Their method was to keep the attack rolling and by-pass minor resistance. This doctrine worked well, and the invaders gained the island with maximum speed and perhaps minimum losses.

Meanwhile the Southern Attack Force had begun its move against Kwajalein, and like the Marines, the 7th Infantry Division first seized adjacent islands and set up artillery to assist in the bombardment of the main objective. At the same time the Navy was shelling Kwajalein. Using only minimum air bombardment, it concentrated on careful and extended naval gunfire, later aided by the infantry division's artillery. About two miles long, Kwajalein is shaped somewhat like a boomerang with blunt ends. Since it curved inward about the lagoon, landings on this side would have exposed the invaders to possible enfilading fire. Rather than risk this or the heavy surf on the seaward side, the attack force made its landings on the blunt western end of the island.

The attack force was more experienced than those going against Roi-Namur. The 7th Infantry Division had taken Attu and occupied Kiska in the Aleutians. While the amphibious tank battalion had seen no action, it had had extensive training in land tanks similar to the

LVT's and proved most competent in the landings. Consequently, since Japanese resistance had been stilled by preliminary bombardment, the landing operation proceeded with gratifying precision. The actual conquest of the island, however, went ahead more slowly than on Roi-Namur. The Japanese followed their pattern of determined fighting from strongly fortified positions. Naval gunfire, air bombardment, tanks, and artillery were important, but in the end it remained for demolition squads of infantrymen to move in to place charges against pillboxes and other defenses. As was the case elsewhere, heavy bombardment was a mixed blessing; it shattered defenses and killed many of the enemy but in the process created rubble from which it was difficult to root out the rest of the foe. By February 6, however, the Army had completed its conquest of Kwajalein Island.

So successful had been the Kwajalein operation that Admiral Nimitz authorized Admiral Spruance to move quickly to the assault of Eniwetok, an extreme western atoll of the Marshalls.[31] Once again fast carrier forces and Army Air Force planes prepared the way and made interdiction raids on Japanese air bases in the Carolines and Marianas. On January 31, a Navy task group raided Eniwetok itself.

Truk, capital of the Carolines under both German and Japanese rule, had the best fleet anchorage in any of the Japanese mandates. The Japanese Combined Fleet had been based in its lagoon since July, 1942, and headquarters of the Commander Sixth Fleet (submarines) was on one of Truk's islands, which unlike most atoll islands were volcanic and reached elevations as high as fifteen hundred feet. Often called the "Gibraltar of the Pacific" early in the war, Truk, although appearing most difficult to take by sea because of its surrounding coral ring and the numerous islands that would have to be seized, proved vulnerable to the kind of air attack which fast carrier forces were able to stage by 1944. Truk was an important air as well as naval base, but it was weak in antiaircraft defenses. On February 4, 1944, a Marine Corps plane from Bougainville took valuable photographs of Truk but at the same time alerted the Japanese to the possibility of air attack, and as a result most of the combatant ships hurried away from the lagoon to the Palaus.

On February 17, Admiral Mitscher's Task Force 58, consisting of three task force groups, each centering about three carriers, raided

---

[31] Crowl and Love, *Gilberts and Marshalls*, p. 333.

Truk.[32] The first wave of planes destroyed about thirty planes in the air and forty on the ground, with a loss of only five American planes. In the afternoon, counterattacking Japanese knocked the *Intrepid* out of action for several months with an aerial torpedo. That night Admiral Mitscher launched the U.S. Navy's first night carrier air attack on shipping. Using radar, a dozen torpedo bombers armed with five-hundred-pound bombs inflicted about one-third of the total damage done to shipping in the entire raid. The next morning, without interference from enemy aircraft, carrier strikes concentrated on such targets as ammunition dumps, hangars, and storage tanks before retiring at noon. The two-day strike had sunk about 200,000 tons of shipping with light losses, made so in part by effective rescue work by submarines and seaplanes. On February 17, Task Group 50.9, cruising around the atoll, sank a number of vessels, including a light cruiser and a destroyer.

The Truk raid was not an isolated venture; rather, it was geared to the invasion of Eniwetok and the encirclement of Rabaul. As a result of its success no enemy planes challenged the seizure of Eniwetok, and Allied planes raiding Rabaul on February 18 encountered none of the usual air opposition. The Truk raid affected Japanese in the homeland; on February 18, Tokyo Radio reported on the attack and stated, "The war situation has increased with unprecedented seriousness—nay, furiousness. The tempo of enemy operations indicates that the attacking force is already pressing upon our mainland." Although planes could still operate from Truk, the atoll's value as a fleet anchorage ended with the attack. The Fleet Admiral did not return.

Two days before the raid on Truk a reorganized attack force left Kwajalein to attack Eniwetok. Joining soldiers from the 27th Division and other units was the 22d Marine Regiment, going into action for the first time after eighteen months' garrison duty in Samoa. There were more Japanese on the atoll islands than the Americans at first realized, but their defenses were hastily contrived. There was no escape for them, and their orders were to fight a delaying action to the death. Instead of challenging the enemy as it attempted to land, the Japanese waited in cleverly concealed underground networks.[33]

[32] For a description of the first raid on Truk, see Morison, *History,* VII, 314–332.

[33] Accounts of the invasion of Eniwetok include *ibid.,* VII, 282–304; Heinl and Crown, *The Marshalls,* pp. 117–151; Crowl and Love, *Gilberts and Marshalls,* pp. 333–365.

For the invaders, once more the problem was that of seizing several islands in an atoll. They took one, Engebi, without much trouble, but had been light on preliminary bombardment of Parry and Eniwetok in the belief that they were undefended. Meeting stiff opposition on Eniwetok, Marines and soldiers took the island after short but hard fighting. Discovering that Parry had large numbers of concealed Japanese, the Americans accorded it somewhat heavier bombardment. After the landings, the Japanese fought from crude but well-hidden underground shelters and for a time their land mines and antitank guns were effective against tanks and personnel. By February 23, however, U.S. forces had one more strategic atoll in their possession.

Tactically, the U.S. forces learned much from the Marshalls operations. They made better use of the versatile DUKW's improved techniques of lifting troops to the assault area, and used naval star shells which facilitated night operations ashore. Perhaps most important of all, the various branches of the service found that they could all work together as an effective fighting unit.[34]

Strategically, occupation of the Marshalls forced the Japanese fleet to retire behind the Philippines–Netherlands East Indies–New Guinea line, and what had appeared to be a major Japanese bastion no longer seemed so important. Deciding not to try to seize Truk, the Allied forces by-passed it and kept it neutralized during the remainder of the war by frequent air raids.[35]

Both Admiral Nimitz and General MacArthur sought variations in the planning schedule for operations approved at the Cairo-Teheran conferences. In January, 1944, Nimitz proposed a schedule for 1944 which provided for approach through the Central Pacific by way of the Marshalls and the Carolines (including Truk but considering the possibility of by-passing it to take the Palaus) to join forces with those of the Southwest Pacific Area in the Philippines. Marshall did not agree but consented to a conference of theater commanders, which was held at Pearl Harbor on January 27–28 with representatives from the three Pacific areas present. Although no decisions were reached, both Army and Navy representatives seemed to feel that more emphasis

---

[34] For appraisals of the Marshalls operations, see *ibid.*, pp. 371–374; Heinl and Crown, *The Marshalls*, p. 151; Morison, *History*, VII, 331–332; Isely and Crowl, *The U.S. Marines and Amphibious War*, pp. 301–309.

[35] In their directive of March 12, 1944, the Joint Chiefs of Staff ordered the by-passing of Truk. Summarized in Matloff, *Strategic Planning*, p. 458.

should be placed on naval and amphibious operations on the New Guinea route to the Philippines than on the Central Pacific route. Conference members did not appear to consider the Marianas important and felt them to be too far from Japan for effective use by B-29's. Acting quickly after the conference, General MacArthur, in a message to Marshall dated February 2, urged the War Department to turn all forces after the Marshalls operation to advance along the New Guinea coast. He also requested diversion of all the B-29's to the area and placing of all naval forces under Admiral Halsey as his naval commander.

To these suggestions Admiral King and the Joint planners objected. They noted that MacArthur as yet had presented no plan for movement along New Guinea's coastline, and King also spoke of the successes of the operations in the Central Pacific. Marshall responded with a suggestion, which was accepted, that the matter be turned over to the Joint Strategic Survey Committee for a report on the best and quickest route or routes to victory against Japan. In the debate which continued in Washington, Army Air Forces leaders argued strongly for seizure of the Marianas, for they felt that B-29's could make good use of air bases in these islands. On February 16, the Joint Strategic Survey Committee proposed that the Central Pacific route be the primary route, that operations be carried out for the conquest of the Marianas and Palau and then for an attack on Formosa or Luzon.[36]

While the debate continued in Washington, several developments in the Pacific affected the decision. On February 15, forces under Halsey occupied the Green Islands, 117 miles east of Rabaul and 220 southeast of Kavieng.[37] By early March Allied forces had built a fighter strip and by the end of the month a bomber field. PT boats had started operating from the islands within two days after the landings. In addition, Washington heard of the devastating raid on Truk, and the opinion grew that Nimitz could by-pass Truk and go into other Caroline Islands or the Marianas by June. On March 5, MacArthur stated that his forces in New Guinea would by-pass Hansa Bay and strike farther

---

[36] Philip A. Crowl, *Campaign in the Marianas* (*United States Army in World War II: The War in the Pacific*) (Washington, 1960), pp. 17–18.

[37] For descriptions of these landings, see John Miller, Jr., *Cartwheel: The Reduction of Rabaul* (*United States Army in World War II: The War in the Pacific*) (Washington, 1959), pp. 312–315; Morison, *History*, VI, 412–419.

west at Hollandia. The debate went on until, on March 12, 1944, the Joint Chiefs of Staff issued a directive establishing new operations targets and schedules.[38] Kavieng, no longer important, would be by-passed in favor of more easily obtainable islands to the north, the Mussaus Islands or Emirau. The directive approved invasion of Hollandia on April 15, and by-passing Truk in favor of landings in the Marianas on June 15. In September, Central Pacific forces would take the Palaus in preparation for advance by Southwest Pacific forces on Mindanao, November 15. A target date of February 15, 1945, was set up for invasion of either Luzon or Formosa, but the Joint Chiefs of Staff did not decide at this time which would be the objective. Although Nimitz seemed to have fared better than MacArthur in this directive, the principle of flexibility remained, as did the dual approach to the Philippines, and the Formosa-Luzon-China Coast continued to be the main target.

While the Joint Chiefs of Staff were reaching these decisions, General MacArthur had been preparing for an attack on the Admiralties, authorized at the Cairo-Teheran conferences.[39] These islands, two hundred miles northeast of New Guinea and 260 miles west of Kavieng, were well located to aid in neutralizing Rabaul and supporting the advance into the Philippines. In addition, they contained two airfields and one of the finest harbors to be found anywhere—Seeadler Harbor, created by the two main islands, Los Negros and Manus, and some islets. MacArthur assigned responsibility for coordinating planning to General Krueger, who decided on the 1st Cavalry Division, reinforced, as the assault force. On the basis of weakening reaction to air attacks, General Kenney recommended that General MacArthur send a small force to land on Los Negros and seize Momote airfield instead of waiting to attack Seeadler Harbor at a later date. Enthusiastic over the possibilities, MacArthur ordered a "reconnaissance in force." By this decision, without benefit of staff study, MacArthur sent a force of a thousand men into an area which original planning called for a whole division to invade a month later than the reconnaissance landings.

[38] Message, Joint Chiefs of Staff to MacArthur and Nimitz, Mar. 12, 1944, summarized in Matloff, *Strategic Planning,* pp. 458–459.

[39] For descriptions of the Admiralties campaign, see Miller, *Cartwheel,* pp. 316–350; Morison, *History,* VI, 432–448; Walter Krueger, *From Down Under to Nippon: The Story of Sixth Army in World War II* (Washington, 1953), pp. 45–55.

MacArthur also ordered a support force of fifteen hundred men to be ready to land two days after D-day if the reconnaissance force remained.

To determine whether the initial force should stay or leave, Mac-Arthur accompanied the invasion force, elements of which landed on unprepossessing Hyane Harbor with comparatively few losses. Mac-Arthur went ashore, decorated the first man to land and ordered the reconnaissance force, which had seized the airfield, to "remain here and hold the strip at all cost." MacArthur's estimate of the situation proved correct; the men fought off Japanese attacks until supporting troops arrived to aid in the conquest of Los Negros and Manus. On March 9, destroyers and mine sweepers led the way for LST's to enter the harbor and discharge cavalry units which completed the conquest of Los Negros. The Americans placed artillery on small islets, and on March 15 made landings on Manus. Resistance in places was heavy, but the invaders moved ahead. Aided by tanks, artillery, and an air strike on stubborn pillboxes, ground forces on March 18 secured the Lorengau airfield. Isolated resistance would continue until May 18, but the Americans had secured their main objectives, the airfields and Seeadler Harbor.

The seizure of the Admiralties brought the Allies many benefits. Base construction moved ahead, and a seven-thousand-foot runway was in operation on Momote airfield on Los Negros by May 18. Since Lorengau did not prove suitable for development, Seabees and Engineers built a new field on Los Negros. Seeadler Harbor became one of the largest naval bases in the Pacific, with repair facilities for all types of vessels. The base serviced the Third, Fifth, and Seventh Fleets in later operations, and the airfields helped support advances in both New Guinea and the Central Pacific.